Communicative English for Engineers and Professionals

Communicative English for Engineers and Professionals

Nitin Bhatnagar

Maharishi Markand•••• •••University
Ambala, Haryana

Mamta Bhatnagar

Ambala, Haryana

Associate Production Editor: Jennifer Sargunar
Composition: Mukesh Technologies Pvt. Ltd, Pondicherry
Printer: Sheel Print N Pack

ISBN: 978-81-317-3204-5

First Impression, 2010

Published by Pearson India Education Services Pvt.Ltd,CIN:U72200TN2005PTC057128.

Head Office: 15th Floor, Tower-B, World Trade Tower, Plot No. 1, Block-C, Sector 16, Noida 201 301, Uttar Pradesh, India.

Registered Office: The HIVE, 3rd Floor, Metro zone, No 44, Pillaiyar Koil Street, Jawaharlal Nehru Road, Anna Nagar, Chennai, Tamil Nadu 600040.
Phone: 044-66540100, Website: in.pearson.com, Email: companysecretary.india@pearson.com

Digitally Printed in India by Repro Books Limited, Thane in the year of 2020.

Contents

Preface

Communicative English for Engineers and Professionals is a product of our long experience and knowledge gained through classroom teaching of communication skills in English and research carried out at the university and college levels. The material in the book has been well tested on learners and professionals and modified after feedback from them. It is designed to give our readers an edge in their careers.

As the title of the book *Communicative English for Engineers and Professionals* indicates, the book is a comprehensive study of oral and written skills in English. It is meticulously written to develop our readers' insight into the learning and enhancement of technical and business communication skills and to help them meet challenges by providing them with some useful practical tips.

The book has a wide range of utility. It is broad enough to cover the syllabi of B.Tech., B.E., Bachelors and Masters in Commerce, Hospitality, B.Pharma., Nursing, Physiotherapy, MBA, and other courses being taught at various universities, professional and technical institutions. It is also suitable for in-job professionals who would like to enhance their oral and written communication skills. We have also taken into consideration aspirants of English proficiency examinations, who wish to sharpen their listening, speaking, reading and writing skills. Above all, teachers will find this book useful as a support material and a ready reference for making their class instructions learner-centered and practical. It will also provide them with answers to some pertinent questions that they might come across during their classes.

The layout of the book has been designed to follow the natural progression of the faculties of listening, speaking, reading, and writing. Chapter 1 is an effective guide for learners, especially beginners, on how to develop and improve oral communication, and it gives readers practical tips to achieve this aim. Chapter 2 is unique as it directs the learners to the field of CALL (Computer Aided Language Learning) and other useful technologies for learning oral and written communication skills. Chapters 3 and 4, valuable sections on vocabulary extension, will not only furnish the readers with a wide range of synonyms, antonyms, homonyms, homophones, one-word substitutes, and technical terms but will also help learners develop an understanding of difficult words by gaining knowledge on roots, bases, and affixes of the English language. Chapter 5 deals with the phonetics of English in the fine tuning of the skills learnt in Chapter 1. Chapter 6 has been especially designed for job seekers and professionals who aspire to gain proficiency in group discussions, interviews, and professional presentations. Chapter 7 concentrates on the fundamentals of grammar and touches the aspects that are normally difficult for learners, supported by examples taken from day-to-day interactions. Developing the skills of reading, note making, note taking and summarizing are dealt with in Chapter 8. Chapters 9 and 10 discuss professional and technical written communication along with the creative aspects of writing slogans, paragraphs, dialogues and developing outlines, which are included in the course contents of many universities. All the features are supported with apt illustrations. Each chapter ends with learner-oriented practice material intended to make the readers apply the concepts to their professional and personal real-life situations.

We have been rather particular to make the book relevant to the current requirements of students, their curricula, and to the prevailing standards of oral and written interactions in the professional sector. The scope of the book is wide enough to cater to the needs of beginners, improvers, and professionals by providing them with the knowledge of the basics and the tools required to practice them. This is just not another theoretical book but a detailed guide for learning and developing your communication skills.

Acknowledgements

We express our heartfelt gratitude to our teachers and parents whose guidance and blessings were a perpetual source of encouragement to us. We are thankful to our colleagues and friends for their cooperation and valuable suggestions, which broadened our horizon. We acknowledge our students for their constructive feedback that helped us in shaping this book. At the same time we appreciate our children, Nivedita and Kushal, for their patience and support provided during the preparation of the book.

Nitin Bhatnagar
Mamta Bhatnagar

About the Authors

Nitin Bhatnagar is currently working as a professor of English at Maharishi Markandeshwar University, Mullana, Ambala. He has been teaching English Language Skills, Professional Communication and English Literature at different levels for more than 26 years. His expertise lies in training learners for oral professional communication using Computer Aided Language Learning (CALL). He has also been guiding students for competitive examinations and preparing them for placements in companies. He has been associated with many reputed universities and institutes as a visiting faculty and has delivered expert lectures on various aspects of professional communication. He did his Ph.D. from Devi Ahilya University, Indore, and is currently supervising many scholars for their doctoral research. He has written many research papers, which have been published in various national and international journals.

Mamta Bhatnagar is a senior lecturer in English at Guru Nanak Institute of Technology, Mullana, Ambala. She has several years' experience of teaching Communication Skills in English, English Grammar, and Professional Interaction at various levels. She has also been engaged in imparting training in oral communication using computerized language labs. In addition to teaching, she has been actively involved in writing articles in magazines and newspapers as well as in editing magazines and newsletters for which she has received many awards. She has authored a book on Communication Skills and has written several papers in national and international journals.

Effective Communication

1

In this unit

- ✓ What do We Mean by Communication?
- ✓ Process of Communication
- ✓ Channels and Media of Communication
- ✓ Barriers to Communication
- ✓ Learning Strategies for Effective Communication:
  - ✍ Listening
  - ✍ Thinking

- ✍ Vocabulary Building
- ✍ Speaking
- ✍ Reading
- ✍ Writing
- ✍ Grammar
- ✍ Body Language

"Effective communication depends not so much on WHAT is said as WHY and HOW it is said."

–Groff Conklin

1.1 What do We Mean by Communication?

Communication is as old as man himself. Since time immemorial, it has been an integral part of man's life. The word 'communicate' is derived from the Latin word *'communicare'* and the French word *'communis'*, and both the words mean 'to give to another'. The Oxford Advanced Learner's Dictionary defines 'communication' as "The activity process of expressing ideas and feelings or of giving people information". Although the growth of communication technology has tremendously changed the ways of communicating ideas, meaning of the word 'communication' remains unchanged. If we look around us, we find people communicating with one another or involved in day-to-day conversations, calls, e-mails, writing letters, sending SMS's, chatting, presentations and so on. Social interaction, which is the basic need of man, is impossible without communication. All living beings communicate, but man has language that is a precious gift of nature. Communication has a survival value as it helps us exist, grow and mould ourselves accordingly.

1.2 Process of Communication

Communication is a dynamic exchange between a sender and a receiver. It is a complex process and not as simple as it appears to be. Mere transmission of message is not sufficient. Along with this, receiver's understanding, feeling and response are to be taken into consideration. A message moves through the following five stages of the process of communication:

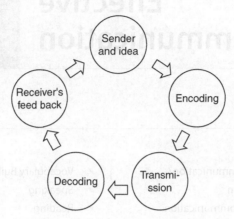

Figure 1.1   Communication Cycle

→ Sender and idea
→ Encoding the idea into a message
→ Transmission of the message
→ Decoding of the message by the receiver
→ Receiver's feedback

The process becomes cyclic in case of a two way oral interaction (See Figure 1.1). Each step of the process is very important *per se* for effective communication.

1.2.1   Communication Cycle

1. Sender and Idea: The process of communication begins with an idea that is generated in the mind of the sender and the selection of a message to be communicated. The scope of the idea depends on the knowledge and abilities of the sender as well as the purpose and the context of communication.

2. Encoding: Encoding is the next step in communication. Here, the sender converts the idea into a message which can be non-verbal, verbal or written. This is called encoding. It involves language selection in addition to the selection of the medium of communication. An appropriate choice of language is necessary for effective encoding. A verbal message requires a common language that can be understood by both the sender as well as the receiver. For example, a receiver who does not understand English cannot decode a message, encoded in English. That's why we use our first language in informal situations and an official language in professional, academic or business situations. The medium of communication should be carefully chosen because the choice of the medium is the beginning of effective communication. A written message should be clearly stated while the choice of words, tone and style are significant in an oral message. The right encoding leads to successful communication because a work, well begun is half done.

3. Transmission: The next step is transmission of the message. Transmission is the flow of message through a chosen channel—verbal, nonverbal, written, visual and audio-visual. A channel of communication uses a medium such as telephone, e-mail, SMS, video conferencing, Internet, letter and face-to-face conversation. The choice of the channel and the medium depends upon the time and place of communication. Suppose you want to take a day's leave from your boss who normally loses his/her temper on such issues. The best way would be to decide whether you should request him/her in the morning, afternoon or evening in his/her office or when he/she is walking down to the waiting car. In such situations one must make one's choices with a cool mind.

4. Decoding: Decoding is the next step in the process of communication. It is the stage when the transmitted message is converted into thoughts so that the receiver may understand its meaning. It is to be noted that the receiver interprets the message by analyzing it according to his/her understanding. A written message is decoded through reading, an oral communication by listening and a non-verbal communication by interpreting signs and symbols. However, all these types of communication have a common aim of grasping the idea as formulated in the mind of the sender. An effective decoding leads to a successful communication. To achieve this aim, the sender should possess good communication skills (verbal mastery and coordinated body language) and the receiver should be a good decoder who should possess the following qualities:

→ Good listening
→ Verbal mastery
→ Ability to read between the lines
→ Empathy

An absence of any of these skills may lead to misinterpretation of the message and may cause confusion and misunderstanding.

5. Receiver's Response or Feedback: Response or feedback is the last stage in the process of communication. It incorporates the reaction of the receiver to the message and assists the receiver in knowing whether the message has been correctly interpreted, misunderstood or rejected. If encoding and decoding match each other, that is, the sender and the receiver of the message are on a common wavelength, transmission of the message is effective and efficient. Communication in this way is perfectly successful. Newton's Third Law of Motion, 'every action has an equal and opposite reaction', seems to work in the case of communication process also. Encoding is the action, whereas decoding is the reaction. If the action (encoding) is effective, the reaction (decoding) will surely correspond to it. Effectiveness or weakness of an action from the sender will generate a corresponding reaction from the receiver. This reaction is always in the opposite direction, that is, the feedback of the receiver goes back to the sender. The communication cycle gets over with the receiver's response.

1.3 Channels and Media of Communication

The various methods of communication have been changing with the passage of time. It started with the non-verbal communication of the primitive man, drums, the use of pigeons and horse messengers, to radio, telegram, telegraph, wireless, and finally has evolved to the electronic media of the modern times. With the advent of technological and management studies, channels and media of communication have changed from simple to complex and slow to fast making it more and more effective. The choice of the channel and the media largely depends on the sender–receiver relationship as well as the need and purpose of communication. Communication may take place through any of these channels and media. A list of channels with the corresponding need and media is given in Table 1.1.

Communication technology is growing at a rapid speed. What was only a figment of imagination yesterday has become a reality today and the process does not seem to stop here. Some of the media, mentioned in Table 1.1 like mobile, television, e-mail and Internet, have brought a revolution in the

Table 1.1   Channels, their Need and Media of Communication

Channels	Need	Media
Nonverbal	• Simplification, explanation and observation	• Face-to-face, charts, graphs, diagrams, OHPs and LCD projectors
Verbal	• One-to-one conversation • Record is not needed • Immediate response	• Face-to-face, telephone, mobile phones, voice mail, audio tapes, Internet, teleconferencing
Audio-visual	• Simplification and more explanation • Marketing • Entertainment • Immediate response	• Television, cinema, video tapes, video conferencing, Internet (through webcams)
Written	• Record is necessary • Immediate response is not required • Communication is detailed, in depth, or complex	• Letters, memos, reports, print, e-mails, fax, SMS on mobile phones, chatting through the Internet

field of communication. 'Grid' is another amazing medium of communication and is soon going to be a reality:

> Grid (a revolution in information superhighway): Scientists in Geneva have claimed to have developed a grid that is made of "thousands of desktops, laptops, supercomputers, data vaults, mobile phones, meteorological sensors and telescopes." This grid will combine the resources of about "100,000 processors from more than 170 sites in 34 countries and will be accessible to thousands of physicists globally". It will share computing power and data-sharing capacity. A scientist can log on from anywhere in the world to process data across the planet with a very high speed. It has been reported that the grid will speed up drug discovery process during the outbreak of epidemics such as swine flu, dengue, etc. This communication explosion is "just weeks away from powering up". The grid will surely be the next giant leap in international communication.

(Source: *The Times of India*. "The Biggest Thing Since the Web". New Delhi/Chandigarh/02 November 2009. It has been registered in the present book on the very date of the publication of this information.)

1.4   Barriers to Communication

Communication is a process through which you convey your idea to someone or a group of people. It is said to be effective if the idea is conveyed clearly and unambiguously. In such a case, the message should reach the receiver with little deformation. Communication becomes successful only if the receiver understands what the sender is trying to convey. If your message is not clearly interpreted or the receiver does not give the desired feedback, you should understand that you are facing a communication barrier. The process of communication may be blocked due to many reasons. Many socio-psychologists believe that there is 50–70% loss of meaning while conveying the message from a sender to a receiver. You should understand these barriers as they can create hurdles in your professional and personal life too. The following are some of the major barriers:

1. **Physical Barriers:**   One of the major barriers to communication is the physical barrier. Physical barriers include large working areas that are physically separated from others. Distracting body movements

can also create physical barriers. Other distraction that could cause physical barriers is the negative environment which is not conducive to healthy talks. Background noise may also affect the whole process of communication. One should try to minimize the elements that cause physical barriers.

2. Psychological Barriers: Your emotions could be a barrier to communication. If you are preoccupied with some emotions, you will have trouble listening to others or understanding the message conveyed to you. It can be due to many other reasons too—hostility, anger, inhibitions, ego-hang-ups, personal prejudices, tiredness, pre-conceived notions, stress, lack of confidence and introvert nature.

3. Linguistic Barriers: Incapability or failure to communicate in a language that is known to both the sender and the receiver is the most crucial barrier to effective communication. Wrong or out of place words, mispronounced sounds, incorrect grammar and syntax as well as difference in accent, lack of clarity, could lead to misunderstanding between the sender and the receiver while conversing or writing.

4. Perceptual Barriers: The problem in communicating with others occurs because we all perceive things differently. This is because we are made and groomed differently due to our varied social, cultural and family backgrounds. If we weren't, we would have no need to communicate. We all see the world from different angles and if we lack the perspective to see other's point of view, we become the victim of the perceptual barrier.

5. Cultural Barriers: Intercultural communication has become more common in the present scenario than ever before. The differences in cultural values cause socio-cultural barriers. When we interact with a cross cultural group and wish to associate with it, we need to adopt the behaviour patterns of the group. The group reverts back by showing recognition and approval. When you are not able to adjust to the new setting, cultural barriers crop in.

These are some of the major barriers which obstruct the process of communication. In addition to them, goal mismatching i.e., communication with conflicting intensions, ineffective listening and impoliteness create barriers that you may encounter during oral and written communication.

How to Overcome Barriers to Communication

The solutions to overcome these barriers are not simple or easy. Remedies are to be adopted according to situation. Here are some solutions to overcome communication barriers:

→ Avoid physical distractions
→ Empathize with your receiver
→ Try to understand your receiver's point of view
→ Encode your message in a language that your receiver can interpret
→ While communicating be calm from within to avoid psychological barriers
→ Listen and read effectively
→ Understand cultural variations

1.5 Learning Strategies for Effective Communication

We have seen that communication cannot be successful unless it moves through all the five stages of the process of communication. Encoding of the message by the sender and its decoding by the receiver are the two stages that need a good level of linguistic and communicative competence.

In the absence of such skills, encoding will be faulty and this in turn will lead to incorrect decoding. If the sender is equipped with such skills and the receiver is not, it will result in the misinterpretation of the message. Communication is required in all walks of life—familial, social and professional and you must strive hard to learn, develop or enhance your skills for an effective communication.

Language plays a vital role in the acquisition of knowledge. English language in India with all its uniqueness is not native to the soil; yet, its importance cannot be underestimated. It enjoys unlimited significance because it is not only a language of international business but also of the cyber world that is playing a significant role in making communication highly effective. David Graddol, the famous applied linguist and researcher on issues related to Global English, in his British Council Commissioned Report, *Future of English?* (1997) commented "English is rapidly becoming something else—a near universal basic skill." The non-native users of English too have now realized that they need to learn English and communicate in it to get a good job in a surging economy. Learning the art of oral interaction in English has become indispensable today for success in occupational sphere and social circles. Efficiency in spoken English is a passport to employment. Good technical, scientific or commercial knowledge fails to yield desired results if one's English is poor or one has weak communication skills. Language learning ability, at a young age, is an unconscious but an effective process. Psychologists and speech therapists have pointed out that a child acquires sufficient ability in listening and speaking at a very early stage. By the age of three, he/she starts understanding elements such as asking questions, requesting, saying no, making past tenses, singulars and plurals, masculine and feminine, etc. The natural language learning ability disappears by the age of five. Henceforth, language is learnt not naturally, but by effort. Now at the present age you cannot go back into time, oral skills can only be learnt and developed through a conscious effort. To become an effective communicator; the following skills are to be mastered:

→ Listening
→ Thinking
→ Vocabulary Building
→ Speaking
→ Reading and Writing
→ Grammar
→ Body Language

Let us discuss each skill in some detail:

1.5.1   Listening

A good communicator has to be a good listener first. Nature has given us an auditory system in our body for the purpose of listening. Although the early humans used sounds and wordless voices to communicate, listening must have been used to listen to the sounds of the surrounding areas. Along with the growth of communication, listening has become more and more vital to make the communication productive. No oral communication is complete without listening. In a communication process, the decoder has to be a good listener. As a student, you require active and efficient listening to understand your lectures, seminars and speeches. Listening is not only a necessary first step in language learning but is also a manifestation of certain virtues in your personality such as patience, tolerance, involvement, understanding and many more. Once you are in a profession, you are required to listen to instructions, telephonic conversations, meetings, presentations, etc. carefully and respond to them in a graceful way.

1. **Listening and Hearing:**   Listening is a conscious process. It requires complete involvement of all your faculties—auditory, mental and visual—and the whole of your body has to support you. Hearing

is more or less an unconscious process. For example, when you are sitting in a class, you are supposed to listen to the lecture. Meanwhile, you may hear sounds of fans, air conditioners, students' voices from outside, etc., but your concentration is on the lecture as you are listening to it.

2. Development of Listening Skills: Development of listening skills has a dual purpose. First, it makes you a good decoder of a communicated message and secondly a regular listening practice of correct English strengthens your spoken English—your accent, pronunciation, fluency, tone and articulation. A learner may practise by making use of television, radio and other audio and audio-visual aids. Prolonged listening to bad English can lead to inculcation of incorrect grammar and communication skills. Table 1.2 gives some skills required for effective listening in contrast with some negative traits associated with ineffective listening:

Table 1.2 A Contrast Between Effective and Ineffective Communication

Effective listening	Ineffective listening
• Remaining silent	• Talking while speaker is speaking
• Listening patiently	• Losing patience during conversations
• Putting speaker at ease through encouraging gestures	• Giving negative signals to show your disinterest
• Maintaining eye contact with the speaker	• Looking here and there but not at the speaker
• Giving positive signals (nodding, etc.) to show your understanding	• Looking at the speaker passively
• Empathizing with the speaker	• Considering yourself too important to share speaker's ideas
• Asking questions at an appropriate time	• Interrupting whenever you disagree
• Staying focused on the context	• Getting distracted or letting the mind wander

With regular listening, the elements of correct English settle down in our mind and they gradually replace the incorrect elements which have been there for a long time. Listening works subconsciously in grasping the nuances of the language and helps us overcome the mother tongue and the regional language barriers.

3. Barriers to Listening: Barriers to an effective listening can be many. However, the major ones have been given in Table 1.3 with their corresponding behavioural responses.

Table 1.3 Major Barriers to Listening with their Behavioural Responses

Barriers	Behavioural response
Pre-conceived ideas	Blocked mind
Lack of interest	Weak concentration

(Continued)

Table 1.3   (*Continued*)

Barriers	Behavioural response
Feeling of self-importance	Disapproval of the speaker's point and no empathy
Fear of the situation or the person	Weak concentration
Previous knowledge of the topic	Overconfidence and no empathy
Lack of self-confidence	Weak concentration
Self-involvement	Ineffective listening
Stress in life	Weak concentration, ineffective listening and no empathy

Barriers to listening can be overcome by a conscious effort. Do not listen to the speaker with pre-conceived ideas, give due importance to him/her and don't let your mind wander while listening. Stress is a part of life; do not let it become an impediment in your listening process.

1.5.2   Thinking

Thinking is one of those faculties which are directly related to the brain. The language of conscious thinking is either the mother tongue or the local dialect of common use. For a learner of oral communication, thinking in English can be very helpful. You may start with short sentences of daily use or of the dealings you are really thinking about without getting conscious of your shortcomings. Initially, you may have to put in a lot of effort but with regular practice, thinking in English will start coming to you naturally. During the process of communication, thinking in English becomes a part of the communication flow in the first two stages of idea generation and encoding by the sender. The effort will not only give strength to the thoughts but will also make the message linguistically impressive.

1.5.3   Vocabulary Building

As words make sentences, you should have the ability to use the right word at the right place. This will help you express yourself correctly as well as assist you to bring fluency in your speech.

How to Increase Vocabulary

Extension of vocabulary is a gradual process. It cannot be done overnight. The most effective tool is to do regular reading and careful listening of English. Memorizing new words is not advisable, as they do not stay long in the head. Moreover, words change their meanings according to context. For instance, the word 'expose' can be used in two ways:

'The media has *exposed* his underworld connections'.
'Near an X-ray machine you may *expose* yourself to radiations'.

Here, you should be able to distinguish not only one word from another but also its different shades of usages. There is a difference between 'understanding' and 'knowing' a word. You may understand a word roughly by knowing its context or you may look at the way it is made up. We cannot know a word or form it a part of our blood stream, unless we use it in our day-to-day life. *The Reader's Digest* describes it as '*passive and active vocabulary.*' Understanding corresponds to the '*passive stage*' that improves the ability to recognize and interpret words. In the '*active stage*' of knowing a word, you should try to fix a useful word in your mind. It becomes a part of your active vocabulary when you know how to use it correctly in the right context.

This can be done in three stages: *First stage*: Understanding is the first stage of knowing a word. Study the structure, spelling, meaning and pronunciation of the word preferably with the help of a dictionary. *Second stage*: Then, try to visualize a picture or a situation corresponding to the word. *Third stage*: When you are sure you have understood the word, bring it in your usage, in speaking as well as in writing. Suppose the word is '*plaudits*' which means '*admiration*'. After understanding the word you may construct a vivid picture of a cricketer, who has scored the fastest century, surrounded by people shouting slogans of admiration, in a word '*plaudits*'. Then, be on a look out of a way to use it in a sentence.

One can also extend one's vocabulary by writing 5–10 new words every day from newspapers, magazines or a speech on a piece of card along with their complete profile. Learn them by making use of the method described above. Compile these newly learnt words in an alphabetical order along with their meaning, pronunciation and use in sentences. This will be a ready reference for you. Another method would be to acquaint yourself with a complete profile of words such as common English roots, affixes, synonyms, antonyms, homophones, homonyms, one word substitutions and familiarizing yourself with the words of daily use. All such elements of word building have been dealt with in Unit 3, *Word Elements* and Unit 4, *Vocabulary Building* in this book.

1.5.4 Speaking

Listening practice, thinking in English and vocabulary building are the perfect launching pads to start the process of speaking. After crossing the initial stage, the practice of all the four skills should be simultaneous. English is widely used in business, education, government offices, research and other formal platforms. In a country like India, where there are a variety of regional languages, English has been universally accepted as the *lingua franca* that is, a common language used between people whose main languages are different. In informal and social circles, especially in big cities and metropolitan towns, the use of oral interaction in English is gaining momentum. To achieve success in one's career, good communication skills in English have become a necessary requirement. In communication process, effective oral skills in English make the encoding part strong, resulting in an equally effective decoding by the receiver.

There are many techniques to develop oral communication in English. The learner should choose them according to his/her own requirement and abilities. The following guidelines can be of great utility to the learners:

1.5.4.1 Barriers in Learning Spoken English

The non-native learners of spoken English come across certain most commonly identified barriers during the process of learning and they should be aware of their specific barriers:

→ Hesitation
→ Limited word power
→ Weak grammar skills

1. Hesitation: A learner may hesitate to communicate in English due to various reasons. Some of the important ones are: (i) *Error syndrome:* A learner is highly error conscious and does not want to take risks of committing mistakes. (ii) *Image syndrome:* Some people may carry the notion that English is a language of prestige. A self-conscious learner, who cherishes this image of English, may not open up due to the fear of hurting his/her public image. (iii) *Weak English background:* Some learners from a weak background in English or non-English background lack strong will power required to groom themselves in the field of spoken English. A hesitant and obsessive nature creates an invisible wall in our mind and stops us from free expression. This wall needs to be broken consciously. All such difficulties and barriers in learning spoken English can be overcome by persistent efffort. With strong will power and you can boldly venture into the path of learning oral skills.

2. Limited Word Power:
A limited vocabulary in English may become an impediment in learning or improving oral skills. A speaker may find himself/herself at a loss to catch hold of the right word and may be forced to use words from his/her mother tongue. During the initial stages of learning, one can mix words of other languages to maintain the flow of speaking and to build self-confidence.

3. Weak Grammar Skills:
Weak grammar skills hamper effective communication. The speakers are not able to express their idea properly and the listener is unable to grasp it in the right perspective of time and action. At the same time, speaker's consciousness about his/her weak grammar causes hesitation.

1.5.4.2 Speaking Practice

The way we speak affects the image we project. You may be bright and deserving but if your speech and manner don't reflect those traits, you are not able to generate the desired response during the oral interaction. If someone doesn't take you seriously, perhaps you are at fault. You can also talk in English in the same way as others do by following the given suggestions:

1. Start with Short Sentences:
Language learning demands practice. As you cannot learn swimming without diving into water, you cannot develop spoken skills without gathering courage to speak in English and that too in public. Along with training your ears, listening exercises and efforts to enrich your English vocabulary of daily use, compile a list of sentences of day-to-day experience and translate them into English. Practice speaking by using them in routine conversations.

2. Mirror Face Test:
Mirror face test is an effective technique to practice speaking practice as it provides you privacy of learning. Choose a common topic, one that you can speak on, stand in front of a mirror and speak on the topic looking at yourself in the mirror. Maintain pleasant expressions while speaking and be calm from inside. Have a mirror session for 5 minutes daily (initially, you can have smaller sessions). Keep a close eye on your shortcomings and try to improve upon them with every session. You will soon notice that the practice will gradually carry over into your normal way of speaking.

3. Control Non-word Fillers:
Many speakers of English habitually use words such as '*you know*', '*um*', '*a…..*', '*like*', '*ok*', etc. as fillers. Every one of us utters occasional fillers, but too many will rob the sentence of its desired effect. At the same time, they will put you in an odd situation or convey to the listener either you are not prepared or you lack confidence. Identify your habitual non-word fillers and use the technique of replacing them with pauses and breathing intervals.

4. Make Role Models:
Make a list of people you have listened to personally, on radio, or on television. This is the part of your listening practice too. Mark the traits that make them sound effective

in their expression, clarity, fluency, energy and self-confidence. Try to overcome your shortcomings with speaking techniques.

5. Take Regular Feedback: Once you have started using the techniques of oral communication in English, take feedback for your improvement. You may ask it as a favour from a friend who is good with his English-speaking skills. Another way is to record your voice and play it back to listen to it objectively. Note down your weaknesses as well as your strong points and work upon them accordingly.

6. Use of Visual Reminders: Once you have identified your problem areas (such as fillers, rambling, trailing off without finishing a sentence, weaknesses related body language, etc.), write them on stickers. Stick them on some approachable spots like your bag, mobile phone, mirror, watch, etc. This will be a constant visual reminder to you for not using them again.

7. Practice Conversation: Indulging in conversations (formal, informal, telephonic) is a good practice to improve your oral skills. When you find that you have gained confidence in speaking short sentences, start participating in conversations. Role plays on day-to-day interactions can be very effective. At the same time, one should keep participating in the real conversations also. One should not shy away from getting into conversations. Tips to develop conversational skills are given as under:

   (i) *Starting a conversation*: Starting a conversation is known as the art of small talk which can be a nightmare for some people but do not let it become your problem area. There are many good starters you can use to open up a piece of conversation. Try to make them as commonplace as possible. For example:

   → *The food looks tempting. Doesn't it?*
   → *The traffic was awful.*
   → *What about parking? Where did you get it?*
   → *The coffee appears good.*

Don't let the starters become an interrogation but make your partner speak and watch for the response. When the ball is in your court, you must keep the conversation going.

   (ii) *Joining a conversation*: Social get-togethers demand mixing with people of different cultures and backgrounds. One should not keep mum when two persons are talking rather be bold and join them. As they might be talking personal, use your common sense and look for the right opportunity to join them with the sentence like, *'I am sure you won't mind if I join you.'*

   (iii) *Ending a conversation*: Be very polite and use the right time to leave the conversation. You can use comments like:

   → *It's been fantastic talking to you.*
   → *I think I should go and finish the job.*
   → *It's quite hot inside; I think I'd go in the fresh air.*

One should have the ability not only to start a conversation but also to help others start and keep it going.

8. Speak with Clarity and with Pauses: Speaking fast in the guise of fluency is not a sign of good spoken English. At least, do not try it during the initial learning stages. The listener might miss some important points that you want to convey. This may also distort the pronunciation and tone of speaking. Speak with clarity and pauses, paying attention to the tone, articulation, accent and pronunciation.

9. Be Friendly and Polite: Respect others' views and use polite expressions to show friendliness, express agreement/disagreement or to make suggestions (be cheerful and courteous during oral interactions).

10. Show Interest: Take active part in conversation by showing your keen interest in the verbal exchange. You may use expressions such as "Really?", "Is it so?" "Oh! My God!", "How interesting!", etc.

11. Be an Active Listener: To be an active conversationalist, be an active listener first. Listen to the speaker carefully without interrupting. Wait for the right opportunity to speak.

1.5.4.3 The Finer Touches: Fluency

Fluency is the flow of words pronounced correctly with proper speech modulation, without the use of unnecessary pauses, non-word fillers and repetitions, spoken with a moderate speed. Students have to understand that fluency is not speaking English fast. Speaking fast produces a jarring effect, mars politeness and mixes up pronunciations. This is a short cut which can be risky as it may make the speaker habitual of speaking fast with mistakes, leaving no room for improvement. It has been found that the average speed of speaking fluent English is 150 words per minute. If you have the habit of speeding up while speaking, do loud reading and count words per minute and then consciously reduce the pace of speaking to reach the desired speed. In functional English people tend to compromise accuracy with fluency. You may take this priviledge at the initial level but as you gain competency, achieve correctness alongwith fluency. There is no short cut to achieve fluency. It comes with regular practice. Once a learner starts speaking long sentences with clarity and pauses, he/she should aim at fluency by improving:

→ Articulation
→ Pronunciation
→ Expression
→ Accent and intonation

1. Articulation: Articulation is a technique to modify voice as well as to use tongue, teeth, lips and other organs to produce sounds. In English, there are 44 sounds, which should be produced distinctly. Regular practice of listening and articulating vowel and consonant sounds bring in good articulation and clarity in speech.

2. Pronunciation: Pronunciation plays an important role in determining the clarity of expression. Wrong pronunciation not only distorts the conversation but may also twist the meaning as understood by the listener. However, J. S. Bright feels, "*When you are conversing, go on speaking fluently even if, you do not know exact words or their pronunciations.*" This approach can be risky as it may provide speakers with a license to carry on talking boldly with their mistakes. One should remedy wrong pronunciations as soon as they are discovered. Human babies are best equipped to learn pronunciations as they have a natural tendency to listen and imitate. When this natural ability is lost, especially in adults, it is, indeed, very difficult to master pronunciations. This is because when one grows up, the die-hard habits of mother tongue, regional language and those of accent and wrong pronunciations, learnt at preprimary or primary stage, are very difficult to break. It requires considerable patience and determination to overcome these habits. Correct pronunciation is one which is understood by the majority of people. In English, received pronunciation (RP) (from British English) is the most acceptable dialect.

The learners of oral skills in English should study elementary phonetics along with various symbols and sounds of English. This will assist them to study pronunciation from dictionaries also. For example, the word 'career' (a person's professional future) is generally mispronounced as 'carrier' (something that carries), although they are two words with different meanings and pronunciations. Such instances of commonly mispronounced words are many. (A list of such words is given in the section on 'Speaking Skills' in 5.4.) Do rigorous listening practice of sounds, words and sentences. You may take one sound at a time, picking out its Englishness and the features which make it different from the nearest sound in your native language and the sounds which are recorded in your memory. Careful matching of the performance with listening will bring you nearer the model English pronunciation that is 'RP.'

3. Expression: Expression in spoken English means adjusting the tone and pitch of your voice according to the type of interaction—formal, informal, telephonic, during presentations, seminars, debates, meetings and group discussions, etc. This is also known as voice modulation. It can be learnt and improved through training and regular practice of listening to good English, recording your voice and getting proper feedback.

4. Accent: Right accent brings fluency in spoken English. Along with this, it lends a particular style which is characteristic of oral interaction. English is a language of stresses. A specific stress is laid on the specific part of a word, while other parts remain unstressed. This is not the case with most of the Indian languages, where parts of the words are given equal significance. Accent develops with regular participation in conversation and careful listening to speakers with good accent. (All these factors contribute to nurture fluency in English and they have been discussed in Unit 5, 'Speaking Skills').

1.5.5 Reading

Today, success in your professional life depends on your ability to read, write and speak well, in a way communicate effectively. All these activities are interrelated and need support of one another to master communication skills. Reading as a skill is very important as it helps you to develop style, word knowledge, sentence structures, which you can carry over in your writing as well as speaking almost unknowingly. Apart from this, reading enhances your knowledge of the outside world. Francis Bacon's comment, "Reading maketh a full man, writing an exact man and conferring a ready man" is quite apt for using language as a tool for communication. Reading skills give a firm background to speaking and writing skills.

1.5.6 Writing

Writing is a significant device to make your communication effective. In professional life, we have to communicate orally as well as in writing. One has to write letters, memos, notices, applications, reports, minutes of a meeting, etc. This requires a good command over grammar as well as use of suitable words and good expressions (formal and informal) in writing. We cannot neglect the skill of effective writing which leads to effective communication. Whenever there is a need for details and to make a record of the communication, writing is always preferred to oral communication. Besides this, creative writing enhances originality, enables you to express yourself on a given topic, helps you use your imagination and makes your communication better on the whole. Learning writing skills is crucial as writing is caught rather than taught. It blossoms in a relaxed atmosphere, depends on systematic acquisition of skills and emerges gradually through practice. The following steps will be helpful in developing effective writing:

Stages in the Development of Writing Skills:

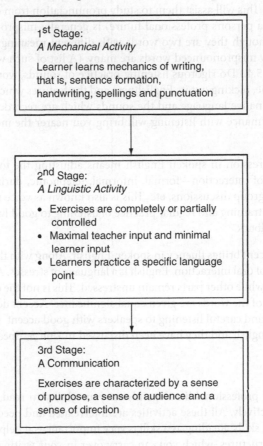

1st Stage:
A Mechanical Activity

Learner learns mechanics of writing,
that is, sentence formation,
handwriting, spellings and punctuation

2nd Stage:
A Linguistic Activity

- Exercises are completely or partially controlled
- Maximal teacher input and minimal learner input
- Learners practice a specific language point

3rd Stage:
A Communication

Exercises are characterized by a sense of purpose, a sense of audience and a sense of direction

Good writing results from effective listening, reading and speaking, and can be achieved through systematic attainment of all the language skills.

1.5.7   Grammar

Grammar has certainly an important role to play in learning written and spoken English. However, the extent of its use depends upon the learning stage of the student. The beginners, ideally speaking, should start with the process of learning grammar. It is advisable to concentrate on the practical aspects of grammatical features like sentence structure—difference between the fundamental structure of any Indian language and that of English, verb patterns, auxiliaries and modals, tenses, comparisons of adjectives and question tags. One should also learn the use of ellipsis for informal talk, for example:

Want a drink? (informal) – Do you want a drink? (formal)
Sounds fine to me. (informal) – It sounds fine to me. (formal)

Use of finite clauses and co-ordinations is preferred in spoken English. For example: instead of '*Getting exhausted, he went home early*', a better sentence in informal talk would be: '*He got so tired that he went home early*'.

Use of contracted forms of auxiliaries is typical of spoken discourse and should be preferred over the full forms. Spoken and written English share the same basic grammar. The variation is only in approach —it is functional or practical in case of the former and theoretical in the latter. The learners of oral communication should know this essential difference so that they may develop confidence in expressing themselves in written as well as in spoken English—in formal as well as in informal situations.

1.5.8   Body Language

Charles Darwin, in his book *The Expression of the Emotions in Man and Animals*, wrote, "The power of communication between the members of the same tribe by means of language has been of paramount importance in the development of man; and the course of language is much aided by the expressive movements of the face and the body". On paper, words are static but in face-to-face conversation message is conveyed at two levels simultaneously—verbal and nonverbal. Body language is a non-verbal communication and is an integral part of oral interaction. Nature has gifted human beings with the body that has a surprising versatility of expression. It keeps on communicating endlessly, round the clock, with an infinite variety of abstract signals, that too without getting tired. Although the most part of non-verbal communication is involuntary, it accounts for a larger part of the total message than the words. A research done by Albert Mehrabin, Professor Emeritus in psychology at the University of California, Los Angeles (UCLA), reports that words are only 7 per cent, voice tonality 38 per cent and body language 55 per cent in a message. Body language gives listeners important clues about thoughts and feelings of a speaker, confirming or contradicting the words he/she speaks. We achieve complete communication when our body works with our ideas. Body language should not be considered in isolation; rather, it should be taken in a broader perspective of personal appearance and grooming, posture, gestures, facial expressions, eye contact, paralinguistic aspects of speech and space (proxemics) and touch. A study of the following aspects of body language can help you acquire a deeper understanding of body language and motivate you to develop the right ones.

1. **Appearance and Dress:**   Appearance and dress are part and parcel of the message that we transmit to the listeners. The first impression is a lasting impression and the first thing we communicate about ourselves is through our appearance. Right from your hair style to your footware, appearance speaks a lot about you. Well-groomed people are generally regarded as people with skills, intelligence and professionalism, while a dishevelled appearance puts them at a disadvantage in the eyes of the observers.

2. **Posture:**   Posture plays an important role in communication and it can be positive or negative according to the situation. Good posture is a natural alignment of the body. A physiotherapist would advise one to keep ears, shoulders and hipbone in a straight line while sitting and on standing the same should be from hip down to the knee. A gait appears confident if a person walks straight and squared shouldered with stomach in. Not only this, holding the head awkwardly puts a lot of strain on the neck and shoulders, extending the tension throughout the body, while an unnatural posture makes the body a mass of stresses resulting in an undue strain on our vocal cords. Crossed arms and legs may indicate an unseen barrier or a negative attitude. Similarly, leaning away from the speaker most likely shows opposition, while leaning forward means that a person is open, honest and interested. A slumped posture presents a person in low spirits while an erect posture shows his/her high spirits, energy and confidence. Posture, as far as possible, should be natural to your body but it should be examined and corrected if it is not up to the mark. With sincere and determined efforts one can get rid of inappropriate traits and develop the right way of walking, sitting and standing.

3. Gestures: Gestures refer to the movements made by hands, arms, shoulders, head and torso. Sincere and meaningful gestures not only drive a point home but also add greater value to what is being said. Gestures clarify ideas and reinforce them; hence, they should be well suited to the audience as well as to the occasion. Too many gestures make a person look theatrical. For example, hand movements should be used to add emphasis to what is being said without waving arms around all over the place. Playing with earrings, wrist watch, fumbling with rings, twisting a key chain, clasping hands tightly, or cracking knuckles not only distracts the listener but also indicates hesitation, nervousness or lack of confidence. For communicating monosyllables such as "yes" or "no" avoid using fingers or head as it may be annoying for some people. Sometimes involuntary gestures such as biting nails and scratching your head, can give a lot of hidden information about a person's mental state. Dr. Alan Hirsch of St. Luke's Medical center, Chicago, explained "*Pinocchio Syndrome*" as something when "blood rushes to the nose when people lie. This extra blood may make the nose itchy." People who stretch the truth tend to either scratch their nose or touch it more often. Positive gestures can make us better communicators. Conscious effort and practice is required to develop the right gestures.

4. Facial Expressions: Face is the index of the mind; it conveys warmth and sincerity and is the most expressive part of our body. Expressions that cross our face send out signals which can be encouraging as well as discouraging. A smile stands for friendliness, a frown for discontent, raised eyebrows for disbelief, tightened jaw muscles for antagonism, etc. It puts the vocal cords at ease and helps the speaker sound interesting. Facial expressions are subtle as the face rarely sends a single message; rather it communicates a series of messages—anxiety, recognition, hesitation and pleasure—at the same time. Facial expressions should be encouraging. It has been seen that people often assume virtual masks which are rigid and incommunicable. For instance, if the mask is that of tight lips and a tense jaw with little expression, speakers may not get enough encouragement to talk. Some faces are very expressive while some are not. Let your expressions be natural and you should be careful enough not to display negative signs such as consistent frowning. At the same time, expressions should match the content of the verbal message.

5. Eye Contact: Eyes are considered to be the window of the soul; hence, eye contact is a direct and powerful form of non-verbal communication. Eyes are a rich source of feedback as a speaker looks at the listeners to find how they are reacting—are they bored, asleep or interested? The listeners too may search for truthfulness, intelligence, attitude and feelings of the speaker. If a speaker or a listener avoids eye contact, it may mean that he/she is guilty of something or is telling a lie. In a small group one should look at everyone at eye level, neither above their heads nor at the walls or at the other places. In a large group one can maintain eye contact by drawing a large imaginary 'M' or 'W' round the room. Maintaining eye contact with only one part of the audience may instil a feeling of neglect amongst the rest. It is not enough that one should look at the listeners, how one looks at them also matters a lot. Consistent eye contact indicates that the person is thinking positively of the speaker. If a person looks at the speaker but makes the arms-crossed-chest signal, the eye contact could be indicative that something is bothering the person. Fiddling with something while looking at the speaker means that the attention is somewhere else. The attention invariably wanders if a person is not being convinced by what the speaker is saying. So, we should be able to analyze the situation, particularly in the professional world and should make pleasant eye contact with the listeners to show that we are confident, concerned and interested.

6. Touch: Touch is an important element of body language. It goes beyond and forges a bond that is more on an emotional and spiritual level than on the physical one. Touch is an inherent desire of almost all the creatures. Children instinctively seek physical contact whenever they are disturbed. As one grows older, one tends to suppress this desire possibly due to fear of social embarrassment. Touch can also convey negative feeling if it is used unwillingly. In India, one has to be careful as touch and the extent of it has its own cultural reservations.

7. The Voice of Silence: Silence can be a very effective means of communication, if used positively and in the right context. The age old saying 'speech is silver; silence is gold' undoubtedly refers to the superiority of silence over verbal communication. A well-timed silence has more eloquence than speech. In face-to-face communication, it can communicate a number of messages. However, with the help of a right posture and proper facial expressions, silence can be highly effective.

8. Cultural Variations in Body Language: These aspects of body language are an integral part of oral interaction and we should try to develop them for effective communication. However, some mannerisms are culture specific. Social status, age, occupation and ethnic background also influence nonverbal signs. People who are enthusiastic about communication should not take cultural differences of body signals lightly. We should know the variations that could cause failure in communication. In a country like India, there can be regional cultural variations too. For example, it has been observed that North Indians like to talk in a more informal tone than the people of the other parts of the country. A handshake, an embrace, a kiss on cheek and lips in public may be a traditional form of greeting in many western countries but in Asian countries such as India, Pakistan and China such gestures are frowned upon and are considered actions reserved for one's private life. In many cultures, 'thumps up' is a positive sign while in Greece it is negative. In the west, most people sit when they wish to remain in place for some time, but in many Asian countries squatting is considered as primitive by some westerners. Bowing as a greeting is traditional in Japan but may be interpreted as a sign of subordination in other cultures. Therefore, one can see that it is not safe to assume that gestures used with all innocence in one country are accepted in the same manner throughout the world.

Task

Answer each of the following questions:

1. What is communication? Discuss its significance for society as well as for an organization.
2. What is the process of communication? Explain how a message moves through different stages of the process to make communication effective.
3. What are the various skills needed for effective communication?
4. Discuss the steps that can be taken for their development.
5. What steps can be taken to develop a good word power?
6. How is body language important in communication?

Write short notes on the following:

1. Right encoding and right decoding are essential for the success of communication.
2. Channel and medium of communication should be need specific.
3. Eye contact of the speaker with the listener is an important part of body language.

Use of Technology in Developing Communication Skills

2

In this unit

- ✓ Introduction
- ✓ Computer Assisted Language Learning (CALL)
- ✓ Effectiveness of CALL for Developing English Language Skills
- ✓ Use of Internet

"Technology can not be a goal in itself. However, a holistic integration of technology in teaching is the need of the hour."

–Mini Joseph

2.1 Introduction

Nothing succeeds like success. This phrase goes well with technology, which has surpassed everything in its progress and the success rate is almost 100%. Out of the various available technologies, communication technology is progressing at the fastest rate and computer is playing a leading role in this advancement. Technological advancement not only makes the communication easier but also has a major share in the communication flow. Media of communication have been changing with the passage of time. Drums, pigeons and horse messengers were some of the early media of communication. With the advancement of technology, more complex media such as radio, telegram, telegraph, wireless, and telephone, have been beautifully realized. Today, mobile phones and Internet have become the most widely used media for both the oral and written exchange of messages. Communication technology is continuously upgraded from slow to fast and simple to complex. The science fiction of yesteryears is becoming a reality today. Teleconferencing, video conferencing, audio-visual aids, television, voice mails, audio tapes, compact discs (CDs), digital video discs (DVDs), pen drives and various types of software have brought a revolution in the field of communication.

It is an undebatable fact that if you want to be professionally successful, you will have to be highly proficient in communication skills. There is always a need not only to learn these skills but also to upgrade them from time to time, depending upon the latest situations that you may come across in the course of your career advancement. Sophistication in computer technology has made it available as a necessary tool for learning and developing the skills of oral and written interactions, commonly referred to as 'Computer Assisted Language Learning' ('CALL'). This new learning of language, especially for the non-native learners of English as a second language (ESL) and English as a foreign language (EFL) is fast gaining acceptance globally and the results are quite encouraging. Teaching technology has offered students those opportunities which no one had imagined before. Consequently, it has also brought marked changes in curriculum as well as in teaching techniques. The best part is that the current technological tools to develop such skills are learner centric, rather than teacher centric. So, as a student of communication skills in English, one must have the knowledge of the technology being used and should make an active use of it as a tool in learning interactive skills.

2.2   Computer Assisted Language Learning (CALL)

For many years, foreign-language teachers have used computer to provide supplemental exercises. CALL used to focus on vocabulary or discrete grammar points was more or less restricted to the basic drill-and-practice software programmes. In recent years, advancements in computer technology have motivated software developers as well as teachers to reassess the use of computer and consider it as an essential part of daily foreign-language learning. Innovative and interactive software programmes, authoring capabilities, CD technology and elaborate computer network are providing teachers with new methods of incorporating vocabulary, grammar, interactive sessions on real-life situations and writing into it. At the same time students gain access to audio, visual and textual information about the culture and language of non-native and native speakers. Simultaneously, they get necessary information and tips on developing the various skills of communication. For example, there are programmes, which are simulations that provide country-specific situations in a task-based format. Many other software programmes provide an entertaining environment for the students to learn the target language through problem solving and other entertaining tasks. There are writing assistants that aid students in writing compositions in English language by providing help in grammar, style, and verb conjugation and their usage.

CD technology (CDs and DVDs) has many uses in teaching foreign language. It includes information retrieval, interactive audio, video and other multimedia programmes. The CD allows us to store a huge amount of information on one disc along with the facility of quick access to the same. Publishers have put complete encyclopaedias, which could fill more than a dozen floppy discs, on one CD. Students and teachers can use the information quickly and efficiently in and out of the classroom. In recent years, many effective foreign language computer programmes for learning communication skills have been loaded on CDs.

Once you have chosen a wide range of tools, available for language learning in CALL, a right kind of technological environment, that can support you in various aspects of language learning, is required. Here, two options are available for you. You can either go for (i) self-learning or (ii) integrated group learning.

2.2.1   Self-learning Through the Use of Technology

The basic hardware requirement for this type of learning is a multimedia computer, a good-quality web camera, a headphone and the study material in the form of software of an interactive language-learning programme or similar type of programmes on CDs. While selecting the software, one should keep the following points in mind:

(a) Competency level of your interactive skills in English.
(b) It should be interactive, activity based and should particularly cover the development of all the required skills—namely listening, thinking, speaking, vocabulary, grammar, reading, writing and body language. (These skills have been dealt in detail in Unit 1, "Effective Communication".)
(c) It should be a reputed product.

The equipment should be set up in a quiet place, which has no echo. Now start using the programme and proceed systematically following the instructions given therein. Good interactive programmes have the facility of feedback, which you can use for self-judgement. The feedback of one's own performance is an essential part of self-learning as it indicates how fast or slow one has to proceed, which items need more practice and so on. Self-learning with technology has its advantages as well as limitations.

Advantages

Some of the advantages are listed below:

→ Good for beginners as it provides privacy of learning; hence, ideal for removing hesitation and building the initial confidence.
→ Useful for people who have time constraints.
→ Helpful for developing listening skills and viewing material to enrich basic vocabulary and grammar.
→ Provides perfect environment for self-analysis by recording one's own voice and viewing body language using the webcam and monitoring it from time to time.

Limitations

Some of the limitations are listed below:

→ Does not provide opportunity for real-life interactions with individuals, and does not provide environment required to gain confidence and fluency.
→ The software is your instructor, which lacks the natural versatility and originality of a teacher. Human understanding and empathy is missing and there is no room for teacher's guidance and doubt-clearing sessions.
→ The software programmes may not be learner specific.
→ Regular sessions may lead to too much dependence upon technology.
→ For a computer-savvy learner, technology may become the aim.
→ Technology (hardware and software) may not be easily affordable.

2.2.2   Integrated Group Learning Using a Multimedia Language Laboratory

State-of-the-art language teaching involves teaching syntax and grammar, phonetics and communication skills besides vocabulary enhancement. The task before the teacher is to motivate the student to speak and to improve his/her oral/aural abilities. The student also needs facility to assess his/her own performance. Multimedia language laboratory is an invaluable tool in this process.

There may be different versions of language laboratories that cater to the various requirements of the learners; the one that is currently gaining acceptance is a fully computerized, software-based and interactive laboratory for gaining competency in a targeted language area. A language laboratory consists of:

(a) A teacher's workstation facing the students, fitted with a computer, a headphone, a console and an auxiliary station for audio and video input.
(b) Student terminals (number of terminals may depend upon the capacity of the laboratory software), each fitted with a computer, headphone and a volume control. All the terminals are duly numbered.
(c) Video projection for common viewing.

Computers of the student terminals are linked together through local area network (LAN). They offer teachers a novel approach for creating new activities for students to provide them with more time and new experience in the targeted language. Certain LAN set-ups allow students and teachers to correspond with one another via computer or to conduct collaborative writing activities. Exercises on such a system enable students and teachers to communicate back and forth. Students may also be engaged in co-operative writing exercises, conversations and problem-solving exercises. Teachers can observe students' activities and progress and provide feedback to individual learners from the teacher's station.

The first requirement of using such a laboratory is that the learner should be able to work on a computer and should understand the working of such a laboratory. A language laboratory of this type normally has the following features:

1. The Interactive Nature: The laboratory is fully interactive with teacher to learner, learner to teacher and learner-to-learner interactions.

2. Audio Link: Oral communication in the first two types is made possible through audio hardware links via headphones, while the to and fro link between learners is established by going into grouping option. Teachers can address all the learners at a time or to a specific learner. A learner can individually communicate with the teacher to ask a question or clarify a doubt.

3. Text Messaging: Text messages can be transferred back and forth at all the three levels of interactions. Learners can take on-line objective type and short-answer type tests prepared by the teacher for testing specific deficient areas. They can also exchange messages and can use them creatively to supplement oral interactive activities.

4. Audio Broadcast: Audio files (recorded lessons through teacher's authoring and other audio software programmes and CDs) can be transferred to student terminals for on-line listening. The broadcast audio lessons are used by the learners to develop and improve listening exercises. Some laboratories even give the option of transcribing the audio material to cross check the effectiveness of their listening.

5. Video Transfer: Watching videos is highly fruitful for the appropriate use of body language as well as for enhancing oral skills. The laboratory software provides you with the option of transferring video CDs and DVDs and videos of a software study material to the monitors of the individual learner or to the common viewing facility through LCD projection. The learners can watch videos with original audio of animations, role-plays, group interactions, interviews, film clippings, speeches and presentations. Apart from using videos from language teaching software and CDs, self-made video shoots will be a rich source of learning and feedback. This will help learners develop and improve their understanding of pronunciations, stress, rhythm, intonation expression and culture. Here, it will be advisable to include videos of both the native and non-native speakers. The teacher's voice, if required, can also be inserted for further explanations.

6. Speech Recognition: Many language laboratories provide the option of speech recognition with in-built pronunciation of some words and a facility to compare the user's voice with the model. Here, the teacher should choose a pronunciation programme using the RP as it has gained a global acceptance. However, to be more user specific, teacher-authored programmes would be more suitable. Recorded files containing correct pronunciation of commonly mispronounced words and sentences, etc., get registered on the teacher's track and thereby transferred to the student terminals. This software has a program disc and various language discs that contain the digitized speech. With such programs, students are able to listen to the pronunciation of a phrase, a word, or even a syllable or a sound and then record their own voice on the student track, following the example. Thereafter, they can listen to the original recording, as well as their own, and compare the two for self-assessment and self-analysis. The learners can record their own voices again and compare the two until they feel their pronunciation has improved or it is correct. In addition to aural comparison, students can compare the two digitalized tracks plotted in waveform and, in this way, can pinpoint their variations to the level of syllable and even to the individual sound. Learners can also use this option for self-study under the effective guidance of the teacher.

7. **Group Formation:**   One essential feature is the formation of multiple groups to carry out paired conversations using role-plays and group discussions. The software allows the teacher to participate in group activity and record them for feedback and self-evaluation. Group discussion is an essential criterion for selection in jobs, while a role-play develops face-to-face conversational skills, confidence and fluency. In a language laboratory, ideally speaking, each student terminal should be provided with partitions on the left and the right of the terminal to ensure privacy of learning. In a group activity, learners can discuss a subject without being exposed to their partners. This reduces their inhibitions to speaking. In a paired conversation, a learner can overcome the fear of being spotted. Once the required confidence has been gained, group interactions should be carried out separately.

8. **Screen Transfer:**   Language laboratories give the option of transferring the teacher's monitor screen to that of the student's and vice versa. This facilitates the teacher to display different types of text information, pictures and videos on student's monitors. Power point presentations on topics can be shown directly on student terminals. Learners can be taught to create power point slides with live demos. A teacher can view their monitor screens for effective monitoring of the class.

2.3   Effectiveness of CALL for Developing English Language Skills

We have seen the various technical options available in a multimedia language laboratory and the activities which can be performed using these options. In fact, such a type of laboratory is an ideal proposition for learning English language skills, oral as well as written, and can be a great supplement to classroom teaching.

Listening exercises carried out in a language laboratory have been found to be highly fruitful. The learners, according to their requirement, are exposed to intensive listening of English sounds, recorded texts, speeches, discussions, stories, reviews and role-plays. Prior to this, a few minutes can be assigned to the aural recognition of vocabulary used and clarification of the other aspects of the listening material. Specific stress should be laid on the development of aural and oral skills. Teaching of phonetic symbols can come at a later stage. Development of listening skills demands training of the ear by an exposure to a wide variety of native and non-native speakers, discussing familiar topics and using normal conversational deliveries. Learners are able to listen to the finer variations of pronunciations and intonation with superior quality of digitalized sound. Listening strengthens the subconscious grasping of the nuances of the language and helps overcome the mother tongue and regional language barrier.

During laboratory sessions, the main concentration is on learner-to-learner interaction by involving them in various activities. In a free conversation or a situational role-play, students should be able to respond intelligently to what someone else has said. To make learning faster and more effective, audiovisual effect can be brought in by making students listen and watch simultaneously. Advance learners may listen and watch CDs of job interviews, interviews of politicians and celebrities, group discussions on various topics. As learners need to use language more independently, activities such as face-to-face interactions, role-plays, mock interviews, group discussions and presentations should be performed and demonstrated more and more in the laboratory. Pictures of people interacting in various situations may be displayed and students may be asked to comment, discuss and converse on them. As the learner's confidence increases, a teacher can introduce more activities such as problem solving, brain-storming sessions, film reviews, debates, open house and mock press conferences. Availability of a language laboratory makes the speaking activities highly effective and productive as all the interactive sessions can be recorded, played and replayed to the students for assessment and error corrections.

Loud reading practice is a tested tool for bringing clarity and fluency in speaking. Reading activities can be recorded in a language laboratory for self-analysis and monitoring the speed of speaking, which should be around 150–160 words per minute. The exercises on grammar items, dealt within classes, may be carried out skilfully in the laboratory relieving the students from the monotony of the classroom teaching. Writing skills should also be made an important part of the laboratory activity. Learners may be asked to write passages on eye-catching visual clues, pictures and video clippings transferred or shown to them on their monitor screens. They may also be given the task of writing words, which are relevant to the given clues. This activity will assist them in vocabulary building. In this way, a multimedia technology of a language laboratory can be proved to be an excellent additional tool for strengthening, not only the listening and the speaking skills, but also the skills of word building, grammar, reading and writing. Above all, the language laboratory sessions remove the tedium of a traditional language learning class.

2.4   Use of Internet

With the focus on language, communication and culture, English language teachers are continually searching for better ways of accessing authentic materials that will improve their students' knowledge and skills in the targeted areas. As the technology of Internet has transformed communication around the world, it is natural that it should play a major role in a multimedia language laboratory for developing English language skills. E-mail, is the most commonly used Internet application today. English language teachers can integrate e-mail-based activities into their curriculum. The search engines such as Goggle and Yahoo take you to sites that enable you to correspond with native speakers of the English language. The infrastructure requirements for e-mail are minimal, making it the most available of all Internet tools. Today's e-mail software can handle text in a wide variety of languages, and can include word-processed files as attachments. The software also allows us to send sound and images as attachments that enhance the context of the written communication. British Broadcasting Corporation (BBC) is doing an excellent job in providing regular on-line lessons on English language learning. Technology has advanced to such an extent that there are sites, which provide you on-line language laboratories giving you listening and speaking practice with recording facility for feedback. A web camera can be a very important tool for on-line video conferencing, which can be used to interact with native and non-native speakers. One such application is Internet Relay Chat (IRC), which enables synchronous "conversation" among participants in different parts of the world.

Technology is growing very fast and we will have newer and newer techniques each day for improving communication skills. However, it cannot be a substitute to the classical method of language teaching. It supplements the basic training system. The teacher is very much on the scene and has a big responsibility. At the same time the teacher has to make learners understand that their aim is not mastering technology but language itself. It is he/she who identifies the weaknesses of the learners, provides them with the correct guidance, motivates them, inculcates confidence in them and makes language-learning experience a real joy.

Task

Answer the following questions:

(a) What is CALL? How can it be effectively used to develop communication skills?
(b) How can a multimedia language laboratory be beneficial to language learning?
(c) Compare the advantages and disadvantages of technology aided self-learning and integrated group learning.

Write short notes on the following:

(a) Use of Internet in language learning
(b) Technology as a teacher
(c) Technology is a good servant but a bad master

3

In this unit

✓ Introduction
✓ Root/Base: The Core of a Word
✓ Affixes

✎ Prefix: The Frontal Element
✎ Suffix: The Tail to Modify Meaning

"Colours fade, temples crumble, empires fall, but wise words endure."

–Edward Throndike

3.1 Introduction

A study of 'Word Elements' plays a significant role in the field of vocabulary building. It is practically intricate for us to remember the wide range of words just by cramming them. Knowledge of the elements of a word: root/base and affix, technically known as morphemes (from the Greek word *'morphe'*) would be a much better proposition to enrich the vocabulary of professionals including the engineers-in-making.

3.2 Roots/Base: The Core of a Word

A root is the basic part of a word that comprises its main meaning and is used to form its derivatives. It is a letter or a group of letters taken from Greek or Latin language in English. Roots and bases are the original or primary words. They are added to a prefix, a suffix or a word to change its meaning or to form a new word. As you study the following chart, you can notice that the Latin or the Greek root word is often simple in meaning: Latin, *anima*, is 'spirit,' or Greek, *dunamis*, is 'power.' The table that follows lists many common roots/bases of English language, their sources (Greek/Latin) along with the shades of meanings they have acquired in English word building:

Root with its meaning	Source of the root with its meaning in English	Sample words
• *act, ag*: do, act, drive	Latin, *agere*: to drive, lead, act	active, actor, agile, agenda
• *am, ami*: love, like	Latin, *amor*: to love, *amicus*: friend	amorous, amicable, amiable
• *anim*: mind, life, spirit	Latin, *anima*: spirit	animal, animate

(Continued)

Root with its meaning	Source of the root with its meaning in English	Sample words
• *aero*: air	Greek, *aero*: air	aerobics, aerodynamics
• *arch*: chief	Greek, *arkhos*: chief, *arkhein*: to rule	architect, archaic, monarch
• *astr, aster*: star	Greek, *astron*: stars	astrology, astronomy, disaster
• *annu, enni*: yearly	Latin, *annus*: yearly	annual, perennial, annals, annuity
• *anthrop*: man	Greek, *anthropos*: man, people	anthropology, anthropoid, misanthrope, philanthropist
• *auc, aug, aut*: to originate, to increase	Latin, *augere*: to originate, increase	auction, augment, authentic
• *aud, audi, audit*: hear	Latin, *audire*: to hear, to examine	audible, audience, auditorium, audition
• *bel, belli*: An act or situation of a war	Latin, *bellum*: war	rebel, belligerent, rebellion, bellicose
• *bene, ben*: good, well, gentle	Latin, *bene*: good	benefit, benevolent, benediction, benign
• *bio*: life	Greek, *bios*: life	biography, biology, antibiotic
• *bible, biblio*: book	Greek, *biblion*: book	bibliophile, bibliography, biblical
• *brev*: short	Latin, *brevis*: short	abbreviate, brevity, brief
• *cad, cap, cas, ceiv, cept, cip, capt, cid*: to take, to seize, to hold	Latin, *capere*: to seize, to fall	cadaver, cadence, capable, occasion, casual, receive, intercept, concept, except, recipient, captive, capture, accident
• *carn*: flesh	Latin, *caro carn*: flesh	carnal, carnivorous, carnival, carnation
• *ced, ceas, cede, ceed, cess*: go, yield	Latin, *cedere*: to go, yield, give way	antecedent, cease, accede, precede, recede, exceed, succeed, excess, success
• *celer*: fast	Latin, *celer*: fast, rapid	accelerate
• *cent*: hundred	Latin, *centum*: hundred	century, centipede
• *chron*: time	Greek, *khronos*: time	chronology, chronic, chronicle, synchronize
• *cite, cit*: quote	Latin, *citare*: set in motion	cite, incite, citation
• *clam, claim*: shout	Latin, *clamare*: to call out, shout	clamour, proclaim

(Continued)

Root with its meaning	Source of the root with its meaning in English	Sample words
• *cogn, gnos*: know to know	Latin, *cognoscere*: to know	recognize, cognition, diagnose, agnostic
• *cord*: heart	Latin, *cor cord*: heart	cordial, accord, record, discord
• *corp, corpor*: body	Latin, *corpus, corporis*: body	corps, corpulent, corpse, corporate, corporation
• *cosm*: universe	Greek, *cosmos*: universe as a well-ordered whole	cosmology, cosmopolitan
• *cre, cresc, crease, cret*: grow	Latin, *crescere*: to grow	create, crèche, crescent, increase, accretion
• *cred*: trust, believe	Latin, *credo, creditum*: to believe	credible, credentials, creed, credit, credulous
• *cour, cur, curr, curs*: run, course	Latin, *currere*: run	discourse, occur, concur, current, cursor, cursive
• *dent*: tooth	Latin: *dens, dent*: tooth	dental, dentist
• *derm, dermat*: skin	Greek: *derma*: skin	epidermis, hypodermic, dermatitis
• *dic, dict*: say, speak	Latin, *dictare, dicere*: to say, speak	dictate, diction, contradict, edict
• *doc, doct*: teach, prove	Latin, *docere*: to teach	docile, document, doctrine, doctoral, doctor
• *dog, dox*: thought, idea	Greek, *dokein*: seem, think	dogma, doxology
• *dec*: suitable	Latin, *decere*: to be suitable	decent, decency
• *duc, duct*: lead	Latin: *ducere*: to lead, to draw	conducive, produce, conduct, ductile
• *dynam*: power	Greek, *dunamis*: power	dynamic, dynamite
• *electric, electro*: electric	Greek, *electrum*: amber	electricity, hydroelectric, electromagnetic, electronic
• *ev, et*: time, age	Latin, *aevum*: lifetime	medieval, eternal
• *fac, fact, fect, fas, fea*: make, do	Latin, *facere*- make, do	fact, facile, factory, manufacture, perfect, affect, fashion, feasible, feature
• *fer, late*: bear, carry	Latin, *ferre*: bear, carry	confer, differ, offer, prefer, relate, collate
• *feign, fain*: shape, make, fashion	Latin, *fingere*: shape, make	feign, fiction, faint, fictitious

(Continued)

Root with its meaning	Source of the root with its meaning in English	Sample words
• *fid*: belief, faith	Latin, *fidere*: to trust	confide, confidence
• *fig*: shape, form	Latin, *figura*: form, shape, figure	figure, configure
• *fix*: fasten	Latin, *figere*: fix	fixation, affix, prefix
• *flu, fluct, flux*: drawing flow	Latin, *fluere*: to flow	fluid, influence, flush, fluently, fluctuate, influx
• *form*: shape	Latin, *formare*: beauty, shape, form	format, form, conform, formulate, perform, formal
• *fract, frag, frai*: break	Latin, *frangere*: to break	fraction, fracture, fragment, fragile, frail, frailty
• *gen, gin*: to give birth, kind	Greek, *genus, gener*: stock, race	generate, genesis, genetics, gingerly
• *geo*: earth	Greek, *ge*: earth	geography, geometry, geocentric, geology
• *grad, gress, gree*: step, go, move	Latin, *gradus*: step	gradual, digress, degree
• *graph, graf*: write, draw	Greek, *graphe*: write, scratch, carve	graphic, biography, autograph, photography, graft
• *her, hes*: to stick	Latin, *haerere*: to stick	adhere, inherent, hereditary, cohesion, hesitate
• *jac, ject*: to throw	Latin, *jacere*: to throw, to lie	ejaculate, adjacent, reject, eject, project, trajectory, inject
• *jug, junct, just*: to join	Latin, *jungere*: to join	juggle, conjugal, junction, justify, adjust
• *labor*: to hit something of somebody by hand	Latin, *labor*: to hit something of somebody by hand	laborious, labourer, laboratory
• *leag, leg*: law	Latin, *lex*: law	legal, legitimate, league, college
• *lect, leg, lig*: choose, gather, select, read	Latin, *legere*: to choose	collect, legible, eligible
• *loco, loc*: place, area	Latin, *locare*: to place	locomotion, location, locally, locality, allocate
• *log*: say, speech, word, reason, study	Greek, *logos*: speech, word, reason	logic, biology, logical
• *luc, lum, lust*: light	Latin, *lucare*: shine, Latin, *lumen*: light, Latin, *lustrare*: light-up	translucent, illuminate, luster, illustrate

(*Continued*)

Root with its meaning	Source of the root with its meaning in English	Sample words
• *man*: hand, make, do	Latin, *manus*: hand	manage, manuscript, manual, manifest
• *mem*: recall, remember	Latin, *memor*: mindful	memory, memo, memento, memorable
• *ment*: mind	Latin, *mens*: mind	mental, mention
• *micro*: very small	Greek, *mikros*: Very small	microwave, microphone, microorganism, microscope
• *min*: little, small	Latin, *minuere*: to lessen	minute, minor
• *mit, miss, mission*: send	Latin, *mittere*: put, send	admit, permit, submit, admission, permission, submission
• *mobile, mob, mov, mot*: move	Latin, *mobilis, movere*: move, movable	automobile, mobilize, mobilization, remove, movable, motor, motion
• *mune, muni*: service	Latin, *munis*: Service	immune, community
• *nasc, nat, gnant, nai*: to be born	Latin, *gnasci* to be born	nascent, native, pregnant, naïve
• *nom, nym*: name	Latin, *nomen, nomin*: name	nominate, ignominious, pseudonym
• *nov*: new	Latin, *novus*: new	novice, novel, renovate, innovate
• *oper*: work	Latin, *opus*: work	operate, co-operate, opus
• *pat, pass*: feel, suffer	Latin, *pati*: suffer	passion, patient, passion
• *path*: feel	Greek, *pathos*: feeling	sympathy, pathology
• *ped*: foot	Latin, *pes, ped*: foot	impede, pedal, pedestrian, centipede
• *pod*: foot	Greek, *pous*: foot	podium, tripod, podiatry, antipode
• *pel, puls*: drive, push	Latin, *pellere*: to drive, push, beat	compel, dispel, expel, impulse, compulsory, repulsive
• *pend, pens, pond*: to hang, weigh	Latin, *pendere*: to hang, to weigh	pendant, suspend, append, pensive, pension, respond, despondent
• *phan, phen, fan, phant, fant*: show, make visible	Greek, *phainein*: show	phantom, phenomenon, fantasy
• *philo, phil*: love	Greek, *philos*: loving	philosopher, philanthropy

(Continued)

Root with its meaning	Source of the root with its meaning in English	Sample words
• *phon*: sound	Greek, *phone*: voice, sound	phonetic, telephone, phonograph microphone, symphony
• *pict*: paint, show, draw	Latin, *pingere*: to paint	picture, depict
• *port*: carry	Latin, *portare*: carry	import, export, transport
• *pli, ply*: fold	Latin, *plicare*: fold	implication, application, reply, ply
• *pon, pos, pound*: put, place	Latin, *ponere*: to lay down, place	opponent, postpone, expose, impose, posture, expound, impound
• *psych*: mind	Greek, *psukhe*: soul, spirit	psyche, psychiatry, psychology, psychosis
• *puter, pute*: to think	Latin, *putare*: to think	computer, dispute, repute
• *quir, quis, quest, quer*: seek, ask	Latin, *quaerere*: seek, ask	inquire, inquisitive, question, query
• *rupt*: break	Latin, *rumpere*: break	rupture, interrupt, abrupt, disrupt,
• *sci, scio*: to know	Latin, *scire*: to know	conscience, conscious, omniscient
• *scrib, scrip*: write	Latin, *scribere*: to write	scribble, inscribe, describe, prescribe, manuscript, script
• *sent, sens*: feel, think	Latin, *sentire*: feel	sentiment, consent, resent, dissent, sense, sensory
• *sequ, secut, sue*: follow	Latin, *sequi*: to follow	sequence, consequence, sequel, prosecute, consecutive, ensue, pursue
• *sist*: to withstand, make up	Latin, *sistere*: to make a stand	insist, assist, persist, resist
• *soci*: to join, companions	Latin, *socialis, socius*: to join, a companion	sociable, sociable, sociology
• *sol*: alone	Latin, *solus*: alone, single	solo, soliloquy, solitary, isolate
• *solv, solu, solut*: loosen, explain	Latin, *solvere*: to loosen, release	solve, absolve, soluble, resolution, resolute, dissolute
• *spec, spic, spect*: look	Latin, *specere*: look, look at	speculate, specimen, specific, aspect, inspect, respect
• *sphere*: ball	Greek, *sphaira*: ball, sphere	sphere, stratosphere, hemisphere, spheroid

(Continued)

Root with its meaning	Source of the root with its meaning in English	Sample words
• *spir*: breath, soul	Latin, *spirare*: breathe	respiration, spirit, conspire, inspire, aspire, expire
• *stab, stat*: stand	Latin, *stare*: to stand	establish, stable, stature, stance
• *strain, strict, string*: bind, pull	Latin, *stringere*: to bind or pull tight	restrain, constraint, constrict, strict, restrict, stringent
• *stru, struct, stroy*: build	Latin, *struere*: to build	structure, instruct, obstruct, destruction, construct, destroy
• *tact, tang, tig, ting*: touch	Latin, *tangere*: to touch	tactile, contact, tangible, contagious, contiguous, contingent
• *tele*: far away	Greek, *tele*: end	telephone, telegraph, telegram, telescope, telecast, telepathy
• *tend, tent, tens*: stretch	Latin, *tendere*: to stretch	extend, contend, pretend, extent, tension, pretence
• *tain, ten, tent, tin*: hold, keep, have	Latin, *tenere*: to hold	retain, contain, abstain, pertain, tenure, detention, retentive, content, pertinent, continent
• *term*: end, boundary, limit	Latin, *terminus*: limit, boundary	exterminate, terminal
• *terr*: earth	Latin, *terra*: earth	territory, terrestrial
• *test*: see, witness	Latin, *testis*: witness	testament, detest, testimony, attest, testify
• *therm*: heat	Greek, *therme*: heat	thermometer, theorem, thermal, thermos bottle, thermostat
• *tor, tors, tort*: twist	Latin, *torquere*: twist	torture, retort, extort, distort, contort, torsion, tortuous
• *tract, trai, treat*: pull, draw	Latin, *trahere*: pull	attract, tractor, traction, extract, trailer, retreat, subtract
• *uni*: one	Latin, *unus*: one	union, uniform, universal, unity, unanimous
• *vac*: empty	Latin, *vacare*: to be empty	vacate, vacuum, evacuate, vacation, vacant
• *ven, vent*: come	Latin, *venire*: to come	convene, venue, avenue, invent, convent, event, prevent
• *very, ver*: true	Latin, *venus*: true	very, verdict, verity, verify

(Continued)

Root with its meaning	Source of the root with its meaning in English	Sample words
• *verb, verv*: word	Latin, *verbum*: word	verbose, verbalize, verify
• *vers, vert*: turn, change	Latin, *vertere*: to turn	diversion, reverse, versatile, convert, advertise, introvert
• *vid, vie, vis*: see	Latin, *videre*: to see; Latin, *videre*: to separate	video, evident, review, preview, visible, revise, vision
• *vit, viv*: live	Latin, *vivere*: to live	vitality, vital, vitamins, revive, survive, vivid
• *voc, voke*: call	Latin, *vocare*: call, voice	vocation, invocation, advocate, vocal, evoke, provoke, revoke
• *volv, volt, vol*: roll, turn	Latin, *volvere*: to roll, turn	revolve, revolt, evolution, voluble, voluminous

3.3 Affixes

Some words are formed with the help of affixes (a prefix or a suffix). They were originally words themselves but they are now letters or groups of letters added to words or to roots to create new words.

3.3.1 Prefix: The Frontal Element

Prefixes [pre (before) + fix (fasten) = fasten before] are groups of letters placed before words or roots. Prefixes modify or extend the meanings of words and roots. Following is the table that lists commonly used prefixes and sample vocabulary:

Prefixes	Meaning	Sample words
A-, Ac-, Ad-, Af-, Ag-, Al-, An-, Ap-, As-, At-	to, toward, near, in addition to	aside, afloat, accord, acclaim, adapt, admire, affix, affair, aggression, aggravate, alleviate, allow, annex, annihilate, apparition, appear, associate, attend, attain
A-, An-	without	amoral, asexual, apart, atheist, anaemic, anaesthetic
Ab-, Abs-	away from, off	abdicate, abduct, abnormal, absent, absolve, abstain
Acer-, Acid-, Acri-	bitter, sour, sharp, keen	acerbic, acid, acrid, acrimony
Acu-	sharp	acute, acupuncture, accurate, acupressure
After-	later	aftercare, afterbirth, afterwards, afternoon
Agri-, Agro-	pertaining to fields or soil	agriculture, agribusiness, agro industry

(Continued)

Prefixes	Meaning	Sample words
Ali-, Alter-	other	alias, alibi, alternate, altercation
Ambi-	on both sides	ambiguous, ambivalent, ambitious, ambiance
Ambul-	to walk	ambulatory, ambulance
Ante-	before	anterior, antecedent, antedate
Anti-	against	antiseptic, antidote, antibacterial, antibiotic
Aq-	water	aquatic, aquaculture, aquamarine
Auto-	self	automotive, autonomy, autocracy, autograph
Bar-	weight, pressure	barograph, barometer, barbarian, barbecue
Bi-	two	biannual, bicycle, biweekly, bilingual, binocular
Be-	on, around, over, about, make, cause, affect	befall, befriend, beside, become, before
By-	subordinate	bypass, byproduct, byline, bygone
Cat-, Cata-, Cath-	down, with	category, catalogue, cataract, catabolism, catholic, catharsis
Cis	on the side	cisalpine, cistern
Circum-	around	circumstances, circumference, circumlocution, circumspect
Co-, Cog-, Col-, Com-, Con-, Cor-	together, with	coexist, coincident, cognate, cognition, collide, colleague, combat, combine, connect, conceive, correlate, correct
Contra-	against	contradict, contraband, contravene
Counter-	back	counter-attack, counterfoil, counterbalance
Cyber-	related to the Internet	cybercafé, cybercrime, cybernetic
De-	to do the opposite, down (negative)	debar, declare, decline, devaluate, debase, descend
Demi-	half	demigod, demitasse, demiparadise
Di-, Dia-, Dif-, Dis-	apart, separate, two, opposite, not	diphthong, dioxide, dialogue, diagonal, differ, diffuse, dissuade, disable, dissolve, disarm
Deci-, Deca-	ten, ten times	decimate, decimal, decennial, decade

(Continued)

Prefixes	Meaning	Sample words
Dec-, Dign-	suitable	decent, decease, dignity, dignitary
Du-	two	duplicate, duplex
E-	related to electronic	e-mail, e-ticket, e-commerce
Ex-	out, out of, from	expel, exclude, exhale, express, extort
Ex-	former	ex-captain, ex-president
En-, Em-	put into	enclose, enact, encircle, empower, emission
Epi-	upon, beside, over	epilogue, epicure, epitome, epicentre, epiglottis
Equi-	equal	equitable, equivalent, equilibrium, equilateral
Eu-	form well, easily	eulogize, euthanasia, euphoria, eucalyptus
Extra-	beyond	extraordinary, extra-large, extracurricular, extraterrestrial
For-	away, off	forbid, forbear, forward, forswear, forlorn
Fore-	before	foretell, forecast, forehead, foresight
Hecto-, Hect-	hundred	hectogram, hectare
Hepta-	seven	heptagon, heptameter
Homo-	same	homonym, homogeneous
Hetero-	different	heterodox, heterogeneous
Hexa-	six	hexagon, hexameter, hexagram
Hyper-	extreme	hyperactive, hypersensitive, hyperbole, hypercorrect
Hypo-	too little	hypothermia, hypothesis, hypodermic, hypothetical
Il-, Im-, In-, Ir	not, in	illiterate, illegible, imperfect, impossible, inaction, insecure, irresistible, irresponsible
Inter-	between	interject, intermingle
Intra-	within	intramuscular, intravenous
Intro-	into, within, inward	introvert, introspection, introduce
Infra-	beneath	infrared, infrastructure
Kilo-	thousand	kilometre, kilogram

(Continued)

Prefixes	Meaning	Sample words
Mal-, Male-, Mali-	bad, ill, evil	malfunction, malnutrition, malefactor, malevolent, malignant, malicious
Mega-	huge	megastar, megaship, megawatt, megaphone
Meta-	changing	metaphysics, metabolism, metaphor, metamorphosis
Mid-	middle	midday, mid-air, mid-path
Milli-	thousand	millisecond, milligram, millibar
Mis-	wrong	misunderstand, misbehave, misspell, mistake
Mini-	small	mini bus, mini skirt
Mono-	one	monologue, monotheism, monomania
Multi-	many	multicolour, multistorey, multifacet
Neo-	new	neophyte, neo-classical
Non-	not	nonsense, non-vegetarian, nonstop, nontoxic
Ob-, Oc-, Of-, Op-	toward, against, in the way	obtain, object, obtuse, occupy, oculist, offend, offence, oppose, oppress
Octo-, Oct-	eight	octopus, octane, octet
Omni-	all	omniscient, omnipotent, omnipresent
Out-	faster	outlive, outgrow, outlook, output
Over-	excessive	overactive, overwork, overdo, overact
Pan-	all	panacea, pandemonium, pantheon, pan-american
Para-	beside	paragraph, paradox
Penta-, Pent-	five	pentagon, pentacle
Per	through, by, utterly, badly	persecute, perpetual, perfect
Poly-	many	polygamy, polythene, polyglot, polytechnic
Post-	after	postpone, postman, postwar, postscript
Pre-	before	prepare, precept, precaution, prefix
Peri-	around	periscope, perigee

(*Continued*)

Prefixes	Meaning	Sample words
Quadri-, Quadr-	four	quadrilateral, quadrille, quadruple
Pro-	for, forward	propose, project, provide, pronoun, profess
Pseudo-	false	pseudonym, pseudo-classical
Re-	back, again	revive, regain, refresh, rebel, revise
Retro-	backward	retrospect, retroactive, retrograde
Se-	apart, move away from	separate, secede, secure, select
Self-	for oneself	self-help, self-interest, self-confidence
Semi-	half	semiconductor, semicircle, semidetached
Sub-, Suc-, Suf-, Sup-, Sur-, Sus-, Sug-, Sum-	under, beneath, near, from below, secretly, above, up, secondary	submarine, subside, succeed, succumb, suffice, suffocate, support, suppose, survive, surface, sustain, suspect, suggest, suggestible, summon, summarize
Super-, sur	over, above	superman, superfast, supernatural, superfine, surcharge, surcoat
Supra-	above	suprasegmental, supranational
Syn-, Sym-	together, at the same time	synchronize, synonym, sympathy, symmetry
Trans-	across, beyond, change	transform, transaction, transport, transmit, transparent
Tri-	three	tricolour, tricycle, triangle
Un-	not, against, opposite	uncommon, unnatural, undo, unwind
Under-	too little	underdog, underestimate, underpaid, underwater
Uni-, Un-	one, single	unity, union, universe, unilateral, unanimous
Ultra-	beyond	ultramodern, ultrahigh, ultrasound, ultraviolet
Vice-	junior	vice-president, vice-chancellor
With-	against, away	withhold, withdraw, withstand

3.3.2 Suffix: The Tail to Modify Meaning

A suffix is a letter or groups of letters attached to the ends of roots, words or word groups and serve a grammatical function. A suffix can indicate the part of speech (noun, verb, adjective, adverb) the word belongs to. It can also modify and extend the meaning of the word, for example, the –al suffix makes an adjective from a noun such as 'national' and 'structural'. The following suffixes are grouped beneath the grammatical function they perform:

1. Nouns:

Nouns perform the function of naming. Nouns name persons, places animals or things, as well as groups, ideas and qualities. In a sentence, nouns can be subjects, objects, or appositives.

Suffix	Meaning	Sample words
-acy, -cy	state or quality	privacy, supremacy, policy, conspiracy
-ade, -age	activity, or result of action	barricade, cascade, brigade mortgage, bondage, leakage
-al	action, result of action	rotational, chemical, arrival, functional
-ance, -ence	action, state, quality or process	fragrance, elegance, diligence, precedence
-ancy, -ency	state, quality or capacity	vacancy, infancy, proficiency, frequency
-ant, -ent	an agent, full of	servant, applicant, independent, pendent
-ary	resembling, related to	library, granary, salary, honorary
-art, -ard	characterized	hand cart, bullock cart, drunkard, wizard, steward, billiard
-ate, -ee, -ey, -y	persons, agents	candidate, employee, payee, attorney, journey, fury, query, economy, society
-ation	action, resulting state	specialization, qualification, imagination, conversation
-crat-, -cracy	rule	autocrat, technocrat, theocracy, democracy
-dom	place, state of being	wisdom, boredom, freedom, seldom
-eer, -ier	person concerned with or described as	mountaineer, engineer, barrier, carrier, brigadier
-er, -or, -ar	one who	porter, painter, inferior, doctor, beggar, circular
-erel	showing small objects, animals, etc.	cockerel, mongrel
-ery, -ry	class or kind	crockery, stationery, dowry, pantry
-ess	denoting females	actress, poetess, hostess, lioness
-et, -ette	denoting small objects, places, etc.	coronet, packet, cigarette, etiquette
-ful	an amount or quantity that fills	tearful, spoonful, dreadful, mouthful
-hood	condition or state	manhood, falsehood
-ia	names, diseases	phobia, mania

(*Continued*)

Suffix	Meaning	Sample words
-ain, -an, -en, -on	referring to persons, agents	captain, villain, pagan, artisan, warden, maiden, sexton, deacon
-iatry	art of healing	psychiatry
-ic, ics, -ique	related to the arts and sciences	artistic, realistic, economics, politics, physique, critique
-ice, -icle	small objects, qualities, feelings, etc.	malice, cowardice, article, particle
-ie	state, condition	birdie, girlie
-ing	material made for, activity, result of an activity	flooring, building, running, swimming
-ion	condition or action	abduction, preposition
-ism	doctrine, belief, action or conduct	socialism, secularism, humanism, heroism
-ist	person or member	plagiarist, dentist, artist, sadist
-ite	product or part	graphite, granite
-itude	range of something	solitude, altitude, magnitude, attitude
-ity, -ty	state or quality	lucidity, nativity, activity, frugality, novelty, honesty, modesty
-ive	condition	protective, active, secretive, creative
-let	very small	booklet, pamphlet, owlet, rivulet
-ment	condition or result	document, derangement, amusement, monument
-monger	persons, agents	war monger, fish monger, iron monger, gossip monger
-mony	denoting condition, state, system	matrimony, harmony, ceremony, economy
-ness	state, condition, quality	kindness, goodness, greatness, sharpness
-ock	referring to small things, animals	bullock, hillock, paddock
-ory	place for, serves for	territory, ivory, victory
-red	denoting feeling, thought	hatred, kindred, shepherd
-ship	status, condition	relationship, citizenship, ownership, fellowship

(Continued)

Suffix	Meaning	Sample words
-ssion, -sion	denoting action or state	admission, commission, succession, tension, supervision
-ster	a person who is connected with or has the quality of	youngster, spinster, trickster, gangster
-th	the action or process of	warmth, wealth, health, growth
-ure,- eur, -our	act, condition, process, function	exposure, enclosure, grandeur, tenure, labour, glamour
-wright	persons, agents	playwright, cartwright

2. Verbs: Verbs make statements about nouns, ask questions, give commands, or show states of being. Verbs can be active or passive. Verbs also show tense or time of action.

Suffix	Meaning	Sample words
-ate, -ite	cause to be	situate, associate, stimulate, dedicate, expedite, ignite
-cogn, -gnos	to know	recognize, diagnose
-ed	past tense	achieved, created, nominated, selected
-en	to cause to become	moisten, shorten, lighten, soften
-er, -or	action	wonder, batter, clamour, tailor
-ify	cause	specify, clarify, glorify, signify
-ing	present participle	doing, swimming, shouting, sealing
-ize	cause	humanize, specialize, realize, utilize, popularize
-ure	act	procure, secure, endure, allure

3. Adjectives: Adjectives describe or modify nouns. Adjectives tell the reader more about the noun used in the sentence.

Suffix	Meaning	Sample words
-able, -ible, -ble, -bile	worth, ability	capable, drinkable, edible, incredible, visible, soluble, illegible, mobile, profile, futile
-al, -ial, -ical	quality, relation	functional, communal, structural, territorial, menial, categorical, illogical
-ant, -ent, -ient	kind of agent, indication	important, triumphant, dependent, ardent, convenient, transient

(*Continued*)

Suffix	Meaning	Sample words
-ar, -ary	resembling, related to	spectacular, familiar, unitary, sanitary
-ed	having the quality	terraced, dreaded, messed, blessed
-en	material	silken, forbidden, molten, frozen
-er	comparative	bigger, better, flicker, dimmer
-ese	related to	Chinese, Portuguese
-esque	like to	picturesque, grotesque
-est	superlative	brightest, sharpest, hardest, quickest
-ful	having, giving, marked by	beautiful, colourful, fanciful, dutiful
-ic, -ique	quality, relation	generic, prolific, antique, unique
-ile	having the qualities of	textile, fertile
-ine	belonging to	masculine, feminine, divine, feline
-ish	having the character of	feverish, sheepish, newish, reddish
-ive, -ative, -itive	having the quality of	festive, co-operative, creative, sensitive
-less	without, missing	motionless, speechless, restless, tireless, childless
-like	similar to, characteristic of	child-like, war-like, woman-like, man-like
-most	extreme	innermost, foremost, utmost, topmost
-ory	denoting place	sensory, advisory, cursory, transitory
-ous, -eous, -ose, -ious	having the quality of, relating to	adventurous, courageous, verbose, fractious
-some	a group of	troublesome, tiresome, wearisome, wholesome
-th	in ordinal number	fifth, sixth, seventh, eighth
-luent, -ulent, -lent,	full of	affluent, flatulent, fluent, violent, virulent
-wise	manner, respect	likewise, lengthwise, clockwise, crosswise
-y	marked by, having	hungry, sandy, healthy, heavy

4. **Adverbs:** Adverbs describe verbs, adjectives and other adverbs.

Suffix	Meaning	Sample words
-ce	showing frequency	once, twice, thrice
-st	showing position	amidst, amongst, co-exist

(Continued)

Suffix	Meaning	Sample words
-fold	in a manner of, marked by	Threefold, manifold
-ly	in the manner of	fluently, quietly, nicely, timely
-ther	in the direction	hither, thither, whither
-ward	in a direction or manner	homeward, inward, onward, outward
-wise	in the manner of, with regard to	clockwise, lengthwise, crosswise, timewise

Task

1. Form words using the following prefixes:
   Bi......, intra....., mega....., micro......., ill...., in......., alter...., anti......, auto....., cata...., ambi...., counter......, cyber...., demi...., epi...., fore...., hyper...., homo..., intro...., infra...., milli...., mono...., omni..., para..., pseudo...., retro....., supra...., sym...., with...., ultra...., trans...., tri....

2. Form words using the following suffixes:
   ....acy, ...ade, ...ant, ...art, ...ation, ...crat, ...eer, ...erel, ...ory, ...ette, ...ain, ..ique, ...icle, ...ism, ...mony, ...monger, ...ster, ...th, ...ure, ...ster, ...eur, ...ment, ...wright, ...ible, ...like, ...most, ...some, ...y, ...fold, ...ward, ...less,... ly

3. Form words using the following bases:
   Areo, arch, aster, biblio, corpus, electrum, facere, gradus, logos, manus, mittere, mobilis, pathos, philos, phone, tele, therme

Vocabulary Building

4

"The knowledge of words is the gate of scholarship."

–Edmund Wilson

4.1 Introduction

Words are the building blocks of spoken or written communication. A rich vocabulary is the area of language competence, which is directly related to all the four skills of listening, speaking, reading and writing. When we pass out from college or university, we feel the need to communicate with the world at the personal, social as well as professional level. For this purpose, we have to extend our vocabulary to express ourselves effectively. In addition to this, all the competitive, school and university examinations make a direct test of vocabulary to evaluate a prospective student on the threshold of word knowledge. For these purposes, we have to increase our vocabulary to express ourselves precisely, accurately and fluently. A good stock of words assists us to differentiate between different shades of meaning and between similarly appearing or sounding words. At the same time, it checks repetitions and brings variety to our language. With a good knowledge of words, we are able to understand and interpret written material in the right perspective.

Choice of words depends upon your relationship with the person with whom you are communicating. Here comes your knowledge of formal and informal vocabulary, which serves a very important social and professional function. Avoid using formal words while interacting with friends and relatives, as it will bring in a lot of formality in your relationships. On the other hand, in a formal situation, such as talking to your principal, teacher, colleague or manager, formal words should be preferred to the informal ones. List of technical words given in this chapter, will provide you with examples of words from formal English. Vocabulary of official communication is dealt with in the chapter on "Technical Communication".

Extension of vocabulary is a gradual process. It cannot be done overnight. The most effective tool is to do an extensive reading and careful listening of English on a day-to-day basis. We should be alert enough to grasp new words—their meaning, context, parts of speech, pronunciation and usage—and make them a part of our system by using them in our communication and interactions.

To make a word a part of your system, study its complete profile. Along with its meaning, pronunciation and usage, study its roots, affixes, synonyms, antonyms, homophones and homonyms. Familiarize yourself with one-word substitutes as well as with the words of common usage. Lists of these elements of vocabulary building have been given under various headings in this chapter.

4.2   Synonyms

To use words appropriately in speech and writing, you should be able to distinguish one word from another with its slight changes in meaning. Synonyms are words that have the same or almost the same meaning but with different shades in different contexts. For example, assist: help/support. The use of synonyms imparts vividness to the expression. One can communicate effectively if one has a good variety of words to use. An antonym is a word opposite in meaning with another. To express contrast between two objects, persons or situations, antonyms are the best options. They can also be formed by using prefixes. For example, partial: impartial, competent: incompetent. A good stock of synonyms and antonyms is essential for an effective language usage. However, while using them you should be careful that the grammatical status of the word does not change. Here are some useful synonyms and antonyms for your ready reference:

Synonyms

Abandon	Discard		Augment	Add
Abhor	Hate		Avoid	Ignore
Abduct	Kidnap		Awful	Terrible
Abridge	Shorten		Awkward	Odd
Absolute	Complete		Baffle	Confuse
Accord	Agree		Banal	Ordinary
Accumulate	Collect		Barren	Unproductive
Adequate	Enough		Behaviour	Conduct
Adversity	Misfortune		Betray	Deceive
Admire	Praise		Benevolent	Charitable
Admission	Entry		Bias	Predisposition
Affection	Love		Bitter	Unpleasant
Affluent	Rich		Blend	Combine
Agile	Swift		Bliss	Happiness
Aggravate	Intensify		Bluff	Cheat
Alien	Foreign		Bold	Daring
Alleviate	Lighten		Bonus	Benefit
Anguish	Distress		Bother	Annoy
Arrogant	Disdainful		Brief	Concise
Astonish	Overwhelm		Brilliant	Clever
Atrocious	Unpleasant		Brisk	Active

Brutal	Cruel	Eliminate	Remove
Cause	Reason	Eminent	Important
Callous	Cruel	Emolument	Salary
Candid	Honest	Encourage	Motivate
Caricature	Cartoon	Endorse	Approve
Casual	Usual	Endure	Last
Category	Class	Envy	Jealousy
Cautious	Careful	Essential	Indispensable
Cease	Stop	Estimate	Guess
Cherish	Relish	Evaluate	Assess
Compassion	Pity	Exceptional	Unusual
Compensate	Recompense	Exhaust	Tire
Competent	Capable	Explicit	Clear
Conceit	Pride	Extreme	Severe
Conceive	Observe	Fabricate	Construct
Confess	Admit	Fabulous	Unbelievable
Consequence	Result	Fastidious	Fussy
Confirmation	Acknowledgement	Fatigue	Weariness
Contradict	Challenge	Feeble	Weak
Cordial	Warm	Feign	Pretend
Courteous	Polite	Fervour	Zeal
Craving	Desire	Feud	Argument
Crazy	Mad	Filth	Dirt
Credulous	Trustful	Flatter	Compliment
Cure	Remedy	Flexible	Changing
Cursory	Superficial	Flimsy	Fragile
Damp	Wet	Forbid	Prohibit
Dare	Challenge	Former	Previous
Decay	Rot	Frail	Weak
Decent	Respectable	Fragment	Scrap
Defer	Postpone	Frivolous	Playful
Dense	Thick	Frugal	Economical
Designate	Appoint	Furious	Angry
Deteriorate	Decline	Generous	Kind
Disclose	Announce	Genuine	Real
Display	Exhibit	Glare	Shine
Dogma	Belief	Gloomy	Dark
Donation	Contribution	Goad	Provoke
Durable	Lasting	Grasp	Grab
Dwindle	Lessen	Grave	Serious
Eager	Keen	Grief	Sorrow
Eccentric	Abnormal	Greed	Avarice
Elaborate	Detail	Guarantee	Assurance

Guile	Cunning	Lean	Slim
Gullible	Naïve	Liberal	Moderate
Habitual	Accustomed	Limitation	Constraint
Hamper	Block	Loyal	Faithful
Handicap	Disability	Lucid	Clear
Harass	Bother	Lucky	Fortunate
Harsh	Cruel	Mad	Insane
Hasty	Hurried	Majestic	Dignified
Hindrance	Obstacle	Malice	Ill-will
Haughty	Arrogant	Manage	Administer
Humiliate	Disgrace	Manipulate	Control
Humility	Modesty	Marginal	Minor
Humorous	Amusing	Match	Equal
Hygiene	Cleanliness	Maze	Confusion
Hypocrisy	Duplicity	Meagre	Small
Ideal	Perfect	Meek	Humble
Idle	Lazy	Meditate	Think
Ignorant	Uninformed	Memorial	Monument
Illogical	Irrational	Mention	State
Illustrious	Famous	Merge	Blend
Imitate	Copy	Misery	Unhappiness
Immense	Huge	Mockery	Ridicule
Impartial	Neutral	Nature	Character
Impatient	Anxious	Negate	Contradict
Implicate	Accuse	Negligent	Careless
Inhuman	Brutal	Negotiate	Bargain
Initiate	Start	Noble	Aristocratic
Innate	Inborn	Novice	Beginner
Indifferent	Disinterested	Nuisance	Annoyance
Industrious	Hard working	Obedient	Faithful
Inevitable	Unavoidable	Objection	Disapproval
Eradicate	Eliminate	Obligatory	Compulsory
Isolate	Detach	Obstinate	Stubborn
Jargon	Slang	Obsolete	Outdated
Journey	Trip	Obtuse	Dull
Jovial	Cheerful	Obvious	Clear
Judge	Evaluate	Offend	Insult
Justification	Reason	Offer	Proposal
Juvenile	Young	Omen	Sign
Keen	Eager	Omit	Remove
Label	Tag	Opportune	Favourable
Labour	Toil	Opulent	Rich
Lead	Direct	Pacify	Calm

Pain	Ache	Superficial	Shallow
Paramount	Chief	Stabilize	Balance
Partisan	Follower	Tame	Domesticate
Passive	Inactive	Tangle	Twist
Pathetic	Touching	Tedious	Dull
Pause	Break	Temper	Mood
Perpetuate	Continue	Temperate	Moderate
Perplex	Astonish	Tendency	Trend
Persecute	Harass	Term	Duration
Prodigal	Extravagant	Thrift	Frugality
Radical	Basic	Tough	Strong
Range	Variety	Transfer	Move
Rank	Arrange	Tumult	Agitation
Realize	Understand	Turbulent	Chaotic
Reconcile	Resolve	Ugly	Repulsive
Regret	Lament	Unique	Unequalled
Reliable	Dependable	Urbane	Polite
Renown	Fame	Urge	Incite
Reticent	Reserved	Vacate	Quit
Rigid	Stiff	Vain	Hopeless
Rude	Harsh	Valid	Authorized
Sanction	Approval	Vanish	Disappear
Sane	Sensible	Variety	Range
Scope	Extent	Verbose	Wordy
Section	Division	Verify	Prove
Shrewd	Cunning	Vigilance	Watchful
Shun	Avoid	Wholesome	Healthy
Significant	Important	Wreck	Ruin
Slight	Trivial	Yearn	Crave
Spontaneous	Unplanned	Yield	Surrender
Spread	Broadcast	Zeal	Passion
Stubborn	Obstinate	Zenith	Peak

Task

Choose the word or phrase which is nearest in meaning to the key word:

1. Lethargy
   (a) Serenity
   (b) Listlessness
   (c) Impassivity
   (d) Laxity
2. Inedible
   (a) Unfit for human consumption
   (b) Polluted
   (c) Vitiated
   (d) Eatable

3. Sadistic
   (a) Smart
   (b) Malicious
   (c) Given to deriving pleasure from inflicting pain on others
   (d) Depressed
4. Amoral
   (a) Loving
   (b) Immoral
   (c) Uninvolved
   (d) Highly ethical
5. Duplicity
   (a) Innocence
   (b) Cleverness
   (c) Double-dealing
   (d) Repetition
6. Coup
   (a) Sudden overthrow of a government
   (b) Small enclosure
   (c) Accident
   (d) Clever reply
7. Concert
   (a) Agreement
   (b) Beauty
   (c) Power
   (d) Musical performance
8. Buoyant
   (a) Child-like
   (b) Brisk
   (c) Sturdy
   (d) Light-hearted
9. Parasite
   (a) Disease
   (b) A loss of motion
   (c) One that clings
   (d) Exterminator
10. Drab
    (a) Dull or colourless
    (b) To brag
    (c) Discouraged
    (d) Shabby
11. Weak
    (a) To twist
    (b) To emit an unpleasant odour
    (c) To inflict
    (d) To sweat
12. Carcass
    (a) Mind
    (b) Association
    (c) Soul
    (d) Dead body
13. Skip
    (a) Overlook
    (b) Introduce
    (c) Insert
    (d) Notice
14. Obscene
    (a) Dirty
    (b) Fraud
    (c) Indecent
    (d) Unwanted
15. Cajole
    (a) Scold
    (b) Intimidate
    (c) Threaten
    (d) Persuade

4.3 Antonyms

Absence	Presence	Always	Never
Absurd	Sensible	Amateur	Professional
Abundant	Inadequate	Ancient	Modern
Accept	Refuse	Approval	Disapproval
Admit	Deny	Arrogant	Humble
Agree	Disagree	Artificial	Natural
Ally	Enemy	Arrival	Departure

Asleep	Awake	Dainty	Clumsy
Attack	Defence	Danger	Safety
Attractive	Unattractive	Deep	Shallow
Attention	Inattention	Decrease	Increase
Awkward	Graceful	Definite	Indefinite
Backward	Forward	Demand	Supply
Bend	Straighten	Despair	Hope
Beginning	Ending	Disappear	Appear
Below	Above	Disease	Health
Blunt	Sharp	Discourage	Encourage
Better	Worse	Dismal	Cheerful
Best	Worst	Dull	Intelligent
Blame	Praise	Dusk	Dawn
Bless	Curse	Ebb	Flow
Bitter	Sweet	Economize	Waste
Borrow	Lend	Eligible	Ineligible
Bravery	Cowardice	Encourage	Discourage
Brutal	Humane	Entrance	Exit
Build	Demolish	Emigrant	Immigrant
Bold	Timid	Employer	Employee
Bright	Dull	Empty	Full
Broad	Narrow	Entrance	Exit
Callous	Tender	Establish	Demolish
Clear	Cloudy	Exceptional	Ordinary
Careful	Careless	Excited	Calm
Calm	Troubled	Expand	Contract
Capable	Incapable	Expensive	Cheap
Captivity	Liberty	Export	Import
Cellar	Attic	Exterior	Interior
Cheap	Expensive	External	Internal
Climax	Anti-climax	Fail	Succeed
Close	Distant	Feeble	Sturdy
Combine	Separate	Flexible	Rigid
Clockwise	Anti-clockwise	Foolish	Wise
Conceal	Reveal	Famous	Unknown
Common	Rare	Forelegs	Hind legs
Comfort	Discomfort	Fold	Unfold
Competent	Incompetent	Frequent	Seldom
Confident	Diffident	Forget	Remember
Courage	Cowardice	Friend	Enemy
Cruel	Kind	Fortunate	Unfortunate
Courteous	Discourteous	Frank	Secretive
Cunning	Simple	Generous	Mean

Gentle	Rough	Lawful	Unlawful
Genuine	Fake	Land	Sea
Gather	Distribute	Landlord	Tenant
Gloomy	Cheerful	Lawyer	Client
Great	Ordinary	Lecturer	Student
Guardian	Ward	Lender	Borrower
Guest	Host	Lengthen	Shorten
Guilty	Innocent	Light	Dark
Happy	Sad	Like	Dislike
Harmful	Harmless	Likely	Unlikely
Hasten	Dawdle	Leader	Follower
Hate	Love	Liberty	Slavery
Healthy	Unhealthy	Load	Unload
Height	Depth	Lofty	Lowly
Hero	Coward	Loud	Soft
Hill	Valley	Loyal	Disloyal
Horizontal	Vertical	Mad	Sane
Hinder	Aid	Magnetize	Demagnetize
Honest	Dishonest	Master	Servant
Humble	Proud	Mature	Immature
Hunger	Thirst	Maximum	Minimum
Imitation	Genuine	Merry	Mirthless
Immense	Tiny	Minority	Majority
Imprison	Free	Miser	Spendthrift
Include	Exclude	Misunder-stand	Understand
Increase	Decrease		
Industrious	Lazy	Mortal	Immortal
Inhabited	Uninhabited	Narrow	Wide
Inferior	Superior	Native	Foreigner
Inside	Outside	Neat	Untidy
Intelligent	Unintelligent	North	South
Inhale	Exhale	Obedient	Disobedient
Interior	Exterior	Odd	Even
Interesting	Uninteresting	Offer	Refuse
Internal	External	Open	Shut
Intentional	Accidental	Optimist	Pessimist
Join	Separate	Optional	Compulsory
Jovial	Gloomy	Organize	Disorganize
Junior	Senior	Pacify	Provoke
Justice	Injustice	Parent	Child
King	Subject	Partial	Impartial
Knowledge	Ignorance	Past	Present
Laugh	Cry	Patient	Impatient

Peace	War	Simple	Complicated
Permanent	Temporary	Slim	Thick
Persuade	Dissuade	Solid	Liquid
Please	Displease	Sober	Excited
Plentiful	Scarce	Speaker	Listener
Poetry	Prose	Sour	Sweet
Possible	Impossible	Sorrow	Joy
Poverty	Wealth	Sow	Reap
Powerful	Feeble, weak	Success	Failure
Polite	Impolite	Tame	Wild
Private	Public	Teacher	Pupil
Prudent	Imprudent	Thrive	Decline
Pretty	Ugly	Tight	Loose
Pure	Impure	Transparent	Opaque
Qualified	Unqualified	Truth	Untruth
Rapid	Slow	Urbane	Impolite
Rectify	Falsify	Unique	Common
Regularly	Irregularly	Vacant	Occupied
Remarkable	Ordinary	Valuable	Valueless
Responsible	Irresponsible	Victory	Defeat
Rough	Smooth	Virtue	Vice
Satisfactory	Unsatisfactory	Visible	Invisible
Security	Insecurity	Voluntary	Involuntary
Scatter	Collect	Vowel	Consonant
Serious	Trivial	Wax	Wane
Second-hand	New	Wisdom	Folly
Sense	Nonsense	Within	Without
Shopkeeper	Customer	Yield	Resist
Singular	Plural	Zeal	Indifference

Task

Pick out the word opposite or nearly so in the meaning of the given words:

1. Accepted
   - (a) Followed
   - (b) Noted
   - (c) Provided
   - (d) Considered
   - (e) Rejected
2. Anger
   - (a) Party
   - (b) Happiness
   - (c) Approval
   - (d) Considered
   - (e) Joy
3. Loved
   - (a) Refused
   - (b) Defamed
   - (c) Distracted
   - (d) Averted
   - (e) Hated

4. Obey
   - (a) Attract
   - (b) Disobey
   - (c) Repel
   - (d) Diffuse
   - (e) None
5. Outwit
   - (a) Laugh
   - (b) Victory
   - (c) Defeat
   - (d) Win
   - (e) None
6. Come
   - (a) Play
   - (b) Fast
   - (c) Go
   - (d) Got
   - (e) None
7. Dull
   - (a) Pale
   - (b) Wise
   - (c) Shining
   - (d) Colourful
   - (e) Foolish
8. Receded
   - (a) Bloomed
   - (b) Advanced
   - (c) Increased
   - (d) Diminished
   - (e) Rebuilt
9. Extrovert
   - (a) Boaster
   - (b) Mixer
   - (c) Introvert
   - (d) Social
10. Urban
   - (a) Rustic
   - (b) Rural
   - (c) Civil
   - (d) Domestic
11. Militant
   - (a) Religious
   - (b) Spiritual
   - (c) Combative
   - (d) Impure
12. Ruthless
   - (a) Militant
   - (b) Might
   - (c) Majestic
   - (d) Merciful
13. Latent
   - (a) Hidden
   - (b) Forbidding
   - (c) Obvious
   - (d) Artificial
14. Antipathy
   - (a) Indifference
   - (b) Willingness
   - (c) Fondness
   - (d) Liking
15. Extravagant
   - (a) Developing
   - (b) Wonderful
   - (c) Disappearing
   - (d) Economical
   - (e) Real
16. Inevitable
   - (a) Unavoidable
   - (b) Eatable
   - (c) Half-baked
   - (d) Uncertain
   - (e) Mutilated

4.4 Homophones

The word 'homophone' has its origin in the combination of two elements—'homo' (same) and 'phone' (sound). Thus, the term *homophone* describes the words that sound the same but have different meanings. For example, the words 'ate' and 'eight' are pronounced in the same way but both have different meanings. The knowledge of homophones helps the learner check the ambiguity in expression as well as to bring clarity to it. They can also be used to create puns to make language interesting. For example, 'he died on his birth'—can be interpreted to have a pun on the word 'berth' that is a homophone of the word 'birth.' However, homophones can be a tricky business, that is, one may find it difficult to know when to use which word. Some common mistakes occur with *your/you're, there/their/they're,* and *hear/here*. Mastery of homophones requires a lot of practice. You may learn them by making a list, use them in complete sentences or make use of flash cards. These things will definitely help you in understanding tricky homophones accurately. Some of them are given below:

1. Aid, Aide
   Aid: Help or assistance: *We should give aid to the poor.*
   Aide: A person who helps: *Farida has been working as a doctor's aide for 5 years.*

2. Airs, Heirs
   Airs: Snobbish and artificial behaviour: *Rajeev put on airs at the dinner party just because he had bought a new car.*
   Heirs: Successors: *Mansi and Gouri are going to be heirs to a large fortune.*

3. Altar, Alter
   Altar: A place of worship: *We offered prayers before the altar of the Goddess Durga.*
   Alter: To change: *You should alter your way of thinking, if you want to succeed.*

4. Artist, Artiste
   Artist: One who practices fine arts: *The person who has made this painting is a real artist.*
   Artiste: A professional dancer, singer, etc.: *Amitabh Bachchan is a famous artiste.*

5. Ascent, Assent
   Ascent: Rise, the way up: *The cart began its gradual ascent up the hill.*
   Assent: To agree: *The director gave his assent to the proposal.*

6. Aural, Oral
   Aural: Connected with hearing and listening: *Students should be given some exercises to improve their aural abilities.*
   Oral: Spoken, not written: *The message was conveyed to us orally.*

7. Aught, Ought
   Aught: Anything: *If there is aught I can do for you, please feel free to tell me.*
   Ought (to):   Should: *Children ought to learn their lessons.*

8. Awe, Oar, Or, Ore
   Awe: Feeling of respect and slight fear: *'It's really wonderful,' she whispered in awe.*
   Oar: A long pole with a flat blade used for rowing a boat: *The sailor pulled as hard as he could on the oars and started rowing the boat.*
   Or: Otherwise: *'Do or die,' was the slogan given by Gandhiji.*
   Ore: Rock, earth, etc. from which a metal can be obtained: *Iron ore is mined in Bihar.*

9. Bail, Bale
   Bail: Security: *He committed another offence while he was out on bail.*
   Bale: A bundle, a parcel: *The bales of cotton got damaged in the fire.*

10. Bait, Bate
    Bait: Food put on a hook to catch fish or in nets, traps, etc. to catch animals or birds: *Fresh bait was put in the hook to catch fish.*
    Bate: Holding (breath) when anxious or excited: *We waited with bated breath for the results to be announced.*

11. **Baize, Bays**
Baize: Thick woollen cloth usually green, used for covering card, billiard, snooker or pool tables: *The peon changed the baize of the snooker table.*
Bays: Part of the sea, or of a large lake, partly surrounded by a wide curve of the land: *We saw a magnificent view across the bays.*

12. **Bald, Bawled**
Bald: Having little or no hair on the head: *He started going bald in his twenties.*
Bawled: Shouted loudly, roared: *Sheela bawled at her servant and asked him to clean the table.*

13. **Band, Banned**
Band: A group of people doing something together: *The band of the musicians played a lovely tune and we all started dancing.*
Banned: Prohibited: *Use of mobile phones should be banned in educational institutions.*

14. **Bare, Bear**
Bare: Without, naked: *One should not go bare footed in the sun.*
Bear: To tolerate: *I can't bear separation from my family.*

15. **Barren, Baron**
Barren: Unfruitful, infertile: *We cannot grow anything on this barren land.*
Baron: A landlord: *People used to respect barons in the middle ages.*

16. **Beach, Beech**
Beach: Seashore: *Beaches of Goa attract a lot of tourists every year.*
Beech: A kind of tree: *Birds have made their nests on the beech tree.*

17. **Bean, Been**
Bean: A seed or pod containing seeds: *We bought some coffee beans from the market.*
Been: Past participle of 'be': *I had been to the US to attend a conference.*

18. **Beer, Bier**
Beer: A kind of wine: *The men took some beer and went to sleep.*
Bier: A frame on which the dead body or the coffin is placed or carried at a funeral: *At the time of Minister's funeral, the bier was full of flowers.*

19. **Bell, Belle**
Bell: A hollow object shaped like a cup that makes a ringing sound: *As soon as the bell rang, children came out of the classes.*
Belle: A beautiful woman: *The belle attracted everyone in the party.*

20. **Bight, Bite, Byte**
Bight: A long curve in a coast: *The bight of Mumbai Marine Drive attracts a lot of tourists.*
Bite: To use teeth to cut into or through something: *Don't go near the dog, it may bite you.*
Byte: A unit of information stored in a computer: *A computer's memory is measured in bytes.*

21. **Billed, Build**
Billed: Having the type of bill: *The billed amount had a calculation error.*
Build: To make something, especially a building: *We have got permission to build two more rooms in our house.*

22. **Birth, Berth**

Birth: To be born: *It was the study of history that gave birth to the social sciences.*

Berth: Place of sleep in a train: *We got our berths reserved in an air-conditioned compartment.*

23. **Bloc, Block**

Bloc: Community, Union: *The EEC has many countries in its bloc.*

Block: A tall building that contains flats or offices: *The post office is three blocks away from the hospital.*

24. **Blue, Blew**

Blue: A colour: *The girl was wearing a beautiful blue gown.*

Blew: The past tense of the verb 'blow': *He blew his trumpet to make an announcement.*

25. **Boar, Bore**

Boar: A wild pig: *We went to the forest to hunt a boar.*

Bore: Past tense of the verb 'bear': *The widow patiently bore ill temper of the society.*

26. **Board, Bored**

Board: A long, thin piece of strong hard material: *I'll write it up on the board.*

Bored: Feeling tired and impatient because you have lost interest: *The children quickly got bored with staying indoors and they wanted to go outside.*

27. **Boarder, Border**

Boarder: A child who lives at school and goes home for holidays: *Boarders have various advantages in this school.*

Border: The place where two countries meet: *Indo–Pak border is a sensitive area.*

28. **Bold, Bowled**

Bold: Brave and confident: *It was a bold step on her part to marry against her parents' wish.*

Bowled: To throw a ball to the batsman: *Zaheer Khan bowled well and took three wickets.*

29. **Born, Borne**

Born: Past tense of 'birth': *Lata Mangeshkar was born in a family with music tradition.*

Borne: Carried: *The dried leaves borne away with a sudden gust of wind.*

30. **Bough, Bow**

Bough: Branch of a tree: *The boughs of the tree were without any leaves in winter.*

Bow: To bend down: *They bowed to the audience to thank them.*

31. **Brae, Bray**

Brae: A steep slope or hill: *The ball came running down the brae.*

Bray: Cry of a donkey, to talk or laugh in a loud unpleasant voice: *Nobody likes braying of a donkey.*

32. **Braid, Brayed**

Braid: Thin-coloured rope used to decorate furniture and military uniforms: *The general's uniform was decorated with gold braid.*

Brayed: Past tense of 'bray': *The villain brayed with laughter to frighten the people.*

33. **Bread, Bred**

Bread: A type of food made from flour: *Bread and butter is my usual breakfast.*

Bred: Rear, raise: *I am born and bred in a cultured family.*

34. Break, Brake
    Break: To destroy: *Don't drop the plate; otherwise it will break into pieces.*
    Brake: Device for stopping vehicles: *He applied brakes and pulled the car to the side of the road.*

35. Brews, Bruise
    Brews: Make tea, coffee: *I like the tea, which is brewed for a few minutes.*
    Bruise: A mark that appears on the skin after somebody has fallen, been hit, etc.: *She slipped on the floor and badly bruised her face.*

36. Bridal, Bridle
    Bridal: Of a bride: *We bought a beautiful bridal dress for our daughter.*
    Bridle: The head gear used to control the horse: *Use the bridle carefully while riding a horse.*

37. Broach, Brooch
    Broach: Mention, bring up: *He was scared to broach the subject of exam results to his father.*
    Brooch: Ornament, trinkets: *The queen gave a gold brooch to the maid on her wedding.*

38. Bury, Berry
    Bury: To hide something in the ground: *They found a treasure buried in the ground.*
    Berry: A kind of fruit: *Birds feed on nuts and berries in the winter.*

39. But, Butt
    But: Except, save for: *I didn't invite him but he came to attend the function.*
    Butt: Interfere (in): *No one likes you to butt in his/her personal matters.*

40. Calender, Calendar
    Calender: Press to give finish to a piece of cloth: *Calender this dress to make it glossy.*
    Calendar: Chart: *This is one of the biggest weeks in the academic calendar.*

41. Canvas, Canvass
    Canvas: A rough cloth: *He was wearing a canvas hat.*
    Canvass: To request for votes: *Canvassing before the election has stopped.*

42. Cast, Caste
    Cast: To throw: *The setting sun cast an orange glow over the mountains.*
    Caste: An exclusive class: *Many social problems occur in India due to caste system.*

43. Caught, Court
    Caught: Fixed, trapped: *The police have caught the criminals.*
    Court: The place where legal trials take place: *If you don't pay your taxes on time, you will have to face court action.*

44. Cease, Seize
    Cease: To stop: *The company ceased trading in June.*
    Seize: To hold: *The boy seized my mobile and disappeared.*

45. Ceiling, Sealing
    Ceiling: Inner roof: *The ceiling of the room had a beautiful painting.*
    Sealing: Fastening with seal: *I sealed the parcel and posted it.*

46. Cell, Sell
    Cell: A room for prisoners in a prison: *The prisoners were not at all comfortable in the cell.*
    Sell: To offer goods for consumption at a cost: *Mrs. Sharma sells paintings at art fairs.*

47. Cemetery, Symmetry

Cemetery: A burial place: *We took the dead body to the cemetery for burial.*

Symmetry: Harmony: *The arrangement of paintings in the room needs symmetry.*

48. Censor, Sensor

Censor: To prohibit free expression: *The news reports have been heavily censored.*

Sensor: An electronic receiver: *The lights are turned on by a moving sensor.*

49. Cereal, Serial

Cereal: A food grain: *Cereals are eaten in abundance in India.*

Serial: A story in parts: *Most of the TV serials have a similar type of story.*

50. Check, Cheque

Check: To examine something or someone quickly: *You should always check your answers before giving your answer sheet to the teacher.*

Cheque: Order for money: *I have received a cheque for Rupees 5000/- from the examination department.*

51. Choir, Quire

Choir: A group of singers: *The school choir sang devotional songs on Guru Purab.*

Quire: Four sheets of paper folded to make eight: *I bought a quire of paper from the stationery shop.*

52. Cite, Site, Sight

Cite: To quote: *He cited his poor health as the reason for his breakdown.*

Site: A place for building, etc: *All the materials are on site so that work can start immediately.*

Sight: View: *The lovely sight inspired him to paint a beautiful picture.*

53. Climb, Clime

Climb: To go up, ascend: *It was very cold when we were climbing up.*

Clime: A country with a particular kind of climate: *I'm heading for sunnier climes next month.*

54. Colonel, Kernel

Colonel: An officer of high rank in the army: *Mr. Vijay is a retired colonel.*

Kernel: The most important part: *The kernel of the fruit is very tasty.*

55. Complacent, Complaisant

Complacent: Self-satisfied: *No one should be complacent about his/her achievements.*

Complaisant: Ready to accept other people's actions and opinions: *A complaisant person can adjust everywhere.*

56. Compliment, Complement

Compliment: An expression of regard, words of praise: *I complimented my son on his fine handling of responsibilities.*

Complement: That which completes: *The team needs players who complement one another.*

57. Cord, Chord

Cord: A string: *The books were tied with a string.*

Chord: String of a musical instrument: *Give me a long chord; I have to repair the violin.*

58. Counsel, Council

Counsel: Advice: *I was grateful for her wise counsel.*

Council: An assembly: *Academic Council of our college takes all important decisions.*

59. Course, Coarse

Course: Path, direction taken: *The rivers change their course with seasons.*

Coarse: Rough: *She found their remarks rather coarse and vulgar.*

60. Creak, Creek

Creak: Squeak or groan: *The table creaked and groaned under the weight.*

Creek: A small stream: *Children were playing near the creek in the village.*

61. Crew, Cruise

Crew: Teams, groups: *The crew were paid off as soon as the ship docked.*

Cruise: A journey by sea, visiting different places, especially as a holiday/vacation: *I'd love to go on a luxury cruise.*

62. Current, Currant

Current: Existing, present: *The Prime Minister is worried about the current anti-government wave.*

Currant: Dried grapes: *We got choicest currants from Kashmir.*

63. Cymbal, Symbol

Cymbal: A musical instrument shaped like a round metal plate: *A crash of cymbals disturbed all of us in our studies.*

Symbol: Sign, emblem: *A list of symbols used on the map is given in the index.*

64. Dam, Damn

Dam: Barrier: *The dam burst under the weight of water.*

Damn: A curse, to be condemned: *That was a damn fool thing to do.*

65. Days, Daze

Days: Calendar days: *He has worked days and nights together.*

Daze: In a confused state: *Survivors of the accident were dazed and frightened.*

66. Dependent, Dependant

Dependent: To depend upon (adjective): *Old parents are dependent on their children.*

Dependant: A person who depends upon others (noun): *Besides the members of his family, he has several other dependants to take care of.*

67. Desert, Dessert

Desert: To abandon: *People deserted the village after the severe drought.*

Dessert: The sweet course of a meal: *Children demanded ice cream for dessert.*

68. Dew, Due

Dew: Very small drops of water that falls on the ground: *The dews were frozen on the ground in winter.*

Due: Owing to: *Most of the problems in India occur due to poverty and illiteracy.*

69. Discreet, Discrete

Discreet: Careful in what you say or do: *One should be discreet in official matters.*

Discrete: Distinct, detached: *The organisms can be divided into discrete categories.*

70. Dissent, Descent

Dissent: Disagreement: *The bill was passed without dissent from the opposition.*

Descent: A movement downwards: *The plane began its descent to Delhi.*

71. Doe, Dough

Doe: A female deer, rabbit or hare: *Children clapped when they saw a doe jumping in the field.*
Dough: A mixture of flour, water, etc. used to make bread, pastry, etc: *Add some water and mix it well until the dough is smooth.*

72. Done, Dun

Done: Finished, completed: *Don't stop until the job is properly done.*
Dun: Greyish-brown in colour: *The old man was wearing a dun jacket.*

73. Dose, Doze

Dose: Of medicine: *You have to take two doses a day of this syrup.*
Doze: Light sleep or to feel sleepy: *The old woman was dozing in the sun.*

74. Draft, Draught

Draft: A rough sketch: *Prepare a rough draft of the letter before you finalize it.*
Draught: A current of air: *I closed the window as there was a draught outside.*

75. Dual, Duel

Dual: Double: *You can't please anyone with your dual policy.*
Duel: A combat between two persons: *He challenged his opponent to a duel and killed him.*

76. Earn, Urn

Earn: To get something that you deserve: *A well-mannered person earns respect of everyone.*
Urn: A tall, decorated container: *A beautiful urn is decorated in the drawing room.*

77. Faint, Feint

Faint: Faded, weak: *We heard a faint sound of the puppy.*
Feint: A movement performed with trick and skill: *You will be asked to perform some standard feints during your driving test.*

78. Fair, Fare

Fair: Just: *He complains that he was not given a fair hearing.*
Fare: Charge to be paid for a journey: *What is the bus fare from Jaipur to Delhi?*

79. Farther, Father

Farther: At or to a greater distance in space or time: *Nothing is farther from truth.*
Father: A male parent: *My father is very loving and caring.*

80. Faze, Phase

Faze: To distress or disturb: *He looked as if nothing could faze him.*
Phase: Stage, period: *The wedding is the beginning of a new phase in Kinshuk's life.*

81. Feet, Feat

Feet: Part of the body: *We touch the feet of elders to seek their blessings.*
Feat: Trick, a deed or skill: *The clown entertained us by his feats.*

82. Find, Fined

Find: Get, locate: *We were amazed to find that no one was injured in the accident.*
Fined: To make somebody pay money as an official punishment: *The student was fined for creating indiscipline in the class.*

83. Fir, Fur

Fir: A kind of tree: *Villagers are very particular about protecting the fir trees of the forest.*
Fur: Hair of animals: *It was very cold and I wore a fur jacket.*

84. Flaw, Floor
    Flaw: Fault, error: *His performance was absolutely flawless.*
    Floor: Ground, base: *The alterations should give us extra floor space.*

85. Flea, Flee
    Flea: Louse, bug: *The dog has fleas, don't let it come in.*
    Flee: Run away: *Many refugees have been forced to flee their homeland.*

86. Flew, Flu
    Flew: To move through the air, using wings: *A wasp bit me and flew away.*
    Flu: An infectious disease like a very bad cold: *Swine flu is a dangerous disease.*

87. Flour, Flower
    Flour: Fine powder made from grains: *The price of wheat flour has gone up.*
    Flower: Blossom: *The garden has flowers of different colours.*

88. Forbear, Forebear
    Forbear: To refrain from: *We could not forebear laughing when he told us a humorous joke.*
    Forebear: An ancestor or forefather: *Our forebears made this house years ago.*

89. Foreword, Forward
    Foreword: Introduction of a book written by someone other than the author: *The foreword of the book explains how its research is useful for the young learners.*
    Forward: Ahead, onward: *Paras moved forward slowly in the line at the fee counter.*

90. Fort, Fought
    Fort: A building or buildings built to defend an area against attack: *We went to see the Mewar Fort.*
    Fought: Struggled: *The freedom fighters fought for the independence of the countrymen.*

91. Forth, Fourth
    Forth: Forward, from this point: *The commander ordered the soldiers to move forth.*
    Fourth: Number between 3 and 5: *We are staying on the fourth floor of the building.*

92. Foul, Fowl
    Foul: Dirty and smelling bad: *There is a foul smell in the room.*
    Fowl: A bird that is kept for its meat and eggs: *I do not relish fish or fowl.*

93. Freeze, Frieze
    Freeze: To be very cold: *It's freezing cold, please close the windows.*
    Frieze: Wall painting: *A frieze collection was displayed beautifully in the exhibition hall.*

94. Gait, Gate
    Gait: Manner of walking: *You should walk with a smart gait.*
    Gate: Opening, entrance: *He pushed open the garden gate.*

95. Gamble, Gambol
    Gamble: A game of chance, stake: *We cannot gamble with our career.*
    Gambol: To skip about: *We all were delighted to see a lamb gamboling in the meadow.*

96. Gays, Gaze
    Gays: Sexually attracted to the people of the same sex: *The quality of life for gays has improved over the last two decades.*
    Gaze: Fix your eyes on: *He sat for hours just gazing into space.*

97. **Genes, Jeans**

   Genes: Genetic material: *Genes are the genetic carriers of characteristics.*

   Jeans: Denim, pants: *Youngsters love to wear jeans as they find them very comfortable.*

98. **Gild, Guild**

   Gild: To cover with gold, brightness: *The golden light gilded the sea.*

   Guild: Association: *The Actors' Guild works for the welfare of the film stars.*

99. **Gilt, Guilt**

   Gilt: A thin layer of gold used on a surface for decoration: *Kushal decorated the birthday greeting card with gilt lettering.*

   Guilt: Remorse, blame: *We have abundant evidence to prove his guilt.*

100. **Great, Grate**

   Great: Big, large: *Our society accords great importance to the family.*

   Grate: To rub food in a grater to cut it into small pieces: *Grate the reddish and add it to salad.*

101. **Greys, Graze**

   Greys: Colour of smoke or ashes, dull: *The students were dressed in greys.*

   Graze: To eat grass that is growing in a field: *The cattle were grazing beside the river.*

102. **Hail, Hale**

   Hail: To greet or to come from: *A voice hailed us from the other side of the street.*

   Hale: Sound, healthy: *Minnie is hale and hearty enough to run five miles daily.*

103. **Hair, Hare**

   Hair: Locks: *He smoothed his hair and adjusted his tie.*

   Hare: An animal like a large rabbit with very strong back legs: *The hare and the tortoise were old friends.*

104. **Hall, Haul**

   Hall: A building or large room for public meetings, meals, concerts, etc.: *When he began his speech, the hall was full.*

   Haul: To pull something, somebody with a lot of effort: *The wagons were hauled by horses.*

105. **Hangar, Hanger**

   Hangar: Shed, shelter: *The aircraft moved out of the hangar.*

   Hanger: A curved piece of wood, plastic or wire, with a hook at the top, used to hang clothes on: *Put these clothes on the hanger.*

106. **Hart, Heart**

   Hart: A male deer: *Everybody was happy to see a hart in the zoo.*

   Heart: The organ in the chest that sends blood around the body: *The patient is suffering from a rare heart disease.*

107. **Heal, Heel**

   Heal: To cure: *Injury is not serious, it will heal soon.*

   Heel: A part of the foot: *He hurt his heel when he was running.*

108. **Hear, Here**

   Hear: Perceive sound: *Did you hear that play on the radio last night?*

   Here: To this position or place: *Here's the money I promised you.*

109. **He'd, Heed**

He'd: Short form of 'he had' or 'he would': *He'd been here for a long time.*

Heed: Pay attention to: *The victims were requesting for help but no one heeded to them.*

109. **Heard, Herd**

Herd: A group of animals: *Neeru pushed her way through a herd of cows.*

Heard: The past tense of 'hear': *I heard a strange kind of noise and came out.*

111. **Heroin, Heroine**

Heroin: An illicit drug: *The boy is addicted to heroin.*

Heroine: The main female character in a story, novel or film: *This is heroine-centred film.*

112. **Higher, Hire**

Higher: Upper, senior: *The case was referred to a higher court.*

Hire: Employ, engage: *You should hire a car if you want to visit this area.*

113. **Him, Hymn**

Him: Objective form of pronoun 'he': *We liked him because of his honesty.*

Hymn: A Christian song praising God: *The church choir sang hymns in praise of God.*

114. **Hoard, Horde**

Hoard: Collect, store: *Ants hoard food during the summer and save it for winter.*

Horde: A large group: *Hordes of people go shopping on festivals..*

115. **Hue, Hew**

Hue: Colour: *His face was glowing with a healthy hue.*

Hew: To cut down: *The statues were hewn out of solid rock.*

116. **Idle, Idol**

Idle: Without work: *An idle man's hands are devil's tools.*

Idol: Image: *Idol of Goddess Durga was kept in the room.*

117. **In, Inn**

In: Within, inside: *There are six people in the room.*

Inn: A small hotel, usually in the country: *We all were tired, so we spent the night in an inn.*

118. **Key, Quay**

Key: A specially shaped piece of metal used for locking a door, starting a car, etc., Input. Solution: *The key to success is hard work, planning and preparation.*

Quay: A platform in a harbour where boats come in to load, etc.: *We were waiting for the ship on the quay.*

119. **Knave, Nave**

Knave: A dishonest man or boy: *Don't trust him, he is a knave.*

Nave: The long central part of a church with most of the seats: *The nave of the church was practically vacant.*

120. **Knead, Need**

Knead: To press and stretch dough, wet clay, etc.: *Add some milk to the flour and knead it into dough.*

Need: Require: *Children need lots of love and affection.*

121. **Knit, Nit**

Knit: Weave: *I have knitted this cardigan myself.*

Nit: The egg or young form of a louse: *The child's hair is full of nits.*

122. Knotty, Naughty

Knotty: Having knots: *I can't use this rope to tie the bundle because it is knotty.*

Naughty: Mischievous: *Suresh is a very naughty boy.*

123. Lac, Lack

Lac: A resinous substance: *The tree stem is oozing out lac.*

Lack: Be short of: *He could not achieve success because he lacked determination.*

124. Lain, Lane

Lain: Past participle of 'lie' means to remain in a flat position on a surface: *The cat has lain fast asleep by the fire.*

Lane: Path, track: *We drove along a muddy lane to reach the farmhouse.*

125. Lead, Led

Lead: The thin black part of a pencil that marks paper: *The fishing nets are weighted with lead.*

Led: Influenced or organized by: *Eating too much sugar led him to health problems.*

126. Leak, Leek

Leak: Seep out, disclose: *The contents of the report were leaked to the press.*

Leek: A vegetable like a long onion with many layers of wide flat leaves: *We all love to cook and eat leeks.*

127. Lessen, Lesson

Lessen: To decrease or make less: *The noise began to lessen after sometime.*

Lesson: Something learnt: *We have learnt a new lesson today.*

128. Liar, Lyre

Liar: Pretender, a person who tells lies: *He is nothing but a liar and a fraud.*

Lyre: An ancient musical instrument with strings: *In ancient Greek, a singer used to sing in accompaniment of a lyre.*

129. Licence, License

Licence: An official document that shows that permission is given: *Lack of punishment seems to give youngsters licence to break the law.*

License: To give somebody official permission to do, own, or use something: *They have licensed the firm to produce the drug.*

130. Lightning, Lightening

Lightning: Electric flash in the clouds: *He was struck by lightning and killed.*

Lightening: Making lighter: *The measures will lighten the tax burden on small businesses.*

131. Loan, Lone

Loan: Anything lent: *The bank is happy to loan money to small businesses.*

Lone: Solitary: *She was the lone worker in the field.*

132. Made, Maid

Made: Completed: *We all relished home-made sweets.*

Maid: A female servant in a house or hotel: *There is a maid to do the housework but she is on leave today.*

133. Mail, Male

Mail: Letters, packages, etc. sent and delivered: *We do our correspondence by mail.*

Male: Related to masculine gender: *The male birds are more colourful than the female ones.*

134. **Main, Mane**
  Main: Chief: *Poor housing and unemployment are the main problems in this area.*
  Mane: Hair on the neck of a horse or a lion: *We all admired the lion's mane.*

135. **Mall, Maul**
  Mall: Shopping centre: *The drug store has a prime position in the mall.*
  Maul: Attack: *The attackers mauled the victim and left him bleeding.*

136. **Mantel, Mantle**
  Mantel: A shelf above a fireplace: *A lovely painting was decorated at the mantel.*
  Mantle: Responsibility: *The vice-president must now take on the mantle of supreme power.*

137. **Mare, Mayor**
  Mare: A female horse or donkey: *The bridegroom selected a healthy and strong mare.*
  Mayor: The head of the government of a town or a city: *The new theatre was inaugurated by the Mayor.*

138. **Marshal, Martial**
  Marshal: An officer of high rank in a police or fire department: *Air Chief Marshal, Mr. Nehra was the chief guest for the occasion.*
  Martial: Connected with fighting or war: *The city remains firmly under martial law.*

139. **Mask, Masque**
  Mask: A covering for part or all of the face: *In group dance, children were wearing masks of the cartoon characters.*
  Masque: A play written in verse: *All the actors played their roles very well in the masque.*

140. **Maze, Maize**
  Maze: Confusion, jumble: *The building is a maze of corridors and stairs.*
  Maize: A corn: *Maize grows in north India in abundance.*

141. **Meddle, Medal**
  Meddle: To interfere: *Somebody had been meddling with my computer.*
  Medal: Award, honour: *Abhinav Bindra has won a gold medal in the Olympics.*

142. **Meet, Mete, Meat**
  Meet: To assemble, get together: *We will meet our old friends today.*
  Mete: To give somebody a punishment: *Severe penalties were meted out by the court.*
  Meat: Flesh that may be eaten: *Being a nonvegetarian, he loves meat, fish and chicken.*

143. **Metal, Mettle**
  Metal: A type of solid mineral substance: *Lead is one of the heaviest metals.*
  Mettle: Courage, spirit: *The next game will be a real test of their mettle.*

144. **Meter, Metre**
  Meter: A device for measuring electricity, gas, water, etc.: *The cab driver demanded hundred rupees as the meter of the cab was not working.*
  Metre: A unit for measuring length: *She came second in the 4×100 metres relay race.*

145. **Might, Mite**
  Might: Power, strength: *I used all my might and pushed the rock aside.*
  Mite: Very little: *The place looked a mite (a little) expensive.*

146. **Miner, Minor**

     Miner: A person who works in a mine: *Coal miners do a very tough job.*

     Minor: Insignificant: *There may be some minor changes to the schedule.*

147. **Mind, Mined**

     Mind: Brain, intellect: *There were all kinds of thoughts running through my mind.*

     Mined: Excavated: *They were mining for gold.*

148. **Missed, Mist**

     Missed: To fail to hit, catch, reach, etc.: *I got late because I missed my train.*

     Mist: Haze, fog: *The hills were shrouded in mist at night.*

149. **Morning, Mourning**

     Morning: The early part of the day: *Early morning mist patches will soon clear.*

     Mourning: Sadness that you show and feel on somebody's death: *He was still mourning his brother's death.*

150. **Nay, Neigh**

     Nay: Used to emphasize something you have just said by introducing a stronger word or phrase: *He is weak, nay he is the weakest one amongst all.*

     Neigh: Cry of a horse: *The horses were neighing in the stable.*

151. **Naught, Nought**

     Naught: Nothing: *All of our plans came to naught.*

     Nought: Zero: *A million is written with six noughts.*

152. **None, Nun**

     None: Not any: *We saw several houses but we liked none.*

     Nun: Priestess: *Mother Teresa was a holy nun.*

153. **One, Won**

     One: Number 1: *This book costs one hundred and fifty rupees.*

     Won: To be the most successful in a competition, race, battle, etc.: *Britain won five gold medals in athletics.*

154. **Packed, Pact**

     Packed: Extremely full of people: *He packed a bag with a few things and was off.*

     Pact: A formal agreement: *They have made a pact with each other that they will not speak about their differences in public.*

155. **Pain, Pane**

     Pain: Ache: *I never meant to cause her pain.*

     Pane: A single sheet of glass in a window: *Ramesh hit a shot and broke the window pane.*

156. **Pair, Pare, Pear**

     Pair: Two things of the same type: *I bought a pair of shoes for the party.*

     Pare: To remove the thin outer layer: *The lemon was pared of its outer layer.*

     Pear: A yellow or green fruit: *Cut some pears and add them to custard.*

157. **Pale, Pail**

     Pale: Whitish complexion: *You look pale. Are you OK?*

     Pail: A bucket: *The servant brought some warm water in a pail.*

158. Pause, Paws
   Pause: Break, gap: *The woman spoke almost without pausing for breath.*
   Paws: Hand, foot: *The cat jumped from the terrace and landed on her paws.*

159. Peace, Piece
   Peace: A sense of calm, absence of war or hostility: *She lay back and enjoyed the peace of the summer evening.*
   Piece: A part or segment of something: *She wrote something on a small piece of paper.*

160. Peak, Peek, Pique
   Peak: The top of a mountain: *The peak of the mountain is covered with snow.*
   Peek: Peep, peer: *I couldn't resist peeking in the drawer.*
   Pique: Annoyed or bitter feelings: *When he realized nobody was listening to him, he left in a fit of pique.*

161. Peal, Peel
   Peal: Loud sound: *The comic show left us into peals of laughter.*
   Peel: To take off the skin: *Peel the apple carefully.*

162. Peer, Pier
   Peer: Person who is the same age or social status as you: *Children are worried about failing in front of their peers.*
   Pier: A long low structure built in a lake, river or the sea and joined to the land at one end: *The diver dived into the river from the pier.*

163. Pedal, Peddle
   Pedal: A flat bar on a machine such as a bicycle, car, etc., pushed down with foot to make parts of the machine move or work: *She pressed her foot down sharply on the brake pedal.*
   Peddle: To try to sell goods by going from place to place: *He was arrested by the police as he was trying to peddle illegal drugs.*

164. Pi, Pie
   Pi: The symbol π used in mathematics: *The teacher asked the students to find out the value of pi (π).*
   Pie: Fruit baked in a dish with pastry on the bottom, sides and top: *Decorate the pie with chocolate sauce.*

165. Plain, Plane
   Plain: Simple not showy: *The interior of the church was plain and simple.*
   Plane: A flat and level surface, a new level, an airplane: *The plane took off an hour late.*

166. Pleas, Please
   Pleas: Urgent emotional request: *Nobody listened to the pleas of the innocent man.*
   Please: To make somebody happy: *He's a difficult man to please.*

167. Plum, Plumb
   Plum: A soft round fruit with smooth red or purple skin: *We had plum pudding after dinner.*
   Plumb: Understanding something mysterious: *She spent her life plumbing the mysteries of the human psyche.*

168. Poll, Pole
   Poll: Voting: *A recent poll suggests some surprising changes in public opinion.*
   Pole: A long stick: *He jumped across the field with the help of a pole.*

169. Pour, Pore
    Pour: To dispense liquid from one container into another: *I poured it carefully, still I spilt some.*
    Pore: A small opening in skin: *Pores are all over our bodies.*

170. Practice, Practise
    Practice: (noun) Do, follow: *She's determined to put her new ideas into practice.*
    Practise: (verb) To do regularly: *He usually wants to practise English speaking with me.*

171. Pray, Prey
    Pray: To offer prayer to God: *She prayed to God for an end to her sufferings.*
    Prey: Hunt or kill: *The lion attacked and killed its prey.*

172. President, Precedent
    President: One who presides, the head of the country: *Dr. Rajendra Prasad was the first President of India.*
    Precedent: Previous example: *There is no precedent for a disaster of this scale in the past.*

173. Principle, Principal
    Principle: Rules, code of conduct: *I refused to lie about it as it was against my principles.*
    Principal: Chief: *Mr. Sharma is the new Principal of our college.*

174. Profit, Prophet
    Profit: The money earned above the expense: *The firm made a healthy profit on the deal.*
    Prophet: A person who can foretell the future and through whom a divine presence speaks: *Prophet Guru Nanak Dev is respected by the people of all the religions.*

175. Rain, Reign, Rein
    Rain: The water that falls from the sky: *In India, agriculture depends mainly on rainfall.*
    Reign: The rule of a king or a queen: *In the field of classical music, he still reigns supreme.*
    Rein: Straps of leather used to control and guide a horse: *She pulled gently on the reins and the horse started running.*

176. Raise, Raze, Rays
    Raise: To grow: *He raised his hand to greet us.*
    Raze: To destroy: *The village was razed to the ground.*
    Rays: A narrow line of light, heat or other energy: *The windows were shining in the reflected rays of the setting sun.*

177. Raw, Roar
    Raw: Uncooked: *This information is only raw and it needs further clarification.*
    Roar: To make a very loud, deep sound: *The lion roared deafeningly in the jungle.*

178. Read, Reed
    Read: Understand writing: *We should have good reading habits to enhance our knowledge.*
    Reed: A tall plant like grass with a hollow stem: *The sea shore was covered with reed beds.*

179. Real, Reel
    Real: Actually existing or happening: *Politicians seem to be out of touch with the real world.*
    Reel: Roll: *We bought reels of magnetic tape.*

180. Reek, Wreak
    Reek: To smell very strongly of something unpleasant: *His breath reeked of alcohol.*
    Wreak: To do great damage or harm: *Their policies would wreak havoc on the economy.*

181. **Rest, Wrest**

   Rest: Relax: *I am very tired, I want some rest.*

   Wrest: To take something such as power or control from somebody with great effort: *He wrested the gun from my grasp.*

182. **Right, Write, Rite**

   Right: Correct: *It seems only right to warn you of the risk.*

   Rite: A ceremony: *The last rites for the grandfather were held in the church.*

   Write: To express oneself in writing: *Write your name at the top of the paper.*

183. **Ring, Wring**

   Ring: To produce sound: *The Principal rang the bell to call the peon.*

   Wring: Squeeze: *Please wring out the wet towel.*

184. **Role, Roll**

   Role: A part in a play or movie: *Mary is playing the role of a mother in her next movie.*

   Roll: To turn over and over: *Dinesh rolled the flat tire into the shop.*

185. **Road, Rode**

   Road: A long path or street to travel on: *My house is situated at the main road.*

   Rode: Past tense of 'ride': *A small boy rode on the elephant's back.*

186. **Root, Route**

   Root: Basis, origin: *Tree roots can cause damage to the buildings.*

   Route: Way, direction: *The house is not on a bus route.*

187. **Rose, Rows**

   Rose: A flower with a sweet smell: *They presented me a bunch of roses on my birthday.*

   Rows: Objects, people arranged in a line: *The vegetables were planted in neat rows.*

188. **Scene, Seen**

   Scene: A place, view: *Nobody was present at the scene of the crime.*

   Seen: Past tense of the verb 'see': *I have not seen any horror movies.*

189. **Seam, Seem**

   Seam: Line of stitching: *Her dress split along the seam.*

   Seem: To appear: *It seems that they know what they are doing.*

190. **Sent, Scent, Cent**

   Sent: Past tense of 'send': *I sent him a lovely bouquet on his birthday.*

   Scent: Fragrance: *The air was filled with the scent of wild flowers.*

   Cent: A hundred: *A successful career requires hundred percent commitment.*

191. **Sew, So, Sow**

   Sew: Stitch: *Surgeons were able to sew the finger back on.*

   So: Therefore: *He was very tired so he went to sleep.*

   Sow: To plant or spread seeds in or on the ground: *The fields around had been sown with rice.*

192. **Shear, Sheer**

   Shear: To cut off: *We shear sheep's wool in the spring.*

   Sheer: Pure, unadulterated: *It was a sheer pleasure to watch the cartoon movie.*

193. Soar, Sore
   Soar: Fly: *The building soared above us.*
   Sore: Causing pain: *He is suffering from sore throat.*

194. Sole, Soul
   Sole: Only: *The sole motive of the drama was to irritate them.*
   Soul: Spirit, essence: *There was a feeling of restlessness deep in her soul.*

195. Stair, Stare
   Stair: Step: *How many stairs are there up to the second floor?*
   Stare: To gaze: *I stared blankly at the paper in front of me.*

196. Stalk, Stork
   Stalk: A thin stem: *The stalk is without leaves.*
   Stork: A large black and white bird: *There is a tradition that says that it is storks that bring people their new babies.*

197. Stationary, Stationery
   Stationary: Still and unmoving: *The lion was stationary until it attacked a deer.*
   Stationery: Refers to writing materials such as paper: *Chirag took out his best stationery to prepare the invitation card for his birthday.*

198. Steel, Steal
   Steel: A strong hard metal: *The photo frame is made of steel.*
   Steal: To take something without permission or intention to return: *She had to steal food just to stay alive.*

199. Storey, Story
   Storey: Refers to a floor of a building: *We stay in a multi-storey building.*
   Story: A tale related in speech or writing: *Children love listening to stories of fairies and magic.*

200. Straight, Strait
   Straight: No bends or curves: *He was too tired to walk straight.*
   Strait: A narrow channel connecting two bodies of water: *The Bering Strait lies between Alaska and Siberia.*

201. Tare, Tear
   Tare: A plant growing where you do not want it: *The garden is full of tare, remove it and plant some grass in its place.*
   Tear: To damage something by pulling it apart: *The car has taken a lot of wear and tear.*

202. Team, Teem
   Team: Group: *The team is not playing very well this season.*
   Teem: To abound in: *The streets were teeming with tourists.*

203. Their, There, They're
   Their: Possessive of 'they': *The boys had finished their games when they came out.*
   There: Refers to a place that is not here: *There are four main branches in our college.*
   They're: A contraction for 'they are': *They're going to meet him tonight.*

204. Threw, Through
   Threw: Tossed, hurled in the air: *She threw the ball up and caught it again.*
   Through: From one end or side to the other: *The doctor pushed his way through the crowd.*

205. Throne, Thrown
     Throne: The position of being a king or queen: *His claims to the throne are baseless.*
     Thrown: Past participle of 'throw', fling: *The problem was suddenly thrown into focus.*

206. Tide, Tied
     Tide: Flood, surge: *Everybody is anxious about the rising tide of crime.*
     Tied: Fasten with string, rope, etc.: *I don't want to be tied to coming home at a particular time.*

207. Tire, Tyre
     Tire: Exhaust: *They soon got tired of the beach and went for a walk.*
     Tyre: A thick rubber ring that fits around the edge of a wheel of a car, bicycle, etc.: *I found a nail sticking in the tyre.*

208. Vane, Vain, Vein
     Vane: Blade that rotates: *A strong wind blew the weather vane off the roof.*
     Vain: Fruitless, without result: *I knocked loudly at the door but it was in vain.*
     Vein: The tubes that carry blood back to the heart: *His veins got cut in the accident.*

209. Verses, Versus
     Verses: Lines of poetry: *Most of the play is written in verse, but some of it is in prose.*
     Versus: In comparison or opposition to: *The benefit of individual study versus self-study depends on the individual.*

210. Wail, Whale
     Wail: Cry: *There is no point wailing about something that happened so long ago.*
     Whale: A large sea animal: *A whale was thrashing the water with its tail.*

211. Vale, Veil
     Vale: Valley: *From the top of a mountain we saw a vale covered with fog and snow.*
     Veil: A covering: *The mountain tops were hidden beneath a veil of mist.*

212. Waist, Waste
     Waist: Refers to the narrow area of a human body between the hips and ribs: *Her hair hung down her back to the waist.*
     Waste: Garbage, use carelessly: *Don't waste your sympathy on him, he does not deserve it.*

213. Wait, Weight
     Wait: Stay, pass the time: *We are waiting for the rain to stop to go shopping.*
     Weight: Heaviness, load: *He staggered a little under the weight of his backpack.*

214. Warn, Worn
     Warn: Caution: *The guidebook warns against walking alone at night.*
     Worn: Weary: *The stone steps were worn and broken.*

215. Wave, Waive
     Wave: To move back and forth: *People were waving back at the film star.*
     Waive: To give up, not require or ask for: *He waived his claims for the property.*

216. Way, Weigh, Whey
     Way: Route: *Infectious diseases can be acquired in several ways.*
     Weigh: To measure somebody/something in weight: *I weighed the benefits of the plan against the risks involved.*
     Whey: The thin liquid that is left from sour milk: *Whey water is good for digestion.*

217. Wear, Ware, Where
     Wear: To have clothing on: *All employees have to wear their name badges.*
     Ware(s):   An article of merchandise, a product (usually in the plural): *He travelled from town to town selling his wares.*
     Where: Indicates place or situation: *Where did you read that?*

218. Weather, Whether
     Weather: Refers to climate: *Bad weather only added to our difficulties.*
     Whether: Means "if" and is used only inside sentences: *It remains to be seen whether or not this idea can be put into practice.*

219. Which, Witch
     Which: What particular choice: *"Which is your favourite book?" I asked him.*
     Witch: A person who practices magic: *It seems that some witch has put a spell on you.*

220. Whither, Wither
     Whither: To what place: *They did not know the place whither they were sent.*
     Wither: To fade away: *The grass withered due to excessive heat.*

221. Wreathe, Wreath
     Wreathe: To encircle, be full of: *The mountain tops were wreathed in mist.*
     Wreath: Flowers arranged in a circle, garland: *The queen laid a wreath at the war memorial.*

222. Yolk, Yoke
     Yolk: The yellow internal part of the egg: *Add an egg yolk to bind the mixture together.*
     Yoke: Something that represents a bond: *We got independence from the British yoke on 15th August, 1947.*

Task

Make sentences using the following pairs of words to bring out their differences:

Air-heir; bread-bred; caught-court; cord-chord; discreet-discrete; fir-fur
Great-grate; hanger-hangar; leak-leek; morning-mourning; plum-plumb; rain-rein;
ring-wring; stationary-stationery

4.5 Homonyms

Everyone wants to be better at writing as well as speaking. There is one thing that we all wish to have in common—using words correctly. English language includes quite a few words that have more than one meaning, depending upon the context in which they are used. Such words are called homonyms. In other words, a homonym is a word, which is spelt like another word or is pronounced like it but has a different meaning. For example, the word 'can' means 'be able to' and 'to put something in a container.'

1. Admission: 1. Admitted to some society or class: *We have got admission in a reputed college.*
   2. Acknowledgement of something as true: *The minister's resignation was an admission that she had lied.*

2. Aim: 1. The purpose of doing something: *She set out the company's aims and objectives in her speech.* 2. The action or skill of pointing a weapon at somebody/something: *The gunman took aim and fired at the lion.*

3. Arm: 1. Wing: *The research arm of the company is working efficiently.* 2. Upper limb: *My left arm is aching badly.*

4. Back: 1. The part of the human body on the opposite side to the chest: *He stood with his back to the door.* 2. To support somebody: *Her parents backed her in her choice of career.*

5. Ball: 1. A round object used for throwing, hitting or kicking in games and sports: *You need to hit the ball accurately.* 2. A large formal party with dancing: *We all are going to the ball tonight.*

6. Band: 1. Group: *He persuaded a small band of volunteers to help.* 2. A range of radio waves: *Short-wave radio uses the 20–50 metre band.* 3. A thin flat strip or circle of any material put around things: *She wore a simple band of gold on her finger.*

7. Bank: 1. An organization that provides various financial services: *She approached the bank for a loan.* 2. The side of a river, canal, etc., and the land near it: *My house is situated on the north bank of the Ganges.* 3. A place where something is stored for use: *I donated blood in the blood bank.*

8. Bark: 1. The outer covering of a tree: *Deer had stripped the bark off the banyan tree.* 2. A loud sound made by a gun or a voice: *The dog suddenly started barking at us.*

9. Bat: 1. A mammal: *His father was as blind as a bat.* 2. To hit a ball with a bat: *This batsman bats well on the front foot.*

10. Bear: 1. To tolerate: *How can you bear to eat that stuff?* 2. An animal: *She has been wounded by a bear.*

11. Bill: 1. Statement: *I always pay my bills on time.* 2. A written suggestion for a new law presented to a country's parliament: *Parliament passed the bill without any amendment.*

12. Bit: 1. A little: *These trousers are a bit tight.* 2. Past tense of 'bite': *The mosquitoes bit us all the night.*

13. Block: 1. A group of buildings with streets on all sides: *There is a supermarket in the next block.* 2. Obstruct: *An ugly new building blocked the view from the window.* 3. Capital: *Write you name in block letters.*

14. Blue: 1. The colour of a clear sky: *He was wearing a blue shirt.* 2. Sad: *Things were going wrong and he was feeling blue all the time.*

15. Box: 1. A container made of wood, cardboard, metal, etc.: *I gave my son a box of chocolates.* 2. To fight: *He won a gold medal in heavy weight boxing.*

16. Bright: 1. Extremely clever: *The school has been criticized for failing to encourage bright pupils.* 2. Very bright: *It was a bright, breezy day.*

17. Broke: 1. Bankrupt: *During the recession, thousands of small businesses went broke.* 2. Past tense of 'break': *The cat jumped upon the table and broke the plate.*

18. Bug: 1. Any small insect: *Sometimes bugs are used to check the overgrowth of plants.* 2. An infectious illness that is usually mild: *I picked up a bug in the office.*

19. Burn: 1. To destroy by fire: *The farmer burnt the dead leaves to clear the field.* 2. To put information on a C. D.: *Copy the data from the file and burn it on a C.D.*

20. Cake: 1. A food mixture that is cooked in a round flat shape: *We all love chocolate cake.* 2. To cover, coat: *Take off your shoes, they are caked in mud.*

21. Can: 1. Modal verb: *With diligence, discipline and determination everybody can achieve success.* 2. A metal container in which food and drink are sold: *A variety of canned food for pet dogs is available in the market.*

22. **Capital:** 1. The most important town or city of a country: *Washington is the capital of the USA.* 2. A large amount of money invested or used to start a business: *Kushal wanted to set up a business with a capital of Rs. 50,00,00,00.*

23. **Case:** 1. Container, holder: *Please put this necklace in a jewellery case.* 2. A question to be decided in court: *The case was dismissed in the absence of any proof.*

24. **Chair:** 1. A piece of furniture: *She rocked backward and forward in her chair.* 2. The person who holds this position: *Who's chairing the meeting today?*

25. **Change:** 1. To become different: *He has changed altogether since joining the army.* 2. Coins rather than paper money: *Do you have any change for the public phone?*

26. **Charge:** 1. The amount of money asked for goods/services: *Tickets are available free of charge from the bank.* 2. Blame: *They decided to drop the charges against the newspaper and settle out of court.* 3. Responsibility: *He took charge of the farm after his father's death.*

27. **Check:** 1. To examine something or someone quickly: *Check the container for cracks or leaks.* 2. To control something from increasing or getting worse: *She wanted to tell him the whole truth but she checked herself as it wasn't the right moment.*

28. **Chicken:** 1. A large bird that is often reared for its eggs or meat: *We ordered butter chicken for dinner.* 2. Cowardly: *He is a chicken-hearted fellow, he won't take any risk.*

29. **Choke:** 1. To block: *Rain water choked the drainage.* 2. A device that controls the amount of air flowing into the engine of a vehicle: *It is difficult to start a two wheeler without a choke in winters.*

30. **Class:** 1. A group of students who are taught together: *The whole class was told to stay back after school.* 2. A high level of skill that is impressive: *There is a real touch of class about this team.*

31. **Club:** 1. A group of people who meet together regularly: *You have to abide by the rules of the club.* 2. One of the four set of cards: *I played a club and won the game.* 3. Unite: *We clubbed together to buy them a new television.*

32. **Coast:** 1. The land beside or near the sea/ocean: *During the vacation we had a trip to the coast.* 2. To move quickly and smoothly, without using much power: *He coasted through his final exams.*

33. **Common:** 1. Something shared by two or more: *We are working together for a common purpose.* 2. Widespread: *Breast cancer is the most common form of cancer among women in this country.*

34. **Company:** 1. A business organization: *Company has given Manish a new flat.* 2. The fact of being with somebody else: *We had a good company for the weekend.*

35. **Country:** 1. Nation: *The whole country will profit from the new economic reforms.* 2. Countryside: *We all wish to spend our vacation in the country.*

36. **Course:** 1. Lessons: *MBA students have to go on a management training course* 2. Direction: *Rivers change their course with the seasons.*

37. **Crash:** 1. Vehicle accident: *I had a car crash.* 2. Sudden loud noise made by falling or breaking: *The tree fell with a great crash.*

38. **Cross:** 1. A mark on paper: *Put a tick if the answer is correct and a cross if it is wrong.* 2. A Christian symbol: *Remove this gold cross from your neck.* 3. To oppose: *She is really nice until you cross her.*

39. **Cut:** 1. Wound, hole: *He cut the paper with scissors.* 2. To hurt somebody emotionally: *His cruel remarks cut her deeply.* 3. The shape and style that a piece of clothing has: *We were impressed by the elegant cut of her dress.*

40. **Dark:** 1. With no or very little light: *Children fear to go in dark.* 2. Hidden and not known about: *There are no dark secrets in our family.*

41. **Dash:** 1. An act of moving suddenly and quickly: *He jumped off the bus and made a dash for the nearest bar.* 2. A small amount of something that is added: *The curtain is adding a dash of decor to the room.*

42. **Dawn:** 1. Daybreak: *We arrived in Sydney as dawn broke.* 2. To become easy to understand: *When the awful truth dawned upon us, we were shocked.*

43. **Deal:** 1. To buy and sell a particular product: *You can often see people dealing in narcotics openly on the streets.* 2. Much, a lot: *It took us a great deal of time to finish this project.*

44. **Delivery:** 1. The way of speaking: *The speech was greatly admired because of his wonderful delivery.* 2. Giving away: *When can we take the delivery of goods?*

45. **Descent:** 1. A movement downwards: *The climbers began their final descent from Mount Everest.* Your ancestry: *We were surprised to know that our friend was of royal descent.*

46. **Desert:** 1. To abandon: *All his friends and relatives deserted him in hard times.* 2. A wasteland: *The Thar Desert, in the north covers a huge area.*

47. **Dog:** 1. An animal: *People love to keep dogs as pets.* 2. A thing of low quality, a failure: *Her last movie was an absolute dog.* 3. To follow somebody closely: *Storm dogged the footsteps of the tired men.*

48. **Dope:** 1. A drug that is taken by a person to influence his/her performance in a race or sport: *When the athlete failed the dope test, it was obvious that he had taken such drugs.* 2. Information or details that are not generally known: *My friend asked me to give him the dope on the new officer.*

49. **Down:** 1. To or at a lower place or position: *She bent down to pick up her glove.* 2. To finish a drink or eat something quickly: *We downed our coffee and left.* 3. Sad or depressed: *After losing the match, the players were feeling a bit down.*

50. **Draw:** 1. To make pictures, with a pencil, pen or chalk: *The teacher drew the diagram beautifully on the blackboard.* 2. A game in which both teams finish with the same number of points: *The match ended in a two-all draw.* 3. Choosing: *The lucky winner of the day was chosen through a draw of lots.*

51. **Drain:** 1. To make something empty by removing all the liquid: *You will need to drain the central heating system before you replace the radiator.* 2. A pipe that carries away dirty water or other liquid waste: *We called the sweeper to clean the drains.* 3. Deplete: *Plight of the highly educated people is a huge drain on the country's resources.*

52. **Drum:** 1. A musical instrument: *As soon as they played the drum, children started dancing.* 2. A large container for oil or chemicals: *Yesterday my father bought a 50-gallon drum.*

53. **Duck:** 1. A bird that lives on or near water: *The duck's feathers shed water immediately.* 2. A batsman's score of zero: *The batsman was out for a duck.* 3. Dodge: *For some time he ducked a few blows; then, he started to fight back.*

54. **Even:** 1. Used to emphasize something unexpected or surprising: *He did not even speak a word in his defence.* 2. Smooth, level and flat: *Spread the sheet on an even surface to draw the picture.* 3. Calm, not becoming upset: *She has a very even temperament and she does not get disturbed easily.*

55. **Fair:** 1. Beautiful, white complexioned: *My daughter is very tall and fair.* 2. Just: *This is not fair on your part to cheat small kids in the game.*

56. **Fall:** 1. Drop down: *They were injured by falling rocks.* 2. Decrease: *Prices continued to fall on the stock market today.* 3. Waterfall: *The falls upstream are full of salmon.*

57. **Fare:** 1. Charge to be paid for a journey: *What is the plane fare from Delhi to Amritsar?* 2. Food provided: *We shared our simple fare with our guests.*

58. **Feet:** 1. Lower part of the legs: *His feet were cold with snow.* 2. A unit of measurement: *The snake I saw was 10-feet long.*

59. **Felt:** 1. A type of soft, thick cloth made from wool or hair: *He wore a big felt hat while dancing.* 2. Experienced, sensed: *She felt that she was wrong.*

60. **Field:**   1. An area of land used for growing crops: *We camped in a field near the village.* 2. A particular subject or activity: *This discovery has opened up a new field of research.* 3. To catch the ball and throw it back: *He fielded the ball very well.*

61. **Figure:**   1. Numeral: *Write your roll number in words not in figures.* 2. The shape of a person seen not clearly: *A tall dark figure appeared and frightened all of us.* 3. Pictures: *The results are illustrated in Figure 3.* 4. Judge: *I could not figure out his bad intention.*

62. **Fine:**   1. Excellent, very good: *I was feeling very fine that morning.* 2. To make somebody pay money as an official punishment: *She was fined for using her mobile in the class.*

63. **Fire:**   1. The flames, light and heat: *The little lamp set the curtains on fire.* 2. Shoot: *He threatened to fire if he did not raise his hands.* 3. To force somebody to leave their job: *Ramesh was fired because he did not follow the instructions of the boss.*

64. **Firm:**   1. A business or company: *We all are working in a US-based firm.* 2. Not likely to change: *He is a man of firm decesions.*

65. **Fit:**   1. Healthy: *After a good night rest, I am feeling fit.* 2. To be the right shape and size: *The dress was loose, it didn't fit me.*

66. **Flight:**   1. A journey made via air: *The next flight from Delhi to Bombay leaves at 5 am.* 2. Running away: *No valid reasons have been given for the sudden flight of refugees from this area.*

67. **Fool:**   1. A person who lacks intelligence or judgement: *He said that he secured first position; I was fool enough to believe him.* 2. A man employed by a king or queen to entertain people: *In the past, kings used to employ fools to entertain the court.*

68. **Form:**   1. Type or a variety: *A gentle form of exercise will increase your ability to relax.* 2. Document: *I have applied on the prescribed application form.* 3. The fact that somebody is performing well: *Yuvraj is out of form so, he is not performing well these days.*

69. **Founder:**   1. Creator: *Mr. Sharma is the founder member of our institution.* 2. To run aground: *The boat foundered in the deep storm.*

70. **Free:**   1. Liberated: *The only ambition I have is to lead a happy life and be free.* 2. Costing nothing: *We are offering a free gift with each copy you buy.* 3. Not busy: *Keep your weekend free; you have to visit Chandigarh.*

71. **Game:**   1. Sport: *Children were playing a game of basket ball.* 2. Secret plan: *I don't want to be a part of his dirty game.*

72. **General:**   1. Usual: *The general opinion is that the show was a success.* 2. An officer of very high rank in the army: *The Chief Guest for the function was Major General Manish Singh.*

73. **Great:**   1. Very large: *People were arriving in great numbers to attend the ceremony.* 2. Very suitable or useful: *This gadget is great for grinding food.* 3. A very well known and successful person: *Sachin Tendulkar has been described as one of the greatest batsmen in the world.*

74. **Ground:**   1. The solid surface of the earth: *I found my shoes lying on the ground.* 2. An area of knowledge: *He managed to cover a lot of ground in a short talk.* 3. Crushed into very small pieces or powder: *We bought some grounded seeds from the market.*

75. **Hail:**   1. To greet or to come from: *My mother hails from Mumbai.* 2. Balls of ice: *Hail and rain stopped us from going out.*

76. **Hand:**   1. The part of the body: *Raise your hand if you know the answer.* 2. A sailor on a ship: *The captain shouted, "All hands on deck!"* 3. To pass or give: *She handed a copy of letter to me.*

77. **Hard:**   1. Firm, stiff: *The doctor asked him to sleep on the hard bed.* 2. Difficult: *It is hard to believe that he has changed his statement.* 3. Without sympathy: *He said some very hard things to me.*

78. **Head:**   1. Part of the body: *He shook his head in disbelief.* 2. Brain: *For some reason, she has got it into her head that no one likes her.* 3. Pain: *I was not feeling well, I really had a bad head this*

morning. 4. To move in a particular direction: *We headed for the classrooms.* 5. To lead or be in charge of something: *She has been given the responsibility to head the marketing team.*

79. **Heart:** 1. Part of the body: *I could feel my heart pounding in my chest.* 2. Feelings, emotions: *The story captured the hearts and minds of the young children.* 3. One of the four sets of cards: *Who has played that king of hearts?*

80. **Hide:** 1. Conceal: *He hides himself away in his study room all day.* 2. An animal's skin: *These belts are made from sheep hide.*

81. **Hold:** 1. Grasp: *She was holding the baby in her arms.* 2. To keep somebody/something in a particular position: *He asked him to hold the door open for the patient.* 3. To own or have something: *We hold 60% shares of the firm.*

82. **Hose:** 1. A long tube made of rubber, plastic, etc.: *The gardener took out a new hose to water the plants.* 2. Trousers, pants worn by men in the past: *In old movies heroes used to wear doublet and hose.*

83. **Hot:** 1. Producing heat: *The day was hot and we all were tired.* 2. Causing strong feelings: *Opposition is getting hotter day by day.* 3. New, exciting and very popular: *This is one of the hottest news of the day.*

84. **Interest:** 1. Wanting to know more: *Do you have any interest in singing?* 2. The extra money that you pay back or receive when you borrow or invest money: *The interest we paid was more than the principal amount.*

85. **Iron:** 1. A metal: *The railings are made of iron and steel.* 2. To make clothes, etc., smooth by using an iron: *I'll need to iron my suit before I wear it.*

86. **Jet:** 1. Plane: *The jet took off an hour ago.* 2. A strong narrow stream of gas, liquid, steam or flame: *The pipe burst and jets of water shot across the room.* 3. A hard black mineral that can be polished and is used in jewellery: *The jewellery was studded with diamonds and jets.*

87. **Just:** 1. Very recently: *He has just left this place.* 2. Exactly: *She is just like her mother in her dealing with kids.* 3. Simply: *Just because you are senior to me doesn't mean you know everything.*

88. **Kind:** 1. Type: *Dresses of this kind are very popular amongst the youngsters.* 2. Gentle, friendly and generous: *My father is a very kind and helpful person.*

89. **Lean:** 1. To bend: *Don't lean forwards, you will fall down.* 2. Thin: *The patient was looking lean and thin.*

90. **Leaves:** 1. Flat green parts of the trees: *The leaves of the tree were loaded with ice and snow.* 2. Goes away from a person or a place: *The plane leaves for Amritsar at 5 pm.*

91. **Left:** 1. Opposite of right: *The car took a turn towards the left.* 2. Past tense of 'leave': *He has left for home.*

92. **Letter:** 1. A written or printed sign representing a sound used in speech: *There are 26 letters in English alphabet.* 2. Correspondence: *The letter was written in her usual humorous style.*

93. **Lie:** 1. Recline: *I was not feeling well so I kept lying in the bed.* 2. To say or write something that you know is not true: *Whatever he told us is nothing but a pack of lies.*

94. **Light:** 1. Glow from lamp, sun: *I can't read this paper without any light.* 2. Not weighing very much: *Mobile phones are very light and easy to handle.* 3. Start to burn: *The room was dark, so I lighted the lamp.*

95. **Line:** 1. A long thin mark: *I drew a thin line across the page.* 2. The edge, outline or shape of somebody/something: *He marked the line of the shadow with his finger.* 3. A particular telephone number: *If you hold the line, I'll see if she is available.*

96. **Long:** 1. Length, distance: *She was wearing a black long coat. He walked down the long corridor.* 2. To wish: *I had always longed for a successful career.*

97. **Lose:** To misplace: *I lost my belongings while travelling in a bus.* 2. Be defeated: *The team did not play well and lost the match.*

98. **Lots:** 1. Plenty: *Lots of spectators were present at the show.* 2. Group, set: *The first lot participants has arrived.* 3. Luck: *She was feeling dissatisfied with her lot.*

99. **Major:** 1. Main: *Corruption and illiteracy are major problems in India.* 2. Serious: *Don't worry, the breakdown is not major.* 3. An officer of fairly high rank in the army: *He is a Major in the Indian army.*

100. **Man:** 1. To work at a place: *These telephones lined are manned 24 hours a day by the volunteers.* 2. A male person: *Ramesh is a good-looking man.*

101. **Marks:** 1. Grade: *I always score good marks in English.* 2. Spot: *My fingers left marks on the glass.*

102. **Match:** 1. Game: *The match took an interesting turn in the last over.* 2. An equal: *He is no match for his brother at singing.* 3. A small stick used for lighting a fire, cigarette, etc.: *Please strike a match and light the fire.*

103. **Material:** 1. A substance that things can be made from: *I have ordered for some building materials.* 2. Connected with money, possessions, etc., rather than with the needs of the mind or spirit: *We should not be too much concerned about the material needs.*

104. **Matter:** 1. Substance, stuff: *Add some fertilizer to improve the soil.* 2. Affair: *Nobody likes any interference in his/her personal matters.* 3. To be important: *It hardly matters whether you like it or not.*

105. **May:** 1. Perhaps: *You may do whatever you like.* 2. Fifth month of the year: *We will be very busy in the month of May.*

106. **Mean:** 1. Suggest, imply: *What do you mean by favouritism?* 2. Not generous: *He is very mean with money.* 3. Average: *Add together all the numbers in a group, and divide the total by the number of numbers to get the mean.*

107. **Might:** 1. Strength: *'Might is right' – is the law of jungle.* 2. Probable: *There were clouds in the sky, it might rain.*

108. **Mine:** 1. Belonging to the person writing or speaking: *These objects are mine.* 2. A deep hole under the ground where minerals such as coal, gold, etc., are dug: *He and his brother work in a coal mine.*

109. **Mission:** 1. Assignment: *It was the army's mission to capture the terrorists.* 2. A building or buildings used by a Christian mission: *The mission has taken the responsibility of charity.*

110. **Miss:** 1. To fail to hit: *Hurry up or you will miss the bus.* 2. Not understood: *I completely missed the point.* 3. Title, form of address: *Miss Teena teaches us English.*

111. **Mistake:** 1. Error: *I made a big mistake by trusting him.* 2. Not understanding or judging somebody/something correctly: *I mistook him for my old friend.*

112. **Mouse:** 1. A small animal: *The cat often plays with the mouse before the kill.* 2. A small device used to control the movement of the cursor on a computer screen: *Click on the print icon with the mouse.*

113. **Note:** 1. A short piece of writing: *He sent me a note to meet him at the mall.* 2. A short comment on a word or passage in a book: *I bought a new grammar book with explanatory notes.* 3. A piece of paper money: *Do you have a five-rupee note?*

114. **Nursery:** 1. Nursery school: *My little daughter goes to the nursery at church.* 2. A place where young plants and trees are grown for sale or for planting somewhere else: *I bought a mango tree at the nursery.*

115. **Order:**   1. Arrangement: *Arrange these points in the correct order before you show them to your teacher.* 2. Instructions: *He gave me an order to do it at once.*

116. **Out:**   1. Away from: *As soon as he opened the box, a frog came out.* 2. At the end: *They had to apologize for their behaviour before the day was out.*

117. **Pack:**   1. A group of animals that hunt together: *The wolf pack killed the zebra.* 2. To put clothes, etc., into a bag in preparation for a trip: *Jasmine has packed her suitcase as she has to go home.*

118. **Page:**   1. Sheet of paper: *I drew a line across the page.* 2. Summon: *Why don't you have him paged at the airport?*

119. **Pants:**   1. Trousers: *He was wearing a lovely set of pants and pullover.* 2. Something you think is of poor quality: *I don't want to see this pants programme.*

120. **Park:**   1. Recreational area: *Children are playing in the park.* 2. To leave a vehicle at a particular place for a period of time: *A red van was parked in front of the house.*

121. **Part:**   1. Piece: *I spent the early part of my childhood at my grandfather's place.* 2. Leave somebody: *He has recently parted from his near and dear ones.*

122. **Party:**   1. A political organization: *Congress and BJP are the two major political parties in India.* 2. Social gathering: *I threw a splendid party when I excelled in exams.*

123. **Peak:**   1. Climax: *The suspense reached its peak in the last scene.* 2. Any narrow and pointed shape, edge, etc.: *Mountain peaks are covered with snow.*

124. **Peel:**   1. To take the skin off fruit, vegetables, etc.: *Please peel the carrot and grate it.* 2. To remove some or all of your clothes: *You are looking tired, why don't you peel off?*

125. **Peer:**   1. Person who has the same age or social status as you: *She enjoys the respect of her peers.* To look closely or carefully at something: *He went to the window and peered out.*

126. **Perspective:**   1. A view from a certain place or position: *From this building you can have a spectacular perspective of the valley.* 2. A mental outlook: *Although Jatin is not very successful in his career, he has a wonderful perspective about his life.*

127. **Pin:**   1. Fasten: *I pinned the identity card on my pocket.* 2. To make somebody unable to move by holding or pressing them: *The robbers pinned the old lady against a wall and took away the valuables.*

128. **Pick:**   1. To choose: *Please pick up the phone.* 2. To allow somebody to get into your vehicle: *The bus will pick the passengers outside the railway station.*

129. **Place:**   1. Position, area: *This area will be a good place for building a house.* 2. To put: *Place this lamp near the window.*

130. **Plain:**   1. Simple not show: *The teacher asked us to write the essay on a plain paper.* 2. A large level region: *He bought a farm on a great plain to grow rice.*

131. **Plane:**   1. A flat and level surface, a new level: *You should clear your basics to understand the equation of a plane surface in mathematics.* 2. An airplane: *Amar landed the plane successfully.*

132. **Play:**   1. To enjoy, rather than work: *Children were playing hide and seek.* 2. A piece of writing performed by actors in a theatre: *Shakespeare's plays are staged for the students of literature.*

133. **Point:**   1. Sharp end: *The scissors have a sharp point.* 2. Show with finger: *It's not polite to point someone while taking meal.*

134. **Police:**   1. An official organization which makes people obey the law and prevents crime: *The police have arrested the criminal.* 2. Monitor: *The organization is policed by its own governing body.*

135. **Pour:**   1. To dispense liquid from one container into another: *My mother poured some juice into the jug.* 2. Rain heavily: *The match was abandoned as the rain was pouring down.*

136. **Print:** 1. To publish: *The address has been printed at the top of the letter.* 2. To make a design on a surface or cloth: *They have printed some unique design on the bed sheets.*

137. **Quarter:** 1. One of the four equal parts: *The cinema hall was about three-quarters full.* 2. Residence: *The soldier's sleeping quarters were crowded.*

138. **Race:** 1. Contest: *Kushal secured first position in hundred-metre race.* 2. A group of people who share the same language, history, culture, etc.: *He admired Indians as a hardy and determined race.*

139. **Raise:** 1.To grow: *The farmers raise wheat in these fields.* 2. To build: *The mason will raise the pillars of the structure by the evening.*

140. **Report:** 1. Description: *I am preparing a report on independence day celebration in the college.* 2. Inform: *The case of theft was immediately reported to the police.*

141. **Rest:** 1. The remaining part: *I don't want to continue this job for the rest of my life.* 2. Relax: *I want to take some rest before I go on a long journey.*

142. **Right:** 1. Correct: *Your answers are absolutely right.* 2. Not left: *Take a right turn and go straight, you will see a school building.*

143. **Rock:** 1. The hard, solid material that forms part of the surface of the earth: *They have done a special course in rock climbing.* 2. A person who is emotionally strong and who you can rely on: *My father is my rock; he is always there to support me.*

144. **Room:** 1. Place to live: *Children are studying in their rooms.* 2. Empty space that can be used for a particular purpose: *There is no room in the bus, let us wait for the next one.*

145. **Root:** 1. Origin, source: *Roots of the banyan tree are very deep.* 2. To settle and live in one place: *After travelling for a long time, I feel that we should put down our roots somewhere.*

146. **Rose:** 1. A flower with sweet smell: *A rose is a lovely flower with sweet smell.* 2. Past tense of 'rise': *The sun rose from the east and set in the west.*

147. **Ruler:** 1. A person who rules or governs: *King Ashoka was a noble ruler.* 2. A straight strip of wood, plastic or metal, marked in centimetres or inches: *Draw a straight line with the help of a ruler.*

148. **Run:** 1. To move very fast: *As soon as they saw a lion, they started running.* 2. To make a service, course of study, etc.: *The institute runs summer courses for B.Tech. students.* 3. To travel on a particular route: *Ambala to Chandigarh is about an hour run.*

149. **Safe:** 1. Protected: *Most of the people avoid taking risk and they want to keep themselves safe.* 2. A strong metal box or cupboard with a lock, used for storing valuable things: *Please keep these valuables in the safe.*

150. **Saw:** 1. To cut something: *He accidentally sawed through a cable.* 2. Past tense of 'see': *I saw a beautiful kite flying in the sky.*

151. **Scale:** 1. The size or extent of something: *It was very difficult to understand the full scale of the damage caused by earthquake.* 2. A series of musical notes moving upwards or downwards: *He is practicing singing on a higher scale.* 3. To climb to the top: *May we all scale new heights each day!*

152. **Seal:** 1. Close: *Seal the packet well before you post it.* 2. A sea animal: *Some grey seals were basking on the rocks.*

153. **Season:** 1. Any of the four main periods of the year: *People wear woollen clothes in winter season.* 2. To add salt, pepper, etc., to a food to give it more flavour: *We added some salt and cheese and seasoned the dish.*

154. **Second:** 1. Ordinal number: *He secured second position in his class.* 2. A unit for measuring time: *It took her 65 seconds to finish the round.* 3. To send an employee to another department,

office, etc., to do a different job for a short period of time: *Each year two employees are seconded to industry for training.*

155. **Set:** 1. To put: *The waiter set the jug down on the table.* 2. To fix something so that others may follow: *The firm works on a set standard of ethics and discipline.* 3. A group of similar things: *I have brought a new set of uniform.*

156. **Sharp:** 1. With a fine edge or point: *The knife is very sharp, use it very carefully.* 2. Exactly: *The meeting will start at seven o'clock sharp.* 3. Intelligent: *My sister is very sharp, she can solve these sums orally.*

157. **Shoot:** 1. To fire a gun: *The orders were given to shoot the criminals at sight.* 2. Acute: *I had a shooting pain in the stomach.* 3. To grow very quickly: *My nephew has shot up a lot since I last saw him.*

158. **Show:** 1. To make something clear: *The results show that you have worked hard on this project.* 2. A theatre performance such as singing and dancing: *We organized a charity show to help the victims of earthquake.*

159. **Sign:** 1. Indication: *His behaviour is rude and he has shown no sign of improvement.* 2. Writing name: *We got the documents signed before filing them.*

160. **Sink:** 1. To go under the surface of a liquid or soft substance: *The ship sank with all the passengers.* 2. Fade: *Her voice sank as she became unconscious.*

161. **Skip:** 1. To move with jumps: *The children were skipping happily in the lawn.* 2. To leave secretly: *The terrorists skipped the country immediately after the blast.*

162. **Slip:** 1. Slide, fall: *I slipped on the ground as it was wet.* 2. A small mistake: *He sang the song beautifully without any slip.* 3. Piece of paper: *I noted his address and contact number on a slip of paper.*

163. **Smart:** 1. Neat and clean: *The kids were looking very smart in winter uniforms.* 2. Quick, brisk: *The thief was struck with a smart crack on his head.* 3. To feel upset about a criticism, failure, etc.: *The players were smarting from the one-sided defeat.*

164. **Sole:** 1. Only: *The sole purpose of our visit is to encourage the kids.* 2. The bottom surface of the foot: *The sole of her feet was badly injured after the fall.*

165. **Sort:** 1. Kind: *This sort of problem is due to changing season.* 2. To separate things of one type from others: *The teacher asked the students to sort out words and phrases.*

166. **Sound:** 1. Something that you can hear: *He came late at night; so, he tried not to make any sound.* 2. Give impression: *She didn't sound shocked when I gave her the news.*

167. **Space:** 1. Empty area: *There is no space left on this page.* 2. Outside Earth's atmosphere: *Kalpana Chawla was the first Indian woman to go into space.*

168. **Spell:** 1. Write the letters of a word in correct order: *How do you spell your father's name?* 2. A short period of time: *She consulted the doctor as she had dizzy spells.* 3. Charm: *I completely fell under her spell.*

169. **Spot:** 1. A small mark: *Small pox left a big spot on his face.* 2. To see or notice a person: *I've just spotted an error in calculation on this page.*

170. **Spring:** 1. Name of the season: *Many beautiful flowers bloom in spring season.* 2. Twisted wire: *The lamp spring has become very loose.*

171. **Stamp:** 1. A small piece of paper with a design on it to stick on an envelope or a package before posting it: *I pasted a 10-rupee stamp on the letter before posting it.* 2. The sign of a particular quality or person: *All his work bears the stamp of authority.*

172. **Stand:** 1. To be on your feet: *She was standing near the gate.* 2. Survive the treatment: *His heart won't stand the strain much longer.*

173. **Star:**   1. In the sky: *There were hundreds of stars shining in the sky.* 2. Celebrity: *Amitabh Bachchan is a superstar of Hindi film industry.*

174. **State:**   1. Permanent condition: *He has gone in a state of shock ever since he has got his results.* 2. Part of the country: *Punjab is a flourishing state of India.* 3. To formally write or say in a careful and clear way: *I don't agree with the facts stated in the report.*

175. **Steer:**   1. Turn: *He steered the boat towards the temple.* 2. To take control of a situation and influence the way in which it develops: *A good conversationalist steers the conversation in the desired direction.*

176. **Stick:**   1. Attach, fix: *We used glue to stick the broken pieces of the paper together.* 2. A thin piece of wood from a tree: *We collected dry sticks to light bonfire.*

177. **Still:**   1. Continuing until a particular point in time: *I joined this post in 2005 and I'm still working on it.* 2. Calm and quiet: *Most of the people feel that time stands still in villages.*

178. **Stole:**   1. Shawl: *The girl was wearing a beautiful stole that matched with the colour of her sari.* 2. To take something without permission: *Somebody has stolen my purse.*

179. **Suit:**   1. A set of clothes made of the same cloth: *The clown was wearing a loose fitting suit.* 2. To be convenient or useful for somebody: *Choose the gadget to suit your particular needs.*

180. **Swell:**   1. Enlarge: *Her leg has swollen a lot since she has fallen.* 2. Very good, enjoyable, etc.: *We had a swell time and we all enjoyed the company of our friends.*

181. **Table:**   1. A piece of furniture: *Food was served to us on the dining table.* 2. Facts or numbers arranged in a special order: *Table 6 shows how crime rate has increased over the past 20 years.* 3. Multiplication: *The teacher asked the kids to learn the table of 8.*

182. **Tear:**   1. Rip, damage: *Handle it carefully it may tear very easily.* 2. A drop of liquid that comes out of your eye when you cry: *His eyes were full of tears when he got the news of his father's death.*

183. **Through:**   1. From one end or side to the other: *The thief broke into the house through the back door.* 2. From the beginning to the end of an activity, a situation or period of time: *My grandfather is too tired to sit through the concert.*

184. **Too:**   1. More than is good, necessary, possible, etc.: *Too much of liberty may be dangerous for anyone.* 2. Also: *After painting the rooms, I'm going to do the kitchen too.*

185. **Top:**   1. The highest point: *She stays on the top floor.* 2. The best: *Kushal has topped the list of successful students in the examination.* 3. A toy: *I was so confused that my mind started spinning like a top.*

186. **Train:**   1. A railway coach: *I am going to Delhi by train.* 2. Educate: *We do our best to train our students in soft skills.* 3. A number of people or animals moving in a line: *We saw a horse train going towards south.* 4. A series of events or actions: *The death of his grandfather caused a train of events that led to his marriage.*

187. **Trip:**   1. Excursion: *Our teacher took us to a zoological park for an educational trip.* 2. To catch your foot on something and fall or almost fall: *Walk carefully or you will trip on the step.*

188. **Trunk:**   1. The thick main stem of a tree: *The trunk of the birch tree was covered with snow in winters.* 2. A large metallic box: *During summers, we keep our woollens in trunks.* 3. The main part of the human body apart from the head, arms and legs: *The injuries were found on the trunk of the injured person.*

189. **Type:**   1. Kind, sort: *She can adjust well with all types of people.* 2. Letters that are printed or typed: *The type of the letter was too small to read.*

190. **Up:**   1. In a higher position: *As we go up, the climate becomes cold.* 2. Completely: *We ate up all the food during the journey.*

191. **Use:**   1. Apply: *I do not know how to use this software.* 2. To take a particular amount of a liquid, substance, etc.: *These types of water coolers use a lot of electricity.*

192. **Walk:**   1. To move or go somewhere on foot: *The baby is just learning to walk.* 2. To disappear: *Lock up your valuables in the cupboard because things seem to walk here.*

193. **Watch:**   1. Observe: *We all watched the show on TV.* 2. A type of small clock that you wear on your wrist: *It is 6.30 pm by my watch.*

194. **Wave:**   1. To move back and forth: *She waved her hand to say good bye.* 2. A swelling in a body of water: *The boats were rocking in the waves.*

195. **Way:**   1. A method, style or manner: *This is not the right way to write the answers.* 2. A route or road that you take: *We had to go a long way before we reached our home.*

196. **Weigh:**   1. Consider: *I weighed the benefits of self-study against group study.* 2. To measure somebody/something in weight: *He weighed the potatoes on the scales.*

197. **Well:**   1. Fine: *We all are doing well in our studies.* 2. Thoroughly and completely: *Add some salt to the lemon juice and mix it well.* 3. A deep hole in the ground to obtain water: *The village women go to the nearby well to bring water.*

198. **Whisper:**   1. Murmur: *Her voice dropped to a whisper and she fainted.* 2. Rumour: *I have heard whispers that he is leaving.*

199. **Will:**   1. Determination: *If you have a strong will you can do whatever you wish.* 2. Auxiliary verb used to refer future: *You will have to finish it on time.*

200. **Yard:**   1. An area outside a building: *They were sitting in the yard.* 2. A unit for measuring length: *The farm spreads over a land of 5000 yards.*

Task

Make sentences using the following words to bring out their different meanings:

Admission; bank; capital; cross; duck; figure; ground; heart; just; matter; nursery; peer; race; sound; whisper

4.6   Words Often Confused

Using the right word in the right place is a crucial skill in professional and technical communication. However, there are several words that may be confusing because they are similar in form, meaning or pronunciation. Learners of English tend to get confused in their use, as they are different in the shades of their meaning and usages. The words such as alter/altar, amiable/amicable may confuse the user. We must learn the following words, their spellings and usage as they are mistaken frequently:

1. **A lot:**   Much, plenty: *He had to do a lot of hard work to achieve success.*
   Allot: To give time, task, money, etc., to somebody: *You have been allotted three crore rupees for this project.*

2. **Ability:**   Skill: *He has an ability to handle difficult situations.*
   Capability: Capacity: *Animals, in the zoo, lose their capability to catch food for themselves.*

3. **Abstract:**   Substance of a document: *Please prepare an abstract of the research paper.*
   Extract: Something that is taken out: *This book contains extracts from the speeches of the famous leaders.*

4. **Abuse:**   Use wrongly: *What she did was an abuse of her position as a manager.*
   Misuse: Use incorrectly: *He has misused the funds allotted for staff welfare.*

5. **Accede:** To agree to a request, proposal, etc.: *Harish finally acceded to accept the presidency of the company.*

   Exceed: To go beyond, to surpass: *Don't exceed the word limit while writing your composition.*

6. **Accept:** To agree to some request, invitation, etc: *I have accepted his proposal to start a new showroom in this area.*

   Acknowledge: To recognize: *He did not acknowledge that he had said anything wrong.*

7. **Accept:** To take, to receive: *It was raining heavily; so, I accepted his offer of a lift.*

   Except: Excluding: *Every student except Ramesh has done well in exams.*

8. **Access:** Approach: *Access to the Internet is very easy these days.*

   Excess: To be more than enough: *If you eat in excess, your health will be affected.*

9. **Accident:** Mishap: *Her mother was killed in an accident three years ago.*

   Incident: Occurrence not very important but interesting: *My grandmother told us some interesting incidents of her life.*

   Event: A planned public occasion: *Sports were the major event of the year in our college.*

10. **Accurate:** Correct and true in every detail: *Facts and figures, given in records, should be accurate.*

    Exact: Correct and as detailed as possible: *Please tell me the exact words he said.*

11. **Admission:** The act of accepting somebody into an institution, organization, etc.: *Most of the students aspire to take admission in IIT's and NIT's.*

    Admittance: Physical entrance: *Hundreds of people were unable to gain admittance to the hall.*

12. **Admit:** To agree (often unwilling): *She has admitted that she was very strict with her students.*

    Confess: Admit (formally): *He confessed that he had stolen my purse.*

13. **Adopt:** To take up, to make one's own: *All the people adopted different approaches to the problem.*

    Adept: Skilled: *He has been very successful on the stage because he is adept in the art of singing.*

    Adapt: To adjust: *A wise man adapts his ways according to the circumstances.*

14. **Adverse:** Unfavourable: *Smoking has an adverse effect on our health.*

    Averse: Unwilling or opposed: *Old people are generally averse to any change.*

15. **Affect:** To produce a change in somebody, something: (a verb): *Every living being will be affected by pollution.*

    Effect: The result (a noun): *His smile had a strange effect on me and I forgot my worries.*

16. **Affectation:** Exhibit, show: *I don't like things done out of affectation without any sincerity.*

    Affecting: Moving, touching: *Tragic stories are full of affecting scenes.*

17. **Ago:** Used when a remote event is referred to: *I joined this institution long time ago.*

    Since: Used for a point of time: *I have been reading this novel since Monday.*

18. **Alive:** Not dead: *He met with a serious accident and is lucky to be alive.*

    Living: Alive now: *Every living creature has to make efforts to reduce pollution.*

19. **All together:** Used for people or things treated as a whole: *We always had fun when we were all together.* To double check this usage, try separating the two words: *We all had fun when we were together.*

    Altogether: Completely: *He has changed altogether since he has joined army.*

20. **Allusion:** Reference to: *While talking to him, his boss did not make any allusion to his poor performance.*

    Illusion: Deception: *In a desert, there is an illusion of water.*

21. **Alone:** Unaccompanied: *He prefers to sit alone when he does some important work.*

    Lonely: Feeling alone: *I don't know anyone in this town and sometimes I feel very lonely.*

22. **Already:** By now: *I did not go to the cinema as I had already seen the film.*
   All ready: Everything completely prepared: *Are you all ready to go for a picnic?*
23. **Alternate:** Every other, by turns: *We have activity periods on alternate days.*
   Alternative: Other choice: *You have no alternative but to work hard.*
   Choice: Choosing between two or more: *The choice is between reading and writing.*
24. **Amiable:** Friendly, good natured and sociable (used for people): *Sheela was very amiable and everyone liked her.*
   Amicable: Friendly (used for agreements or relationships): *After discussing for a long time, we came to an amicable agreement.*
25. **Amoral:** Not following any moral rules: *Amoral behaviour of the terrorists cannot be justified.*
   Immoral: Bad, lacking good principles: *Stealing is an immoral act.*
26. **Amusement:** That occupies free mind: *The rich amuse themselves by playing games.*
   Recreation: That refreshes the mind after hard work: *Students should play some outdoor games for recreation.*
27. **Anonymous:** Unidentified, nameless: *I received an anonymous letter yesterday.*
   Unanimous: Fully in agreement: *We are all unanimous regarding whom to choose our next president.*
28. **Answer:** Something that one writes, says or does in response to questions or situations: *You have to write the answers on the sheet provided.*
   Reply: Say or write something as an answer to what one said or an advertisement or a letter: *I asked her a question, she only replied with a smile.*
29. **Antic:** Tricks: *The antics of the juggler amazed us.*
   Antique: Old, ancient: *Most of the people love to preserve antique things.*
30. **Anticipate:** To expect some trouble or difficulty: *The Indian government is anticipating troubles from both Pakistan and China.*
   Forestall: To take steps to prevent troubles: *The Indian government forestalled the evil intentions of Pakistan by sending troops to Kashmir promptly.*
31. **Antipathy:** Dislike: *Antipathy to manual labour does not help anyone.*
   Apathy: Indifference: *Most of the government officers have a general apathy towards work.*
32. **Apart:** In pieces, separately: *The two houses stood 500 metres apart.*
   A part: One section of: *I did not feel bad while losing as it was a part of the game.*
33. **Apprehend:** To grasp, get a hold on the meaning of a thing: *I can apprehend principles of the Theory of Relativity.*
   Comprehend: Understand fully: *He cannot comprehend the full implications of his remarks.*
34. **Apprise:** Describe: *The personal assistant apprised the director of the situation.*
   Appraise: Evaluate: *The director must appraise all staff.*
35. **Artful:** Cunning, crafty: *We were misled by his artful designs.*
   Artistic: Beautiful: *I love artistic patterns.*
   Artificial: Not natural: *Some states of India have a highly efficient artificial irrigation system.*
36. **Aspire:** To desire for: *She aspired to pursue a scientific career.*
   Expire: To come to an end: *The insurance policy will expire on 31st March.*
37. **Assay:** To test, to evaluate: *Examination is not a fair assay of a candidate's knowledge.*
   Essay: A literary composition: *The students were asked to write an essay on 'The causes of the First World War.'*
38. **Assure:** To guarantee: *I assured my father that the mistake will not be repeated in future.*
   Ensure: To make sure by double checking: *Before leaving for college, we ensured that all the rooms were locked.*
   Insure: To provide insurance: *It is wise to get your house insured against flood, fire, or theft.*

39. **Attain:**   Accomplish, to succeed in getting something after a long effort: *Most of the students of this college attain 'A' grade in their exams.*

    Acquire: To get hold of: *She has acquired a good command on spoken English.*

40. **Avoid:**   Keep away from: *The name of the firm was changed to avoid confusion.*

    Prevent: Stop or check someone from doing something: *The boundary wall prevents the dogs from getting into the garden.*

41. **Award:**   Honour: *'Ashoka Chakra' is an award given for bravery in war.*

    Reward: Something given in return: *The poor servant was rewarded for his honesty.*

42. **Bad:**   Evil: *We should not do bad things.*

    Bed: *I go to bed at 11 p.m.*

    Bade: Ordered, commanded: *I bade my servant to clean the room.*

43. **Battle:**   An armed fight between two armies: *The battle of Panipat is very famous in Indian history.*

    War: A series of battles: *The government does not want to go to war unless all other alternatives have failed.*

    Fight: A clash between two or more persons: *Two boys have been expelled from the college for fighting in the campus.*

    Duel: An armed fight between two persons: *In the Middle Ages, it was very common for a knight to challenge the other for a duel.*

44. **Beautiful:**   Full of beauty (generally used for women): *The girls were looking very beautiful in the party.*

    Handsome: Dignified, noble (generally used for men): *A handsome boy was called to conduct the show.*

45. **Because:**   Since, as, for the reason that: *They have achieved success because of us.*

    Cause: To make something happen: *Illiteracy is the major cause of exploitation.*

    Reason: Explanation: *He refused to do it but he didn't give any reason.*

46. **Begin:**   Start, a general word used for any action: *I begin my day with yoga.*

    Commence: Used for the beginning of some formal, important and dignified programme: *The ceremony commenced at 5 a.m.*

    Start: Initiate, used for physical movements: *As soon as we got ready, it started raining.*

47. **Belief:**   A noun: *I admire his passionate belief in what he is doing.*

    Believe: A verb: *He believes in what he does.*

48. **Beside:**   Next to: *The lamp was kept beside the bed.*

    Besides: Additionally: *Besides being a successful businessman, he is a kind-hearted person too.*

49. **Between:**   Used for two: *C comes between A and B in the English alphabet.*

    Among: Used for three or more: *I found the letter amongst his papers.*

50. **Blank:**   Without written or printed words: *Give me a blank sheet of paper to write a letter.*

    Empty: Containing or carrying nothing: *There was an empty jug in the fridge.*

    Vacant: Not occupied: *Several seats are vacant in the hall.*

51. **Blunder:**   A serious mistake: *The teacher blundered in suspending the innocent boy.*

    Error: A minor mistake: *I think you have made an error in calculating the amount.*

    Mistake: Something incorrectly done: *Leaving school so young was the biggest mistake of my life.*

52. **Bold:**   Courageous: *She is bold enough to face the challenges of life.*

    Strong: Physically powerful: *He is strong enough to lift this weight.*

53. **Borrow:**   To take something on loan: *I have borrowed five books from the library.*

    Burrow: A hole, rabbit's home: *The rabbit lives in a burrow.*

54. **Bought:** Past tense of the verb 'to buy': *I bought a bungalow last year.*
    Brought: Past tense of the verb 'to bring': *She brought her friends home to have dinner with them.*
55. **Boundary:** Edge, an area of land within a country: *The fence marks the boundary between my property and hers.*
    Border: The place where two countries meet: *Wagha border in Amritsar separates India and Pakistan.*
56. **Canvas:** A rough cloth: *He was wearing a canvas hat.*
    Canvass: To request for votes: *Party workers are busy canvassing local residents.*
57. **Capture (verb):** Seize: *He was captured by his enemies.*
    Captivate (verb): Fascinate: *He was captivated by her beauty.*
58. **Casual:** Incidental, occasional: *He tried to sound casual, but I knew he was worried.*
    Causal: Denoting cause: *There is a causal relationship between dirt and disease.*
59. **Ceiling:** Inner roof: *Children were playing in a large room with a high ceiling.*
    Roof: Upper covering of a house: *During the summer season, we sleep on the rooftop.*
60. **Centre:** More precise and definite: *There was a table in the centre of the room.*
    Middle: Approximately near the centre: *They were sitting in the middle of the row.*
61. **Ceremonious:** Observing formalities: *The chief guest lighted the lamp and inaugurated the show ceremoniously.*
    Ceremonial: Related to a ceremony: *We use these articles only on ceremonial occasions.*
62. **Chair:** A movable seat for one person: *The old man fell asleep in his chair.*
    Seat: A place to sit as found in cinema, train buses, etc.: *Those seats in the bus are still vacant.*
63. **Check:** To examine something or someone quickly: *Check your answer sheet well before handing it in.*
    Control: To manage, direct: *The police had no control over the mob.*
64. **Childlike:** Like a child, innocent: *We all love our teacher because of his child-like simplicity*
    Childish: Immature, foolish: *Everybody laughs at him because of his childish behaviour.*
65. **Cite:** To quote something as an example: *He cited his poor health as the reason for delay in work.*
    Quote: To repeat the exact words of another person: *People often quote, 'Life is meaningless without love.'*
66. **Cloth:** Fabric: *Clean the surface with a damp cloth.*
    Clothes: Garments, attires: *I bought some new clothes for winter.*
67. **Coma:** A deep unconscious state: *Nobody can meet the patient as he is in coma.*
    Comma: A punctuation mark: *A comma is used to separate more than two words in a sentence.*
68. **Common:** Something shared by two or more: *We all share a common interest in photography.*
    Ordinary: Commonplace, not unusual: *This was no ordinary task but we performed it efficiently.*
    Mutual: Reciprocal: *The two friends have mutual love and respect for each other.*
69. **Comprehensive:** All inclusive: *He gave me a comprehensive summary of the poem.*
    Comprehensible: That which can be understood: *The book was easily comprehensible to the average reader.*
70. **Compulsion:** Pressure to do something due to circumstances: *Students demand that there should be no compulsion on them to attend classes.*
    Obligation: Commitment, duty: *She is not under any obligation to tell him the truth.*

71. **Confident:** To be sure of: *He is confident of achieving success.*
    Confidant: One entrusted with secrets: *Nitin is my trusted confidant, he knows all my secrets.*
72. **Conform:** To be conventional: *He refused to conform to the local customs.*
    Confirm: To make sure: *I came back to confirm whether the room was locked or not.*
73. **Conscience:** Sense of right and wrong: *My conscience does not allow me to exploit the weaker ones.*
    Conscious: Mindful, awake and aware: *Jasmine was still conscious after banging her head on the wall.*
74. **Considerable:** Moderately large: *A considerable number of people think that smoking is injurious to health.*
    Considerate: Thoughtful for the feelings of others: *My friend was considerate enough to understand my problem.*
75. **Contagious:** Diseases that spread through physical contact: *Most of the skin diseases are contagious.*
    Infectious: Transmitted by germs through air or water: *Jaundice is an infectious disease.*
76. **Contemptible:** Deserving hatred: *Ramesh is such a contemptible fellow that no one prefers to work with him.*
    Contemptuous: Disdainful, scornful: *We all felt hurt when our colleagues gave us a contemptuous look.*
77. **Continuous:** Uninterrupted: *We could not sleep because of continuous drumming of rain on the window panes.*
    Continual: Repeated with breaks in between: *The patient was not well; so, the doctor's visit to his place became continual.*
    Continuation: The act of carrying: *The continuation of this project depends on getting the next instalment.*
78. **Convince:** To make one believe something: *Manish has convinced me that he has not stolen the book.*
    Persuade: To talk someone into doing something: *I persuaded my friend to help me in preparing the report.*
79. **Cool:** Opposite of warm: *Let us enjoy the cool shade of the mango tree.*
    Cold: Opposite of hot: *It was very cold outside; so, we did not go out.*
80. **Corpse:** Dead body: *After the war, many corpses were lying on the ground.*
    Corps: A division of an army: *Every student should have the membership of National Cadet Corps.*
    Core: The innermost part: *The hostess welcomed the guest from the core of her heart.*
81. **Credible:** Believable: *The witness did not give any credible argument in support of his evidence.*
    Creditable: Praiseworthy: *It is really creditable for him to attain success under these circumstances.*
    Credulous: One who believes things easily: *Mansi is very credulous and she trusts everybody easily.*
82. **Crime:** Offence against law: *Crime rate is increasing day by day.*
    Sin: Offence against God: *It is a sin to torture the poor.*
83. **Custom:** Tradition, convention: *It is our custom to equate guests with God.*
    Costume: The outfit worn to represent a particular time, event, or culture: *She has four costume changes during the play.*

84. Dairy: A farm where milk and milk products are produced: *Tania has grown up on a dairy and she knows how to churn butter.*

Diary: The daily journal kept: *Karan writes in his diary every night.*

85. Damp: Moist, slightly wet: *Don't sit here, the seat is damp.*

Humid: Warm and sticky: *It is very hot and humid.*

86. Decided: Certain: *It is almost decided that I will not attend the function.*

Decisive: Final: *The decisive shot came from the bat of Sachin Tendulkar.*

87. Defer: To postpone: *The Director has deferred the meeting till Monday.*

Differ: To disagree: *The two friends differ from each other in many respects.*

Deference: High esteem: *The flags were lowered out of deference to the martyrs.*

88. Defy: Challenge: *We should not defy the rules, they are meant for our safety.*

Deify: Worship, idolize: *Heroes are deified by everyone.*

89. Delightful: Pleasant (to the senses): *It was a delightful journey and we all enjoyed it.*

Delicious: Tasty, mouth-watering: *They served us many delicious dishes in dinner.*

90. Deliverance: Freedom: *Oh God! Grant us deliverance from poverty, cruelty and disease.*

Delivery: The way of speaking: *His thoughtful speech was ruined by his poor delivery.*

91. Deny: Contradict (used for statements): *It can't be denied that we need to devote some more time to solve this problem.*

Refuse: Turn down (used for actions): *He refused to give me his notes.*

92. Device: An instrument used to perform a task: *Nowadays there are several electronic devices to help us.*

Devise: To plan: *You have to devise a plan to finish your work in the given time.*

93. Discriminate: To point out minute differences: *Only an expert can discriminate between the different shades of the same colour.*

Distinguish: To recognize broad differences: *Even a child can distinguish between red and black.*

94. Discussion: Conversation, dialogue: *We arrived at a conclusion after a long discussion.*

Argument: A quarrel: *The boys had an argument with the conductor about the bus fare.*

95. Disease: Illness: *He is suffering from a rare blood disease.*

Decease: Death: *The government decided to give fifty thousand rupees to the family of the deceased.*

96. Divers: Several: *Divers ways were used to overcome the hurdles.*

Diverse: Unlike: *Their views were so diverse that they could not find a solution.*

97. Doubt: Disbelief (used for statement): *I doubt the fact he has stated in the report.*

Suspect: Not to trust someone (used for persons): *Whom do the police suspect in theft?*

98. Draught: A current of air: *There is a draught outside, please close the door.*

Drought: Want of rain: *The whole of north India is suffering from drought due to scanty rainfall.*

99. Drown: Used for living objects: *Three people drowned in the river yesterday.*

Sink: Used for lifeless objects: *The boat sank all of a sudden and all the passengers drowned.*

100. Economic: Concerning material needs of a person: *Economic necessities compelled him to sell his house.*

Economical: Not wasteful: *He is an economical person; he spends his money wisely.*

Economics: A subject: *He is studying economics in the college.*

101. Egoist: One who believes that man is selfish by nature: *He is an egoist because he believes that self-interest governs the actions of a man.*

Egotist: A self-centred person: *Those who are egotist by nature are not liked by anyone.*

102. **Elect:** Choose by ballot: *Mrs. Sareen has been elected as the new M.L.A. of Ambala.*
  Choose: Select: *The board has chosen its new president.*

103. **Elemental:** Fundamental: *Air, water, earth, and fire are elemental forces.*
  Elementary: Basic: *His elementary knowledge of the subject is very weak.*

104. **Eligible:** Qualified: *Only a postgraduate is eligible to teach in this institution.*
  Illegible: Unreadable: *His handwriting is so illegible that no one can understand it.*

105. **Elusive:** Mysterious: *Pratap is an elusive person, you cannot trust him.*
  Illusive: Deceptive: *The hope of controlling terrorism in India proved illusive.*

106. **Emerge:** To come out: *Many evils emerge from poverty.*
  Immerge: To go down into: *He immerged into water and took out the lost ring.*

107. **Emigrant:** A person who leaves his native country to settle in another: *There are many emigrant workers in USA.*
  Immigrant: A person who moves to a new country: *Many immigrants settle in this country every year.*

108. **Eminent:** Well known: *An eminent scholar presented his research paper at the seminar.*
  Imminent: About to happen: *We all waited for an imminent announcement about his resignation.*

109. **Empire:** Kingdom: *The British Empire ruled India for a long time.*
  Umpire: Referee: *Nowadays, players challenge umpire's decision in a cricket match.*

110. **Envelop:** To surround, encircle: *Clouds enveloped the mountain tops.*
  Envelope: A cover, a flat container: *I wrote a letter and put it in an envelope.*

111. **Enviable:** Good and desirable: *He is in the enviable position of having two job offers to choose from.*
  Envious: Feeling envy: *He saw the envious look in the other boy's eyes.*

112. **Envy:** Painful awareness of the advantages enjoyed by others with the desire to have the same: *She felt a pang of envy at the thought of his success.*
  Jealousy: Hostility towards one who is believed to enjoy an advantage: *Children often feel jealous when a new baby arrives.*

113. **Estimate:** Calculate approximately: *We estimated that it will take three weeks to complete this project.*
  Estimation: Opinion: *Freedom fighters stand high in the estimation of the world.*

114. **Excite:** Motivate, stimulate: *The prospect of the new job greatly excited her.*
  Incite: Provoke: *They were accused of inciting the workforce to come out on strike.*

115. **Excuse:** To apologize for an ordinary offence: *Excuse me for coming late.*
  Pardon: To exempt from penalty: *The governor pardoned the convict.*
  Forgive: Act of pardoning at personal level: *Don't say anything wrong; otherwise, he will never forgive you.*

116. **Exhausting:** Tiring: *The journey was exhausting, I need some rest.*
  Exhaustive: Thorough: *The notes, our teacher gave us, are quite exhaustive; we don't need anything else.*

117. **Expect:** To wait for: *I did not expect to finish it today.*
  Hope: To think with some confidence: *I hope to win the first prize in the competition.*

118. **Famous:** Well known for being good: *Kalidas is a famous Sanskrit poet.*
  Notorious: Well known for being bad: *Ramesh Bahadur is a notorious terrorist.*

119. **Famous:** Popular: *Chetan Bhagat is internationally famous because of his novels.*
  Renowned: Celebrated, distinguished: *She is renowned for her patience.*

120. **Fatal:**   Deadly: *Cholera is a fatal disease.*
     Fateful: Decisive, significant: *She looked back to that fateful day when she decided to join this firm.*
     Fatalist: One who believes in fate: *Nipun is a fatalist; he believes that all the happenings are decided by fate.*
121. **Felicity:**   Happiness: *True felicity results from contentment.*
     Facility: Ease, comfort: *The hostels of our college are equipped with every facility.*
122. **Floor:**   Ground, base: *The body was lying on the kitchen floor.*
     Flour: Fine powder made from grains: *Wheat flour is used to make bread.*
123. **Forceful:**   Impressive: *Everybody was impressed by his forceful speech.*
     Forcible: Aggressive: *The criminal was sent to the jail forcibly.*
124. **Formally:**   Ceremoniously: *The chief guest was formally welcomed by the students.*
     Formerly: Previously: *My father is a teacher but formerly he was in military.*
125. **Founder:**   Creator: *Dr. Gupta is the founder member of this trust.*
     Flounder: To struggle to move or get somewhere: *She was floundering around in the deep end of the swimming pool.*
126. **Freedom:**   Independence: *In democracy, everybody has freedom of speech.*
     Liberty: Being free from slavery: *The slaves were set at liberty.*
127. **Get:**   Receive something: *What present did you get on your birthday?*
     Obtain: Achieve, to get something by making efforts: *To obtain the overall score, add up the totals in each column.*
128. **Goal:**   Aim: *Our ultimate goal must be the preservation of the natural resources.*
     Gaol: Jail: *The thief who tried to steal the jewels has been put in the gaol.*
129. **Ghostly:**   Like a ghost: *A ghostly figure appeared in the dark.*
     Ghastly: Pale, frightening: *The patient looked ghastly as he was very weak.*
130. **Godly:**   Pious, holy: *Guru Nanak Dev is a Godly figure.*
     God-like: Like God: *Mother Teresa was God-like in her kindness and generosity towards the poor.*
131. **Graceful:**   Pleasing, charming: *Everyone admired her graceful personality.*
     Gracious: Kind: *A gracious boss is loved by his subordinates.*
132. **Gypsy:**   A race of people who move from one place to another and traditionally live in caravans: *A gypsy camp has come to settle here for some time.*
     Vagabond: A person who wanders from place to place without settled home or job: *Rajesh has passed the whole of his life as a vagabond.*
133. **Hanged:**   Past tense of 'hang', used for executing someone with a rope around the neck: *The murderer was hanged.*
     Hung: The past tense of hang (used for other things): *Leela's son never hung up his clothes.*
134. **Haste:**   Speed in doing something: *Don't write your answers in haste or you will make a number of mistakes.*
     Hurry: Quickness with compulsion: *Hurry up or you will be late for your classes.*
135. **Haven:**   A place for retreat: *This island is a safe haven for smugglers.*
     Heaven: Paradise: *The joys of heaven are a myth.*
136. **Healthy:**   One who has good health: *A healthy man enjoys the bliss of life.*
     Strong: Physically powerful: *He is strong enough to carry this burden.*
137. **Historical:**   Chronological: *You must analyse these events in their historical context.*
     Historic: Notable: *Today is a historic occasion for our institution.*
138. **Honorary:**   To serve without salary: *He is working on an honorary post.*
     Honourable: Respectable: *Dr. Abdul Kalam is an honourable person.*

139. **Human:**   Related to mankind: *All human beings want love and praise.*
     Humane: Kind: *We should be humane in our treatment towards the sufferers.*
140. **Humiliation:**   Disgrace: *She suffered the humiliation of being criticised in public.*
     Humility: Modesty: *She did not refuse the task due to her humility.*
141. **Idle:**   Without work: *An idle mind is a devil's workshop.*
     Lazy: Lethargic (habit): *He does not finish his work due to his laziness.*
142. **Idle:**   Without work: *We should not sit idle.*
     Idol: Image: *The Hindus believe in idol worship.*
     Ideal: Perfect: *This place is ideal for building a shopping complex.*
143. **Ill:**   Suffering from a disease: *I could not attend the meeting as I was ill.*
     Sick: Tired: *I felt sick of the dull routine of life.*
144. **Immemorial:**   That which is beyond time: *These costumes have been here in this museum since time immemorial.*
     Immortal: Eternal: *Virtues such as kindness, honesty and truthfulness are immortal.*
     Immoral: Not nice, unethical: *Telling lies is an immoral act.*
145. **Industrious:**   Hard working: *We have to be industrious to achieve success in our life.*
     Industrial: Related to industry: *Industrial Revolution has played an important role in the history of civilization.*
146. **Intelligent:**   Clever, bright: *Anuj is a very intelligent boy.*
     Intelligible: Understandable: *This article is readily intelligible to all the students.*
147. **Invent:**   To create, to originate: *Graham Bell invented telephone.*
     Discover: To find out, notice: *Columbus discovered America.*
148. **Judicial:**   Related to a judge or justice: *The committee has ordered judicial inquiry against the accident.*
     Judicious: Thoughtful, sensible: *We must be judicious while taking important decisions.*
149. **Jump:**   To leap, to skip: *The kids were jumping in the field.*
     Pounce: To attack suddenly: *The cat pounced upon the rat.*
150. **Kill:**   Slay (unintentionally): *His brother was killed in a car accident.*
     Murder: Put to death (intentionally): *Amir murdered his brother for property.*
151. **Kind:**   Generous: *A kind-hearted person helps everyone.*
     Kindly: Graciously: *Mr. Bhargav has kindly consented to inaugurate the function.*
152. **Keep:**   To put something for a long time: *Keep your passport in a safe place.*
     Place: To put something for the time being: *A bomb has been placed under the seat in a theatre.*
153. **Later:**   Afterwards: *As we were very tired, we decided to do it later.*
     Latter: Second: *Out of the two solutions, the latter one was better.*
154. **Lay:**   To set, to arrange, to put down: *The table was laid for four people.*
     Lie: Remain in a certain place: *He kept lying in the bed because he was not feeling well.*
155. **Lend:**   To give something to someone temporarily: *Can you lend me your car this evening?*
     Loan: Something borrowed: *Most people get a bank loan to buy a house or to start a business.*
     Borrow: To receive something from someone temporarily: *Members can borrow up to 10 books from the library at a time.*
156. **Literal:**   Usual meaning of a word or a phrase: *I am not referring to 'small' people in the literal sense of the word.*
     Literary: Related to literature: *Prem Chand is a literary figure.*

157. **Loose:** Not tight: *The knot was tight but after sometime it came loose.*
Lose: To misplace, be defeated: *If you don't play well, you will lose the game.*

158. **Lovely:** Beautiful: *There were many lovely flowers in the garden.*
Lovable: Worthy of love: *People admire him because of his lovable nature.*

159. **Luggage:** A traveller's trunks, suitcase, etc.: *You stay there with the luggage while I find a taxi.*
Baggage: Traveller's luggage, tent and provisions, etc. for an army: *The army loaded their baggage into the car.*

160. **Marry:** To wed: *Vineet decided to marry a girl of his choice.*
Merry: Full of joy: *It was festival time and we all were busy making merry.*

161. **Marital:** Related to marriage: *Vasu and Meena are facing marital difficulties.*
Martial: Refers to war or warriors: *Anuj has got a black belt in martial arts.*

162. **Mob:** A large gathering of people in a disorderly and uncontrolled manner: *The mob was going to storm the building.*
Crowd: A large gathering of people: *Salman Khan left the hotel surrounded by a crowd of journalists.*

163. **Momentary:** Short-lived: *When results were announced there was a momentary confusion.*
Momentous: Significant: *The decision to devaluate the rupee is momentous.*

164. **Monetary:** Financial: *Vishal is facing monetary problems these days.*
Monitory: Giving warning or advice: *We should listen to the monitory advice of the elders and teachers.*

165. **Nation:** A country considered as an economic or political structure: *China is one of the strongest nations of the world.*
Country: The area a person comes from: *Most of the leaders in our country are corrupt.*

166. **Negligible:** Not of much value: *There was a negligible error in calculation.*
Negligent: Careless: *Don't be negligent about your duties.*

167. **Notable:** Important, worth noting: *The town is notable for its ancient harbour.*
Noticeable: That which can be seen: *Marks were noticeably higher for girls than for boys.*

168. **Odious:** Horrible: *What an odious act!*
Odorous: Having unpleasant smell: *The room is full of odorous gases.*

169. **Old:** Not new or young: *Rahim is an old man of 60.*
Ancient: Not modern: *Women were not kept in purdah in ancient India.*

170. **Overdo:** To exaggerate something: *Isha overdoes her makeup and she looks like a clown.*
Overdue: Something that has missed its deadline: *You must pay these overdue bills immediately.*

171. **Overtake:** Leave behind, surpass: *It's dangerous to overtake on a bend.*
Takeover: Taking control of a company by buying its shares: *The company's takeover has lifted its shares in the market.*

172. **Patrol:** A party of soldiers or guards: *Police patrol visits this place regularly at night.*
Petrol: A kind of liquid used as fuel in car engines, etc.: *There has been an increase in petrol prices.*

173. **Personal:** Private, individual: *All the travellers should take care of their personal belongings.*
Personnel: Human resources: *Personnel are currently reviewing pay scales.*

174. **Perspective:** A mental outlook: *Nivedita is only 15-years old but she has a wonderful perspective on life.*
Prospective: Likely to happen: *Children have several prospective opportunities before them.*

175. **Possible:** That which is achievable: *If possible, please try to help him get a job.*
Probable: That which is likely to take place: *It is probable that the disease is genetic.*

176. **Praise:** Compliment, to approve of something: *We all are full of praise for the progress he has made.*
     Admire: Esteem, regard: *I don't agree with her, but I admire her for sticking to her principles.*
177. **Precede:** To come or go before: *The flower girl preceded the bride in the procession.*
     Proceed: To move forward: *The MLA and his group proceeded to the guest house for lunch.*
178. **Presence:** The state of being near: *The presence of our near and dear ones comforts us in the time of sorrow.*
     Presents: Gifts: *We received many presents on Diwali.*
179. **Propose:** To suggest: *He proposed to his friend that they should have an outing.*
     Purpose: Object: *The purpose of education is overall development of a child.*
180. **Prosecute:** Put on trial: *Those who do not follow the traffic rules will be prosecuted.*
     Persecute: Maltreat, harass: *Why are the media persecuting him in this way?*
181. **Pursue:** Follow: *We should pursue our goals with strong determination.*
     Persuade: Influence: *I persuaded him to come with me.*
182. **Quiet:** Calm, silent: *We are supposed to be quiet in hospitals, schools and libraries.*
     Quite: Completely, rather: *She was quite alone that Saturday afternoon but she kept herself busy with house keeping.*
183. **Remember:** To keep in memory: *I remember the days when I was in school.*
     Remind: To help someone remember something: *Could you remind me to pay the bill?*
     Recollect: To recall with an effort: *As far as I can recollect, she wasn't there on that occasion.*
184. **Respectable:** Deserving respect: *Our elders always teach us to be respectable in public.*
     Respectful: Showing respect: *We were brought up to be respectful of authority.*
     Respective: Individual: *The kids were taken to their respective cabins after the play.*
185. **Sale:** The selling of something: *Every big sale means a lot of commission for the salesman.*
     Sail: To go in a boat, the material used to catch wind on a boat: *The sail fluttered in the wind as the boat sailed across the water.*
     Sell: To offer goods for consumption at a cost: *Mrs. Chawla sells her pottery at art fairs.*
186. **Sensitive:** Easily and actually affected: *He is very sensitive, don't say anything bad to him.*
     Sensible: Wise, prudent: *A sensible person takes every step carefully.*
187. **Sever:** To cut through completely: *The two countries have severed all diplomatic links.*
     Severe: Strict, hard: *The party suffered severe losses during the last election.*
188. **Shade:** A place sheltered from the sun: *The travellers rested in the shade of the tree.*
     Shadow: The dark spot cast by a body: *The shadows lengthened as the sun went down.*
189. **Shore:** A beach: *We all wish to spend vacation on the shore.*
     Sure: Without doubt: *I am sure that we will win the prize.*
190. **Sight:** View: *The lovely sight inspired him to paint a beautiful picture.*
     Vision: An idea or a picture in your imagination: *We have a vision of the world in which there will be no poverty, corruption and war.*
191. **Social:** Related to society: *We have joined a social club to make new friends.*
     Sociable: Friendly: *I'm not feeling very sociable this evening.*
192. **Steal:** To take something without permission: *Someone has stolen my belongings from the room.*
     Rob: To take property unlawfully: *The robbers robbed the travellers of their valuables.*
193. **Suit:** A set of clothes: *The manager was wearing a nice business suit.*
     Suite: A set of rooms: *We rented a three-piece suite with two armchairs and a sofa.*
     Soot: Black substance in smoke: *The lamp soot blocked the pipes.*

194. **Superficial:** Shallow: *He has a very superficial knowledge of the subject.*
     Superfluous: Unnecessary, excess: *She gave him a look that made words superfluous.*
195. **Tamper:** To meddle: *Someone appears to have tampered with the glasses.*
     Temper: Disposition: *We should not rely on those who have an unpredictable temper.*
196. **Temporary:** Short-lived: *I don't want to apply against a temporary vacancy.*
     Temporal: Worldly, earthly: *A ruler has only temporal authority.*
197. **Tenor:** Character or meaning of something: *I was discouraged by the tenor of his remarks.*
     Tenure: Period of holding the office: *The president effected many changes during his tenure.*
198. **Travel (v):** To change location: *My job requires a lot of travelling.*
     Trip (n): Used when the travelling distance is short: *How was your trip to the amusement park?*
     Voyage (n): A long journey by boat: *The voyage to South Africa took 6 weeks.*
     Journey (n): Travel between two or more points: *I got very tired because the journey was very long.*
199. **Unity:** The state being joined together to form one unit: *India is known for her unity in diversity all over the world.*
     Union: Association: *The labourer union has called off the strike but no one is satisfied with the decision.*
200. **Urban:** Of the city: *The urban population has a lower percentage of voting than the rural one.*
     Urbane: Polite, smooth: *Everyone loves him because of his urbane manners.*
201. **Unqualified:** Not having sufficient qualification: *He is unqualified for the post as he cannot write anything in a systematic manner.*
     Disqualified: Debarred: *He was disqualified from military services because of his health problems.*
202. **Vacation:** Holiday: *During the summer vacation we are planning to attend music classes.*
     Vocation: Profession: *She is fortunate that she has found her true vocation in life.*
203. **Verbal:** Spoken, unwritten: *The company has received both oral and written complaints.*
     Verbose: Full of words: *He is a verbose speaker without much substance in his speeches.*
204. **Vicious:** Cruel and violent: *Police were shocked by the viciousness of the attack.*
     Viscous: Thick and sticky: *Honey and tar are viscous material.*
205. **Wander (v):** To walk aimlessly: *She wandered aimlessly around the streets.*
     Wonder (v): Consider or question some issue: *I was wondering whether you'd like to come to a party.*
     Wonder (n): A feeling of surprise and admiration for something beautiful, unusual or unexpected: *The pyramids are the real wonder of the world.*
206. **Wary:** Distrustful and cautious: *The police will need to keep a wary eye on this area of the town.*
     Weary: Tired and worn: *After working the whole day, I was very weary.*
207. **Were:** Past tense of 'are': *Mansi and her fiancé were at the ball last weekend.*
     We're: A contraction for 'we are': *We're planning to finish this project today.*
208. **Wish:** To want something to happen: *I wish you all success in your future endeavours.*
     Hope: A feeling of expectation or desire: *We hope to finish it today.*
209. **Womanish:** Related to a woman, used in a negative sense: *People make fun of him because of his womanish habits.*
     Womanly: Related to a woman, used in a good sense: *The nurse treated the patients with womanly gentleness and gestures.*
210. **Yet:** Up till now (often used in negative and interrogative sentences): *We haven't got the letter yet.*
     Still: Continuing/even now: *I wrote to them last month and I'm still waiting for a reply.*

Task

Fill in the blanks using suitable words from those given in the brackets:

1. The noise outside _____my performance. (affected/effected)
2. She _____her friends home to have dinner with them. (brought/bought)
3. You should always ____oil, water and tyres before taking your car on a long trip. (check/cheque)
4. The _____of the book explains how its thesis fits in with current thinking. (foreword/forward)
5. His poor health _____him for military services. (disqualified/unqualified)
6. The rich _____ themselves by playing cards. (amuse/recreate)
7. He _____ her about the quality of the item. (assure/ensure)
8. Fill the amount of your payment in the _____ space. (empty/blank)
9. She _____ him on his fine handling of the official work. (complemented/complimented)
10. A _____ is used to separate more than two words in a sentence. (coma/comma)
11. He was awarded a gold _____ for securing first rank. (medal/meddle)
12. I liked only the _____ half of the movie. (latter/later)
13. I _____ him of my sincere help. (assured/insured)
14. Kalidas is one of the _____dramatists of India. (eminent/imminent)
15. The hunter walked two miles _____in the forest and found a dead lion. (further/farther)

4.7   One Word Substitution

Single words often express the ideas of phrases. We should learn them, as they are very useful when we want to put our ideas in brief. Francis Bacon's old statement, "Brevity is the soul of wit," is apt even today as conciseness and brevity are the call of modern communication. One-word substitutes help us in summarizing, précis writing and all types of official communication. Listed below are some commonly used one-word substitutes:

1. A partner in crime   ↔   Accomplice
2. Written declaration made on an oath   ↔   Affidavit
3. A list of things to be discussed at a meeting   ↔   Agenda
4. One who doubts the existence of God   ↔   Agnostic/Atheist
5. One who is a habitual drunkard   ↔   Alcoholic
6. A legal defence by which an accused person tries to show that he was somewhere else when the crime was committed   ↔   Alibi
7. A person who lives in a foreign country   ↔   Alien
8. One who takes part in sports and other activities for enjoyment only   ↔   Amateur
9. A statement that is open to more than one interpretation   ↔   Ambiguous
10. A general pardon of political offender   ↔   Amnesty
11. One who is out to destroy the government   ↔   Anarchist
12. Absence of government   ↔   Anarchy
13. The science of the structure of human body   ↔   Anatomy
14. An instrument used for measuring force of the wind   ↔   Anemometer
15. A medicine which produces insensitivity   ↔   Anaesthetic
16. A book written by an unknown author   ↔   Anonymous
17. The study of man   ↔   Anthropology
18. A medicine used to counteract poison   ↔   Antidote
19. One who studies things of the past   ↔   Antiquarian

20. A substance which kills germs   ↔   Antiseptic
21. An artificial pond or a tank used for keeping live fish, water plants, etc.   ↔   Aquarium
22. A study of ancient things   ↔   Archaeology
23. One who prepares plans for buildings   ↔   Architect
24. A place where government and public records are kept   ↔   Archive
25. A government by the nobility   ↔   Aristocracy
26. A study of stars and planets and their influence on human affairs   ↔   Astrology
27. One who flies a space vehicle   ↔   Astronaut
28. The study of stars   ↔   Astronomy
29. Animals that live in water   ↔   Aquatic
30. Space or room which is immediately below the roof of a house   ↔   Attic
31. Something that can be heard   ↔   Audible
32. A record of one's life written by oneself   ↔   Autobiography
33. A government by one   ↔   Autocracy
34. The right of self-government   ↔   Autonomy
35. A place for keeping birds   ↔   Aviary
36. An unmarried man   ↔   Bachelor
37. One who is unable to pay off one's debt   ↔   Bankrupt
38. A building used for lodging soldiers   ↔   Barrack
39. Hastily erected barrier across a street   ↔   Barricade
40. One who is engaged to be married   ↔   Betrothed
41. A great lover of books   ↔   Bibliophile
42. One who can speak two languages   ↔   Bilingual
43. An instrument used by both the eyes to see a distant object in an increased shape   ↔   Binocular
44. A record of one's life written by somebody else   ↔   Biography
45. A study of plants   ↔   Botany
46. A bunch of flowers   ↔   Bouquet
47. A collection of flags   ↔   Bunting
48. A government by the officials   ↔   Bureaucracy
49. A list which contains dates and days   ↔   Calendar
50. The art of beautiful writing   ↔   Calligraphy
51. One who eats human flesh   ↔   Cannibal
52. The dead body of an animal   ↔   Carcass
53. One who lives on flesh   ↔   Carnivorous
54. A place with gambling tables   ↔   Casino
55. Soldiers on horses   ↔   Cavalry
56. One who is unmarried   ↔   Celibate
57. One who is more than hundred years old   ↔   Centenarian
58. Situation in which everything happens in a confused way   ↔   Chaotic
59. One who mends shoes   ↔   Cobbler
60. People who work together   ↔   Colleagues
61. A person belonging to one's own country   ↔   Compatriot
62. One who is completely self-satisfied   ↔   Complacent
63. One who sells sweets and pastries   ↔   Confectioner
64. Belonging to an individual from birth   ↔   Congenital
65. One who believes in keeping things and customs as they are   ↔   Conservative
66. A number of stars grouped together   ↔   Constellation

67. Smuggled goods   ↔   Contraband
68. One who lives at the same time   ↔   Contemporary
69. One for whom the world is home   ↔   Cosmopolitan
70. One who easily believes what others say   ↔   Credulous
71. A number of sailors working on a ship   ↔   Crew
72. A war of religion   ↔   Crusade
73. One who questions everything   ↔   Cynic
74. A person who has been appointed or selected to attend or speak at a conference   ↔   Delegate
75. A government by the people   ↔   Democracy
76. A language of a region with its own way   ↔   Dialect
77. Shy, timid unwilling to face a situation   ↔   Diffident
78. A book which contains telephone addresses   ↔   Directory
79. A game in which no one wins   ↔   Draw
80. Extremely dry weather without rainfall   ↔   Drought
81. One who deals in cattle   ↔   Drover
82. A person who is slow in learning   ↔   Dunce
83. One who has strange habits   ↔   Eccentric
84. Something that can be eaten   ↔   Edible
85. One who thinks and talks too much about himself/herself   ↔   Egoist
86. A poem written to mourn the death of someone   ↔   Elegy
87. The most capable part of group, class of society or a country   ↔   Elite
88. The art of effective speaking   ↔   Elocution
89. A book containing information on all branches of knowledge   ↔   Encyclopaedia
90. One who is given to the pleasures of flesh   ↔   Epicure
91. A speech made by the dramatist at the end of the play   ↔   Epilogue
92. Words inscribed on a tomb about the person buried therein   ↔   Epitaph
93. A statement open to more than one interpretations   ↔   Equivocal
94. The act of spying   ↔   Espionage
95. A study of the origin of words   ↔   Etymology
96. To shift people from a place of danger to a safer place   ↔   Evacuate
97. A speech made without preparation   ↔   Extempore
98. Short stories with an element of moral   ↔   Fable
99. One who is not easily pleased   ↔   Fastidious
100. A disease which ends in death   ↔   Fatal
101. One who believes in fate   ↔   Fatalist
102. Animals of a certain region   ↔   Fauna
103. One who champions the rights of women   ↔   Feminist
104. One who is engaged to marry   ↔   Fiancé/Fiancée
105. A person with showy character   ↔   Flamboyant
106. A number of battle ships   ↔   Fleet
107. A number of sheep   ↔   Flock
108. Plants and vegetation of a certain region   ↔   Flora
109. Murder of a brother   ↔   Fratricide
110. Large band of stars encircling the heavens   ↔   Galaxy
111. The study of rocks and soil   ↔   Geology
112. One who eats too much   ↔   Glutton

113. Storehouse of grains ↔ Granary
114. One who is easily deceived ↔ Gullible
115. Language that has been very much used ↔ Hackneyed
116. A cluster of houses in a village ↔ Hamlet
117. A place for shelter of ships ↔ Harbour
118. A place for the collection of dried plants ↔ Herbarium
119. Descending from father to son ↔ Hereditary
120. One who acts against religion ↔ Heretic
121. Murder of a human being ↔ Homicide
122. Words different in meaning but similar in sound ↔ Homophones
123. Serving without pay ↔ Honorary
124. One who is sympathetic to mankind ↔ Humanitarian
125. One who pretends to be what he/she is not ↔ Hypocrite
126. The house of an Eskimo ↔ Igloo
127. Something which is unlawful ↔ Illegal
128. Something which cannot be read ↔ Illegible
129. One who cannot read or write ↔ Illiterate
130. One who settles in another country ↔ Immigrant
131. Free from infection ↔ Immune
132. Not planned ahead of time ↔ Impromptu
133. Something which cannot be heard ↔ Inaudible
134. Not of good omen ↔ Inauspicious
135. Something that cannot be corrected ↔ Incorrigible
136. Something that cannot be described ↔ Indescribable
137. Something that cannot be eaten ↔ Inedible
138. Something that cannot be avoided ↔ Inevitable
139. One who does not make mistakes ↔ Infallible
140. Murder of an infant ↔ Infanticide
141. The soldiers on foot ↔ Infantry
142. Liable to catch fire ↔ Inflammable
143. Something which cannot be imitated ↔ Inimitable
144. Something which cannot be satisfied ↔ Insatiable
145. To examine one's thoughts and feelings ↔ Introspect
146. Having no force, null and void ↔ Invalid
147. Something which cannot be conquered ↔ Invincible
148. A decision that cannot be taken back ↔ Irrevocable
149. A plan for the route to be followed ↔ Itinerary
150. A professional rider in horse races ↔ Jockey
151. One who has an irresistible tendency to steal ↔ Kleptomaniac
152. A place where food is kept ↔ Larder
153. A book of account showing debit and credit ↔ Ledger
154. Something which is lawful ↔ Legal
155. Something which can be read ↔ Legible
156. One who compiles a dictionary ↔ Lexicographer
157. Number of books housed in one building ↔ Library
158. Pertaining/related to moon ↔ Lunatic

159. A place where mad men are kept   ↔   Lunatic asylum
160. A speech made for the first time   ↔   Maiden
161. Animals that suckle their young ones   ↔   Mammals
162. A book or a paper written by hand   ↔   Manuscript
163. Killing on a large scale   ↔   Massacre
164. Murder of a mother   ↔   Matricide
165. Negotiating between the opposite parties to settle their dispute   ↔   Mediate
166. Personal reminiscences in a narration form   ↔   Memoir
167. The world in miniature   ↔   Microcosm
168. One who imitates voice and gestures of another person   ↔   Mimic
169. A place where money is coined   ↔   Mint
170. One who hates mankind   ↔   Misanthrope
171. A person who loves money and hates spending it   ↔   Miser
172. A hater of women   ↔   Misogynist
173. A rule by the mob   ↔   Mobocracy
174. A government by a king or a queen   ↔   Monarchy
175. A treatise on a subject   ↔   Monograph
176. A speech delivered by one person   ↔   Monologue
177. Mental derangement confined to one idea   ↔   Monomania
178. Exclusive possession or control of any one thing   ↔   Monopoly
179. A place where dead bodies are kept for identification   ↔   Morgue
180. A place where dead bodies are kept before they are cremated or buried   ↔   Mortuary
181. A place where ancient works are kept   ↔   Museum
182. Favouring one's friends and relatives   ↔   Nepotism
183. Taking neither side in the dispute, remaining impartial   ↔   Neutral
184. A hollow space in a wall for a statue   ↔   Niche
185. One who is new to a profession   ↔   Novice
186. A word no longer in use   ↔   Obsolete
187. One who is 80-years old   ↔   Octogenarian
188. A government by the few   ↔   Oligarchy
189. Possessing unlimited powers   ↔   Omnipotence
190. One who is all powerful   ↔   Omnipotent
191. One who is present everywhere   ↔   Omnipresent
192. One who knows everything   ↔   Omniscient
193. Flesh- and vegetable-eating animals   ↔   Omnivorous
194. Something through which light cannot pass   ↔   Opaque
195. One who is able to make an eloquent speech   ↔   Orator
196. Curved path of a planet, satellite   ↔   Orbit
197. An authoritative decree or law of the government   ↔   Ordinance
198. A study of birds   ↔   Ornithology
199. The study of mountains   ↔   Orology
200. A place where orphans are housed   ↔   Orphanage
201. One who looks at the bright side of things in life   ↔   Optimist
202. A cure for all diseases   ↔   Panacea
203. Belief of God in nature   ↔   Pantheism
204. One that lives on others   ↔   Parasite

205. A document allowing persons to travel abroad ↔ Passport
206. Murder of a father ↔ Patricide
207. One who loves one's own country ↔ Patriot
208. One who shows too much concern for small details of learning or teaching ↔ Pedant
209. One who walks on foot ↔ Pedestrian
210. A doctor who specializes in the treatment of children ↔ Paediatrician
211. One who looks at the dark side of things ↔ Pessimist
212. One who loves mankind ↔ Philanthropist
213. One who collects postage stamps ↔ Philatelist
214. The study of languages ↔ Philology
215. A study of human body ↔ Physiology
216. Deeply religious ↔ Pious
217. A writer who steals ideas from another writer ↔ Plagiarist
218. A government by the rich ↔ Plutocracy
219. The science of government ↔ Political science
220. One who knows many languages ↔ Polyglot
221. Something which can be carried or moved easily ↔ Portable
222. Occurring after death ↔ Posthumous
223. Examination of a dead body ↔ Post-mortem
224. A child of unusual or remarkable talent ↔ Prodigy
225. A speech made by the dramatist in the beginning of the play ↔ Prologue
226. A person who preaches religion and is considered to be a messenger of God ↔ Prophet
227. To write under a different name ↔ Pseudonym
228. A doctor who specializes in mental illness ↔ Psychiatrist
229. The study of human mind ↔ Psychology
230. One who retires from society to live a solitary life ↔ Recluse
231. Too much official formality ↔ Red tapism
232. An institution meant for reforming young offenders ↔ Reformatory
233. Murder of the king ↔ Regicide
234. A place for improving one's health ↔ Resort
235. One who speaks less ↔ Reticent
236. A person who lives in a countryside far from the humdrum of society ↔ Rustic
237. One who gets pleasure in others' trouble or pain ↔ Sadist
238. A room where idols of God are kept ↔ Sanctorum
239. A very private room ↔ Sanctum
240. Bitter or ironic remark, specially one ironically worded ↔ Sarcasm
241. Person who is made to bear blame due to others ↔ Scapegoat
242. Someone who knows a lot about the subject ↔ Scholar
243. One who carves in stones ↔ Sculptor
244. A state in which all the religions have equal freedom ↔ Secular
245. A case in which sword is kept ↔ Sheath
246. A speech made to one self ↔ Soliloquy
247. One who walks in one's sleep ↔ Somnambulist
248. One who talks in one's sleep ↔ Somniloquist
249. An older woman who is unmarried and is not likely to get married ↔ Spinster
250. A sudden rush of a large number of frightened people or animals ↔ Stampede

251. Social position or rank ↔ Status
252. One who loads and unloads ships ↔ Stevedore
253. One who is indifferent to pain and pleasure ↔ Stoic
254. Murder of self ↔ Suicide
255. Name shared by all the members of a family ↔ Surname
256. A person's last utterance ↔ Swan Song
257. One who always keeps to himself ↔ Taciturn
258. One who does not drink wine ↔ Teetotaller
259. An instrument used to send messages to long distances ↔ Telegraph
260. An instrument which transmits spoken words to long distances ↔ Telephone
261. One who believes in God ↔ Theist
262. Something through which light can partly pass ↔ Translucent
263. Something through which light can pass ↔ Transparent
264. One who changes sides ↔ Turncoat
265. A decision on which all agree ↔ Unanimous
266. A place where everything is perfect ↔ Utopia
267. A person who lives a wandering life ↔ Vagabond
268. To spend life without purpose and initiative ↔ Vegetate
269. One who is gifted with several talents ↔ Versatile
270. One who offers one's services ↔ Volunteer
271. One who is given to the sensual pleasures of body ↔ Voluptuary
272. A place where clothes are kept ↔ Wardrobe
273. A woman whose husband is dead ↔ Widow
274. A man whose wife is dead ↔ Widower
275. An unexpected piece of good fortune ↔ Windfall
276. Highest point in the sky directly above the observer ↔ Zenith
277. A study of animals ↔ Zoology

Task

Give one-word substitutes for the following expressions:

1. That which cannot be explained
2. One who thinks only of oneself
3. An exact copy
4. A word or law no longer in use
5. One who possesses many talents or gifts
6. One who always looks at the dark side of life
7. The collection and study of stamps
8. That which cannot be avoided
9. A doctor who specializes in the diseases of the children
10. Those who work in the same organization
11. A statement open to more than one interpretation
12. Belonging to an individual from birth
13. A person who walks on foot
14. One who walks in sleep
15. Government by the officials
16. One who is present everywhere

4.8 Idioms and Phrasal Verbs

Oxford dictionary defines an idiom as a group of words whose implied meaning is different from the meaning of the individual words. 'The couple has three children but Amit is *an apple of their eyes*,' refers to the fact that out of the three children Amit is their favourite. We can see that *an apple of one's eye* is a group of words whose meaning has nothing to do with that of the individual words. Idioms are an indispensable part of English language. An idiomatic language is always better equipped to communicate as it lends charm and expression to a routine language. Idioms and phrases are language specific and also vary from culture to culture. However, excessive use of idioms may not be advisable as it makes the language showy and may give an impression that the speaker wants to impress the listener.

4.8.1 Some Commonly Used Idioms

1. A bed of roses: A comfortable position.
2. A bed of thorns: An uncomfortable position.
3. A bird in the hand is worth two in the bush: Having something that is certain is much better than taking a risk for more.
4. A bird's eye view: A brief general view.
5. A blessing in disguise: Something good that isn't recognized at first.
6. A bolt from the blue: Any calamity that overtakes somebody suddenly.
7. A chicken-hearted fellow: A timid person.
8. Achilles heel: A point of vulnerability.
9. A doubting Thomas: A skeptic who needs physical or personal evidence to believe something.
10. A drop in the bucket: A very small part of something.
11. A fair weather friend: One who betrays in difficulty.
12. A fish out of water: A person in uncomfortable surroundings.
13. A fool and his money are easily parted: It is easy for a foolish person to lose his/her money.
14. A hen-pecked husband: A person servile to his wife.
15. A leopard can't change his spots: You cannot change what you are.
16. A penny saved is a penny earned: Saving money little by little.
17. A picture paints a thousand words: A visual presentation is far more descriptive than words.
18. A piece of cake: A task that can be accomplished very easily.
19. A red letter day: An important day.
20. A slap on the wrist: A very mild punishment.
21. A snake in grass: A deceitful person.
22. A taste of your own medicine: When you are ill-treated the same way you ill-treat others.
23. At loggerheads: Engaged in a head-on dispute.
24. Actions speak louder than words: It's better to do something in reality than just talk about it.
25. Add fuel to the fire: To do something to make a bad situation even worse than it is.
26. Against the clock: To do something fast to finish it before a particular time.
27. All bark and no bite: Someone is threatening or aggressive but not willing to engage in a fight.
28. All Greek to me: Meaningless and incomprehensible like someone who cannot read, speak, or understand any of the Greek languages.

29. All in the same boat: When everyone is facing the same challenges.
30. An axe to grind: To have a dispute with someone.
31. An apple of someone's eye: Someone who is cherished above all others.
32. As high as a kite: Anything that is high up in the sky.
33. At the drop of a hat: Willing to do something immediately.
34. Back-seat driver: People who criticize from the sidelines, much like someone giving unwanted advice from the back seat of a vehicle to the driver.
35. Back to square one: Having to start all over again.
36. Beat a dead horse: To force an issue that has already ended.
37. Beating about the bush: Avoiding the main topic. Not speaking directly about the issue.
38. Between a rock and a hard place: Stuck between two very bad options.
39. Bite off more than you can chew: To take on a task that is way to big.
40. Bite your tongue: To avoid talking.
41. Black sheep: A person who is considered a disgrace to a family.
42. Blood is thicker than water: The family bond is closer than anything else.
43. Blow one's own horn: To praise your own abilities and achievements.
44. Blue moon: A rare event or occurrence.
45. Break the ice: To remove the tension, hesitation at the first meeting or at the opening of a party, etc.
46. Burn the midnight oil: To stay awake late at night to work or to study.
47. By hook or by crook: By whatever means possible, fair or unfair.
48. Carry a torch: To be infatuated with.
49. Chew someone out: To scold someone verbally.
50. Chip on his shoulder: Angry today about something that occurred in the past.
51. Chip off the old block: People who closely resemble their parents in some way or the other.
52. Clean slate: To make a new start by clearing records.
53. Cock and bull story: An unbelievable tale.
54. Crocodile tears: Pretending to be sad, in an attempt to manipulate the situation.
55. Cross your fingers: To hope that something happens the way you want it to.
56. Cry over spilt milk: When you complain about a loss from the past.
57. Cry wolf: Intentionally raise a false alarm.
58. Curiosity killed the cat: Being inquisitive can lead you into a dangerous situation.
59. Dark horse: One who was previously unknown and is now prominent.
60. Devil's advocate: Someone who takes a position for the sake of argument without believing in that particular side of the argument.
61. Don't count your chickens before they hatch: Don't rely on something until you are sure of it.
62. Don't put all your eggs in one basket: Do not put all your resources in one possibility.
63. Drastic times call for drastic measures: When you are extremely desperate you need to take extremely desperate actions.
64. Draw the line: To set a limit, as of accepted behaviour.
65. Drink like a fish: To drink very heavily.
66. Drive someone up the wall: To irritate and/or annoy very much.
67. Dropping like flies: A large number of people either falling ill or dying.
68. Every cloud has a silver lining: Be optimistic, even difficult times will lead to better days.
69. Everything but the kitchen sinks: Almost everything and anything has been included.
70. Eye for eye: Revenge.

71. **Feather in one's hat:** An accomplishment a person can be proud of.
72. **Field day:** An enjoyable day or circumstance.
73. **Finding your feet:** To become more comfortable in whatever you are doing.
74. **Fixed in your ways:** Not willing to change from your normal way of doing something.
75. **Flash in the pan:** Something that looks promising in the beginning but fails to deliver anything in the end.
76. **Flesh and blood:** Material of which people are made of, or it can refer to someone's family.
77. **Fools' gold:** A worthless rock that resembles real gold.
78. **From pillar to post:** From one place or thing to another.
79. **From rags to riches:** To go from being very poor to being very wealthy.
80. **Fuddy-duddy:** An old-fashioned and foolish type of person.
81. **Get over it:** To move beyond something that is bothering you.
82. **Get up on the wrong side of the bed:** Someone who has a horrible day.
83. **Give him the slip:** To get away from, to escape.
84. **Go down like a lead balloon:** To be received badly by an audience.
85. **Go out on a limb:** Put yourself in a tough position to support someone/something.
86. **Go the extra mile:** Making extra efforts for the task at hand.
87. **Good Samaritan:** Someone who helps others when they are in need with no thought of a reward.
88. **Great minds think alike:** Intelligent people think like each other.
89. **Green room:** The waiting room, especially for those who are about to go on stage, a TV or radio.
90. **Gut feeling:** A personal intuition that something may not be right.
91. **Haste makes waste:** Quickly doing things results in a poor ending.
92. **Hat trick:** Three scores made continuously without break in a sport, such as three wickets in cricket or three soccer goals.
93. **Have a finger in every pie:** To be involved in a lot of different activities and have influence over them.
94. **He lost his head:** Angry and overcome by emotions.
95. **Head over heels:** Very excited and/or joyful, especially when in love.
96. **Hell in a hand basket:** Deteriorating and headed for complete disaster.
97. **Hit below the belt:** An unfair or cruel remark.
98. **Hit the books:** To study, especially for a test or exam.
99. **Hit the nail on the head:** Do something exactly right or say something exactly right.
100. **Hold your horses:** Be patient.
101. **Icing on the cake:** Something extra that is added to an already good situation.
102. **Idle hands are the devil's tools:** You are more likely to get into trouble if you have nothing to do.
103. **If it's not one thing, it's another:** When one thing goes wrong, then another, and another.
104. **In the heat of the moment:** Overwhelmed by what is happening in the moment.
105. **It takes two to tango:** A two-person conflict where both people are at fault.
106. **It's a small world:** You frequently see the same people in different places.
107. **It's anyone's call:** A competition where the outcome is difficult to judge or predict.
108. **Jack of all trades master of none:** Someone good at many things but excellent at nothing.
109. **Keep an eye on somebody:** You should watch a person carefully.
110. **Keep body and soul together:** To earn a sufficient amount of money to keep yourself alive.
111. **Keep your chin up:** To remain joyful in a tough situation.

112. **Kitty-corner:** Diagonally across, sometimes called Catty-Corner as well.
113. **Knee jerk reaction:** A quick and automatic response.
114. **Knock on wood:** Knuckle tapping on wood to avoid some bad luck.
115. **Know the ropes:** To understand the details.
116. **Last but not the least:** An introduction phrase to let the audience know that the last person mentioned is no less important than those introduced before him/her.
117. **Lend me your ear:** To politely ask for someone's full attention.
118. **Let bygones be bygones:** To forget about a disagreement or argument.
119. **Let sleeping dogs lie:** To avoid restarting a conflict.
120. **Let the cat out of the bag:** To share a secret that wasn't supposed to be shared.
121. **Level-playing field:** A fair competition where no side has an advantage.
122. **Like a chicken with its head cut off:** To act in a frenzied manner.
123. **Liquor someone up:** To get someone drunk.
124. **Loose cannon:** Someone who is unpredictable and can cause damage if not kept in check.
125. **Maiden speech:** The first speech made by a person.
126. **Make no bones about:** To state a fact so there are no doubts or objections.
127. **Mumbo jumbo:** Nonsense or meaningless speech.
128. **Nest egg:** Savings set aside for future use.
129. **Never bite the hand that feeds you:** Don't hurt anyone who helps you.
130. **New kid on the block:** Someone new to the group or area.
131. **No dice:** Not to accept a proposition.
132. **No room to swing a cat:** An unusually small or confined space.
133. **Not playing with a full deck:** Someone who lacks intelligence.
134. **Off on the wrong foot:** Getting a bad start on a relationship or task.
135. **Off the hook:** No longer have to deal with a tough situation.
136. **Off the record:** Something said in confidence that the one speaking doesn't want attributed to him/her.
137. **On pins and needles:** Anxious or nervous, especially in anticipation of something.
138. **On the fence:** Undecided.
139. **On the same page:** When multiple people all agree on the same thing.
140. **Out of the blue:** Something that suddenly and unexpectedly occurs.
141. **Out on a limb:** When people put themselves in a risky situation.
142. **Out on the town:** To enjoy yourself by going out.
143. **Over the top:** Highly excessive.
144. **Pass the buck:** Avoid responsibility by giving it to someone else.
145. **Pedal to the metal:** To go full speed, especially while driving a vehicle.
146. **Peeping Tom:** Someone who observes people in the nude or sexually active people, mainly for his own gratification.
147. **Pick up your ears:** To listen very carefully.
148. **Pig out:** To eat a lot and eat it quickly.
149. **Pipe down:** To shut up or be quiet.
150. **Pour oil on troubled waters:** To calm a disturbance.
151. **Practice makes perfect:** By constantly practicing, you will become better.
152. **Pull the plug:** To stop something. To bring something to an end.
153. **Pulling your leg:** Tricking someone as a joke.
154. **Put a sock in it:** To tell noisy person or a group to be quiet.

155. **Queer the pitch:**   Destroy or ruin a plan.
156. **Raining cats and dogs:**   A very loud and noisy rain storm.
157. **Read between the lines:**   To pay attention to what is implied in writing or speech.
158. **Ring fencing:**   To protect a particular sum of money by putting restrictions on its use.
159. **Rise and shine:**   Time to get out of bed and get ready for work/school.
160. **Rome was not built in one day:**   If you want something to be completed properly, then it is going to take time.
161. **Rule of thumb:**   A rough estimate.
162. **Run out of steam:**   To be completely out of energy.
163. **Saved by the bell:**   Saved at the last possible moment.
164. **Scapegoat:**   Someone else who takes the blame.
165. **Show your true colours:**   To reveal your true intentions, personality or behaviour.
166. **Sick as a dog:**   To be very sick (with the flu or a cold).
167. **Sitting shotgun:**   Riding in the front passenger seat of a car.
168. **Sixth sense:**   Intuition; a special ability to know something without using any of the five senses.
169. **Smell a rat:**   To detect someone in the group who is betraying others.
170. **Smell something fishy:**   Detecting something isn't right and there might be a reason for it.
171. **Southpaw:**   Someone who is left handed.
172. **Spitting image:**   The exact likeness or kind.
173. **Start from scratch:**   To do it all over again from the beginning.
174. **Strike while the iron is hot:**   Act quickly when the opportunity is still available.
175. **The ball is in your court:**   It is your decision this time.
176. **The best of both worlds:**   There are two choices and you have them both.
177. **The bigger they are the harder they fall:**   While the bigger and stronger opponent might be a lot more difficult to beat.
178. **The last straw:**   When one small burden after another creates an unbearable situation, the last straw is the last small burden that one can take.
179. **The whole nine yards:**   Everything.
180. **Third times a charm:**   After no success the first two times, the third try is a lucky one.
181. **Tie the knot:**   To get married.
182. **To be in one's good books:**   To be favoured.
183. **To build castles in the air:**   Imaginary projects.
184. **To call a spade a spade:**   To be plain and outspoken.
185. **To carry the day:**   To be victorious.
186. **To eat humble pie:**   To have to apologize.
187. **To pay lip service:**   To pretend to be faithful.
188. **To steal someone's thunder:**   To take the credit for something someone else did.
189. **To the backbone:**   Thoroughly.
190. **Tongue and cheek:**   Humour, not to be taken seriously.
191. **To nip in the bud:**   To put a stop to a thing in the beginning.
192. **Turn a blind eye:**   Refuse to acknowledge something you know is real or legitimate.
193. **Under the weather:**   Feeling ill or sick.
194. **Up a blind alley:**   Going down a course of action that leads to a bad outcome.
195. **Use your loaf:**   Use your head. Think smart.
196. **Variety is the spice of life:**   The more experiences you try the more exciting life can be.

197. Wag the dog: A diversion away from something of greater importance.
198. Water under the bridge: Anything from the past that isn't significant or important anymore.
199. Wear your heart on your sleeve: To openly and freely express your emotions.
200. When pigs fly: Something that will never ever happen.
201. Wild and woolly: Uncultured and without laws.
202. Wine and dine: When somebody is treated to an expensive meal.
203. Without a doubt: For certain.
204. X marks the spot: A phrase that is said when someone finds something he/she has been looking for.
205. You are what you eat: To stay healthy you must eat healthy food.
206. You can't judge a book by its cover: Decisions shouldn't be made primarily on appearance.
207. Your guess is as good as mine: I have no idea.
208. Young Turk: An insurgent person trying to take control of a situation.
209. Zero tolerance: The policy of applying laws very strictly so that people are punished even for mild offences.

4.8.2   Phrasal Verbs

Phrasal verbs are verbal compounds with a grammatical structure of *verb + preposition and/ or adverbs*. They form a fixed group of words with an idiomatic meaning. They are expressions (also known as verbal idioms) whose real meaning cannot be detected from that of the constituent words. Like idioms, phrasal verbs are widely used in English and they make our expression rich and fresh. Phrasal verbs are better suited to informal speech. You would complain about your friend who has not kept his/her promise by saying, "He has backed out at the last moment." On the other hand if you are a buyer, you would better express the similar idea formally to a supplier who has not supplied the ordered goods by writing, "we are sorry to say that you have not fulfilled your commitment."

4.8.3   Some Common Phrasal Verbs

1. Abide by: Respect or obey the law, a decision, a rule
2. Account for: Explain, give a reason
3. Add up: Make sense, seem reasonable
4. Agree with: Have the same opinion as somebody else.
5. Allow for: Take advantage of something (an opportunity)
6. Answer back: Reply rudely
7. Apply for: Make a formal request for something (job, permit, loan, etc.)
8. Avail (oneself) of: Take into consideration, include in a calculation
9. Back away: Move backwards, in fear or dislike
10. Back down: Withdraw, concede defeat
11. Blow up: Explode; be destroyed by an explosion
12. Back up: Give support or encouragement; make a copy of (file, program, etc.)
13. Black out: Faint, lose consciousness
14. Block off: Separate using a barrier
15. Boil down to: Be summarized as
16. Break down: Go out of order, cease to function; lose control of one's emotions
17. Break out: Start suddenly
18. Break into: Enter by force

19. Bump into: Meet by accident or unexpectedly
20. Burn out: Stop (something) working; become exhausted from overworking
21. Butt in (on something):   Interrupt impolitely
22. Call back: Return a phone call
23. Call off: Cancel
24. Call on/upon something: Formally invite or request
25. Calm down: Become more relaxed, less angry or upset
26. Carry on: Continue
27. Carry out: Do something as specified (a plan, an order, a threat); perform or conduct (test, experiment)
28. Check in: Register at a hotel or airport
29. Check out: Pay one's bill and leave (a hotel); investigate
30. Clam up: Refuse to speak
31. Close down: Stop operating (company, restaurant, cinema)
32. Come across: Find by chance; appear
33. Come forward: Present oneself
34. Conk out: Stop working; stop or fall asleep from exhaustion
35. Come up against: Be faced with or opposed by
36. Count on: rely or depend on (for help)
37. Cross out: Remove by drawing a line through
38. Cut down on: Reduce in number or size
39. Cut out: Remove using scissors; stop doing something
40. Deal with: Handle, take care of (problem, situation)
41. Die down: Calm down, become less strong
42. Dress up: Wear elegant clothes; disguise oneself
43. Do without: Manage without
44. Drag on: Last longer than expected
45. Draw up: Write (contract, agreement, document)
46. Drop in: Visit, usually on the way somewhere
47. Drop out: Leave school without finishing
48. Drop off: Deliver someone or something; fall asleep
49. Ease off: Reduce, become less severe or slow down (pain, traffic, work)
50. Even out: Eliminate differences of opinion; become level or regular
51. Fall through: Fail; doesn't happen
52. Figure out: Understand, find the answer
53. Fill out: Complete (a form/an application)
54. Find out: Discover or obtain information
55. Focus on: Understand; find a solution
56. Figure out: Concentrate on something
57. Get at: Imply
58. Get away: Escape
59. Get back at: To get revenge on somebody
60. Get in: Enter
61. Get into (+noun):   Manage to cope or to survive
62. Get off: Leave (bus, train, plane); remove
63. Get on: Board (bus, train, plane)
64. Get on with (something):   Continue to do; make progress

65. Get out: Leave
66. Get on (well) with (somebody):   Have a good relationship with
67. Get out of: Avoid doing something
68. Get over: Recover from (illness, disappointment)
69. Give up: Stop doing something
70. Get rid of: Eliminate
71. Get together: Meet each other
72. Get up: Rise, leave bed
73. Go through: Experience
74. Grow up: Spend one's childhood; develop; become an adult
75. Hand in: Distribute
76. Hand out: Submit (report, homework)
77. Hang out: Spend time in a particular place, or with a group of friends
78. Hang up: End a phone conversation
79. Hit at: Aim a blow at
80. Hit back: Retaliate; reply to an attack
81. Hit on/upon: Find unexpectedly or by inspiration
82. Hold on: Wait; grip tightly
83. Hurry up: Be quick, act speedily
84. Iron out: Resolve by discussion, eliminate differences
85. Join in: Participate
86. Join up: Engage in, become a member of, meet and unite with
87. Jot down: Take quick notes
88. Keep on: Continue doing something
89. Keep up with: Stay at the same level as someone or something
90. Kick off: Begin, start
91. Leave out: Omit, not mention
92. Let down: Disappoint
93. Look after: Take care of
94. Look ahead: Think of the future
95. Look down on: Consider as inferior
96. Look on: Be a spectator at an event
97. Look for: Try to find something
98. Look forward to: Await or anticipate with pleasure
99. Look up to: Admire
100. Make fun of: Laugh at/ make jokes about
101. Make up: Invent (excuse, story)
102. Mix up: Mistake one thing or person for another
103. Move in: Arrive in a new home or office
104. Move out: Leave your home/office for another one.
105. Nod off: Fall asleep
106. Note down: Write something
107. Opt out: Leave a system or decide not to participate
108. Own up: Admit or confess something
109. Pass away: Die
110. Pass out: Faint

111. Pay back: Reimburse
112. Put off: Postpone, arrange at a later date
113. Put on: Turn on, switch on
114. Put out: Extinguish
115. Put up: Accommodate, give somebody a bed
116. Pick up: Collect somebody
117. Point out: Indicate/direct attention to something
118. Rely on: Count on, depend on, trust
119. Rule out: Eliminate
120. Run away: Escape from a place or suddenly leave
121. Run into: Meet by accident or unexpectedly (also: bump into)
122. Run out of: Have no more of something.
123. Set off: Start a journey
124. Set up: Start a business
125. Shop around: Compare prices
126. Show off: Brag or want to be admired
127. Show up: Appear/arrive
128. Stick up for: Defend
129. Take after: Resemble, in appearance or character
130. Take care of: Look after
131. Take off: Leave the ground
132. Take on: Hire or engage staff
133. Tell off: Reprimand/criticize severely
134. Think over: Consider
135. Try on: Wear something to see if it suits or fits
136. Turn down: Refuse
137. Use up: Finish a product (so that there's none left)
138. Vouch for: Express confidence in, or guarantee something
139. Watch out: Be careful
140. Wear out: (1) Become unusable (2) Become very tired
141. Work out: (1) Do physical exercise (2) Find a solution or calculate something
142. Wipe off: Clean (board, table)

Task

Make sentences with the following idioms:

1. Clean slate
   Dark horse
   A blessing in disguise
   Achilles heel
   A penny saved is a penny earned
   At loggerheads
   Break the ice
   Every cloud has a silver lining
   From pillar to post
   Gut feeling

2. Make sentences with the following phrases:
    Break down
    Come across
    Ease off
    Kick off
    Look forward to
    Move in
    Pass out
    Put out
    Rule out
    Take after

4.9   Technical Terms

Technical vocabulary is a special feature of communication that includes words of specialized terminologies, formal words and expressions and scientific vocabulary. These terms are indispensable parts of various types of formal and technical communication. Hence, their knowledge and usage is necessary to make our written and oral interaction effective.

4.9.1   Some Commonly Used Technical Terms

1. Absolute pressure transducer: A transducer that measures pressure in relation to zero pressure.
2. Absolute pressure: Gage pressure plus atmospheric pressure.
3. Absolute zero: Temperature at which thermal energy is at a minimum. Defined as 0 Kelvin.
4. Absorption :   In *physiology*:   a process by which nutrients move from the lower digestive tract (small and large intestine or colon) into the blood stream to be utilized by the body.
5. AC: Alternating current; an electric current that reverses its direction at regularly recurring intervals.
6. Acceleration: A change in the velocity of a body or particle with respect to time.
7. Accelerometer: A device which converts the effects of mechanical motion into an electrical signal that is proportional to the acceleration value of the motion.
8. Acoustics: The degree of sound.
9. Adapter: A mechanism or device for attaching non-mating parts.
10. ADC: Analogue-to-digital converter: An electronic device which converts analogue signals to an equivalent digital form.
11. Address: The label or number identifying the memory location where a unit of information is stored.
12. Adult stem cell: A specialized cell that is needed for growth, wound healing and tissue regeneration.
13. Alphanumeric: A character set that contains both letters and digits.
14. Ambient compensation: The design of an instrument such that changes in ambient temperature do not affect the readings of the instrument.
15. Amino Acid: Building block of proteins and enzymes.
16. Ammeter: An instrument used to measure current.
17. Ampere (amp):   A unit used to define the rate of flow of electricity (current) in a circuit; units are one coulomb (6.28×10^{18} electrons) per second.

18. **Amplifier:** A device which draws power from a source other than the input signal and which produces as an output an enlarged reproduction of the essential features of its input.

19. **Amplitude:** A measurement of the distance from the highest to the lowest excursion of motion, as in the case of mechanical body in oscillation or the peak-to-peak swing of an electrical waveform.

20. **Amplitude span:** The y-axis range of a graphic display of data in either the time or frequency domain.

21. **Analogue output:** A voltage or current signal that is a continuous function of the measured parameter.

22. **Anemometer:** An instrument for measuring and/or indicating the velocity of air flow.

23. **Anion:** A negatively charged ion (Cl^-, NO_3^-, S_2^- etc.)

24. **ANSI:** American National Standards Institute.

25. **Application program:** A computer program that accomplishes specific tasks, such as word processing.

26. **ASME:** American Society of Mechanical Engineers.

27. **Assembler:** A program that translates assembly language instructions into machine language instructions.

28. **ASTM:** American Society for Testing and Materials.

29. **ATC:** Automatic temperature compensation.

30. **Atom:** The smallest unit of matter as recognized by chemical properties of molecules.

31. **Auto-zero:** An automatic internal correction for offsets and/or drift at zero voltage input.

32. **AWG:** American Wire Gage.

33. **Axis of Rotation (Spin Axis):** The axis of rotation (spin axis) is that straight line about which a body rotates.

34. **Backup:** A system, device, file or facility that can be used as an alternative in the case of a malfunction, loss of data or electricity failure.

35. **Bacteria:** Single-cell organisms and most prevalent form of life on the Earth.

36. **Bandwidth:** A symmetrical region around the set point in which proportional control occurs.

37. **Bile:** The digestive juice released from liver (stored in gall bladder) into the digestive tract to help solubilize and absorb fat soluble nutrients.

38. **Biodegradable:** A property of molecules or chemicals that refers to their usefulness as food because they can be metabolized (metabolism) by organism.

39. **Biodiversity:** The collective richness and variety of all forms of life—bacteria, archaea, eukarya and associated viruses.

40. **Bioelectricity:** The term bioelectricity refers to the use of charged molecules and elements (= ions) in biological systems.

41. **Biotechnology:** Application in biology to manipulate the structure and function of biological systems into forms not found in nature.

42. **Bulb (Liquid-in-glass thermometer):** The area at the tip of a liquid-in-glass thermometer containing the liquid reservoir.

43. **Byte:** A unit of information stored in a computer.

44. **Carbohydrates:** Biochemical name for sugar-containing molecules including single sugar (monosaccharides) such as glucose and galactose.

45. **Carbon:** The element that defines the chemical properties of all life.

46. **Calorie (Cal):** A unit for measuring how much energy food will produce.

47. Calibration: The process of adjusting an instrument or compiling a deviation chart so that its reading can be correlated to the actual value being measured.

48. Calorie: The quantity of thermal energy required to raise the temperature of one gram of water by 1 °C.

49. Cation: A positively charged ion (Na^+, H^+).

50. Cavitation: The boiling of a liquid caused by a decrease in pressure rather than an increase in temperature.

51. Cell: Smallest unit of life (single-cell organism or bacteria) or unit of higher organisms, that is, multicellular organisms.

52. Celsius (centigrade):   A temperature scale defined by 0 °C at the ice point and 100 °C at boiling point of water at sea level.

53. Center of gravity (Mass Centre):   The point in an object at which its weight is considered to act.

54. Centripetal force: A force exerted on an object moving in a circular path which is exerted inward towards the centre of rotation.

55. Cholesterol: Important lipid found only in animals. Chronically high concentration of cholesterol in blood results in insoluble deposits that can clog arteries and restrict blood flow contributing to heart problems.

56. Chromosome: The physical unit of genetic material in a cell.

57. Clone, cloning: A clone is a genetic copy of a parent cell or organism.

58. Conduction: The conveying of electrical energy or heat through or by means of a conductor.

59. Convection: 1. The circulatory motion that occurs in a fluid at a non-uniform temperature owing to the variation of its density and the action of gravity. 2. The transfer of heat by this automatic circulation of fluid.

60. Coulomb: A measurement of the quantity of electrical charge, usually expressed as pico coulomb (10–12 coulombs).

61. Current: The rate of flow of electricity.

62. Database: A large amount of data stored in a well-organized manner. A database management system (DBMS) is a program that allows access to the information.

63. DC: Direct current; an electric current flowing in one direction only and substantially constant in value.

64. DNA: Short for deoxyribonucleic acid; makes up the genetic component of each cell.

65. Ecosystem: A specific characteristic biological system in a location or area with a unique mix of living organisms and physical consistency such as minerals, soil and air.

66. Electrolyte: Any substance which, when in solution will conduct an electric current. Acids, bases and salts are common electrolytes.

67. Electron: Subatomic particle carrying a negative electric charge in atoms or molecules.

68. Element: An atom with a unique number of protons (atomic number). There are 102 different elements and some additional synthetic elements that are not found in nature.

69. Endothermic: Absorbs heat. A process is said to be endothermic when it absorbs heat.

70. Enzyme: A protein (complex) that catalyzes a chemical reaction in a living cell.

71. Evolution, theory of: The theory of evolution as initially formulated by Charles Darwin in 1859 is the central theory of biology. All processes that enable life are the result of the process of evolution over a period estimated to be more than 3 billion years.

72. Fatty acids: Most common form of lipids found in all cells.

73. Flow: Travel of liquids or gases in response to a force (i.e., pressure or gravity).

74. Frequency: The number of cycles over a specified time period over which an event occurs.

75. **Gene:** A gene is an hereditary unit of an organism that cannot be partitioned any further into smaller units; it is made of DNA.
76. **Glucose:** The major carbohydrate in starch and fruit sugar. The latter is also known as sucrose and contains fructose with every glucose molecule.
77. **Galvanometer:** An instrument that measures small electrical currents by means of deflecting magnetic coils.
78. **Hardware:** The electrical, mechanical and electromechanical equipment and parts associated with a computing system, as opposed to its firmware or software.
79. **Haemoglobin:** A protein that binds and transports molecular oxygen in animals.
80. **Hormones:** Messenger substances synthesized in the body and secreted by the endocrine glands. Hormones regulate the digestive system, growth, hunger, thirst, blood glucose and cholesterol levels, fat burning and storage, absorption and excretion, internal clocks such as day and night cycles, menstrual cycles and sex drive.
81. **Hypothesis:** A testable idea that can be proved right or wrong with study and experiments.
82. **Immunology:** Immunology is the science of molecular self-defence of organisms against infections.
83. **Infrared:** An area in the electromagnetic spectrum extending beyond red light. It is the form of radiation used for making non-contact temperature measurements.
84. **Insulin:** A protein hormone that regulates the use of glucose after a carbohydrate rich meal.
85. **Inorganic:** Compounds that do not contain carbon, such as minerals and water.
86. **Ions:** Positively or negatively charged molecules.
87. **Joule:** The modern unit in physics for energy, used in place of calorie. 1 cal equals 4.184 J.
88. **Kilowatt (kw):** Equivalent to 1000 watts.
89. **Kilowatt hour (kwh):** 1000 watthours. Kilovolt amperes (kva): 1000 volt amps.
90. **Kinetic energy:** Energy associated with mass in motion.
91. **Latent heat:** The quantity of heat absorbed or released by a substance undergoing a change of state.
92. **Lipid:** A lipid is a water-insoluble (hydrophobic) substance and is the name of a large class of structurally and functionally diverse molecules.
93. **Melting point:** The temperature at which a substance transforms from a solid phase to a liquid phase.
94. **Mica:** A transparent mineral used as window material in high-temperature ovens.
95. **Microcomputer:** A computer, which is physically small. It can fit on top of or under a desk.
96. **Modem:** A device that transforms digital signals into audio tones for transmission over telephone lines and does the reverse for reception.
97. **Metabolism, metabolic:** The totality of all chemical processes in cells and all living organisms.
98. **Molecule:** A chemically unique aggregate of at least two atoms (see also elements).
99. **Nanotechnology:** A technology that creates small materials at the scale of molecules by manipulating single atoms. The name nano comes from the size of molecules which is measured in nanometers.
100. **Natural selection:** The process described by Darwin's theory of evolution that favours certain genotypes and disfavours others.
101. **Nutrient:** Molecules that can be used by cells or living organism to extract energy through metabolic processes.
102. **Organic:** Compounds that contain carbon, such as vitamins, carbohydrates, proteins and fats, but not minerals.

103. **Pharmacology:** Pharmacology is the study of drugs and their interactions with the human body (A branch of medicine).

104. **Phenotype:** The characteristic of a species or of an individual of a species that is inherited from generation to generation.

105. **Protein:** Proteins are macromolecules made from 20 different types of amino acids. It is very useful for body building.

106. **Read only memory (ROM):** Memory that contains fixed data. The computer can read the data, but cannot change it in any way.

107. **Quantum mechanics:** The physical theory of the composition and behaviour of atoms and subatomic particles; explains the duality of light as wave and particle, the existence of chemical bonds and radioactivity.

108. **Software:** Generally, programs loaded into a computer from external mass storage but also extended to include operating systems and documentation.

109. **Species:** A group of organisms (individuals) that can interbreed and reproduce with each other.

110. **Specific gravity:** The ratio of mass of any material to the mass of the same volume of pure water at 4°C.

111. **Specific heat:** The ratio of thermal energy required to raise the temperature of a body by 1° to the thermal energy required to raise an equal mass of water by 1°.

112. **Spectrum:** The resolving of overall vibration into amplitude components as a function of frequency.

113. **Statistics:** The mathematical procedure to describe probabilities and the random or non-random distribution of matter or occurrence of events.

114. **Stomata:** The pore openings underneath plant leaves that can open and close according to the metabolic needs of the plant. They are the ports for exchange of oxygen and carbon dioxide gas for photosynthesis, but also release excess water into the air.

115. **Telecommunication:** Synonym for data communication. The transmission of information from one point to another.

116. **Thermal conductivity:** The property of a material to conduct heat in the form of thermal energy.

117. **Thermodynamics:** The physical theory of heat and energy distribution in the universe.

118. **Ultraviolet:** That portion of the electromagnetic spectrum below blue light (380 nanometers).

119. **UV Radiation:** Ultraviolet radiation, an invisible, high-energy component of sunlight, can cause skin damage including cancer.

120. **Vacuum:** A state when pressure is much less than atmospheric pressure.

121. **Velocity:** The time rate of change of displacement.

122. **Virus:** Smallest of all organisms and often not considered alive because they strictly depend on a cellular host organism (bacteria, plant, animal) to reproduce. Viruses have no metabolism of their own and depend on passive carriers to transport them around.

123. **Voltage:** An electrical potential, which can be measured in volts.

124. **Voltmeter:** An instrument used to measure voltage.

125. **X-chromosome:** One of the two sex chromosomes in higher organisms that defines the gender of the adult. In almost all sexually reproducing organisms, the X-chromosome defines female characteristics.

126. **Y-chromosome:** One of the two sex chromosomes in higher organisms that defines the gender of the adult. In almost all sexually reproducing organisms, the Y-chromosome defines male characteristics.

4.9.2　Foreign Expressions

Some non-English terminologies, borrowed from foreign languages such as Greek, Latin, French, etc., are used in formal English communications in their original form. The following are some of such expressions:

1. Ad hoc:　Temporary
2. Ad antiquo:　Since ancient times
3. Ad infinitum:　Forever
4. Ad interim:　In between
5. Alma mater:　The place where one is educated
6. Alumni:　Pass out students of an institution
7. Alter ego:　Friend who is very close
8. Ad verbum:　Exactly same word for word
9. Agent provocateurs:　Plotters and culprits working from behind the curtain
10. Au courant:　Up to date
11. Bona fide:　Genuine, real or legal; not false
12. Bon vivant:　A person who lives luxuriously
13. Carpe diem:　'Seize the day': enjoy the present and do not worry about the future
14. Coup d'état:　A sudden, illegal and often violent, change of government
15. Carte blanche:　Full liberty to do something
16. Charge d'affaires:　An official who takes the place of an ambassador in a foreign country when he or she is away
17. De jure:　By legal act
18. De facto:　In reality
19. De novo:　A new beginning
20. Dramatis personae:　Characters of a drama
21. En route:　On the way
22. Enfant terrible:　An outrageously outspoken or bold person
23. Ex officio:　By virtue of one's post
24. Ex parte:　One-sided decision
25. Ex post facto:　After the fact, retroactively
26. Fait accompli:　Something that has already happened or been done and that you cannot change
27. Ipso facto:　In reality
28. In camera:　Away from public eyes, secret
29. Laissez faire:　The policy of allowing private businesses to develop without government control
30. Lingua franca:　Language of the common man
31. Locus standi:　Right to take part in something
32. Mala fide:　Bad, criminal intentions
33. Magnum opus:　The best product, work, etc.
34. Mano a mano:　Hand to hand: competition between two people when they try to out do each other.
35. Modus operandi:　The style of working
36. Par excellence:　Of a high quality
37. Per capita:　Related to an individual

38. Per se: By itself
39. Prima facie: Something that at first seems to be true, may be proved false later
40. Subjudice: Under consideration, it is still being discussed in court
41. Ultra vires: Beyond your legal power or authority
42. Viva-voce: Oral test
43. Vis-à-vis: Compared with, in relation with
44. Tete-e-tete: Informal or private conversation between two people
45. Sine die: For an indefinite time
46. Sine qua non: Something that is essential before you can achieve something else
47. Sang froid: The ability to remain calm in a difficult or dangerous situation
48. Status quo: The current or existing state of affairs

4.9.3   Group Names

1. Ants: A colony
2. Arrows: A sheaf
3. Bats: A cloud
4. Bees/flies: A swarm or hive
5. Bells: A peal
6. Birds/stairs: A flock, flight
7. Camels: A train
8. Cattle/deer/goats: A herd or drove
9. Cotton/wool: A ball
10. Devils: A legion
11. Directors/trustees: A board
12. Elephants: A herd
13. Fish: A shoal or school
14. Flowers: A garland or wreath or bouquet
15. Followers: A retinue
16. Fruits: A bunch
17. Girls/ladies: A bevy
18. Goods: A consignment or stock
19. Grapes/keys: A bunch
20. Grass: A tuft
21. Hair: A lock
22. Hounds/playing cards: A pack
23. Island: A group
24. Lectures: A series or course
25. Merchants/pilgrims/travellers: A caravan
26. Mountains: A chain
27. Musicians: A band
28. Natives: A tribe
29. People: An assembly or crowd or multitude or throng
30. Persons: A group
31. Pigs/pups: A litter
32. Players: A team
33. Quails: A bevy

34. Rain/arrows: A shower
35. Rioters: A mob
36. Robbers/thieves/prisoners: A gang
37. Rooms: A suite
38. Sailors: A crew
39. Scouts: A troop
40. Ships: A fleet
41. Shoes: A pair
42. Shots/bullets/stones/arrows: A volley
43. Singers: A choir
44. Soldiers: An army or regiment or troop
45. Spiders: A cluster
46. Stamps/coins: A collection
47. Stars: A cluster/constellation
48. Sticks/hay: A bundle
49. Stones/ruins: A heap
50. Students: A class
51. Tourists: A flock
52. Trees: A clump or grove
53. Wagons: A train
54. Whale/dolphins: A school or pod
55. Wolf: A pack
56. Worshippers: A congregation
57. Years: A century

4.9.4.   The 'Logies' of Day-to-day Use

1. Cardiology: The study of the heart
2. Conchology: The study of shells
3. Cosmology: The study of the universe
4. Dermatology: The study of the skin
5. Entomology: The study of insects
6. Etymology: The study of the origin of words
7. Graphology: The study of handwriting
8. Haematology: The study of blood
9. Histology: The study of the tissues
10. Horology: The science of measuring time.
11. Meteorology: The study of weather
12. Neurology: The study of the nervous system
13. Oenology: The study of wine
14. Oncology: The study of cancer and tumours
15. Ophthalmology: The study of the eyes
16. Ornithology: The study of birds
17. Osteology: The study of the bones
18. Pharmacology: The study of medical drugs
19. Seismology: The study of earthquakes
20. Sinology: The study of China

Speaking Skills

5

In this unit

- ✓ Introduction
- ✓ IPA Symbols of Received Pronunciation (RP)
- ✓ Phonetic Transcription Using IPA Characters
- ✓ IPA Transcription of Words Often Mispronounced
- ✓ Word Stress
- ✓ Weak Forms in English
- ✓ Intonation

"Our accent and our speech generally show what part of the country we come from and what sort of background we have."

–Ralph W. Emerson

5.1   Introduction

Despite being a small minority, the speakers of English in India are those individuals who lead India's economic, industrial, political, professional and social life. English is no longer a second language for them rather it is a medium in which a great number of interactions take place. In recent years, English has gained a lot of importance among the educated class, particularly the youth, who appears to be using it as a mother tongue and not as a foreign or a second language. Young Indians "think of English as an empowering skill, like Windows, and are comfortable mixing it with their mother tongue." (Gurcharan Das) This has led to the usage of the language such as Hinglish (Hindi + English), Tamlish (Tamil + English), Benglish (Bangla + English), etc. Mixing English with mother tongues has been going on since pre-independence days. In spite of the great stress on good English in higher circles in India, the accent varies greatly from those learning pure English to those learning Indian-language-tinted speech. All native languages of India lack the sound /ʒ/ and substitute it with /dʒ/ or /z/. Subcontinentals do not differentiate between /v/ and /w/ and 'wine' is pronounced as 'vine'. In some parts of the Northern India, people tend to double the consonants whenever they are spelled double like, 'happy,' 'butter,' 'little' and many more. South Indians curl their tongue more on the sounds /l/ and /n/, Biharis substitute /dʒ/ for /z/ and in Bhojpuri, all instances of /ʃ/ are spoken as /s/. The following lines of Kamla Das from her poem "An Introduction" express the way and pattern of English speaking in India:

. . . . The language I speak
Becomes mine, mine alone. It is half English, half
Indian, funny perhaps, but it is honest,
It is as human as I am human . . . .

The problem arises when these people face interviews, attend conferences or seek higher jobs in their own country as well as in other countries where use of such language is considered faulty and a sign of incomplete or poor education. The youngsters who get so much used to speaking English with regional pull find themselves at a loss to understand what the correct pronunciation is and how it can be acquired.

The fact is there is nothing like correct pronunciation as the pronunciation of English varies not only in India due to regional languages but also among the English-speaking countries such as America, Australia, Canada, Scotland, Britain and Northern Ireland. One particular accent called 'Received Pronunciation' (RP) has been accepted as 'accepted' or 'standard' pronunciation. 'Accepted' or 'standard' pronunciation is clearly understood by the people whereas 'unaccepted' pronunciation creates ambiguity. For example, those who cannot differentiate between /dʒ / and /z/ will not be able to pronounce 'Siege' and 'Seize' clearly. To acquire standard English pronunciation, fluency and accent, you should have knowledge of basic phonetics—English sounds, word accent, weak forms and intonation.

5.2   IPA Symbols of 'Received Pronunciation'

5.2.1   'Received' or 'Accepted Pronunciation'

Received pronunciation (RP), popularly known as 'the Queen's English' or 'BBC English,' is the accent of Standard English in England. The early use of the term can be found in H. C. Wyld's *A Short History of English* (1914) and in Daniel Jones's *An Outline of English Phonetics*. The word 'received' conveys its original meaning of 'accepted' or 'approved.' Traditionally, 'RP' was the everyday speech in the families of Southern England where menfolk were educated at well-known public boarding schools. Received pronunciation is an accent or a form of pronunciation, rather a dialect or a form of vocabulary. Sometimes, it is referred to as 'Oxford English' as well. This is not because it was traditionally the common speech of the city of Oxford, but specifically of the Oxford University and the production of dictionaries gave Oxford University prestige in the matters of language. The versions of the Oxford English Dictionary give 'RP' guidelines for each word.

A Chart of IPA Symbols

Vowels							
iː Reel	ɪ Sit	ʊ Book	uː Stool	e Set		æ Mat	ɒ Not
ɔː Fall	ʌ Sun	ə About	ɜː Bird	ɑː Park		eɪ Gate	əʊ Slow
ɑɪ Delight	ɑʊ Cloud	ɔɪ Soil	ɪə Steer	eə Dare		ʊə Poor	
Consonants							
p Polish	b Balloon	t Table	d Door	k Kite	g Gate	tʃ Church	dʒ Judge
m Man	n New	ŋ Thing	f Flight	v Vanish	θ Throat	ð These	s Sight
z Zone	ʃ Shiver	ʒ Vision	h Heat	l Lamp	r River	j Yellow	w Water

5.2.2   IPA Symbols

Effective speaking is difficult without the knowledge of basic English sounds. There are 44 sounds in English—20 vowels sounds and 24 consonant sounds. These sounds are represented by International Phonetic Alphabet (IPA) symbols, which are used to transcribe sounds, words and sentences of any language phonetically. The symbols and the transcription of words are conventionally written within the slashes to distinguish them from the rest of the text.

5.2.2.1   English Consonants

Consonants are produced when the speech organs form an obstruction to the stream of breath. English consonants can be categorized as 'voiced'—articulated with simultaneous vibration of the vocal cords—/d/, /b/, /g/, /dʒ/, /v/, /ð/, /z/, /ʒ/, /m/, /n/, /ŋ/, /l/, /j/, /w/, /r/ (all vowels are voiced) and 'voiceless'—articulated without simultaneous vibration of the vocal cords—/p/, /t/, /k/, /tʃ/, /f/, /θ/, /s/, /ʃ/, /h/.

1. **/p/** Generally represented by the spellings—*p, pp, ph*—*pin*, *map*, *period*, *partial*, *poor*, *pale*, *happy*, *sloppy*, *copper*, *dipper*, *shepherd*.
2. **/b/** Generally represented by the spellings—*b, bb*—*bid*, *bear*, *obey*, *tribe*, *bread*, *shrub*, *blind*, *bulb*, *beam*, *ribbon*, *rubber*, *dubbed*, *clubbed*.
   Comparison of /p/ and /b/:

Pill – Bill	Pulp – Bulb	Simple – Symbol
Peach – Beach	Played – Blade	Pore – Bore
Cup – Cub	Pack – Back	Patter – Batter
Rope – Robe	Lap – Lab	Pull – Bull
Pest – Best	Pin – Bin	Palm – Balm

3. **/t/** Generally represented by the spellings—*t, tt*—*team*, *tribe*, *obtain*, *take*, *trade*, *atlas*, *truth*, *matter*, *butter*, *bitter*, *chatter*, *litter*.
4. **/d/** Generally represented by the spellings—*d, dd*—*sad*, *cried*, *afraid*, *garden*, *badly*, *demand*, *drive*, *dozen*, *middle*, *sudden*, *shudder*, *plodded*.
   Comparison of /t/ and /d/:

Ton – Don	Hit – Hid	Water – Warden
Built – Build	Tin – Din	Bet – Bed
Ten – Den	Plot – Plod	Latter – Ladder
Let – Led	Writer – Rider	Height – Hide
Metal – Medal	Petal – Pedal	Shutter – Shudder
Tore – door	Two – Do	Dose – Toes

5. **/k/** Generally represented by the spellings—*k, c, ck, ch, cc, qu, x*—*keen*, *kite*, *cut*, *can*, *thick*, *sick*, *Chemist*, *cholera*, *account*, *accuse*, *question*, *queen*, *taxi*, *box*.
6. **/g/** Generally represented by the spellings—*g, gg, gh, x*—*gate*, *green*, *beg*, *grass*, *greet*, *beggar*, *ragging*, *ghost*, *aghast*, *exist*, *example*.
   Comparison of /k/ and /g/:

Class – Glass	Bicker – Bigger	Rusk – Rug
Lacked – Lagged	Crew – Grew	Came – Game
Echo – Ego	Coal – Goal	Lack – Lag
Leak – League	Cot – Got	Tack – Tag

7. **/tʃ/** Generally represented by the spellings—*ch, s + ion, t + ure*—*chair*, *choice*, *charm*, *catch*, *batch*, *question*, *suggestion*, *feature*, *torture*, *fixture*.
8. **/dʒ/** Generally represented by the spellings—*j, g, dg, gg, di, dj*—*jump*, *jug*, *germ*, *urgent*, *huge*, *judge*, *ridge*, *suggest*, *suggestive*, *soldier*, *adjust*, *adjoining* .
   Comparison of /tʃ/ and /dʒ/:

Choke – Joke	Larch – Large	Batch – Badge

| Lunch – Lunge | Perches – Purges | Chest – Jest |
| Cheer – Jeer | Chin – Gin | Char – Jar |

9. **/m/** Generally represented by the spellings—*m, mm*—ma*n*ner, *m*atter, *m*ustard, s*m*oke, com*m*it, com*m*unity, drum*m*er, slim*m*er, trim*m*er.

10. **/n/** Generally represented by the spellings—*n, nn*—ru*n*, k*n*it, sig*n*, *n*eedle, s*n*eeze, co*n*duct, ba*n*ner, ru*nn*ing, fa*nn*ing, su*nn*y.
   Comparison of /m/ and /n/:

Maim – Name	Simmer – Sinner	Some – Son
Seem – Scene	Met – Net	Mock – Knock
Melt – Knelt	Mum – Nun	Boom – Boon
Dim – Din	Same – Sane	Mere – Near
Scream – Screen	Deem – Dean	Gleam – Glean
Moon – Noon	Smack – Snack	Sum – Sun

11. **/ŋ/** Generally represented by the spellings—*ng, nk, nc, nch, nx*—thi*ng*, fi*ng*er, la*ng*uage, thi*nk* , a*nk*le, u*nc*le, a*nch*or, a*nx*iety, a*nx*ious.
   Comparison of /n/ and /ŋ/:

Thin – Thing	Banner – Banger	Mountain – Mounting
Kin – King	Sin – Sing	Run – Rung
Din – Ding	Ran – Rang	Pin – Pang
Ban – Bang	Clan – Clang	Ton – Tongue

   Comparison of /ŋ/ and /ng/:

| Longing – Longest | Singer – Finger |

   Comparison of /ŋ/ and /ŋk/:

| Thing – Think | Bang – Bank | Hang – Hank |

12. **/f/** Generally represented by the spellings—*f, ff, gh, ph*—*f*at, *f*ile, *f*ather, of*f*er, of*f*ence, laugh*t*er, rou*gh*, *ph*oto, tro*ph*y.

13. **/v/** Generally represented by the spellings—*v, f,* (only 'o*f*') *ph* (only 'ne*ph*ew')—*v*ain, *v*ein, *v*anish, can*v*as, *v*owels, belie*v*e, *v*ery, sil*v*er.
   Comparison of /f/ and /v/:

Fail – Veil	Few – View	Fairy – Vary
Fear – Veer	Focal – Vocal	Fast – Vast
Surface – Service	Belief – Believe	Fine – Vine

   Comparison of /f/ and /p/:

Fat – Pat	Fail – Pale	Fast – Past
Fall – Pall	Feel – Peel	Four – Pour
Fool – Pool	Fill – Pill	

   Comparison of / b/ and /v/:

Bat – Vat	Best – Vest	Bent – Vent
Buy – Vie	Bold – Volt	Ban – Van
Bane – Vein	Beer – Veer	

14. **/θ/** Generally represented by the spelling—'*th*'—*th*in, *th*ought, *th*rough, *th*rew, e*th*ics, ba*th*, clo*th*, fai*th*, leng*th*, me*th*od.

15. **/ð/** Generally represented by the spelling—'*th*'—*th*at, *th*is, *th*ese, *th*em, *th*ey, ei*th*er, nei*th*er, lea*th*er, bro*th*er, al*th*ough, *th*ence.
   Comparison of /θ/ and /ð/:

| Thigh – Thy | Ether – Breather |

   Comparison of /t/ and /θ/:

| Tank – Thank | Tick – Thick | Tree – Three |
| Trust – Thrust | Taught – Thought | |

Comparison of /d/ and /ð/:

Day – They	Dare – There	Dose – Those
Dense – Thence	Load – Loathe	Ladder – Leather
Dine –Thine	Den – Then	

16. **/s/** Generally represented by the spellings—*s, ss, sc, c, x*—*s*ee, *s*ame, lo*ss*, dre*ss*, *sc*ene, a*sc*ent, fan*c*y, i*c*y, ta*x*, e*x*ercise.

17. **/z/** Generally represented by the spellings—*z, zz, s, ss, x*—*z*eal, graze, craze, dazzle, puzzle, flim*s*y, rea*s*on, he*s*itation, sci*ss*ors, de*ss*ert, e*x*aggerate, e*x*ample.

Comparison of /s/ and /z/:

Seal – Zeal	Cease – Seize	Niece – Knees
Once – Ones	Fancy – Pansy	Peace – Peas
False – Falls	Sip – Zip	Price – Prize

Comparison of / dʒ/ and /z/:

Sedge – Says	Jest – Zest	Gauge – Gaze
Jones – Zones	Junk – Zink	Budge – Buzz
Siege – Seize	Rage – Raise	

18. **/ʃ/** Generally represented by the spellings—*sh, ch, sch, sci, s, ss, ti, ce, ci*—*sh*all, *sh*arp, ma*ch*ine, mous-ta*ch*e, *sch*edule, *sch*lep, con*sci*ence, con*sci*ous, A*si*an, *s*ugar, pre*ss*ure, a*ss*ure, na*ti*onal, e*ss*en*ti*al, o*ce*an, o*ce*anarium, spe*ci*al, cru*ci*al.

Comparison of /s/ and /ʃ/:

Sip – Ship	Ass – Ash	Suit – Shoot
Soar – Shore	Sun – Shun	Same – Shame
See – She	Save – Shave	Seer – Sheer
Soap – Shop	Said – Shade	Self – Shelf
Mess – Mesh		

19. **/ʒ/** Generally represented by the spellings—*si, s, z, ge*—revi*si*on, deci*si*on, confu*si*on mea*s*ure, plea-*s*ure, vi*s*ual, u*s*ual, sei*z*ure, a*z*ure, gara*ge*, sabota*ge*, presti*ge*,

Comparison of /ʒ/ and /ʃ/:

| Pleasure – Pressure | Vision – Fission |

Comparison of /z/ and /ʒ/:

| Bays – Beige | Caesar – Seizure | Composer – Composure |

20. **/h/** Generally represented by the spellings—*h, wh*—*h*at, *h*eat, *h*atred, a*h*ead, *h*appy, *h*erbal, *h*ouse, *h*airy, *wh*ose, *wh*ole, *wh*o.

21. **/l/** Generally represented by the spellings—*l, ll*—*l*et, *l*ime, *l*ight, *l*esson, *l*ean, g*l*ass, cana*l*, roya*l*, reso*l*ve, a*ll*ow, hi*ll*, ye*ll*ow, fe*ll*ow.

22. **/r/** Generally represented by the spellings—*r, rr, rh, wr*—*r*ace, *r*ude, b*r*ave, *r*adio, ca*rr*y, hu*rr*y, ca*rr*ier, a*rr*ive, *rh*yme, *rh*ythm, *rh*ea, *rh*etorical, *wr*ite, *wr*ought, *wr*inkle, *wr*ing.

Comparison of / l/ and /r/:

Lush – Rush	Light – Right	Lighter – Writer
Lake – Rake	Lies – Rise	Alive – Arrive
Light – Right	Late – Rate	Lice – Rice
Low – Row	Lain – Rain	Load – Road
Lead – Read	List – Wrist	

23. **/j/** Generally represented by the spellings—*y, i, eau, eu, ew, ewe, ieu, iew, u, ue*—*y*et, *y*esterday, *y*ear, on*i*on, opin*i*on, b*eau*ty, *eu*logize, *eu*thanasia, n*ew*, d*ew*, *ewe*, l*ieu*, rev*iew*, *u*nit, *u*niverse, val*ue*, arg*ue*.

24. **/w/** Generally represented by the spellings—*w, wh, u, q + u*—*w*est, *w*aist, *w*inter, *wh*en, *wh*ere, lang*u*age, ling*u*ist, eq*u*al, sq*u*are, q*u*estion.

Comparison of / w/ and / v/:

Wail – Veil	West – Vest	Wet – Vet
Wine – Vine	Worse – Verse	Whim – Vim
Why – Vie		

5.2.2.2   English Vowels

Vowels are produced by the free movement of breath through the mouth. There are two types of vowels in English—pure vowels or monothongs and diphthongs.

Pure Vowels

1. **/iː/**: Represented by the spellings—*ay, e, ea, ee, ei, eo, oe, ey, i, ie, ae*—quay, legal, be, bead, read, deed, see, perceive, seize, people, peon, foetus, foetal, key, geyser, unique, police, achieve, aegis, aesthetic.

2. **/ɪ/**: Represented by the spellings—*a, ai, e, ee, ei, ey, i, ia, ie, o, u, ui, y*—village, captain, pretty, ticket, coffee, foreign, storey, miss, marriage, ladies, women, busy, build, city.

   Comparison of /ɪ/ & /iː/:

Hit – Heat	Fit – Feet	Bit – Beat
Dip – Deep	Lid – Lead	Pick – Peak
Sill – Seal	Chit – Cheat	Did – Deed
Lip – Leap	Chick – Cheek	Knit – Neat
Grin – Green	Nil – Kneel	Fill – Feel
Sit – Seat	Ship – Sheep	Live – Leave

3. **/e/**: Represented by the spellings—*a, ai, ay, e, ea, ei, eo, ie, u, ue*—many, said, says, bend, best, pleasure, wealth, leisure, leopard, friend, lieutenant, bury, guess.

4. **/æ/**: Represented by spellings—*a, ai*—rat, matter, gap, ban, fan, man, damp, plait, plaid.

   Comparison of /e/ & /æ/:

Bet – Bat	Peck – Pack	Bed – Bad
End – And	Men – Man	Beg – Bag
Bend – Band	Led – Lad	Lend – Land
Dead – Dad	Beck – Back	Said – Sad
Pen – Pan	Pet – Pat	Vet – Vat
Kettle – Cattle	Guess – Gas	Merry – Marry

   Comparison of /e/, /æ/, /ɪ/ & /iː/:

/e/	/æ/	/ɪ/	/iː/
Set	Sat	Sit	Seat
Bet	Bat	Bit	Beat
Bed	Bad	Bid	Bead
Dead	Dad	Did	Deed
Peck	Pack	Pick	Peak
Ate	At	It	Eat
Led	Lad	Lid	Lead

5. **/ʊ/**: Represented by the spellings—*o, oo, ou, u*—woman, wolf, look, took, hood, hook, would, should, pull, full.

6. **/uː/**: Represented by the spellings—*oo, u, ou, ui, ew, ue, wo*—soon, boon, jute, rude, coupon, group, fruit, bruise, flew, grew, blue, true, two.

   Comparison of /ʊ/ & /uː/

Pull – Pool	Full – Fool	Soot – Suit
Shook – Shoot	Would – Wooed	Stood – Stool
Could – Cool	Look – Loot	Good – Goose
Took – Tool	Cook – Coolie	Nook – Noon
Foot – Food	Put – Pooh!	

7. **/ɒ/**: Represented by the spellings—*a* (after 'w'), *au, o, ou, ow*—watch, water, because, cauliflower, college, cobweb, cough, trough, knowledge.

   Comparison of /ʊ/ & /ɒ/:

Put – Pot	Good – God	Could – Cod
Shook – Shock	Nook – Knock	

8. /ɔː/: Represented by the spellings—*a, ar, au, aw, oa, oar, oor, or, ore, ou, our*—ball, call, warn, warden, caught, caution, shawl, laws, broad, boar, floor, shortage, store, thought, course.

Comparison of /uː/ & /ɔː/:

Boon – Born	Fool – Fall	Shoe – Shaw
Shoot – Short	Pool – Paul	

Comparison of /ɒ/ & /ɔː/

Cot – Caught	Not – Naught	Pot – Port
Cock – Cork	Spot – Sport	Chock – Chalk
Stock – Stork	Lost – Lord	Bomb – Born
Don – Dawn	Hock – Hawk	Rot – Wrought

9. /ʌ/: Represented by the spellings—*o, oe, oo, ou, u*—son, month, does, flood, blood, young, double, must, fuss.

10. /ɜː/: Represented by the spellings—*ear, er, ir, or* (preceded by 'w'), *our, ur*—search, heard, perk, perfect, bird, shirt, word, work, journey, journal, nurse, church.

Comparison of /ʌ/ & /ɜː/

Hut – Hurt	Cut – Curt	Shut – Shirt
Puck – Perk	Bud – Bird	Thud – Third
Such – Search	Ton – Turn	Gull – Girl
Luck – Lurk	Bun – Burn	Thud – Third
Mutter – Murmur	Fun – Fern	

11. /ə/: Represented by the spellings—*a, ar, e, er, i, o, or, ou, ough, our, re, u, ur, ure*—about, cassette, beggar, circular, problem, mother, sensible, polite, comfort, famous, thorough, neigbour, metre, suggest, surmount, measure.

12. /ɑː/: Represented by the spellings—*a, al, ar, au, uar, ear, er*—pass, task, calm, balm, car, farm, laugh, aunt, guard, heart, sergeant.

Comparison of /ɑː/, /ɒ/, /ɑː/ &/ɔː/

/ɑː/	/ɒ/	/ɑː/	/ɔ/
Guard	God	Part	Port
Heart	Hot	Hard	Hoard
Dark	Dock	Art	Ought
Cast	Cost	Bard	Bored
Last	Lost	Cart	Court
Dart	Dot	Card	Cord
Sharp	Shop		
Card	Cod		

Diphthongs: A diphthong is a combination of two vowel sounds. Two dots (ː) are never used in diphthongs. The following diphthongs are used in English:

1. /eɪ/: Represented by the spellings—*a, ai, ay, e, ea, ei, ey*—bake, sake, vain, faith, train, tray, hay, clay, fete, great, break, weight, veil, grey, they.
2. /əʊ/: Represented by the spellings—*o, oa, oe, ou, ow, eau, ew, oo*—go, home, boat, foam, toe, foe, mould, soul, slow, show, flow, plateau, beau, sew, brooch.
3. /aɪ/: Represented by the spellings—*i, is, ais, ei, eye, ie, uy, y, ye*—like, bike, hike, high, island, aisle, either, neither, eye, lie, die, buy, guy, try, dry, bye, dye.
4. /aʊ/: Represented by the spellings—*ou, ow*—house, round, found, clown, town, down, brown.
5. /ɔɪ/: Represented by the spellings—*oi, oy, uoy*—toil, noise, boil, soil, coin, joy, employ, buoy.
6. /ɪə/: Represented by the spellings—*e, ea, ear, eer, eir, eo, ere, ia, ier, io, iou, iu*—serious, period, idea, area, fear, rear, cheer, steer, weird, theory, theorem, sphere, here, India, fierce, pierce, impious, harmonium, gymnasium.
7. /eə/: Represented by spellings—*a, ae, air, ar, are, ear, eir, ere*—Mary, scary, aerobics, aerospace, fair, pair, scarce, care, share, fear, tear, their, heir, there, compere.

8. /ʊə/: Represented by spellings—*oor, our, u, ua, ue, uou, ure*—*poor, moor, tour, gourd, jury, fury, usual, visual, cruel, fuel, tortuous, pure, procure, cure.*

Comparison of sounds – /eɪ/ and /e/:

Taste – Test	Late – Let	Gate – Get
Date – Debt	Raid – Red	Mate – Met
Pate – Pet	Bait – Bet	Eight – Ate
Cane – ken	Bade – Bed	Tail – Tell
Say – Said	Bale – Bell	

/eɪ/	/aɪ/	/ɔɪ/
Tail	Tile	Toil
Fail	File	Foil
Cane	Kinetic	Coin
Lane	Line	Loin
Bale	Bile	Boil

/ɪə/	/eə/	/ʊə/
Beer	Bear	Boor
Pierce	Pears	Poor
Dear/Deer	Dare	Doer
Sheer	Share	Sure
Tear (n)	Tear (v)	Tour
Here	Hair/ Hare	_
Fear	Fare/ Fair	_
Spear	Spare	_
Cheer	Chair	_

/aɪ/ and /ɔɪ/		
Buy – Boy	Try – Troy	Ally – Alloy
Tie – Toy	Isle – Oil	Bile – Boil
Vice –Voice		

/əʊ/ and /ɒ/		
Goat – Got	Note – Not	Own – On
Wrote – Rot	Road – Rod	Hope – Hop
Soak – Sock	Coat – Cot	

/aʊ/ and /əʊ/		
Now – No	Bout – Boat	Howl – Whole
Gout – Goat	Out – Oat	Doubt – Dote
Foul – Foal		

/eə/ and /eɪ/		
Pair – Pay	There – They	Dare – Day
Hair – Hay	Rare – Ray	Bare – Bay
Stare – Stay		

5.3   Phonetic Transcription Using IPA Characters

5.3.1   What is Phonetic Transcription?

The word, 'phonetic' means 'using special symbols to represent each different speech sound' and 'transcription' refers to 'something that is represented in writing.' International Phonetic Alphabet (IPA) is used to represent the sounds of English language and is often useful in describing pronunciation patterns or transcribing the words phonetically. Phonetic transcription is, thus, a kind of alphabetical writing in which each phonetic alphabet represents each sound. English pronunciation cannot be understood by letters; therefore, knowledge of phonetic symbols along with an ability to transcribe them according to sounds may be very helpful in acquiring correct pronunciation along with understanding it. Every good dictionary contains correct pronunciation together with the spelling of a word. Nowadays, these dictionaries are available on CD ROMs as well as online and a learner can not only read the correct pronunciation of the word but may also have a direct access to the audio.

5.3.2 Purpose of Transcription

The purpose of phonetic transcription is to represent the pronunciation of a word, phrase or sentence unambiguously. Most of the dictionaries provide pronunciation of individual words. Phonetic transcription helps in correcting pronunciation and it enables us to compare the sounds of different languages as well as different varieties of the same language.

5.3.3 Guiding Principles for Correct Pronunciation/Transcription

English pronunciation creates a lot of problems for the non-native speakers. Some of these hurdles can be overcome, if we understand some guiding principles related to correct pronunciation, which will automatically lead to correct phonetic transcription of words as well:

5.3.3.1 Silent Letters

1. *b* is silent in a word when it is preceded by 'm' or followed by 't' at the final position:

climb/klaɪm/	thumb/θʌm/	bomb/bɒm/
crumb/krʌm/	plumb/plʌm/	succumb/səkʌm/
jamb/dʒæm/	comb /kəʊm/	tomb /tuːm/
dumb/dʌm/	numb/nʌm/	lamb/læm/
womb/wuːm/	doubt/daʊt/	debt/det/

➜ *b* is also silent in: subtle/sʌtl/, plumber/plʌmə/, bomber/bɒmə/, redoubtable/rɪdaʊtəbl/.

2. *d* is silent in a word when it is followed by 'j' or 'g' and in some other words like:

adjacent/ədʒeɪsnt/	adjust/ədʒʌst/	adjourn/ədʒɜːn/
adjudge/ədʒʌdʒ/	adjoin/ədʒɔɪn/	adjunct/ædʒʌŋkt/
adjective/ædʒɪktɪv/	badge/bædʒ/	judge/dʒʌdʒ/
pledge/pledʒ/	fridge/frɪdʒ/	knowledge/nɒlɪdʒ/
edge/edʒ/	porridge/pɒrɪdʒ/	sludge/slʌdʒ/
bridge/brɪdʒ/	handkerchief/hæŋkətʃɪf/	handsome/hænsəm/

3. *p* is silent in a word when it is followed by 's', 't' or 'n' at the initial position and in some other words such as:

pneumonia/njuːməʊnɪə/	psychology/saɪkɒlədʒɪ/	psalm/saːm/
pseudo/suːdəʊ/	psyche/saɪkɪ/	ptarmigan/taːmɪgən/
Ptolemaic/tɒləmeɪɪk/	empty/emtɪ/	cupboard/kʌbəd/

➜ *p* is also silent when it is followed by 't' at the final position in the word: receipt/rɪsiːt/.

4. *g* is silent when it is followed by 'm' or 'n' in the same syllable:

resign/rɪzaɪn/	foreign/fɒrən/	gnat/næt/
sign/saɪn/	feign/feɪn/	assign/əsaɪn/
campaign/kæmpeɪn/	gnaw/nɔː/	champagne/ʃæmpeɪn/
diaphragm/daɪəfræm/	phlegm/flem/	

➜ *g* is not silent when it is followed by 'm' or 'n' in different syllables:

signature/sɪgnətʃə/	ignore/ɪgnɔː/	ignite/ɪgnaɪt/
phlegmatic/flegmætɪk/	resignation/rezɪgneɪʃn/	malignant/məlɪgnənt/

5. *h* is silent when it is preceded by 'g' and at the final position:

ghost/gəʊst/   aghast/əgɑːst/   ghetto/getəʊ/   ah/ɑː/ oh/əʊ/

h is also silent in:

hour/aʊə/   honest/ɒnɪst/   heir/eə/   exhaust/ɪgzɔːst/

rhythm/rɪðəm/   exhibit/ɪgzɪbɪt/   annihilate/ənaɪəleɪt/

6. *k* is silent in a word when it is followed by 'n' at the initial position:

know/nəʊ/   knee/niː/kneel/niːl/   knit/nɪt/

knave/neɪv/   knife/naɪf/   knot/nɒt/   knight/naɪt/

knob/nɒb/   knock/nɒk/   knowledge/nɒlɪdʒ/

7. *l* is silent in a word when it is followed by 'k' or 'm' and in some modal auxiliaries:

chalk/tʃɔːk/   would/wʊd/   could/kʊd/   should/ʃʊd/

alms/ɑːmz/   almond/ɑːmənd/   half/hɑːf/   palm/pɑːm/

psalm/sɑːm/   balm/bɑːm/   yolk/jəʊk/   calm/kɑːm/

salmon/sæmən/   walk/wɔːk/   folk/fəʊk/   talk/tɔːk/

8. *n* is silent after 'm' when both of them occur in the same syllable:

autumn/ɔːtəm/   damn/dæm/   hymn/hɪm/   condemn/kəndem/

→ When combination of 'n' and 'm' occurs in two different syllables both the letters are pronounced:

autumnal/ɔːtʌmnəl/   damnable/dæmnəbl/

condemnation/kɒndemneɪʃn/   hymnal/hɪmnəl

9. *t* is silent when it occurs between 's' and 'l' and 's' and 'en' or followed by 'en' in some words :

castle/kɑːsl/   hustle/hʌsl/   bustle/bʌsl/   wrestle/restl/

apostle/əpɒsl/   whistle/wɪsl/   bristle/brɪsl/   listen/lɪsn/

glisten/glɪsn/   soften/sɒfn/   often/ɒfn/   fasten/fɑːsn/

→ *t* is silent before 'ch' in most of the words:

kitchen/kɪtʃɪn/   ditch/dɪtʃ/   watch/wɒtʃ/   witch/wɪtʃ/

batch/bætʃ/   catch/kætʃ/   match/mætʃ/   latch/lætʃ/

→ *t* is also silent in many words of French origin:

ballet/bæleɪ/bouquet/bʊkeɪ/   buffet (n)/bʊfeɪ/

depot/depəʊ   debut/deɪbjuː/

10. *w* is silent at the final position. It is also silent at the initial position when it is followed by 'r' or sometimes when followed by 'h':

wreath/riːθ/   wrist/rɪst/   wrinkle/rɪŋkl/   write/raɪt/

wrong/rɒŋ/   wrestle/restl/   wrap/ræp/   wreck/rek/

wrath/rɒθ/   saw/sɔː/   draw/drɔː/   flaw/flɔː/

flow/fləʊ/   snow/snəʊ/   show/ʃəʊ/   blow/bləʊ/

who/huː/   whom /huːm/   whose /huːz/   whole/həʊl/

11. *s* is silent before 'l':

island/aɪlənd/   isle/aɪl/   islet/aɪlət/   aisle/aɪl/

5.3.3.2   Pronunciation of the Suffixes

1. Word endings —*s, es, 's*—are pronounced/s/after/p/,/k/,/t/,/f/and/θ/:

caps/kæps/   stops/stɒps/   cooks/kʊks/   Mick's/mɪks/

cat's/kæts/   fits/fɪts/   fights/faɪts/   laughs/lɑːfs/

chief's/tʃːfs/   moths/mɒθs/

→ -*s, -es, 's*—are pronounced/ɪz/ after/s/,/z/,/ʃ/,/ʒ/,/tʃ/and/dʒ/:

passes/pɑːsɪz/   crosses/krɒsɪz/   roses/rəʊzɪz/

organizes/ɔːgənaɪzɪz/   washes/wɒʃɪz/   slashes/slæʃɪz/

garages/gærɑːʒɪz/   churches/tʃɜːtʃɪz/   benches/bentʃɪz/

judges/dʒʌdʒɪz/   edges/edʒɪz/

→ -*s, -es, 's*—are pronounced/z/after the rest of the sounds:

he's/hiːz/   buds/bʌdz/   bulbs/bʌlbz/   leaves/liːvz/

bags/bægz/   signs/saɪnz/   loves/lʌvz/   boys/bɔɪz/

pulls/pʊlz/   keys/kiːz/   names/neɪmz/   goes/gəʊz/

2. Word endings—*-d, -ed*—are pronounced/ɪd/after/t/and/d/:

wanted/wɒntɪd/   chanted/tʃaːntɪd/   mended/mendɪd/   granted/graːntɪd/

➜ *-d, -ed*—are pronounced/t/after/p/,/k/,/f/,/θ/,/tʃ/,/s/,/ʃ/:

capped/kæpt/   shaped/ʃeɪpt/   cooked/kʊkt/

lacked/lækt/   laughed/laːft/   coughed/kɒft/

earthed/ɜːθt/   berthed/bɜːθt/   thatched/θætʃt/

watched/wɒtʃt/   passed/paːst/   cursed/kɜːst/

pushed/pʊʃt/   blushed/blʌʃt/

➜ *-d, -ed*—are pronounced/d/after the rest of the sounds:

rubbed/rʌbd/   pulled/pʊld/   bagged/bægd/   allowed/əlaʊd/

judged/dʒʌdʒd/   annoyed/ənɔɪd/   seized/siːzd/   sawed/sɔːd/

wronged/rɒŋd/   loathed/ləʊðd/   frayed/freɪd/   crammed/kræmd/

3. Word endings—*-cial, -sial* and *-tial*—are pronounced/ʃl/:

crucial/kruːʃl/   racial/reɪʃl/   official/əfɪʃl/

controversial/kɒntrəvɜːʃl/   substantial/səbstænʃl/   potential/pətenʃl/

4. Word ending—*-cian*—is pronounced/ʃn/:

Magician/mədʒɪʃn/   technician/teknɪʃn/

beautician/bjuːtɪʃn/   electrician/ɪlektrɪʃn/

5. Word endings—*-cious* and—*tious*—are pronounced/ʃəs/:

delicious/dɪlɪʃəs/   judicious/dʒʊdɪʃəs/   ambitious/æmbɪʃəs/   cautious/kɔːʃəs/

6. Word ending—*-stion*—is pronounced/stʃən/:

suggestion/sədʒestʃən/   question/kwestʃən/

digestion/daɪdʒestʃən/   exhaustion/ɪgzɔːstʃən/

7. Word ending—*-age*—is pronounced/ɪdʒ/:

hostage/hɒstɪdʒ/   breakage/breɪkɪdʒ/   carriage/kærɪdʒ/   package/pækɪdʒ/

8. Word ending—*-ate*—is pronounced/ət/ in adjectives:

fortunate/fɔːtʃənət/   incarnate (Adj)/ɪnkaːnət/   immediate/ɪmiːdɪət/

passionate/pæʃənət/   temperate/tempərət/   moderate/mɒdərət/

➜ However, in verbs—*-ate*—is pronounced/eɪt/:

educate/edʒʊkeɪt/   hesitate/hezɪteɪt/   fascinate/fæsɪneɪt/

celebrate/selɪbreɪt/   associate/əsəʊʃɪeɪt/

9. Word ending—*-tain*—is pronounced/teɪn/in verbs:

retain/rɪteɪn/   sustain/səsteɪn/   maintain/meɪnteɪn/   attain/əteɪn/

➜ *-tain*—is pronounced/tən/,/tɪn/or/tn/ elsewhere:

fountain/faʊntən/   mountain/maʊntən/   captain/kæptɪn/

certain/sɜːtn/   curtain/kɜːtn/

10. Word endings—*-ance* and *-ence* are pronounced/əns/whereas endings—*-ant* and *-ent* are pronounced/ənt/:

distance/dɪstəns/   resistance/rɪzɪstəns/   reference/refrəns/

preference/prefrəns/   instant/ɪnstənt/   distant/dɪstənt/

different/dɪfrənt/   current/kʌrənt/

11. Word endings—*est and -et* are pronounced/ɪst/and/ɪt/, respectively when they occur in an unstressed syllables:

safest/seɪfɪst/   hardest/haːdɪst/   ticket/tɪkɪt/   pocket/pɒkɪt/

5.3.3.3   Spelling Sequence

1. 'ng':

➜ Spelling sequence 'ng' is pronounced as /ŋ/ at the final position:

sing /sɪŋ/   wrong/rɒŋ/   ring /rɪŋ/   long/lɒŋ/

→ 'ng' is pronounced / ŋ/ at the medial position also if the word has been derived from a verb:
longing/lɒŋɪŋ/   hanger/hæŋə/   singing/sɪŋɪŋ/   bringing/brɪŋɪŋ/

→ 'ng' is pronounced/ ŋ/ only when the plural maker 's' is added to nouns ending in / ŋ/:
songs /sɒŋz/   rings /rɪŋz/   things /θɪŋz/   cuttings/kʌtɪŋz/

→ 'ng' at the medial position are pronounced as /ŋg/if the words are not derived from verbs:
longer /lɒŋgə/   finger /fɪŋgə/   anger /æŋgə/   hunger/hʌŋgə/

→ The sound / ŋ/ does not occur at the initial position. It occurs at the final position only after the short vowels: /ɪ/, /e/, /ɒ/, /æ/ and /ʌ/ :
throng/θrɒŋ/   hung /hʌŋ/   blank /blæŋk/   drink/drɪŋk/

2. **'th':** Spelling 'th' is pronounced /θ/ or /ð/ but in English names it is pronounced as /t/:
Thames/temz/   Thailand/taɪlənd/   Thomas/tɒməs/   Thompson/tɒmpsən/

3. **'ch':** Spelling 'ch' may be pronounced /tʃ/, /k/ or /ʃ/:
change/tʃeɪndʒ/   chamber/tʃeɪmbə/   chord/kɔːd/
chorus /kɔːrəs/   chef/ʃef/   machine/məʃiːn/

4. **'ss':** Spelling 'ss' may be pronounced /s/, /z/ or /ʃ/:
classes/klɑːsɪz/   assert/əsɜːt/   assist /əsɪst/   dissolve/dɪzɒlv/
dessert/dɪzɜːt/   mission/mɪʃn/   aggression/əgreʃn/   session/seʃn/

5.3.3.4   Letters

1. **'r':**
→ r is silent when it is preceded by a vowel:
park/pɑːk/   occur/əkɜː/   church/tʃɜːtʃ/   charm /tʃɑːm/

→ r is pronounced when it follows a vowel:
drive/draɪv/   crave/kreɪv/   marine/məriːn/   curry/kʌrɪ/

→ r is also silent at the final position:
car/kɑː/   sir/sɜː/   near/nɪə/   meter/miːtə/

→ r is pronounced at the final position in phrases or compound words when the first element ending with 'r' is followed by a word beginning with a vowel sound:
far off/fɑːrɒf/   care of/keərəv/   runner-up /rʌnərʌp/
commander-in-chief/kəmɑːndərɪntʃiːf/   teacher-in-charge/tiːtʃərɪntʃɑːdʒ/

2. **'g':** 'g' may be pronounced/g/,/dʒ/or/ʒ/:
gain/geɪn/   green/griːn/   generous/dʒenərəs/
gym/dʒɪm/   mirage/mɪrɑːʒ/   rouge/ruːʒ/

3. **'t':** 't' may be pronounced as/t/,/tʃ/or/ʃ/:
late/leɪt/   stale/steɪl/   nature/neɪtʃə/
capture/kæptʃə/   mention/menʃn/   edition/ɪdɪʃn/

4. **'s':** is pronounced as/s/,/z/or/ʃ/:
scene/siːn/   system/sɪstəm/   busy/bɪzɪ/
these/ðiːz/   vision/vɪʒn/   pleasure/pleʒə/

5.3.3.5   Double Consonants

All double consonants except 'cc' are pronounced as single consonant sounds:
rubber/rʌbə/   dimmer/dɪmə/   letter/letə/   running/rʌnɪŋ/
'cc' may be pronounced as/ks/when followed by 'e,' 'i,' or 'y' or/k/when followed by the rest of the letters:
accord/əkɔːd/   accurate/ækjərət/   account/əkaʊnt/
accent/æksent/   access/ækses/   accident/æksɪdənt/

5.3.3.6   Sounds

1. /θ/ and /ð/:

→ Many words have sound/θ/but with suffixes 's/es' /θ/becomes/ð/:
  mouth /maʊθ/– mouths/maʊðz/
  youth/juːθ/– youths/juːðz/
  cloth/klɒθ/– clothes/kləʊðz/
  wreath/riːθ/– wreathes/riːðz/

→ Some words have/θ/sound but their derivatives have/ð/sound:
  north/nɔːθ/– northern/nɔːðən/
  south/saʊθ/– southern/sʌðən/
  breath/breθ/– breathe/briːð/
  mouth (n)/maʊθ/– mouth (v)/maʊð/
  heath/hiːθ/– heathen/hiːðn/

2. /j/:

→ /j/does not occur at the final position and after/dʒ/, /tʃ/and /r/:
  juice/dʒuːs/   jute/dʒuːt/   chew/tʃuː/
  rule/ruːl/   grew/gruː/

→ /j/does not occur after/l/when it is preceded by a consonant:
  blue/bluː/   flew/fluː/   glue/gluː/

→ /j/is pronounced when/l/is preceded by an accented vowel:
  failure/feɪljə/   value/væljuː/

Task

Transcribe the following words using IPA symbols:

Woman, bright , raise, address, deserve, palm, design, indict, twelfth, once, women, flower, waist, grams, fragile, cloud, aim, sheep, like, chalk, acquire, career, hurt, oblige, flake, authority, short, rhyme, record (v), single, thumb, deserve, wives, berth, guide, crowd, savage, mother, young, shoes, coil, long, tomb, title, cyst, relate, scarce, army, apple, home, clear, choice, boat, day, foot, give, saw, tour, good, slapped, bouquet, doubt, murder, gaining, liberate, coffee, pudding, school, applaud, polite, chapter, virtue, bird, family, wealth, hurry, hate, crawl, queen, running, single, wives, savage, export (v), battle, pool, shout.

5.4   IPA Transcription of Words Often Mispronounced

The following is the IPA transcription of words which are often mispronounced:

Ability /əbɪlətɪ/

Academician /əkædəmɪʃn/

Accommodation /əkɒmədeɪʃn/

Advantage /ədvɑːntɪdʒ/

Advertise /ædvətaɪz/

All /ɔːl/

Analysis /ənæləsɪs/

Apology /əpɒlədʒɪ/

Assistance /əsɪstəns/

Academic /ækədemɪk/

Accept /əksept/

Adequate /ædɪkwət/

Advantageous /ædvənteɪdʒəs/

Advertisement /ədvɜːtɪsmənt/

Always /ɔːlweɪz/

Analytical /ænəlɪtɪkl/

Apple /æpl/

Association /əsəʊʃɪeɪʃn/

Atmosphere /ætməsfɪə/

Bear /beə/

Breakfast /brekfəst/

Breathe /briːð/

Buffalo /bʌfələʊ/

Calendar /kælɪndə/

Captain /kæptɪn/

Carrier /kærɪə/

Celebrity /səlebrətɪ/

Choreography /kɒrɪɒgrəfɪ/

Clarity /klærətɪ/

Committee /kəmɪtɪ/

Compere /kɒmpeə/

Competitive /kəmpetətiv/

Concept /kɒnsept/

Continue /kəntɪnjuː/

Correspond /kɒrəspɒnd/

Crèche /kreʃ/

Crush /krʌʃ/

Demonstrate /demənstreɪt/

Determine /dɪtɜːmɪn/

Dialogue /daɪəlɒg/

Director /dərektə/

Echo /ekəʊ/

Enough /ɪnʌf/

Envelop /ɪnveləp/

Environment /invaɪrənmənt/

Exact /ɪgzækt/

Except /ɪksept/

Executive /ɪgzekjətɪv/

Faculty /fækltɪ/

Garage /gærɑːʒ/

Government /gʌvənmənt/

Guardian /gɑːdɪən/

Hare /heə/

Here /hɪə/

Interrogative /ɪntərɒgətɪv/

Loose /luːs/

Loss /lɒs/

Measure /meʒə/

Memory /memərɪ/

Mutual /mjuːtʃʊəl/

Observe /əbzɜːiv/

Olympic /əlɪmpɪk/

Onion /ʌnjən/

Oven /ʌvn/

Pan /pæn/

Balcony /bælkənɪ/

Birthday /bɜːθdeɪ/

Breath /breθ/

Bowl /bəʊl/

Calcium /kælsɪəm/

Call /kɔːl/

Career /kərɪə/

Cassette /kəset/

Character /kærəktə/

Cigarette /sɪgəret/

Colleague /kɒliːg/

Compare /kəmpeə/

Competition /kɒmpətɪʃn/

Competitor /kəmpetɪtə/

Confusion /kənfuːʒn/

Continuous /kəntɪnjʊəs/

Correspondence /kɒrəspɒndəns/

Cricket /krɪkɪt/

Data /deɪtə/

Determination /dɪtɜːmɪneɪʃn/

Develop /dɪveləp/

Direction /dərekʃn/

Dramatic /drəmætɪk/

Embarrass /ɪmbærəs/

Enthusiasm /ɪnθjuːzɪæzəm/

Envelope /envələʊp/

Ethics /eθɪks/

Example /ɪgzɑːmpl/

Expect /ɪkspekt/

Extempore /ekstempərɪ/

Formality /fɔːmælətɪ/

Gigantic /dʒaɪgæntɪk/

Guarantee /gærənti:/

Hair /heə/

Heart /hɑːt/

Indecisive /ɪndɪsaɪsɪv/

Leisure /leʒə/

Lose /luːz/

Maroon /məruːn/

Memento /məmentəʊ/

Menace /menəs/

Negative /negətɪv/

Obvious /ɒbvɪəs/

Omelette /ɒmlət/

Opportunities /ɒpətjuːnətɪz/

Pain /peɪn/

Parents /peərənts/

Patriotism /peɪtrɪətɪzəm/
Pen /pen/
Photograph /fəʊtəgrɑːf/
Photography /fətɒgrəfɪ/
Plumber /plʌmə/
Political /pəlɪtɪkl/
Positive /pɒzətɪv/
Potential /pətenʃl/
Preference /prefrəns/
Priority /praɪɒrətɪ/
Pronunciation /prənʌnsɪeɪʃn/
Psychologist /saɪkɒlədʒɪst/
Quality /kwɒlətɪ/
Quiet /kwaɪət/
Receipt /rɪsiːt/
Resume (n) /rezjumeɪ/
Said /sed/
Says /sez/
Sewing machine /səʊɪŋ məʃiːn/
Shoulder /ʃəʊldə/
Success /səkses/
Thorough /θʌrə/
Vehicle /viːəkl/
Wallet /wɒlɪt/
Wool /wʊl/

Patron /peɪtrən/
People /piːpl/
Photographer /fətɒgrəfə/
Pizza /piːtsə/
Police /pəliːs/
Pollution /pəluːʃn/
Posture /pɒstʃə/
Precious /preʃəs/
Pretty /prɪtɪ/
Privacy /prɪvəsɪ/
Psychological /saɪkəlɒdʒɪkl/
Psychology /saɪkɒlədʒɪ/
Question /kwestʃən/
Quite /kwaɪt/
Repetition /repətɪʃn/
Resume (V) /rɪzuːm/
Saturday /sætədeɪ/
Secretary /sekrətrɪ/
Shepherd /ʃepəd/
Soldier /səʊldʒə/
Suggestion /sədʒestʃən/
Tortoise /tɔːtəs/
Village /vɪlɪdʒ/
Want /wɒnt/
Wednesday /wenzdeɪ/

5.5 Word Stress

"Give me the right word and the right accent and I will move the world."

–Joseph Conrad. (a personal record)

Word stress is the key to understand spoken English. Native speakers of English use it naturally. When non-native speakers talk to native speakers, both of them find it difficult to understand each other. The situation becomes worse when the inhabitants speak fast, fluent and conversational English. Especially in a multilingual country like India where so many languages are spoken with so much variation in accent, it is very difficult to acquire standard accent. Nevertheless, we cannot ignore the fact that word stress is an important feature of spoken English. Complete and correct pronunciation means both articulating the sounds correctly and placing the stress at the right place.

5.5.1 What is a Syllable?

To understand word accent, we should first know what is a syllable? A sound is the smallest unit of spoken English. The combination of sounds makes a syllable and the combination of syllables makes a word. Each syllable has one vowel sound and may have one or more consonant sounds. A word can have one, two, three or more syllables. Syllabic division is marked by a hyphen (-):

→ Monosyllabic words: girl /gɜːl/   thoughts /θɔːts/   boys /bɔɪz/   farm/fɑːm/.

→ Disyllabic words: teacher /tiː-tʃə/, doctor /dɒk-tə/,   mother /mʌ-ðə/,   college /kɒ-lɪdʒ/.

→ Three syllabic words: remember /rɪ-mem-bə/,   consonants /kɒn-sən-ənt/, extinguish /ɪks-tɪŋ-gwɪʃ/, fortunate /fɔː-tʃə-nət/.

→ Words with four or more syllables: satisfactory /sæt-ɪs-fæk-tə-rɪ/, electricity /ɪ-lek-trɪ-sə-tɪ/, ridiculous /rɪ-dɪ-kjə-ləs/, civilization /sɪ-və-lɑɪ-zeɪ-ʃn/.

→ Consonants, 'm', 'n', and 'l' have sonority compared to that of some vowels. They are called syllabic consonants and they function as syllables in words such as: button /bʌ-tn/, cotton /kɒ-tn/, kettle /ke-tl/, brittle /brɪ-tl/, shuttle /ʃʌ-tl/, etc.

5.5.2   What is Word Stress?

In English, we do not say each syllable with the same force, strength or emphasis. We accentuate on a particular syllable, that is, all the syllables combined into a word are not uttered with the same degree of prominence. We say one syllable very loudly and all the other syllables very softly or quietly. The following points should be kept in mind regarding word stress:

1. One word, one stress. One word cannot have two stresses. If you have heard two stresses, you have heard two words, not one.
2. Stress is always placed on a syllable.
3. Stress is marked by a vertical bar (') above and before the syllable.
4. Vowel sounds, /ɪ/ and /ə/ are weak sounds. Syllables with these sounds are generally not stressed:
   provide /prə'vaɪd/   disdain /dɪs'deɪn/
   abroad /ə'bɔːd/   merry/'merɪ/
   contain /kən'teɪn/   below/bɪ'ləʊ/
   obtain /əb'teɪn/   sentence /'sentəns/

5.5.3   Ascertaining Word Stress Using Parts of Speech

Use of word stress reveals grammatical relationship between words. There are many words in English like 'absent', 'present' and 'rebel' which may be used as noun/adjectives as well as verbs. In these words stress is placed on the first syllable when the word is used as a noun or an adjective and on the second syllable when the word is used as a verb. For example:

Noun/Adjective	Verb
'absent	ab'sent
'addict	ad'dict
'conduct	con'duct
'contrast	con'trast
'decrease	de'crease
'desert	de'sert
'export	ex'port
'import	im'port
'object	ob'ject
'permit	per'mit
'present	pre'sent
'record	re'cord

5.5.4 Word Stress Related to Prefixes

Weak prefixes—*a-, de-, be-, dis-, mis-, re-, il-, im-, in-, ir-, pre-, un-*—are not stressed in a word. Words with these prefixes are stressed on the root word:

a-: a'ghast, a'rise, a'lone, a'far
de-: de'mand, de'fuse, de'clare, de'generate
be-: be'neath, be'low, be'cause, be'come
dis-: dis'miss, dis'able, dis'own, dis'colour
mis-: mis'shapen, mis'lead, mis'conduct, mis'deed
re-: re'gain, re'call, re'new, re'vise
il-: il'legal, il'lerate, il'logical, il'legitimate
im-: im'movable, impo'lite, im'perfect, imma'ture
in-: in'active, in'accurate, in'capable, in'discipline
ir-: ir'rational, ir'radiate, ir'regular, irre'coverable
pre-: pre'caution, pre'pare, pre-'book, pre'amble
un-: un'sound, un'do, un'comfortable, un'like

5.5.5 Word Stress in Compound Words

1. Compound words ending in '*-ever*', '*-self*' or '*-selves*' take primary stress on the second element:

him'self	how'ever
her'self	what'ever
my'self	who'ever
your'self	when'ever
them'selves	which'ever

2. Compound words with two nouns take stress on the first element:

'postmaster	'lifeboat	'crossword	'hairbrush	'raincoat
'bookshelf	'milkman	'tea-party	'batsman	'classmate
'mainland	'newsprint	'snowfall	'water-supply	'waistline
'waiting-room	'dining-table	'looking-glass	'pickpocket	'footprint

3. Compound words with an adjective plus a noun take stress on the second element:

Prime 'minister	post'graduate	good-'looking	home'made
vice-'chancellor	after'noon	bad-'tempered	ex-o'fficio
self'study	forth'coming	ever'lasting	never'ending

4. Compound adjectives with a numeral plus a noun take stress on the second element:

half-'yearly	'bi'cameral	half-'day	two'edged
one'liner	three'piece	three-'cornered	four-'square
second-'class	first-'rate	second-'hand	first-'class

5.5.6 Word Stress Related to Suffixes

1. Word endings—*ette, -ee, -eer, -ier, -aire, -ean, -een, -oo, -ese, -ique, -esque, -eum, -eur, -ental, -illa, -iety, -escent,*—carry stress on them:

cas'sette	ga'zette	bu'rette	ciga'rette
pay'ee	nomi'nee	devo'tee	exami'nee
engi'neer	ca'reer	muske'teer	pio'neer
briga'dier	ca'shier	dos'sier	chande'lier
millio'naire	question'naire	doctri'naire	soli'taire
Euro'pean	Jaco'bean	hercu'lean	can'teen

four'teen	six'teen	bam'boo	ta'boo
Chi'nese	Bur'mese	Japa'nese	Portu'guese
an'tique	cri'tique	pictu'resque	gro'tesque
mu'seum	peri'neum	po'seur	mas'seur
'dental	pa'rental	acci'dental	orna'mental
va'nilla	ma'xilla	pro'priety	va'riety
so'ciety	ado'lescent	'crescent	

2. Words ending in suffixes—*ial, -ian, -ion, -ious,- eous, -uous, -ic, -ics, -ive, -graphy, -grapher, -logy, -meter, -metry, -sophy, -cricy,- cracy, -gamy,- nomy, -phony, -pathy, -tomy, -logist, -sopher, -sophist, -scopy,- nomer, -nomist, -ical, -ially , -ically, -itive, -iative,-utive, -ative, -atory*—are stressed on the syllable preceding the suffix:

me'morial	confi'dential	re'medial	cere'monial
ci'vilian	ma'gician	phy'sician	mu'sician
appli'cation	deco'ration	fasci'nation	combi'nation
no'torious	cere'monious	'various	fe'rocious
'piteous	cou'rageous	'gorgeous	advan'tageous
'sumptuous	'virtuous	vo'luptuous	'sensuous
apolo'getic	ener'getic	ter'rific	pro'lific
pho'netics	'physics	me'chanics	sta'tistics
de'cisive	sub'missive	ag'gressive	di'visive
pho'tography	radi'ography	ste'nographer	bi'ographer
soci'ology	bi'ology	ba'rometer	ther'mometer
trigo'nometry	ge'ometry	the'osophy	phi'losophy
hy'pocrisy	au'tocracy	de'mocracy	po'lygamy
'bigamy	e'conomy	a'stronomy	te'lephony
'symphony	home'opathy	al'lopathy	a'natomy
hyste'rectomy	zo'ologist	bi'ologist	phi'losopher
the'osophist	mi'croscopy	spec'troscopy	a'stronomer
e'conomist	gram'matical	po'litical	eco'nomical
philo'sophical	com'mercially	fi'nancially	confi'dentially
po'litically	pho'netically	eco'nomically	gram'matically
com'petitive	re'petitive	in'tuitive	in'quisitive
i'nitiative	ap'preciative	'palliative	as'sociative
con'secutive	e'xecutive	dis'tributive	at'tributive
'sedative	af'firmative	al'ternative	inter'rogative
pre'paratory	ob'servatory	la'boratory	inter'rogatory

3. Disyllabic verbs ending in—*ate*—are stressed on the last syllable while verbs with three or more syllables take stress on the third syllable from the end:

nar'rate	mi'grate	re'late	dic'tate
'educate	par'ticipate	ac'commodate	as'sociate
'generate	fa'cilitate	'cultivate	' formulate

→ Adjectives and nouns ending in '*ate*' with more than two syllables are stressed on the third syllable from the end:

| in'animate | 'adequate | 'correlate | 'passionate | 'surrogate |

4. Disyllabic verbs ending in '*-ise*' or '*-ize*' are stressed on the last syllable; verbs with three or four syllables are stressed on the third syllable from the end, whereas the verbs with five or six syllables are stressed on the fourth syllable from the end:

| bap'tize | re'vise | de'vise | ad'vise | cap'size |
| 'maximize | 'agonize | 'idealise | 'characterize | 'eulogize |

5. Words ending in suffixes—*ity, -fy, -icy and -crat*—are stressed on the third syllable from the end:

fa'cility	u'tility	a'bility	fu'tility
'glorify	'magnify	e'lectrify	'purify
'policy	'aristocrat	'bureaucrat	'democrat

5.5.7 Shifting of Stress

1. Stress shifts from the first syllable to the second, the third, the fourth syllable as the longer words are derived from the shorter ones:

'mechanism	me'chanical	mecha'nician	mechani'zation
'family	fa'miliar	-	famili'arity
-	a'cademy	ac a'demic	acade'mician
'telephone	te'lephony	tele'phonic	-
'capital	-	capita'listic	capitali'zation
'telegraph	te'legraphy	tele'graphic	-
'photo	pho'tography	photo'graphic	-
'politics	po'litical	poli'tician	politici'zation
'democrat	de'mocracy	demo'cratic	-
'hypocrite	hy'pocrisy	hypo'critical	-
'diplomat	di'plomacy	diplo'matic	-
'diphthong	diph'thongal	-	diphthongi'zation

2. The inflexional suffixes—*-d, -ed, -s, -es, -ing*—and derivational suffixes—*-age, ance, -en, -er, -ess, -ful, -hood, -ice, -ish, -ive, -less, -ly, -ment, -ness, -or, -ship, -ter, -ure, -zen, -y*—do not affect the stress:

re'late – re'lated	'fade – 'faded
'pass – 'passed	sub'mit – sub'mitted
com'pose – com'poses	di'sease – di'seases
'mass – 'masses	'edge – 'edges
'write – 'writing	'ask – 'asking
'take – 'taking	'think – thinking
'Carry – 'carriage	'marry – 'marriage
ap'pear – ap'pearance	at'tend – at'tendance
'fast – 'fasten	'dark – 'darken
'work – 'worker	'suffer –'sufferer
'waiter – 'waitress	'host – 'hostess
'beauty – 'beautiful	'duty – 'dutiful
'father – 'fatherhood	'brother – 'brotherhood
'coward – 'cowardice	'three – 'thrice
'fever – 'feverish	'white – 'whitish
sug'gest – sug'gestive	a'buse – a'busive
'home – 'homeless	'job – 'jobless
'certain – 'certainly	'former – 'formerly
ar'range – ar'rangement	a'chieve – a'chievement
'dark – 'darkness	'good – 'goodness
col'lect – col'lector	'elevate –'elevator
'friend – 'friendship	'citizen – 'citizenship
'laugh – 'laughter	'gang – 'gangster
e'xpose – e'xposure	'city – 'citizen
'greed – 'greedy	wealth – 'wealthy

Task

Mark primary stress in the following words:

limit(v), waiter, stupidity, rational, courteous, donation, fortunate, professional, management, repent, monkey, trouble, dissolve, minimum, parliament, grandmother, reason, seldom, fluently, precious, familiar, article, office, philosophy, romantic, translate, marginal, subtle, agree, prism, journey, surprise, digest, register, object, (n), perfect, behaviour, umbrella, admirable, inflation, postpone, angular, geographic, produce, equality, supplement, logical, official, rainbow, explanation, horizontal, annual, resonant, appropriate, vicinity, self-study, outcry, record (n), sentence, familiar, article, understand, transport, argument, contrast, frustrate, basement, tomato, factory, invention, popular, product, engineering, terrorists, allow, capacity, velocity, digital, artistic, fortunate, academician, career, record, contemplate, matches, anxious, politician, collect, disclose, than, severe, veteran, placard, haggard, lagoon, ransack.

5.6 Weak Forms in English

Sound is the smallest unit of spoken English. The combination of sounds makes syllables; some of them are stressed while some are unstressed. Similarly, in connected speech some words are stressed while some are not. Sometimes choice of the syllables receiving primary accent depends upon the message the speaker wants to convey. In English language prominent syllables occur at regular breaks in spite of the weak syllables occurring between them. This arrangement of weak and strong syllables imparts rhythm in speech.

5.6.1 What are Weak Forms?

English is very different in refinement and style as it has special, reduced 'weak' forms for many 'function' words, such as pronouns, prepositions, conjunctions, articles and auxiliary verbs. 'Weak forms' are the reduced pattern of their 'strong forms.' As the words indicate 'strong forms' are pronounced strongly with emphasis in such a way that they stand out of the rest while the weak forms are uttered weakly or neutrally in a flow. Most of the words, in English, have at least one stressed syllable; hence, they have no separate strong or weak forms. All words, which do have distinct strong and weak forms, are monosyllables and are usually function words. The main words with weak forms in 'RP' are: *a, am, an, and, are, as, at, be, been, but, can, could, do, does, for, from, had, has, have, he, her, him, his, me, must, of, shall, she, should, some, than, that, the, them, there, to, us, was, we, were, who, would, you.*

5.6.2 Use of Weak Forms

'Weak' forms are used in various styles of speech in most of the cases. First, their use adds to the general fluency of a speaker's English. However, it cannot be ignored that 'weak' forms are one of the major reasons for the non-native speakers to have difficulty in understanding conversational English spoken fluently by the native speakers. A good knowledge of the use of 'weak' forms, can be extremely helpful in understanding listening comprehensions, conversations and interactions and attaining fluency in spoken English. All these factors finally lead to the overall development of communication skills.

5.6.3 Use of 'Function' Words in Strong Forms

These 'function' words are used in strong forms only in exceptional circumstances:

1. When a 'function' word is stressed, emphasized or 'cited:
   → I said a journey *to* Delhi not *from* Delhi.
2. When these words occur at the end of a sentence or a phrase:
   → What are you looking *for*?
   → I know what I *am*.
3. When these words are uttered individually: 'and,' 'for,' 'than,' 'been', etc.

4. When the words like 'have,' 'had' 'do,' etc., are used as full verbs rather auxiliary verbs:
   → He does not *do* his work on time.
   → I don't *have* anything with me.
   → I have *had* my lunch.
5. When 'that' is used as a determiner not as a conjunction or 'there' is used as an adverb not as an empty subject:
   → *That* book is mine.
   → I went *there* to meet my old friend.

5.6.4 Strong and Weak Forms of the 'Function' Words

Word	Strong Form/s	Weak Form/s	Examples
1. Auxiliary Verbs			
Am	/æm/	/əm/	I am doing my work. /əm/
Are	/aː/	/ə/ (before consonants)	We are playing games. /ə/
	/aːr/	/ər/ (before vowels)	You are eating apples. /ər/
Is	/ɪz/	/ɪz/ (after /s/, /z/, /ʃ/, /ʒ/, /tʃ/ and /dʒ/)	The judge is in the court. / ɪz/
		/z/ (after/d/, /b/, /g/, /v/, /ð/, /m/, /n/, /ŋ/, /l/, /j/, /w/, /r/) and vowels	My friend is working in this firm./z/
		/s/ after/p/, /t/, /k/, /f/, /θ/ and /h/)	It is raining. /s/
Was	/wɒz/	/wəz/	The child was playing. /wəz/
Were	/wɜː/	/ wə/ (before consonants)	The boys were going to school./ wə/
	/wɜːr/	/ wər/ (before vowels)	They were accusing us. / wər/
Has	/h æz/	/h əz/ (initially)	Has he done his work? /həz/
		/ əz/ after /s/, /z/, /ʃ/, /ʒ/, /tʃ/ and /dʒ/)	My purse has been stolen. / əz/
		/z/ / (after/d/, /b/, /g/,/v/, /ð/, /m/, /n/, /ŋ/, /l/, /j/, /w/, /r/) and vowels	The bird has gone. /z/
		/s/ (after/p/, /t/, /k/, /f/, /θ/, and /h/)	The cat has killed the rat. /s/
Had	/ hæd/	/ həd/ (initially)	Had they finished their work? / həd/
		/d/ (after personal pronouns)	I had done it before he came. /d/
		/əd/ (elsewhere)	The children had gone home. /əd/

(Continued)

Word	Strong Form/s	Weak Form/s	Examples
Have	/hæv/	/həv/ (initially)	Have you done your work? / həv/
		/v/ (after personal pronouns)	We have done our duty. /v/
		/əv/elsewhere)	The players have played many games. /əv/
Do	/du: /	/də/ (before consonants)	How do you do? /də/
		/dʊ/ (before vowels)	Why do I do it? /dʊ/
Does	/dʌz/	/dəz/	He does it nicely. /dəz/
Can	/ kæn/	/kən/	Come on. You can do it. /kən/
Could	/kʊd/	/kəd/	I could ride a horse when I was young. /kəd/
Shall	/ʃæl/	/ʃəl/	We shall go home. /ʃəl/
Should	/ʃʊd/	/ʃəd/	We should obey the elders. /ʃəd/
Must	/mʌst/	/məs/ (before consonants)	They must leave now. /məs/
		/məst/ (before vowels)	We must eat nutritious food. /məst/
Will	/ wɪl/	/l/ (after personal pronouns and consonants except /l/)	I will do it now. /l/ The child will do it. /l/
		/əl/ (after vowels and /l/	The boy will do it but the girl will not. /əl/
Would	/wʊd/	/wəd/ (initially)	Would you please help me? /wəd/
		/d/ (after personal pronouns)	If I had money, I would buy this car. /d/
		/əd/ (elsewhere)	All would agree to the proposal. /əd/
2. Conjunctions			
And	/ænd/	/ən/	I bought a red and green ball. /ən/
As	/æz/	/əz/	Do as you please. /əz/
Than	/ðæn/	/ðən/	She is more intelligent than her brother. /ðən/
But	/bʌt/	/bət/	He is simple but honest. /bət/
That	/ðæt/	/ðət/	He said that he was lying. /ðət/
He	/hi: /	/hɪ/ (initially)	He is my old friend. /hɪ/
		/ɪ/ (elsewhere)	He said that he wanted a pen. /ɪ/

(Continued)

Word	Strong Form/s	Weak Form/s	Examples
3. Pronouns			
She	/ʃi:/	/ʃɪ/	She is doing MBA. /ʃɪ/
His	/hɪz/	/hɪz/ (initially)	His mobile is missing. /hɪz/
		/ɪz/ (elsewhere)	This is his book. /ɪz/
We	/wi:/	/wɪ/	We are playing a game. /wɪ/
Us	/ʌs/	/s/ (after 'let')	Let us go home. /s/
		/əs/ (elsewhere)	The teacher did not allow us to go. /əs/
You	/ju:/	/jʊ/	You are an honest person. /jʊ/
Me	/mi:/	/mɪ/	He asked me to go. /mɪ/
Who	/hu:/	/hʊ/ (initially)	Who is there? /hʊ/
		/u:/ (elsewhere)	The boy who came here yesterday is my brother. /u:/
Him	/hɪm/	/ɪm/	I gave him a book. /ɪm/
Her	/hɜ:/	/hə/ (initially)	Her project was very good. /hə/
		/ə/ (elsewhere)	Neelam is her cousin. /ə/
Them	/ðem/	/ðəm/	Let them do their work. /ðəm/
4. Prepositions			
At	/æt/	/ət/	Somebody is knocking at the door. /ət/
For	/f ɔːr/	/fər/ (before vowels)	This gift is for Anuj. /fər/
	/f ɔː/	/fə/ (before consonants)	This is for Kushal. /fə/
Of	/ɒv/	/əv/	The table is made of wood. /əv/
To	/tu:/	/tʊ/ (before vowels)	We are going to Amritsar. /tʊ/
		/tə/ (before consonants)	They are going to Delhi. /tə/
From	/frɒm/	/frəm/	I got this book from Meenu. /frəm/
5. Articles			
A	/eɪ/	/ə/	I have a beautiful watch. /ə/
An	/æn/	/ən/	She has an orange. /ən/

(Continued)

Word	Strong Form/s	Weak Form/s	Examples
The	/ðiː/	/ðə/ (before consonants)	The grapes are sour. /ðə/
		/ðɪ/ (before vowels)	The oranges are fresh. /ðɪ/
6. Miscellaneous Words			
Some	/sʌm/	/səm/	Give me some food. /səm/
Sir	/sɜː/	/sə/ (before consonants)	Sir Tomar teaches us English. /sə/
		/sər/ (before vowels)	Here comes Sir Abraham. /sər/
Be	/biː/	/bɪ/	I will be there on time. /bɪ/
Been	/biːn/	/bɪn/	The work has been done very well. / bɪn/
There	/ðeə/	/ðə/ (before consonants)	There were books on the shelf. /ðə/
		/ðər/ (before vowels)	There are few people in the hall. /ðər/

From the above-cited examples, it may be clearly observed that there is a pattern in changing the function words into weak forms. All the words which begin with the sound /h/—*her, his, he, has, have, had, who*—retain /h/ only at the initial position in a sentence, otherwise '/h/' is not pronounced. In the words ending in 'r'—*were, are, her, for, sir, there*—/r/ is pronounced when the word following them begins with a vowel sound. Moreover, long sounds /iː/ and /uː/ change into /ɪ/ and /ʊ/, respectively and the sounds – /æ/, /e/, /ɜː/, /ʌ/, /ɑː/, /eɪ/, /eə/ and /ʊ/ – are replaced by /ə/.

Task

Transcribe the following underlined words in weak forms using IPA symbols:

1. Tell him the truth.
2. Do you know the fact?
3. He is going to the station.
4. I will come in an hour.
5. I told you that I couldn't leave.
6. Harry is an honest worker.
7. He wants to have a cake.
8. I have just finished doing it.
9. She was the first one to leave.
10. Remember me to them.
11. I am going to do it now.
12. This is very true.
13. Can you present her with a bouquet?
14. He said that he was joking.
15. I would love to have a cup of tea.
16. He has gone to take a test.

5.7   Intonation

5.7.1   What is Intonation?

Intonation is the 'music' of a language, and is perhaps the most important element of a correct accent. When we speak, our vocal cords vibrate and the frequency of vibration decides the pitch of the voice. Sometimes, the pitch rises and sometimes it falls or remains level. The way the pitch of the voice varies forms intonation of a language. In other words, intonation is the word used for some pattern in speech which is related to rise and fall of the voice in speaking, affecting the meaning of what is being said.

5.7.2   Patterns of Intonations

Broadly speaking variation in tone may be of four types:

1. Falling Tone [↘] Pitch changes from a higher level to a low level.
2. Rising Tone [↗] Pitch rises from a low level to a high level.
3. Falling–rising Tone [ˇ] Pitch falls and rises.
4. Rising–falling Tone [ˆ] Pitch rises and falls.

The degree of change in the pitch depends upon the intention of the speaker or on the message to be communicated. Intonation is marked on the syllable on which the pitch rises or falls through the above-mentioned symbols.

5.7.3   Purpose of Intonation

Intonation is used with a purpose to convey the moods or the attitudes of the speaker to the listener. It indicates some grammatical forms such as interrogative sentences, orders or statements. The correct use of intonation keeps the speaker as well as the listener in tune with each other while the wrong use of intonation affects such harmony. The following moods and attitudes are generally conveyed by the use of the four intonations:

5.7.3.1   Falling Tone

The falling tone conveys the mood of casualness, aloofness, lack of interest and indifference. Sentences, which are uttered with this tone, are:

1. *Definite and complete statements:*
   I 'don't 'feel 'like ↘ doing it.
   The 'book is 'not ↘ interesting.
2. *Wh-questions asked casually:*
   'When did you ↘ do it?
   'Why are you ↘ calling him?
3. *Commands:*
   'Shut the ↘ door.
   'Don't for'get to ↘ take it from him.
4. *Invitations:*
   Come 'over for a cup of ↘ coffee.
   Why 'don't you 'come and ↘ stay with us?
5. *Exclamations:*
   What a 'beautiful ↘ scene!
   'How ↘ nice of you!

6. *All question tags forcing the listener to agree:*
   You'll ↘ do it, ↘ won't you?
   It 'isn't ↘ wrong, ↘ is it?
7. *Greetings (Cheerful and hearty):*
   Good ↘ morning.
   Good ↘ day.

5.7.3.2 Rising Tone

The rising tone conveys interest, concern, politeness, courtesy, surprise and encouragement. The following tone groups are generally used in rising tone:

1. *Yes/ No questions:*
   Has he ↗ come?
   Are you 'ready for the ↗ show?
2. *Statements proposed to ask questions:*
   He 'isn't ↗ doing it?
   You 'don't 'want to ↗ help him?
3. *Polite requests:*
   'Pass me the' book, ↗ please.
   'Please 'come and ↗ help me.
4. *Commands which sound like requests:*
   'Close the ↗ door.
   'Don't 'call me at ↗ late ,hours.
   'Do 'come in and sit ↗ down.
5. *Wh-Questions asked to show concern or friendliness:*
   'How is your ↗ son?
   'What will you ↗ do now?
6. *Repetition of Wh-questions* (repeating the listener's question or asking him/her to repeat certain information):
   ↗ What did I ,say?
   (It costs two thousand rupees.) ↗ How ,much?
7. *To show courtesy:*
   ↗ After you, 'ma'am.
   'Do ↗ come in 'sir.
8. *To encourage someone:*
   That's ↗ O.K.
   'Don't lose ↗ heart.
9. *Question tags seeking listener's confirmation:*
   You're ↘ coming with me. ↗ Aren't you?
   He'll 'finish it to ↘ day. ↗ Won't he?
10. *Greetings (Done as a duty):*
    Good ↗ evening.
    Good ↗ bye.

5.7.3.3 Falling–rising Tone

The falling–rising tone conveys doubt, reservation on the part of the speaker and polite inquiries. The following tone groups are generally used in falling–rising tone:

1. *Incomplete statements:*
   If you 'don't˅ finish it…
   If he 'doesn't be˅have…

2. *Statements intended to be a correction of the information*:
He 'teaches 'French. ⌄German.
He 'can't 'speak 'English⌄ fluently.
3. *Sentences expressing warning, reproach or concern*:
⌄Careful.
You should have 'shared it with your⌄ brother.
4. *Statements showing a kind of reservation on the part of the speaker*:
He is⌄ good. (but no one likes him.)
I'll 'do it to⌄morrow. (not today)

5.7.3.4 Rising–falling Tone

The rising–falling tone conveys enthusiastic agreement, wonder, appreciation or sarcasm. The following tone groups are generally used in rising–falling tone:

1. *Statements showing enthusiastic agreement*:
It was ter^rific.
Of ^course.
2. *Questions showing indignation, suspicion or mockery*:
'Will you be 'able to ^do it?
'What is he ^doing?
3. *Exclamations showing sarcasm or irony*:
'How ^ clever of you!
Oh, ^ really.
Good ^morning.
4. *Imperatives expressing haughtiness*:
'Go and 'break your ^ head.
'Come and 'see the ^ result.

Task

Mark intonation in the following sentences:

1. May God bless you!
2. When are you coming back?
3. Stop doing that.
4. May I please borrow your car?
5. We saw him yesterday.
6. He sings well. Doesn't he?
7. Are you leaving for Mumbai today?
8. You don't want to come with me?
9. How can you say a silly thing like that?
10. Can you prepare my assignment, please?
11. I am fond of chocolate cake.
12. Where does he live?
13. This is my new office.
14. I am satisfied.
15. You can drive the car, can't you?
16. Give me the money.
17. Are you sure he will help me?
18. What a nice weather!
20. Many happy returns!
21. When is the wedding?

Professional Interaction 6

In this unit

✓ Introduction

✓ Group Discussion

✓ Job Interviews

✓ Professional Presentation

"Regardless of the changes in technology, the market for well-crafted messages will always have an audience."

–Steve Burnett

6.1 Introduction

Speaking well has a striking effect on your professional and personal life. In today's world, where everyone is career oriented, we communicate at various levels for success in a profession. For procuring a job your knowledge, confidence, attitude and team skills are tested through group discussion where you interact with the other participants. Through interviews, you interact with your prospective employer. Once you get into a profession, you keep interacting professionally for expansion of business as well as for your personal growth. All professional exchanges of views are carried out with a purpose. Official meetings, presentations, conferences, seminars, etc., are some of the platforms where we all communicate, discuss or inform people from various professional backgrounds. In order to acquire techniques of professional interaction, the students should focus on the skills of group discussion, interview presentation.

6.2 Group Discussion

Group discussion is a specialized version of group interaction. It is usually carried out for the specific purpose of judging employability of the prospective candidates for a particular job. So, let us first see what group interaction means in general.

6.2.1 Group Interaction

A group interaction is a normal group activity that can be performed in a formal or an informal situation. Formal group interactions are carried out in offices, institutions, at meeting places or at recruitment centres through the activities like meetings, conferences, presentations and group discussions. Such official group interactions may take place within a small or a large group where the members sit together with a common purpose. On the other hand, an informal group interaction can crop up at any place like a college canteen, garden, hostel room, campus, classroom teaching, free periods, restaurants, waiting lounge, mess of an office, in a train or a bus or even at home. Why do people discuss? In an official situation, we interact to arrive at a common viewpoint, take a decision, exchange ideas, update information, seek a better perspective of an issue or to find out a common solution to a problem. Apart from these aims, we all interact for our basic need for socialization, entertainment or sometimes to pass our time. In short, we should exchange views for the development of a business, for personal relations as well as for the society and humanity as a whole.

6.2.2   What is a Group Discussion?

A group discussion, popularly abbreviated as GD, is one of the interactive group activities, with a specific objective of testing employability of the candidates for a particular job profile. It is an oral communication in a formal situation in which participants exchange their ideas and opinions with one another on a given topic, problem or situation, in a systematic manner to share information or to arrive at a common solution. It is an ideal exercise widely used as a type of personality test for evaluating many participants at a time. Normally, it is meant for those candidates who have qualified a written test and are supposed to be shortlisted for the final interview.

6.2.3   Relevance

Companies, today, select candidates not only on the basis of their knowledge but also, in some cases, perhaps more than that, on the basis of their soft skills. The ability to communicate effectively in a group as well as to lead the group successfully is the primary trait of a good personality that a company may require to carry out its business locally as well as globally. In this way, your overall personality has to be evaluated, and GD is an appropriate activity to judge a candidate on the above lines. Moreover, GD, has become a very popular recruitment drive, as it is time and cost effective and is conducted with ease without much hassle.

6.2.4   Purpose

The purpose of participating in a GD is manifold. The primary need, as has been mentioned earlier, is to judge the suitability of a candidate for a job. Apart from this, a regular practice of GD is helpful to:

1. Improve English-speaking skills and abilities.
2. Expand group interaction, persuasive skills, team spirit and leadership qualities.
3. Inculcate analytical ability and the habit to remain to the point.
4. Build up tolerance.
5. Update your knowledge and share the same with others.
6. Make an effort to come to a common viewpoint instead of confrontation.

6.2.5   The Process of Communication in a GD

Prior to the study of the methodology and the various components of a GD, let us first understand how a message flows in a GD. This will enable you to grasp the modalities of this type of interaction better. The message transmission in a GD follows a complex path and is not as direct as it is between a pair of a speaker and a listener. Ideally speaking, in a GD, an idea is encoded at one time, but it is simultaneously transmitted to multiple receivers. Each receiver decodes the message according to

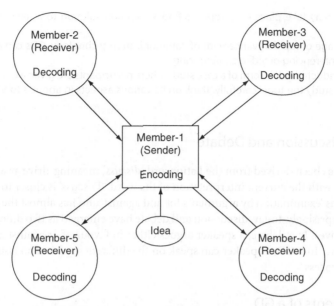

Figure 6.1 Process of communication in a GD.

his/her understanding. If the message is direct, clear and to the point and the receivers are in tune with the speaker, it is decoded perfectly and helps the discussion achieve the purpose of arriving at a common viewpoint. However, if the message lacks language competency, clarity and conciseness, it may get distorted or interpreted differently by different participants. As a result, the feedbacks received are conflicting and this may result in a chaotic situation. Such a communication becomes a barrier to the smooth flow of a GD. You can observe the complexity of the message flow from Figure 6.1.

6.2.6 Mechanism and Formats of GD

Group discussion is a group interaction within a small group, ranging from 5 to 10 members. The participants are asked to sit in a circle or a semicircle, in front of a circular or a semicircular table with their chest members. The evaluator announces the topic and the total time given for the discussion may vary from 15 to 20 minutes. He/she observes the dialogue closely and evaluates the participants to qualify for the next round, may be for the final round of the GD or for the interview. This is the most commonly adopted format of a GD. However, the observer may opt for different formats by using novel ideas for discussion:

1. A topic is declared beforehand or a group is asked to choose a topic from the given ones. The partici-pants may get 2 to 5 minutes to think.
2. In the usual format, anyone may initiate the discussion but a particular candidate may also be asked to express his/her views in brief initially, and others may follow him/her one by one so that the members may get acquainted with one another's stands.
3. In the same way, any one of the members may come forward and conclude the GD or the participants may be asked to summarize it one by one.
4. The group may be asked to decide the procedure of the GD mutually or it may be given to them beforehand.

5. The discussion may take place on a topic to find a common solution to a given problem or a case study.
6. In the modern age of rapid advancement of communication technology, GDs can also be conducted through teleconferencing or video conferencing.
7. GDs may be conducted in the form of a case study where participants are given a case on a topic in written form. They study the topic carefully, think on its various aspects in about 3 to 5 minutes and then discuss it.

6.2.7 Group Discussion and Debate

The word 'discuss' has been derived from the Latin word '*discuss*', meaning 'drive away' or 'declare', and it has nothing to do with the current interpretation of the word. 'Discuss' is closer to the Latin '*discussionem*' which means 'examination by arguments for and against' and has almost the same meaning as that of a 'debate'. Surprisingly, today, discussion and debate have emerged as two different formats with two different objectives. In a debate, a speaker argues either in favour of or against a topic and so it is competitive in nature. In a GD, a speaker can speak on the different angles of an issue. It is basically a supportive group process.

6.2.8 Components of a GD

The success of a GD depends upon how far the members have worked together for the common goal of a group consensus. No doubt, many group interactions fail as they are not able to reach a common viewpoint. It is, therefore, important for us to know the following components of an effective GD:

→ Personality
→ Communication skills
→ Group dynamics
→ Leadership qualities
→ Knowledge

Here, it has to be noted that these components are complementary to one another. Their individual merit should not be judged through the order of the sequence given above. In fact, their importance is relative, depending upon the preference of one component to the other by a specific employer. The characteristics of these components are discussed here along with the strategies for an effective GD.

6.2.9 Strategies for an Effective GD

6.2.9.1 Personality

A good first impression of a pleasing personality helps win the attention of the examiner. Personality manifestation is an important component of a GD as it gives others a complete picture of your attitude, confidence and team spirit. Personality is judged on the following lines:

1. Dress and appearance: Dress and appearance matter a lot in creating a first impression about yourself even before you have spoken a single word. You should be careful about your dress as well as your looks and follow these tips:
   → Your dress should be sober, neat and well stitched. It need not be costly, new or of latest fashion as newly acquired clothes can make you self-conscious, cause discomfort and affect your performance. A well-dressed participant feels confident.

→ Your footwear should be formal, polished and clean with socks drawn tight on your legs and not falling down.

→ Hair should be cut neatly in a style that suits your personality.

→ You have to mind your nails if they are overgrown.

→ Take care of personal hygiene.

→ Dark trousers, a light-coloured matching shirt with a sober tie may be an ideal dress for both boys and girls. However, girls may go for the other decent official dresses too.

2. Body Language: Body language is a non-verbal communication signal that you as a participant, transmit to the other members of the group. Your body cues help others judge your confidence, openness, composure, cooperativeness, friendliness, alertness, insecurity, nervousness, positive or negative attitude and so forth. Some of the important non-verbal pointers that you should try to adopt are as follows:

→ Maintain eye contact with the listeners as well as the speaker and do not look here and there.

→ Never address or look at the panel of the observers.

→ Exhibit cheerful and friendly expressions.

→ Let your eyes radiate confidence.

→ Do meaningful hand gestures.

→ Do not put your hands in your pockets or sit with your hands crossed.

→ Do not fiddle with things such as pen, wristwatch, bangle, button, tie and hair.

→ Sit erect and neither slouch nor sit with your legs crossed.

→ Do not touch other participants of the group while interaction is going on.

→ Do not use aggressive body language.

→ Above all, do not get conscious of your non-verbal signals. "Be energetic outside but composed from within", is the mantra that helps you exhibit a positive body language.

3. Behaviour: Your public behaviour is again a judgement of your personality. The first impression on the viewers is affected by your etiquettes too. What you give so shall you get. If you show good manners, you get the same in return. This is beneficial for the whole group as well. The following etiquettes should be adopted in a GD:

→ Be courteous, polite and helpful to the co-participants.

→ Be assertive but maintain politeness.

→ Get involved in the discussion and do not be indifferent.

→ Be appreciative and considerate.

→ Refute/oppose/disagree with others' views respectfully.

→ Be ready to admit your mistake.

→ Shake hands with co-participants at the start as well as at the end.

6.2.9.2   Communication Skills

The ability to express your knowledge orally in an effective way is a necessary requirement of a GD. As most of the GDs today are carried out in English, you should possess good communication skills in English that will help you speak confidently and express your views convincingly. Remember, during the discussion your speaking skills are judged minutely. Adopt the following strategies to attain effective speaking and fluency:

→ Have good group-listening skills for effective participation and leadership.

→ Use simple and appropriate words with the right pronunciation.

→ Use grammatically correct sentences, concise and unambiguous expressions.

→ Use simple language without exaggeration and flowery expressions.

→ Maintain clarity of expression for the right understanding by the listeners.

→ Speak fluently but with a moderate speed, pauses and volume.

→ Use tone variation and do not let your speech become monotonous.

→ Tone should be pleasing and not commanding.
→ Do not interact just in monosyllables such as "yes" or "no."
→ Do not use non-word fillers such as 'you know'; 'you see'; 'like'; 'well,' etc., too often.
→ Filler-sounds like 'aaaaaa.....' 'eeerrr' and 'ummmm.....' must be checked.
→ GD is an official interaction, do not use slangs.
→ Use linking phrases to link arguments.
→ Make use of polite expressions to disagree or to interrupt.
→ Avoid using technical terms. Explain complex concepts in simple language.

6.2.9.3 Group Dynamics

Employers, today, search for self-motivated candidates who can work in a team-orientated environment. So, group-management skills are a must for the participants of a GD. The organizers test you whether you can get along with the other people or whether you are a self-obsessed person. For this reason, participants have to understand that in a GD they will all succeed or fail together. If a member is not contributing, he/she will not only hurt himself/herself but also the group as a whole. You can manage a group well by using the following tactics:

→ Generate agreement on a common viewpoint and every member should work for it.
→ Be adaptable and adjust with the other members.
→ Show positive attitude towards others' views even if you do not agree with them.
→ Do not indulge in needless talks and private dialogue with your neighbour as it may distract others.
→ Accept criticism sportingly.
→ Motivate other participants to contribute and to be cooperative.
→ Deal with hostile members and conflicts tactfully; otherwise, the whole team will be a loser.
→ To join the discussion, drive yourself in at the earliest suitable moment of a pause, when a speaker has completed his/her arguments or when a speaker is needlessly prolonging the arguments or the discussion is in a state of confusion and chaos or when you find a weak speaker unable to contribute.
→ Never enter the discussion with a disagreement. First agree with the speaker and then present your views.
→ Do not make personal remarks or show anger.
→ Have a shared leadership as there is no elected leader in a GD.

6.2.9.4 Leadership Qualities

Employers look not only for team workers but also for leaders; so, in every GD they seek an element of leadership. They observe the participants very closely and pinpoint those who have good leadership traits. The success or failure of a GD depends a lot on the utilization of the elements of leadership. All GDs provide their participants with numerous opportunities to exhibit their leadership qualities as well as to steer the discussion to its success. Every member should try to be the first to grab the chances to show his/her leadership traits. Some of the important leadership qualities are as follows:

→ Persuade the members to agree on the format of the GD if it has not been announced by the observer.
→ Take an initiative to start the discussion and to promote maximum participation.
→ Maintain a relaxed atmosphere.
→ Handle chaotic situations confidently without losing your temper.
→ Be empathetic and respectful to other's views and beliefs.
→ Sum up the previous speaker's point before expressing your own views or asking the next one to speak.
→ Encourage reticent members to contribute.
→ Make an effort to keep the discussion on the track of the given topic.

→ Be impartial and objective.
→ Look at the group as a whole and monitor each member.
→ Neither allow any one member to speak for long nor dominate the GD.
→ Steer the group to a common viewpoint.
→ Keep track of the allotted time.
→ Do not lose heart if you are not able to initiate. Try to be the first to give a balanced sum up emphasizing agreements to indicate the common viewpoint.

In a nutshell, there is a lot of scope to show team spirit and leadership qualities. With your knowledge, tactfulness and good interactive skills you can always make your presence felt.

6.2.9.5 Knowledge

Knowledge is power but ignorance is surely not bliss, especially during the recruitment activities such as GDs and interviews. If one lacks knowledge, other skills of GD are meaningless. On the contrary, the presence of knowledge strengthens each one of them. The initial good impression on the observers will soon wither away, if you are not able to justify your stand with the latest facts and knowledge. If you have a good stock of information, you are confident, more fluent and relevant. To achieve this aim, you must read a lot and gather facts from different sources. At the same time, you have to keep in mind that knowledge is not static. Facts and information keep on changing; so, you should always try to update yourself. Support your ideas with facts and do not bluff if you are not aware of certain facts or if you are proved wrong. On the contrary, show eagerness to enhance your knowledge. If you have no information on the topic, listen to others, analyze the ideas quickly, take a stand and enter the GD at the first chance.

6.2.9.6 Taking a Stand

The techniques discussed above in various points under the heading 'Strategies for an Effective Group Discussion', are practical tips that you should adopt during a GD. However, some useful dos and don'ts, that could not be included in this part, are given as follows:

→ You are free to take stands that may be for or against or you can take both. Stick to your point with conviction; otherwise, it will reflect indecisiveness, lack of confidence as well as knowledge. Only in a rare situation you may alter your stand tactfully, if a member gives a solid counter-argument which is difficult to negate.

6.2.10 Preparation of a Group Discussion

If you are participating in a GD, it is important to make sure you're prepared beforehand. Well-prepared participants communicate their ideas to one another confidently and the discussion blossoms naturally and spontaneously. On the other hand, if they are not prepared, the purpose of the discussion is defeated.

To make sure that you are prepared for GDs, there are a number of guidelines you should follow. You should be aware of the issues that are being taken for GDs currently, read a lot about them, gather information on them and their past links as well. Do regular net surfing for facts and watch informative TV programmes. The tips given in this chapter are very practical but they need a lot of practice for their best use. Carry out mock GDs regularly with your friends as well as with those whom you do not know. Record or video shoot your GD for analysis. Groom your personality to develop the required soft skills. Work on your communication skills. Learn group dynamics by interacting with groups informally also. Remember that a GD cannot be prepared overnight; rather, it needs careful grooming, thorough study and whole-hearted effort.

6.2.11   Range of Topics

The range of topics for a GD is wide and a long list of topics can be prepared. However, we can roughly classify them for our convenience into seven categories. Some category-wise examples are as follows:

1. Current: Corruption is the price we pay for democracy/Cut-off marks for IIT entrance should not be increased from 60% to 80%.
2. Social: Euthanasia (mercy killing) should be legalized/Cricket is overemphasized in India.
3. Political: Value-based politics is the need of the hour/Women's reservation is the call of the day.
4. Economic: The current economic recession has not affected India's economy/Sixth pay commission is a burden on the government.
5. Management: Women are better managers than men/Rush for MBA is really a rush for big money.
6. Abstract/creative: The wheel is turning round and round/When I woke up in the morning I saw......./A white dot/Blue grass.
7. Case studies: A swine flu case; Downfall of an xyz company.

6.2.12   Some Useful Phrases

The success of a GD, to a large extent, depends on your communication skills. You should use a variety of appropriate and polite phrases to agree, disagree, support opinions, give opinions, motivate, etc. The category-wise list of some useful phrases to be used in a GD is as follows:

1. To initiate a GD: Well friends, may I have your attention please?/My dear friends, we have been given the task of performing a GD on.../Hello everybody, can I have your attention for a minute...? We should begin the discussion now/shall we start?

2. Asking for Views: What do you think/feel about this?/Well, sir, do you have anything to say?/ Does anybody have any comments to add?/Ma'am have you any views on this?/Well friends any more suggestions?

3. Giving Views: Friends, I believe that.../According to me.../I think personally it is.../I'm pretty convinced that.../As far as I'm concerned.../I have no doubt in saying that.../I think it is perfectly clear to everybody that.../From my point of view/You may be right but the way I see it is a bit different/ It appears to me/I might agree with you but it seems to me....

4. Showing Agreement: My friend, I completely agree/I'm sure it's an excellent idea/That's a great proposal, isn't it?/Of course, you are right/Yes, why not?/Yes, certainly/Exactly/I agree with you/I think that is fine/Well said, sir or madam/Sounds OK.

5. Showing Disagreement: My friend, I'm sorry, I don't agree/Excuse me dear, I disagree/I beg your pardon friend but I feel we all differ/You may have a valid point but I have a different view/Of course, not/I'm afraid, this is not acceptable/I appreciate but....

6. Expressing Common View Point: OK friends, thank you very much for contributing your precious arguments. In the end, we are happy to say that we all agree to some major points like.../I think that is the best solution/We all completely favour this/There may be some dissimilarities in our thinking but that is quite human, isn't it?

6.2.13   Evaluation Process

Evaluation of the candidates in a GD is normally done taking into consideration its various components of personality, oral communication skills, leadership qualities, group dynamics and knowledge.

Nonetheless, the assessment can be company specific as the observers may be looking for some particular traits in the prospective candidates.

Task

1. What is a GD? Discuss its relevance and purpose.
2. Elaborate the various components of a GD.
3. Write short notes on:
    (a) Communication process involved in a GD
    (b) Various formats of a GD
4. Perform a mock GD with your friends/colleagues on the following topics:
    (a) Justice delayed is justice denied
    (b) Examinations should be abolished
    (c) Female foeticide is a crime against God

6.3 Job Interviews

A job interview is a systematic and planned method of oral interaction between an employer and a prospective candidate to gather relevant information about the applicant for a specific job position or promotion.

6.3.1 Introduction

The word 'interview', which was formerly used as *'enterview'*, originated from a 16th century French word *'entrevoir'*, which means 'to see each other'. The original meaning of the word appears to be very close to its modern context that considers an employment interview as an interaction between the interviewee and the interviewer. The purpose of an interview may vary from seeking opinions to interrogation, from recruitment and promotions to admissions. Print and electronic media journalists interview politicians, film stars, sports personnel, etc., as well as common man to gather information or to seek their opinion. A doctor interviews a patient, police interrogate a suspect, students are interviewed in viva voce tests and an employer interacts with an employment seeker for different purposes.

6.3.2 Job Interviews

In the current professional environment, job interviews have become much more complex and challenging than what they used to be earlier. The reason is the growing competition, changing demands of the job market and focus on the personality traits of the candidates. Normally, you have to go through a four-tier system of selection where short listing of applicants takes place through:

→ Screening of resumes
→ Written aptitude test
→ Group discussion
→ Interview

Experts consider interviews as the most apt method to judge the suitability of candidates for a particular job. There may be a single interview to complete the selection process or multiple rounds may also be used to shortlist a large number of candidates or to carry out a careful selection for a challenging and demanding job. Unlike a GD, a job interview is a planned exercise with a purpose to achieve the desired results. At the same time, it is conducted with a little informality so as to motivate candidates to feel free and to express their best.

6.3.3   Myths about Job Interviews

Most people believe that job interviews are frightening situations in which they will be grilled by the probing questions of the interviewers. You need not worry as, in the current scenario, job interviews are all about making the best matches in the current scenario. It is no longer a one-sided affair; rather, it is a kind of conversation with a specific purpose. Although, the interaction takes place between the interviewer and the interviewee through questioning, the challenge of judgement is equally on both the sides. Hence, job interviews require certain skills that an applicant should acquire along with becoming aware of their different types and formats to improve his/her chances of success.

6.3.4   Objectives

The primary objective of all the job interviews, as the name suggests, is to ascertain the suitability of a candidate for a particular job profile. There are secondary goals as well depending on the type of interview, requirements of the company and its future prospects. The interviewers, especially human resource managers, aim to judge a job-seeker's personality, attitude, ability to put across his/her ideas, sense of values, etiquettes, character, mental stability, honesty, problem-solving skills, strengths, weaknesses, knowledge, etc. The secondary objectives play a crucial role in taking an interviewer to the final aim of recruiting a suitable candidate.

6.3.5   Venues

Traditional venues of the job interviews have been the human resource departments and the recruitment offices of the companies. Today, HR personnel move out of the four walls of their offices and visit campuses of various universities and institutions. This is cost effective and gives them an opportunity to evaluate students in the natural environment of their institutions. Lunch interviews in hotels have become quite popular as they help the recruiters test personality traits of the applicants in an informal environment. Rapid advancement in the field of information technology has given rise to telephone and videoconferencing interviews that can be attended while sitting at home also.

6.3.6   Types of Job Interviews

There are different types of job interviews. Employers use them according to the requirement of the vacant position and their convenience. They choose the type of interview also according to the stage of selection of a prospective candidate. The *modes* of interviews frequently used by the companies today are:

1. **Traditional Interviews:**   A traditional interview is a face-to-face interview taken by one or maximum two interviewers trying to evaluate abilities of the applicants, their knowledge, oral skills and manners. Such interviews are generally structured wherein the experts ask the same type of questions in the same style. Their questions are broad based such as, 'Why do you want to work for this company?' and 'Tell me about your strengths and weaknesses,' etc. Success or failure in the interview is often based more on your knowledge and ability to communicate than on your attitude.

2. **Panel Interviews:**   In panel interviews, the interviewers sit in a panel of three to eight members. The candidate is supposed to answer their questions that are shot at him/her randomly from different members. It is a test of nerves and patience as well as knowledge when so many pairs of probing eyes are looking intently at one person. Each expert may limit his/her queries to a specific aspect of evaluation.

3. Behavioural Interviews: Behavioural job interviews are based on the concept that past is the best indicator of the future behaviour. It provides insight on how a candidate's mind works. You are made to recall some specific instances based on your experience, such as: 'Tell us about an experience when you failed to achieve a goal'/'Give us a specific example when you managed several projects at a time,' etc.

While answering such questions, speak the truth and do not make any guesses. Be very specific about the incident and the year or the month of its happening. It would be better if you can recall the date and time too. Tell them what your reaction was and how you managed to deal with it successfully. You will have several follow-up questions. Students facing campus interviews and the recent passouts should focus on class projects and college-level group situations. Hobbies and volunteer work may also provide examples.

4. Situational Interviews: In situational interviewing, a candidate may be asked to respond to a specific situation he/she may face on the job. The questions are specifically designed to draw out the best of a person's analytical and problem-solving skills as well as the way to handle them at a short notice. Situational interviews are similar to behavioural interviews, except the fact that the latter give thrust on a past experience while the former focus on a hypothetical situation. In a situational interview, the expert may ask: 'How would you handle a discontented employee in your department who has made a habit of arriving late to work and causing problems during the day?' whereas, in a behaviour interview the same question may be, 'Give an example from the past when you have handled a difficult person.'

5. Stress Interviews: Today, all of us have to learn to live with long and hectic official schedules and to balance them with our domestic responsibilities. Stress interviews are ideal to find out how a person handles pressure situations. The experts may test behaviour of the candidates in a busy environment; question them about handling heavy workloads, parallel projects and conflicting situations. Moreover, such interviews may take place late nights, the interviewees are deliberately kept waiting and the interviewer usually behaves in an uninterested or hostile manner. He may avoid eye contact, yawn, roll his/her eyes or sigh at the candidate's answers, interrupt, keep on eating something, take phone calls, or ask questions in an insulting, sarcastic or challenging tone. The goal is to irritate you purposely and to test how you cope up with such conditions. Candidates may also be asked to deliver a presentation to both, the selection panel as well as the other candidates, perform role-plays or participate in games. This is obviously stressful and is therefore useful to know how the candidate will perform under the similar circumstances. For example: "If you caught your boss cheating on his expenses, what would you do?"/"(A deep sigh) Well, if that's the best answer you can give … (shakes head), we cannot help you out."/"I don't feel like we're getting to the crux of the matter here. Start again…tell me what you *really* mean" The best way to deal with stress-giving questions is to generalize the process and be relaxed. Once you realize that there is nothing personal behind the interviewer's approach, it is easier to handle the questions.

6. Technical Interviews: Technical Interviews are usually carried out prior to the HR interviews to test the basic understanding of the specific trade. Although companies do train their employees after hiring, they expect them to have basic technical knowledge of the particular field. Incomplete or incorrect information indicates that the applicants do not take things seriously. So, be thorough with your subjects and have the latest updates on them.

7. Telephone Interviews: Telephone interviews take place if a recruiter wishes to shortlist a large number of candidates or a job applicant is at a significant distance from the location of the hiring company. It saves cost and time. Along with this, it may be a test of your telephonic skills as well. Take the call of the interviewer at a quiet place, with your resume and other notes highlighted for your ready reference. If you have to make a call, do it within 24 hours of receiving your prospective employer's calling you. Telephone them at a time convenient to them. Listen carefully, and speak with energy, proper expressions and interest. Treat the call as important as a face-to-face interview.

8. Lunch or Dinner Interviews: Companies use lunch or dinner interviews to test the informal side of a candidate's personality. How would you behave at a business lunch or dinner? The best way to deal with this situation is to take it as an official meal by observing all the protocols of a formal get together. Do not get too informal with your prospective bosses and colleagues and give them their due respect. Do not consume alcohol. Take it as an opportunity to show your best conduct.

6.3.7   Preparation for Job Interview

Even before you have received your interview call letter, you should start preparing for your interview systematically. It may not be your first interview; still proper homework helps you win more than half the battle. This will boost your confidence level required to support your candidature and give you the desired strength to deal with anxiety as well as with stress questions. The best jobseekers not only prepare answers to typical interview questions but also anticipate the type of interview expected. The guidelines given as under will help you prepare for your interview:

Analyze Yourself: Start your homework with self-analysis to explore yourself as well as your past. Identify your technical and personal skills. Know your strengths—at least three—relevant to the requirement of the job. Rehearse speaking on them and relate them to the requirement of the job. Explore your weaknesses too, find out how you utilize them positively and what you are doing to overcome them. Be sure about your short and long term career goals and how you plan to achieve them. Spot your special interests and hobbies. Assemble evidences on how and what you have achieved in the past—proof puts you ahead. This will assist you in dealing with behavioural interviews (for details see Section 6.3.6).

Research the Organization: Once you have analyzed yourself, try to learn as much as you can about the organization, its history, management, priorities, products, standing, competitors, work culture, hiring and promotion policies, training programmes and find out what it expects the most from its ideal employees. Your awareness will surely reveal your initiative along with your genuine interest in the organization and will put you in a strong position. Tailor your skills, interests and talents to company's requirements and rehearse speaking on them so that you may satisfy all the queries in this regard. Remember you have to market yourself as the best product and sell what the buyer is buying. Don't forget to evaluate your future with the company and the job profile.

Develop your Soft Skills: Personality traits, etiquettes and oral skills in English are the basic requisites for various types of job interviews. Be a "can do" person. As a daily exercise, practice being more optimistic by giving a positive turn to events and situations you would normally regard as negative. In this way, you will raise your level of optimism. Get into an enthusiastic and alert mindset. Do not have baseless fear about failure or success as you are not a victim rather an active participant in a healthy dialogue. To deal with stress questions, develop the habit of remaining calm in real life pressure situations. Regular yoga and meditation will help you achieve this goal.

Brush up your Oral Skills: A job interview is also a test of your oral skills in English. If they need improvement, do it without delay as they take time to develop. Practice expressing yourself in English by speaking for 1 or 2 minutes on various topics. Study 'Learning Strategies for Effective Communication' dealt with in this book at 1.5. Build up effective telephoning skills for telephone interviews.

Use the Right Body Language and Manners: You can groom them by practicing during the mock interviews. (Study them in detail in Section 6.3.8.).

Prepare an Attractive Resume: Your resume should be up to date and presentable. You should be honest about the information given in it and should be able to satisfy the queries on each point. At the same time, your resume should include and highlight all the skills, achievements and qualities required for the particular post. Look at the weak areas of your CV and prepare yourself to give positive answers of those points.

Be Thorough with the Basics: You should be thorough with the basic concepts of your trade in addition to their practical applications, especially, in relation to your job profile. Read a lot, surf net for facts, watch informative programmes on TV, discuss with friends and teachers to have knowledge of the current affairs and keep yourself in touch with the happenings around you.

Rehearse your Answers: Practice answering the possible questions from 30 seconds to 2 minutes in front of a mirror or with a friend. Don't try to memorize answers word for word, jot down a few key words for each answer.

Carry out Mock Interviews: Participate in mock interviews to have a virtual experience of the interview. You can audio- or video record the sessions for analysis and improvement.

6.3.8 Appearing for an Interview

When you have prepared for your job interview properly and have gained confidence, study the various techniques to be used for making a successful appearance in a job interview. Remember that the first impression creates a lasting impact on the mind of the interviewers. During the interview, you are assessed on the grounds of dress, appearance, etiquettes, attitude, body language, oral communication skills, knowledge, experience and achievements. All these can be summed up under three major heads:

→ Personality
→ Oral communication skills
→ Knowledge

These factors are important individually as well as jointly to judge the suitability of an applicant for a specific job profile. Go through the following tips for facing an interview and make your preparations according to that.

6.3.8.1 Personality

→ Make a good first impression by wearing a conventional, sober and dignified dress. Avoid wearing new clothes. Wear dark trousers, light matching shirt and a tie. Girls can go for other decent official dresses too. A well-fitting dress is good to boost your confidence. Be well groomed and wear sober, official and polished footwear with socks drawn tight on your legs. Hair and nails should be neatly cut. Do not use clunky or flashy jewellery. Avoid strong perfumes and cigarettes.
→ Be punctual. Nonpunctuality can cost you your job. Reach the venue half-an-hour earlier to remain calm and confident. If you are getting late, inform the office.
→ While waiting for your turn, after the interview and during lunch or dinner show your best manners and converse cheerfully. Use your mobile phone sparingly and switch it off as soon as your turn comes.

Stand up to meet people. Do not boast, as somebody from the company might be observing you. Do not smoke or eat things like chewing gum, etc. Most important thing: do not argue or misbehave with the receptionist as he/she might be deliberately testing you as per the instructions of his/her boss.

→ Self-confidence comes automatically when you are well prepared, your personality is properly groomed for an interview, you have good oral skills and an impressive past record. In spite of this, you may feel nervous, as it is natural due to some negative thoughts of failure, etc. Think positively and try to divert your mind. One option is to do backward counting and this will surely calm you down.

→ Walk into the room with straight back, confident gait and pleasant expressions on your face. Greet the interviewers cheerfully and smartly maintaining eye contact with all members of the panel in one glance. Wish the lady members first, if any, and then the gentlemen. Shake hand firmly but not aggressively, and do it only if you are offered the same.

→ You should not sit unless asked or should seek permission. Sit erect at the front half of the chair, slightly leaning forward. Do not drag the chair, if required, lift it gently without making any sound. Put your arms on your lap. If the chair has arms do not put your elbows on them. Do not sit cross legged, place your legs parallel to each other. You should not wrap your arms around the chest as it indicates a personality that does not like to open up.

→ Carry a good and clean leather folder containing fresh copies of your resume and updated documents arranged chronologically. Put the folder on the table in front of you or keep it on your lap if the table is not provided. Do not hand over your folder unless you are asked to do so.

→ Maintain eye contact while speaking as well as listening and do not stare at the interviewers. Do not look here and there as it shows lack of interest, diffidence or short attention span. Give equal response to all the members even if a few of them are actively participating. Look at all the interviewers while answering a question, even though it may be asked by one. Most of the interviewers may feel offended and lack of eye contact has been proved one of the major causes of the failure of a job interview. While listening, show your reaction by nodding or making listening sounds as "um" or "yes".

→ Do not avoid gestures; rather, use them meaningfully.

→ Be energetic externally but remain calm and poised from inside. Do not be self-conscious.

→ Questions on strengths and weaknesses are important to assess your personality. Remember, they can be eliminator questions as well. So, deal with them tactfully.

→ Always be eager to learn and let the interviewers feel that you are ready to update yourself.

→ Follow the basic etiquettes while speaking—do not touch your hair, shake legs or fiddle with your neck tie, pen, earrings, rings or bangles. Lolling in the chair, putting your hands in the pocket or over your mouth, cracking your knuckles, etc., should be strictly avoided because all such non-verbal clues send negative signals.

→ Do not exaggerate your present salary. A good interviewer can estimate your income fairly well.

→ Do a follow up of your interview by sending a short note of thanks within 24 hours reminding them of key points from the interview.

→ Develop a chart for keeping a track of your performance, your strengths and weaknesses during the interview and the areas where you need improvement.

6.3.8.2 Oral Communication Skills

A candidate's manner of talking affects the first impression created by his/her dress, appearance and body signals. Good oral skills comprise both content as well the way of presentation and experts can judge your personality even by your way of communicating. So, keep in mind the following guidelines to communicate effectively in a job interview.

→ Make use of the tips for developing your interactive skills in English that you have learnt during your preparation sessions.

→ Be a good listener and save yourself from the embarrassing situation of saying 'pardon' or 'sorry' again and again in addition to help you understand the questions correctly as well as answer them promptly.

→ Speak carefully, clearly and confidently.

→ Your tone matters a lot. Speak in an enthusiastic tone––few things are more disheartening to the interviewers than the lack of enthusiasm. Interest in the candidate is automatically lost. Talk in a natural conversational tone and it should not appear that you have crammed your contents.

→ Be fluent but do not speak fast. Do not use non-word fillers such as "you know", "like" repeatedly. Check the use of sounds such as "aaaa…..", "urrr…" "ummm" by giving pauses whenever you feel like uttering such sounds. The occasional pause will make you sound confident plus your habit of thinking before speaking.

→ Do not speak too loud or too soft. Modulate the pitch of your voice. Drop the pitch of your voice on the last syllable of the final sentence of your answer.

→ Speak to the point, be brief and avoid speaking for more than 1 minute continuously. Talking too much may expose your weak points. At the same time, neither give one-word answers, nor interact in mono-syllabic words such as "yes" or "no".

→ Use correct pronunciation. Speak naturally but with correct accent. Artificial accent will never impress the interviewers.

→ Use simple but appropriate words. Do not use jargons or flowery language. Use plain and direct sentences. To describe a trait of your personality, make use of a crisp phrase occasionally, for example, 'I take failures as a stepping stone towards success.'

→ When asked about your personal strengths, speak about them convincingly. Relate them to the requirement of the job; give examples when and where you have demonstrated them and how you have developed them.

→ Regarding your weak points do not say—'I'm weak in this…' say 'I've little difficulty with …' Choose a weakness that you can disguise as your strength and relate it to your job profile. For instance, you can say: 'I like to work with a sense of urgency but everyone is not always on the same wavelength.' Or you can state a weakness that is related to your habit not to your job directly, for example, 'Sometimes, when the pressure of work is too much, I forget certain things.' Further, convey what steps you have taken to overcome this problem like 'I maintain a diary' or 'I don't leave any work pending.' Best strategy—strengths related to your job—weakness related to day-to-day life.

→ Do not speak against your last company or boss. It conveys a negative picture about you.

→ Be assertive but do not forget that you have to be polite as well. Be tactful but don't argue. If you disagree, you may say "Sir, I think you're right/I respect your views but I think a bit differently."

→ Show your appreciation for the interview, thank for the opportunity given to you to have a fruitful interaction and show your keenness for the position.

6.3.8.3   Knowledge

Along with evaluating your personality and judging your communication skills, interviewers test your knowledge, which is also a key factor in ascertaining your suitability for a particular job. The knowledge part includes your domain knowledge as well as your awareness of things around you. The company is interested in testing your subject knowledge, which shows how serious you have been as a student. Your extent of information of the world around you is an indication of your eagerness to know facts and it definitely gives you an edge over the other candidates. So, read a lot to collect information and brush up your subjects thoroughly. However, it is not possible to know each and every thing. In case you do not know a particular answer, be honest and say 'I'm sorry, I need to check it, sir. I will be grateful if you kindly tell me the answer.'

6.3.9   Potential Interview Questions

You have to prepare thoroughly for the answers of the probable questions, and this will surely benefit you a lot. Remember, no preparation can anticipate thousands of possible variations on these questions. Furthermore, questions asked in an interview are not many and most of the questions arise from the answers given by the applicant. The important thing is to develop your strategies for each answer. Memorize a few key words that let you recall your answer to the various questions instantly. The following are some of the commonly asked questions in different types of interviews. Go through them and tailor your honest responses relating them to your job profile:

→ Tell us about yourself/What are your major strengths?/What are your major weaknesses?
→ Why do you want to leave your present job?/What is your job profile?
→ Why should we hire you?/How are you different from others?/What makes you unique?
→ You have been leaving jobs frequently, why?/Why have you been out of job for a long time?
→ What are your short-term and long-term goals?/Who has been your ideal person/role model and why?
→ Describe your ideal company/Why do you want to join our company?
→ How do you pass your free time? What good books have you read recently?
→ Tell me one head line of today's newspaper.
→ Was there a situation when your work was criticized?/What is the toughest decision you have ever had to make?
→ Give us instances where you have displayed team spirit and leadership qualities?/Are you a leader or a follower?
→ Critically assess yourself on a scale of 1 to 10/How can you improve your career prospects?
→ How do you take failure and success?
→ How long do you want to stay with us?/What will be your future plans if we do not hire you?
→ Are you ready to relocate?/How does your family like your being away on an official trip?
→ Our experience with women has not been good. What do you feel about this?
→ Don't you feel you are little too old/young for this job?
→ Would you lie for your company?/Can you work under stress?/What makes you angry?
→ Have you ever witnessed a person doing something that you felt was against the company policy? What did you do and why?
→ What has been the most boring assignment for you?/Describe a time you had to work with someone you didn't like.
→ Tell me about a project you worked on and the requirements changed midstream. What did you do?
→ Tell us honestly about the strengths and weaknesses of the boss of your company.
→ Have you heard anything negative about our company?/On a scale of 1 to 10, rate our company/me as an interviewer.
→ What do you think about euthanasia (mercy killing)/ragging in colleges?
→ If you win Rs. 10 million lottery, what will you do?/Can there be life outside the earth?
→ How do you deal with difficult people or settle disputes?
→ When have you been most creative in your life?
→ How many hours a day do you usually work?/What message would you like to give to the younger generation?
→ How much salary do you expect?

6.3.10   Interviewing the Interviewers

You are usually invited to ask questions at the end of your interview. Even if you are not asked, first seek permission and then satisfy your queries skillfully and politely. Whatever you enquire should be to the point, positive and direct. Do not take liberties. Do not forget that you are not in the driving seat. It is you who is going to be selected. However, such initiative will count in your favour. These are some of the questions that you can ask your prospective employer: Will there be opportunities for training?/ If you don't mind my asking, what is the scope of promotion?/Does the company plan to expand in future?/When will I learn about my status?

6.2.11 Evaluation of Performance

An interview is a judgement of the overall personality of a candidate—a mix of the qualities of intellect, body and spirit. Interviewers use interviews to select an applicant for a specific position and evaluate candidates normally on the following grounds of (a) personal traits, (b) leadership qualities, (c) communication skills and (d) knowledge.

Task

1. What is a job interview? Discuss the various types of job interviews.
2. How will you prepare yourself for a job interview?
3. Write short notes on:
   (a) Personality traits required for a job interview.
   (b) Techniques of effective communication needed during a job interview.
4. Write down answers for the following interview questions:
   (a) What are your major strengths and weaknesses?
   (b) What are your short-term and long-term goals?
   (c) Give us instances where you have displayed team spirit and leadership qualities?

Carry out a panel/telephone mock interview with your friends for the post of project manager.

6.4 Professional Presentation

6.4.1 What is a Professional Presentation?

A professional presentation is a kind of an oral talk delivered by a speaker to a group of audience. It is formal in nature, communicated with a specific purpose, usually with the help of some audio/visual aids. Presentations are not as interactive as a GD or an interview as interaction in a presentation takes place in the form of a brief question–answer session in which the speaker satisfies queries of the audience.

In today's professional and academic environment, oral presentations carry a lot of weight. All of us should know its intricacies as we all have to give presentations at some or the other time during our student and professional life. A good presentation can fetch excellent marks in seminars or project reports, help you obtain your dream job or have a rewarding business deal. You need not be a good orator for giving an effective presentation. What you need is good planning, knowledge, effective delivery techniques, confidence to face the audience and to have know-how of the visual aids.

6.4.2 Types of Professional Presentations

Professional presentations, generally in use, are seminars, presentations during meetings and conferences, research paper presentations, university/institution/department/company profile presentations, product marketing, academic presentations, workshops and recruitment presentations. All the forms of oral presentations are purpose specific as well as audience oriented.

6.4.3 Preparation and Research

In an oral presentation, relevant information has to be conveyed to the audience in a limited time. This needs proper planning, research and preparation. The given guidelines will be useful for the ground work required in making a successful presentation:

6.4.3.1 Plan the Presentation

Plan your presentation well analysing the following peripheral factors:

Audience: As a presentation should be audience centred, the first step would be collecting details about the audience—their age, gender, profession, attitude, number, needs, expectations and subject knowledge. Try to match your objectives with their outlook.

Purpose of Presentation: Make sure on which occasion the presentation is to be given; who have organized it and with what purpose. At the same time, ascertain the type of presentation and where it is going to be presented. Are you making your presentation in a seminar, conference or for marketing or launching a product, etc.? Base your presentation according to these requirements.

Time Duration: You should know when and how long you have to speak. If the organizers have given you only vague information about time and you have the flexibility, try to limit your presentation somewhere around 30 to 45 minutes. It has been found that the attention span of an average audience is not more than 30 to 40 minutes. If you go beyond this, you need to employ some strong techniques to draw their attention. If there are more speakers, you need to know if you are preceding or following them. In both the cases, your approach should be different.

Infrastructure: You may also inquire whether you would be speaking from behind a dais or from a platform, what type of microphone will be provided and which audio-visual and visual aids will be available.

6.4.3.2 Collect Material

After analysing the above factors, start collecting your material. Examine the subject matter of your presentation, put yourself in the position of your audience, and consider their needs, expectations and possible questions. Brainstorm yourself, jot down relevant points and arrange them systematically. Now, do some research on the topic to have latest information by reading books, visiting libraries, discussing with people and using Internet. Find out illustrations, facts and figures that may assist you in supporting your points. You also need to include humour, quotations and short narratives to mitigate the boredom of hard facts. Think of the ways to make audience identify with you, as you have to address both their mind and heart.

6.4.3.3 Structure the Presentation

First of all, consider the key areas you would like to cover. Prepare an outline of the presentation in a systematic manner. It should be economical and instead of full sentence, write down key phrases, headings and subheadings. Keep in mind that the same outline will help you in making your power point slides. Use note-making skills to organize your material. (See details of note making in the chapter on 'Note Making and Note taking in Section 8.3 of this book.) Now, structure your data by dividing it into three heads: introduction, body and conclusion.

Introduction: Well begun is half done. If you are able to attract the listener's attention with your effective opening, you are on your way to success. Plan your introduction well. Draw the outline of the approach you would like to take for the beginning—asking an interesting question, using an element of surprise through an unexpected or controversial statement (supported by an explanation later), using humour, narrating a very short story or an event, reminding the listeners why they have assembled, thanking the organizers, making use of a catchy quotation, etc. Introduce the topic and talk about its relevance in short. Whatever approach you plan, consider the mood and attitude of the audience first.

Main Body: The body consists of the major contents of the presentation. As you have researched a lot, you may be tempted to include many details, but exercise restraint and take into account only the main ideas. You may divide your material into points and ideas of primary and secondary importance. Use the former in your notes, and keep the latter in reserve for additional explanations, if required. Write them down clearly, preferably on cards. If you are using a power point or an OHP, mark where they are to be utilized. With every main idea jot down the supporting details, facts, figures, helpful illustrations and anecdotes. Include the element of humour and motivational phrases and place them at intervals. Prepare a few questions that you may ask your listeners to maintain their interest as well as to know if they are getting your point or not. Underline the portions that you want to highlight as well as the parts that may be left out if time is short or you do not receive positive response from the listeners. Structure the notes in the same sequence as you wish to present them before the audience.

Conclusion: Conclusion is a short summary of the overall presentation. Plan which ideas you would like to repeat at the end so that you may finish your speech with a positive note. Write down the central idea of the presentation. Anticipate the expected queries of the listeners; prepare their satisfactory answers and try to include them in your presentation. You may conclude with some unanswered questions to motivate the listeners to analyze your discussion even later on.

6.4.3.4 Plan your Visual Aids

Visual and audio-visual aids enhance the effectiveness of your presentation. Charts, figures, drawings, maps, pictures, graphs, etc. are traditional visual supports that speakers employ. If you want to use them, indicate them in your notes at proper places. Make handouts of the visuals for distribution before the presentation. These visual aids have their own effect, but for much better impact you may go for a technology-aided presentation, where you can make use of gadgets such as an overhead or an LCD projector. LCD projectors aid you in the projection of a power point presentation in front of the audience. Slides are the best equipped means to communicate various types of visuals, audio, and audio-visual material and they can be conveniently prepared on a computer. Once you have structured your notes, use them to prepare slides for power point presentation. Keep in mind the following guidelines:

- → The opening slide should convey the topic of the presentation along with the name of the presenter, followed by a slide that displays all the major points to be discussed.
- → Make one slide for each important idea with a few supporting points. Leave elaboration for the oral delivery.
- → Use simple and direct language—plain words, familiar phrases and short sentences to convey an idea.
- → Slides should not be ornamental. Pay more attention to arrange your thoughts and contents as well as present them in a clear, organized and uniform manner.
- → If required, include graphs, pictures, maps, etc., in the slides. You can incorporate relevant audios and videos also.
- → Plan your notes to elaborate the points displayed in the slides.

Do not be dependent upon the electronic presentation. Plan the use of technology only as support; otherwise, this may carry a negative impression about you as a speaker. You should also be prepared to carry on with your presentation even in the case of a malfunctioning of the electronic system. Remember technology is a good servant but a bad master.

6.4.3.5 Rehearse your Presentation

Practice makes man perfect. You should rehearse your presentation with and without the visual aids of your already prepared power point presentation. Keep track of time. It is always better to finish a little before you are expected to do. You may practice in front of a mirror or with a friend. You may also record your voice for analysis and listen to it carefully keeping in mind the guidelines given under the heading 'Communication Skills'. Practice will not only boost your confidence but will also make you aware of the important points that you might have missed.

6.4.4 Effective Delivery

To make an impact on the audience, delivery of the presentation has to be extremely effective. The following factors that influence its quality should be kept in mind during the preparation of the presentation as well as at the time of presenting it.

6.4.4.1 Dress and Appearance

Professional presentation is a formal activity in which the speaker has to present his/her discourse in front of an educated gathering. His/her dress and appearance should be suitable to the occasion as they make their own impact on the audience. Follow all the norms of formal dressing and grooming, dealt with in 'Group Discussion', in Section 6.2.9.1.

6.4.4.2 Body Language

When you are on the dais, it is your body that speaks the first. So, be careful about your body signals. The art of public speaking requires its own body language. A born speaker may have good body signals as an inherent quality, but it can always be developed by practice. Get on the dais with a positive, happy and relaxed mind set. Keep the following guidelines in mind while giving a presentation:

→ Your body language should match the nature of your subject. It can be motivating, sober, aggressive, mild or humorous. A clever speaker may use a lot of variations in his/her body language many times during a single presentation.

→ Stand with your legs a little apart, distributing your body weight equally on both the legs. Do not stand behind a lectern continuously, as it may indicate lack of confidence or fear of facing the audience. Move around the platform to maintain listener's interest, but the movement should not be too much. Stand erect with your chin parallel to the floor to make your vocal cords work freely.

→ Do not deliver your presentation with wooden expressions. Expressions should be cheerful and you should vary them as per the situation. Do not give blank expressions or be lost in your thoughts.

→ Maintain continuous eye contact with listeners to create a positive impact and to get proper feedback from them. In a small gathering, try to rest your eyes on everyone present. With a big audience, you may randomly fix some points around the room. Rest your eyes on someone at each point and then move on to a point that may be placed across the room. Do not give a furtive glance or look at only one side of the gathering. Your notes and visual aids should not distract you from your speech. Keep your eyes at the viewers most of the time.

→ Use relevant gestures. Be careful if you have any habitual gesticulations, for example, shrugging your shoulders, opening your arms, etc. Too much use of any one of them may make you a laughing stalk or divert the attention of the listeners. Employ them economically to emphasize significant points.

→ Avoid irritating mannerisms such as waving a finger, shaking a fist, fiddling with something like a book, papers and pen kept on the lectern or your clothing.

→ Neither fold your arms nor put them in your pockets. Leave them free for gesticulations. If you are using PowerPoint slides, you may use a pointer whenever it is required.

6.4.4.3 Modes of Delivery

Generally, there may be three types of delivering a presentation: first, when you know your subject well and feel confident, you can carry the main points in your memory and utilize your material with suitable visual aids. Second, you may prepare outline notes and take them on cards or papers along with visual support. The third one is to take along the whole script for reading it out. It has been observed that audience find the first one the most impressive but one should go for this type of presentation only if one is confident, has deep knowledge of the subject or has given presentations on the same or similar topic earlier. Otherwise, the safest one would be to have contents in the form of notes and outline, supported with visual aids. The third proposition should be avoided as it detaches you from your listeners. Whatever type of mode of delivery you may choose, it should be prepared thoroughly and researched well. It should have relevance, plainness and conciseness and should generate genuine interest in the audience. Its second reading will further help you at this stage.

6.4.4.4 Communication Skills

You need not be an orator for giving a professional presentation. The flowery language and the rhetoric of an oration do not find any appreciation in a professional presentation. Oral presentation has its own techniques of communication, which can be developed with help of the tips given below:

- → Use short and simple sentences in a language that is understood by the whole audience. You may use specific vocabulary if the listeners are familiar with the subject.
- → Be careful about the words that have different meaning in different context.
- → Avoid clichés. Whether you're writing or speaking, clichés will weaken the effect of your message. You should use original material as well as expression. For instance, in place of 'Last but not the least' you may use 'in the end' and 'part and parcel' can be replaced by 'a part of'. If someone else has already said what you are going to say, express it in a different manner. Remember, the audience will not forgive you for being boring.
- → Speak with right pronunciation and commonly understood accent. Use pitch and pace variations—a slower speed and lower volume helps emphasize a point and indicate the end of a major idea. Increase in pitch may assist in motivating the viewers or making new points. Tone variations are necessary to maintain listeners' interest.
- → Address the gathering using pauses at the right time as pauses are an essential aspect of public speaking. You may begin your discourse with a pause. Use it to create suspense, state important statements, facts, cite quotations or a humour, to take breath, to put your ideas in order for the next point or to let the listeners take in what you have said. You can also indicate a pause by sipping water or changing your position.
- → Stage fright is normal, but it has to be controlled as it affects your overall performance. If you are well prepared and your thought process is crystal clear, you can cope up with your stage fear. To control the pre-speech nervousness, remain calm, talk freely, and if possible, mix up with the crowd. Go with a positive mindset and do not let baseless apprehensions grip you.

6.4.4.5 Check the Equipments

Before your presentation, see that the aids you are going to use—microphone, computer, laptop, slide projector, OHP or an LCD projector, are in good working condition. Make sure that your visual material as well as the supporting aids is arranged in the right sequence. Prefer a clip or a portable microphone, if available, as they give you freedom of movement. In case of a sudden malfunctioning of a system, do not get panicked or feel guilty, call a technician. Rest assured that the audience knows that such breakdowns can occur any time. Carry on with your presentation without the visual aids. You may continue in the absence of microphone, if the gathering is not large.

6.4.5 Audience Questions

Before you begin your speech, let the audience know that you are willing to satisfy their queries. Make sure that the questions asked are clearly heard by the rest of the listeners. You may also repeat the query, which will give you an extra time to think for your answer. Give your response energetically and it has to go to all the listeners. It should not appear that you are trying to avoid the matter. If you do not know an answer, admit it and convey that you will let the questioner know the answer later. In case, a member objects or confronts you, do not get offended or give similar signals. Tackle the situation calmly. If the problem persists, request the member not to get into a private discussion, break the eye contact and address the rest of the audience.

Task

Answer the following questions:

1. What is a professional presentation and how is it different from a speech?
2. How will you prepare a presentation seminar to be delivered in near future?
3. Discuss the features of an effective delivery of a professional presentation.
4. Prepare presentations on the following topics and give mock presentations in front of a friend or a mirror:
    (a) Developing oral communication in English is not an impossible task
    (b) Economic recession and India
    (c) Mobile phones

Functional Grammar

7

In this issue

- ✓ Introduction
- ✓ Correct Usage: Nouns
- ✓ Correct Usage: Pronouns
- ✓ Correct Usage: Adjectives
- ✓ Correct Usage: Articles

- ✓ Correct Usage: Adverb
- ✓ Correct Usage: Prepositions
- ✓ Correct Usage: Conjunctions
- ✓ Correct Usage: Tenses
- ✓ Correct Usage: Subject–Verb Agreement

"Ignorant people think it's the noise which fighting cats make that is so aggravating, but it ain't so; it's the sickening grammar they use."

–Mark Twain

7.1 Introduction

Grammar is the most discussed aspect of language learning and learners have different opinions about it. Some people are interested in learning the rules of grammar and solving numerous grammar exercises while others criticize grammar and feel that it is the dullest part of learning a new language. Whatever opinion you have, you cannot escape from grammar as it is the word for the rules of using a language. All of us need to understand and use grammar rules in the same way as we need rules in a game, traffic or an activity. If there are no rules or if everybody follows his/her own way, everything will end in chaos and confusion. Without learning the rules of a language, we will not be able to communicate properly with other people.

Experts in the business of teaching second language courses claim that the students, with little or no effort, may begin to speak the target language from the very first day. In this method, they teach students sets of words, phrases and sentences related to day-to-day situations under the direction of the teacher who carefully guides them through virtual conversations. However, this method inculcates the habit of speaking without understanding. An educated person is expected to read, write and speak well. Without the knowledge of grammar, even bright students have problems in writing as they repeat the same errors over and over, misspell words (despite "spell-check"), write incomplete sentences, give improper citations and referencing and do unintentional plagiarism. Most of the teachers and employers believe that the inability of students/employees to write clearly is a major problem.

Of course, we do not learn the rules of our mother tongue as we grow up but we do not make a grammatical mistake in its usage too. It is possible to learn a second language in the same natural way, if you have enough time and an appropriate atmosphere. Hence, one should understand grammar and notice the aspects that are the same as or similar to those in one's language. If you notice grammar similarities and differences, you will probably learn the rules rather quickly. Reading a lot of English books as well as listening to correct and good English equips you with models of correct grammar that will definitely help you when you express your ideas in speaking or writing or when you come to check your work. Concentrate on the aspects of grammar you personally find most difficult and focus on them while writing, speaking or editing your work. Making mistakes reflects poor learning. Good English means correct English. The best way to learn a language is practicing the correct usage in real-life situations. Without grammar, language does not exist. A solid knowledge of all the rules is necessary to use a language well.

7.2 Correct Usage: Nouns

7.2.1 What is a Noun?

A noun is the name of a person, animal or living object, place, thing, action, feeling or quality. In other words, nouns are the naming words. For example: *man, Kushal, girl, Nivedita, horse, Delhi, city, book, pencil, computer, hatred, greatness, sadness, honesty, etc.*

7.2.2 Classification of Nouns

Basically, there are two types of nouns: abstract nouns and concrete nouns.

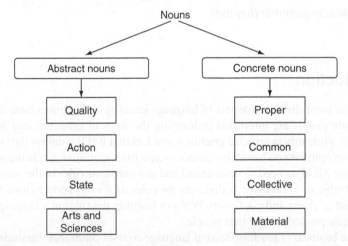

1. Abstract Nouns: An abstract noun is something that can't be sensed by our five senses, that is, smell, touch, hear, see or taste. Abstract nouns are the names of quality, action, state or the names of arts and sciences considered apart from the object to which they belong; such as quality—*freshness, beauty, cowardice, intelligence*; action—*running, walking, robbery, growth*; state—*childhood, loneliness, happiness, slavery, poverty*; the names of the arts and sciences—*music, chemistry, physics, dramatics, etc.*

2. Concrete Nouns: Concrete nouns refer to those living and non-living objects that can be touched, felt, held, seen, smelt, tasted, or heard. Concrete nouns have objective reality. These nouns can further be classified into the following groups:

i) Proper Nouns: A proper noun is the specific name of a place, person or thing. The first letter of a proper noun is always represented by a capital letter; such as people—*Rachna, Karan, Tania, Mansi*; places—*Delhi, Agra, India, Haryana, Madhya Pradesh*; months and days—*January, February, Monday Wednesday*;

books—*War and Peace, Arabian Nights, Communicative English for Engineers and Professionals, The Alchemist*; Company—*Microsoft, Amazon, Nike*; title of the people—*The President of India, The Mayor of Indore*.

ii) Common Nouns: 'Common' means 'shared by' or 'belonging to all in a group.' A common noun is a name given to every person or thing of the same kind or class; such as *dog, house, picture, computer, table, woman, writer, etc*. Common nouns may be used in the singular as well as the plural form and they are represented by lower case letters.

iii) Collective Nouns: Collective nouns refer to things or people taken together or spoken as a collection, group or unit; such as *family, police, class, team, crew, bunch, fleet, army, jury, etc*.

iv) Material Nouns: Material nouns are those nouns, which refer to the substance or the material that things can be made from; such as *water, air, gas, cotton, oil, paint, coffee, tea, rice, etc*.

7.2.3 Countable and Uncountable Nouns

Nouns can also be classified as countable and uncountable nouns. Countable nouns refer to those people or objects that can be counted, for example, *pen, house, leader, apple, potato, etc*. Proper nouns, common nouns and collective nouns belong to this category. Uncountable nouns are names of substances, materials, concepts, etc., that we cannot divide into separate elements. We cannot count them. For example, we cannot count *rice* but can count *bags* of rice. Some uncountable nouns are: *air, water, milk, sugar, goodness, cruelty, faith, music, art, love, happiness, advice, information, news, furniture, luggage, rice, butter, electricity, gas, power, money, currency, etc*. We usually use uncountable nouns in singular form. For example: 'This *news is* very interesting.' 'The *milk is* in the jug.' We neither use the indefinite article *a/an* with uncountable nouns nor do we represent them by a number. We cannot say 'a sugar' or 'a luggage.' However, we can say 'a something of': 'a piece of news,' 'a bottle of milk,' 'a kilo of sugar,' 'three items of luggage', etc.

7.2.4 Compound Nouns

Compound nouns are made up of two nouns. These nouns form their plurals by:

→ Adding s/es in the second element when both the words are nouns: *boy friends, girl friends, toothbrushes, tea bushes*.
→ Adding s/es in the main word of a compound noun formed with a preposition or a gerund: *Sisters-in-law, men-of-war, lookers-on, runners-up, commanders-in-chief, professors-in-charge, ladies-in-waiting, walking-sticks, dressing tables, etc*.
→ Making both the parts plurals when the first noun is 'man' or 'woman': *men-servants, women-doctors, etc*.

7.2.5 Possessive (Genitive) Case of Nouns

7.2.5.1 Formation of Possessive Case

→ Possessive case is formed by adding ('s) to the singular noun or the plural noun not ending in s/es, for example, *Ram's book, child's toy, women's dresses, India's army, etc*.
→ Plural nouns ending in s/es form their possessives only by adding ('): *a girls' hostel, boys' school, birds' nest, workers' union*.
→ Proper nouns ending in s/es may use (') or ('s) to form their possessives: *Keats's poems or Keats' poems, Jones's car or Jones' car*.
→ Compound nouns and the titles with several words form their possessive by adding ('s) to the last word: *My sister-in-law's house, her boy friend's name, the Prime Minister's visit, King George, the Eighth's son, etc*.

→ When two nouns are joined with 'and' and they show possession of the same person, place or object ('s) is added only to the second one. However, ('s) is added to both when they refer to different people, places or objects: *Veena and Neena's father is* a doctor. *Veena'a and Neena's fathers* are doctors.

7.2.5.2   Use of Possessive Case

1. Show possession:

→ For people, countries and animals, for example, *Rini's book, horse's hair, America's President.*
→ For ships and boats, for example, *the ship's deck, the boat's sail.*
→ For time expressions, for example, *a week's holiday, an hour's journey, 10 minutes' exercise.*
→ For the expression of money, for example, *a rupee's value, a dollar's worth.*
→ For the expressions of distance: *a mile's race, the land's end.*
→ Words—house, shop, church, school—are not used after ('s) or ('). *Today I'll stay at my uncle's.* (*house*)
→ The use of double possessives is wrong: *The guests of my wife's brother* (not *my wife's brother's guests*) *are coming today.*

2. Change letters, figures and abbreviations in plural: *all A's, all 6's, B.A.'s, B. Tech.'s.*

3. Form contractions: Do not—*don't*, cannot—*can't*, shall not—*shan't*, will not—*won't* , are not—*aren't*, etc.

7.2.6   Correct Usage of Nouns

1. Some nouns are singular in form but plural in sense and take a plural verb; such as *cattle, gentry, peasantry, clergy, poultry, mankind, majority, etc.* For example:
    → *Cattle are* grazing in the field.
    → *The gentry* of the show *were* good.

2. Some nouns are plural in form but singular in meaning and take a singular verb; such as *means, innings, news, mathematics, physics, economics, comics, summons, politics, optics, etc.* For example:
    → *That is* great *news.*
    → *Mathematics is* an interesting subject.
    → They lost the match by *an innings.*
    → *Summons has been* sent to her to appear in the court.
    → *Is* there any *means* of contacting him?

3. Some nouns are always used in plural form and take plural verbs only; such as *spectacles, glasses, thanks, lodgings, clothes, orders, savings, compasses, tidings, premises, trousers, jeans, socks, shoes, goods, alms, breeches, credentials, customs, amends, annals, etc.* For example:
    → *Thanks are* due to all those who worked hard for many months.
    → My *clothes have* been washed.
    → Big *savings are* made on fuel bills.
    → My *spectacles were* misted with fog and smoke.

4. Some nouns are always used in singular form and take a singular verb only; such as *information, scenery, knowledge, furniture, advice, machinery, stationery, abuse, issue, bedding, poetry, rice, sugar, mischief, abuse, wheat, dust, luggage, alphabet, expenditure, offspring, etc.*
    → *The scenery is* magnificent.
    → Little *knowledge is* a dangerous thing.
    → He has *no male issue.*
    → *The luggage is* kept in the waiting room.

5. Some nouns are used in the same form in singular as well as in plural; such as *sheep, deer, fish, series, species, wages, etc.*

→ *Sheep were/was* grazing in the fields.

→ *Fish are* abundant in the lake.

→ *The fish has* a lot of bones.

→ *Wages have* not increased for a long time.

→ *Wages* for the workers *is* very low.

6. Nouns indicating length, weight, measurement, money or number remain unchanged when they are preceded by a numeral; such *as a 10-foot high wall, a 10-kilo pack, a 5-rupee note, a 2-hour journey, a 3-year old, a 5-judge bench, 10-dozen egg, a 4-year course, etc.* However, if the numeral added is indefinite, these nouns can be used in plural also; *such as dozens of eggs, scores of times, hundreds of rupees, hours of entertainment, etc.*

→ *B. Tech. is a 4-year* degree course.

→ *A 5-judge bench was* appointed to decide the case.

→ *Hundreds of rupees were* spent on the gift.

→ *Dozens of eggs were* used in making the New Year cake.

7. Collective nouns—*jury, committee, team, class, flock, audience, company, staff*—are used as singular subjects when they refer to the whole unit or the group and as plural subjects when they refer to the individuals. For example:

→ *The jury has* given its verdict.

→ *The jury have* given their views about the case.

→ *The flock of sheep is* grazing in the field.

→ *The flock were* running here and there in the ground.

→ *The audience was* clapping to cheer the performers.

→ *The audience were* cheering the winners.

8. Proper, material and abstract nouns are not used in plural sense when they refer to substance or material. For example:

→ This house is made of *brick*.

→ *Beauty lies* in the eyes of the beholder.

→ Each drop of *water is* precious.

→ *Cotton is* used to make bandages.

When proper, common and material nouns are used in plural, they become common nouns; such as coppers = *copper coins*, tins = *cans made of tins*, woods = *forest*, waters = *the water in a particular lake, river, sea or ocean, etc.*

9. Noun followed by a preposition and the same noun repeated takes a singular form and a singular verb: The old man had to *go door to door* asking for help.

10. The subject 'one of the' is followed by plural noun: He is *one of the best boys* of his class.

11. 'Word' when used in the sense of one's promise, assurance or message does not take plural form and is not preceded by indefinite article: We should keep our *word*. He sent *word* (not *a word*) to me.

7.2.7   Common Errors in the Use of Noun Expressions

1. Fifteen candidates sent their applications for *lectureship*.(not lecturership).
2. Four students have applied for *free studentship*. (not freeship).
3. My brother lives in *a boarding house*. (not boarding).
4. Kinshuk and Anuj are *the members of my family*. (not my family members).
5. Mrs. Gupta is our *teacher of French*. (not French teacher).
6. Prashant and Kintu are my *cousins*. (not my cousin brothers).
7. I want some *blotting paper*. (not blotting).
8. We have got *pass marks* (not passing marks) in chemistry.
9. My father is leaving by *12:15 train*. (not by 12–15 o'clock train).
10. Where did you spend summer *vacation?* (not vacations).

7.2.8 Nouns with Two Forms in Plural with Different Meanings

The following nouns have two forms in plural with different meanings:

1. Brother – *Brothers*: Brothers by blood; *Brethren*: Members of a society or a community
2. Cloth – *Cloths*: Pieces/kinds; *Clothes*: Garments
3. Genius – *Geniuses*: Men and women having genius; *Genii*: Spirits
4. Index – *Indexes*: Tables of contents; *Indices*: Alphabetical exponents
5. Penny – *Pennies*: Separate coins; *Pence*: Collective sum
6. Staff – *Staves*: Sticks; *Staffs*: Used only in military sense
7. Die – *Dies*: Stamps for coining; *Dice*: Small cubes used in games

The above-mentioned words should be used carefully according to their meaning.

7.2.9 The Nouns with Different Meanings in Singular and Plural

Some nouns have different meanings in singular and plural forms; so, they should be used carefully.

1. *Circumstance*: Facts; *Circumstances*: Conditions
2. *Air*: Atmosphere; *Airs*: Affected behaviour
3. *Custom*: Habit; *Customs*: Habits/Duties on goods
4. *Good*: High quality; *Goods*: Commodities
5. *Iron*: A metal; *Irons*: Fetters made of iron
6. *Respect*: Regards; *Respects*: Compliments
7. *Physic*: Medicine; *Physics*: Natural sciences
8. *Return*: Come back; *Returns*: Statistics
9. *Sand*: Particles of dust; *Sands*: Sea-shore
10. *Quarter*: One-fourth; *Quarters*: Lodgings/fourth part
11. *Force*: Strength; *Forces*: Army
12. *Content*: satisfaction/substance; *Contents*: Things contained
13. *Pain*: Ache; *Pains*: Efforts
14. *Minute*: Sixty seconds; *Minutes*: Proceedings of a meeting
15. *Spectacle*: Sight; *Spectacles*: Glasses
16. *Copper*: A metal; *Coppers*: Coins made of coins
17. *Tin*: A metal; *Tins*: Cans made of tin
18. *Wood*: Material of tree trunk; *Woods*: Forest
19. *Light*: Radiance; *Lights*: Lamps
20. *People*: Nation/men and women; *Peoples*: Nations
21. *Study*: The activity of learning or gaining knowledge; *Studies*: A particular person's learning activities.

Task

Correct the following sentences

1. We read pages after pages.
2. My uncle has no male issues.
3. Most of the people feel that life is full of miseries and worries.
4. Have you read the poetries of Browning?
5. He has sold all of his furnitures.
6. I have many works to do.

7. The atom bomb did much damages in Japan.
8. We have undergone great many difficulties.
9. They built a house of stones.
10. I am comfortable with my study.
11. The judge passed order for his release.
12. The road is closed for repair.
13. They are walking in the centre of the road.
14. Read two first chapters of the book.
15. He is a man of his words.
16. These news will create panic.
17. My house's roof is leaking.
18. His English knowledge is very poor.
19. He has read three fourth of the novel.
20. I saw a snake crawling on the ground in the room.

7.3   Correct Usage: Pronouns

7.3.1   What is a Pronoun?

The word 'pronoun' means 'for a noun.' Pronouns are the words, which are used in place of nouns. They are used to avoid repetition of nouns such as 'Kamayani is a good girl, *she* is very hard working', etc. Nevertheless, a fresh paragraph should not start with a pronoun; it should start with a noun.

7.3.2   Classification of Pronouns

Pronouns are of nine types – *Personal, Reflexive, Emphatic, Demonstrative, Indefinite, Interrogative, Relative, Reciprocal and Distributive.*

1. **Personal Pronouns:**   Personal pronouns refer to persons; I person, the speaker—*I, we;* II person the person spoken to—*you* and III person, the person spoken of—*he, she, it, they.* Personal pronouns have various forms.

A summary of the forms of the personal pronouns is listed in the table given below.

Person	Number	Subjective case	Objective case	Possessive adjective	Possessive pronoun	Reflexive pronoun
I Person (the speaker)	Singular	I	me	my	mine	myself
	Plural	we	us	our	ours	ourselves
II Person (the person spoken to)	Singular and plural	you	you	your	yours	yourself (singular) yourselves (plural)

(Continued)

Person	Number	Subjective case	Objective case	Possessive adjective	Possessive pronoun	Reflexive pronoun
III Person (the person spoken of)	Singular (masculine)	he	him	his	his	himself
	Singular (feminine)	she	her	her	hers	herself
	Singular	it	it	its	its	itself
	Plural	they	them	their	theirs	themselves

2. Reflexive Pronouns:

A reflexive pronoun refers or reflects back to the subject of the sentence or the clause. Reflexive pronouns end in '-self' (singular) or '-selves' (plural). There are eight reflexive pronouns formed from the personal pronouns: Singular—*myself, yourself, himself, herself, itself* and plural—*ourselves, yourselves, themselves*.

The verbs—*absent, present, avail, apply, exert, enjoy, cut, hurt, oversleep,* etc.—should be followed by *reflexive pronouns*:

→ Ram *absented himself* from the class.
→ He *availed himself* of the opportunity.
→ They all *enjoyed themselves* at the party.
→ He has *hurt himself* while running.

3. Emphatic Pronouns:

All the above-mentioned reflexive pronouns can also act as emphatic pronouns but their function and usage are different. An emphatic pronoun emphasizes its antecedent. For example:

→ I *myself* made it.
→ Ramesh *himself* is to blame.
→ She *herself* spoke to me.
→ The examination *itself* wasn't difficult, but examination room was horrible.

4. Demonstrative Pronouns:

A demonstrative pronoun points out, indicates, shows or demonstrates persons, places, amounts or things such as:

→ near in distance or time (*this, these*)
→ far in distance or time (*that, those*)

5. Indefinite Pronouns:

An indefinite pronoun does not refer to any specific person, thing or amount. It is vague and is used for people and objects in a general way. Some indefinite pronouns are: *all, another, any, anybody/anyone, anything, each, everybody/everyone, everything, few, many, nobody, none, one, several, some, somebody/someone.*

6. Interrogative Pronouns:

Interrogative pronouns ask questions about people or objects we do not know. There are four main interrogative pronouns: *who, whom, what, which.* Possessive form of 'who'—'whose' and compounds of 'who,' 'what' and 'which'—'whoever,' 'whatever' and 'whichever' are also used to show emphasis, confusion or surprise. 'Who' is used for persons only, 'what' is used for things only while 'which' can be used for both persons as well as objects, for example:

→ *Who* spoke to you yesterday?
→ *Which* is your friend?
→ *Which book* do you like the most?
→ *What* have you done?

7. Relative Pronouns:

A relative pronoun refers or relates to some noun or pronoun going before it or in other words its antecedent. Words, *who, whose, whom, which, that* and *what* are relative pronouns. For example:

→ The person *who* called me last night is my teacher.
→ These are the students *whom* we praise.
→ This is the girl *whose* exercises are done well.
→ The book *which* I bought yesterday is very useful.
→ Take anything *that* you like.
→ I say *what* I mean.

1. The relative pronoun, 'who' is used for persons and 'which' is used for objects:
   → This is the *boy who* came here yesterday.
   → Give me the *book which* I gave you.

2. The relative pronoun, 'that' is used for persons as well as objects and it may refer to singular as well as plural numbers:
   → This is *the boy that* I told you of.
   → I know *the house that* he has bought.

3. 'That' is used after the adjectives in superlative degree, interrogative pronouns and words such as all, nothing, none, only, same, anything, anybody, nobody:
   → Raheem is the *kindest man that* has ever lived in the village.
   → *What* is *that* troubles you?
   → *All that* glitters is not gold.
   → There is *nothing that* is farther from truth.
   → I don't say *anything that* can hurt others.
   → There is *nobody that* can help me.
   → Man is the *only animal that* has intelligence.

4. 'That' is used after two antecedents when one of them is a human being and the other one is an object or an animal:
   → The *lady* and *her dog that* I saw yesterday have gone.

5. A relative pronoun should agree with its antecedent in gender, number and person and it should be placed near it, like for example:
   → It is *he who* is to blame.
   → The *boy who* came here yesterday is my brother. (Not the boy is my brother who came here yesterday.)

6. If the pronoun has two or more antecedents, the relative pronoun should be used according to the nearest one:
   → I respect anyone and *anything that* reminds me of my attainments.
   → I like everything and *everyone who* helps me in progress.

7. 'Same' is followed by 'as' whereas, 'such' may be followed by 'that' or 'as':
   → *Such* students *as* avoid hard work always suffer.
   → This is the *same* necklace *as* I bought yesterday.
   → He gave *such* an example *that* no one liked.

8. Reciprocal Pronouns: The word, 'reciprocal' is an adjective which means 'given or done in return.' Reciprocal pronouns express mutual or reciprocal relationship. *Each other* and *one another* are reciprocal pronouns. 'Each other' is used for two persons and 'one another' is used for more than two, for example:

→ The two sisters love *each other*.
→ Ten prisoners were blaming *one another*.

9. Distributive Pronouns: Distributive pronouns refer to persons or things taken one at a time. For this reason, they are always singular and are followed by a singular verb. There are three distributive pronouns: *each, either* and *neither*. 'Each' is used to denote every one of persons or things; 'either' means one or the other of two and 'neither' indicates not the one or the other of two. 'Either' and 'neither' should be used when we speak of two persons, places or things. When more than two are referred to, 'any,' 'no one' and 'none' should be used.

7.3.3   Correct Usage of Pronouns

1. When a personal pronoun is used instead of a noun, it must have of the same number, gender and person as the noun it stands for:
   → *All the students* were supposed to bring *their* notebooks.
   → *Joy* has got *his* ticket.
   → *Mansi* left *her* laptop at home.
   → *We* had had *our* dinner.

2. A pronoun used to represent two singular nouns joined by 'and' should be plural in number:
   → *Swati and Shweta* have finished *their* work.
   Note: If two nouns joined by 'and' refer to the same subject, the pronoun should be singular:
   → *Our teacher* and *warden* is not doing *his* duty.
   → *My teacher* and *guide* has given me *his* best.

3. Two nouns joined by 'and' preceded by 'each' or 'every' are treated as singular:
   → *Each boy* and *each girl* has to be prepared for the test.
   → *Every man* and *every woman* was doing the job very well.

4. When two or more singular nouns are joined by 'or', 'nor', 'either—or', 'neither—nor', the pronouns should be used in singular:
   → *Rajesh or Ramesh* has given me *his* book.
   → *Neither Ram nor his friend* has done *his* work.
   Note: If one singular and the other plural nouns are joined by 'or,' 'nor' 'either—or', 'neither—nor', the pronoun used for them must be plural:
   → *Neither the officer nor his assistants* di d *their* duty.

5. According to etiquettes, when pronouns of different persons are used together, second person comes first, third person second and first person comes last:
   → *Jasmine* and *I* went on a picnic.
   → *You* and *Jyoti* can leave now.
   → *You* and *Gopal* and *I* can do this together.
   → *You, he* and *I* have to attend a party tonight.
   However, if the pronouns are in plural or some fault is to be admitted, the first person comes first, the second person comes second and the third person comes last:
   → *We, you* and *they* have to leave now.
   → *I, you* and *he* are equally to blame.

6. A pronoun followed by a preposition should be used in its objective form, for example, *me, us, them*, etc.:
   → *Between you* and *me*, I don't trust him (not between you and I …).
   → This is *for you* and *him* (not you and he.).

7. Pronouns used after 'Let' should take an objective form:
   → Let *him* do it.
   → Let *them* find the solution.

8. When 'but' is used as a preposition, it means 'except.' The pronoun following the preposition 'but' must be in the objective form:
   → Everybody came *but him*.
   → None *but me* could solve the problem.

9. 'Than' and 'as' are conjunctions joining two clauses. The pronoun followed by 'than' and 'as' should be used in the same case as the pronoun preceding it:
   → *He* is taller *than she* (is).
   → *I* know you better *than he* (knows you).
   → *You* helped me *as* much *as he*.
   → *I* trust you *as* much *as she*.
   Examples such as 'I know *you* better than *him*. (I know him)' and 'I trust *you* as much as *her*. (I trust her)' are also correct.

10. Pronouns used as the complements of the verb 'to be' – *is, are, am, was, were* – should be in subjective form:
    → It is *he*.
    → This is *I*.

11. The possessive form of the pronoun, 'one' is 'one's' and its reflexive form is 'oneself':
    → One should do one's duty (not his duty).

12. 'Everybody,' 'everyone,' 'each one,' 'someone,' 'anyone,' 'anybody' are followed by 'his' or 'her' not 'one's':
    → *Everybody* is doing *his* best.
    → *Someone* has given me *his* book.
    → *Anyone* can get *his* health checked up in the hospital.
    → *Each one* should have *his* share in success.

13. Possessive forms of pronouns—*my, our, his, her, its, their, your*—are used as possessive adjectives only, that is, they are followed by a noun, for example:
    my book, your pen, his mobile, your shoes

14. Possessive pronouns—*mine, ours, yours, hers, his, theirs*—are not followed by nouns, for example:
    → This book *is mine*.
    → That coat *is yours*.

15. A pronoun used for a collective noun should be placed in singular number, neuter gender if the noun conveys the idea of a group and in plural number if it refers to the members individually:
    → *The army* has decided to disobey *its* commander.
    → *The jury* were divided in *their* opinion.

16. If subject of the sentence are nouns/pronouns of the first person and any of the two persons, the possessive pronoun will be in the first person. If the subject is the second person and the third person, possessive pronoun will be in the second person:
    → *You* and *I* have done *our* duty.
    → *You* and *he* have done *your* work.

17. Use of 'It': The pronoun 'It' is used:
    1. For inanimate objects: This is *my car*, I love *it*.
    2. For small animals, birds and insects:
       → This is a *cat*. *It* is white.
       → There is a *bird* in the sky. *It* is flying high in the sky.
       → There is a *fly* in the soup. Take *it* out.
    3. For little children when sex is not clearly pointed out: *The baby* is crying. *It* is hungry.
    4. For facts and statements which have already been referred to: He answered *the question* as he knew *it*.
    5. As an imaginary subject of the verb 'to be' when the real subject comes later: *It* is difficult *to solve this problem*.

6. To emphasize a noun or a pronoun: *It* was *he who* came late.
7. Used as a subject in the sentences referring to time and weather:
   → *It* is two o'clock.
   → *It* is very cold today.

7.3.4 Some Common Errors in the Use of Pronouns

1. There is no need to use a pronoun when the noun it stands for is already present in the clause:
   → The boy who works hard *will win*. (Not 'The boy who works hard he will win.')
   → Whoever does the best *will get a prize*. (Not 'Whoever does the best he will get a prize.')
2. An emphatic pronoun (e.g., myself, himself, themselves, yourself) cannot be used as the subject of a sentence:
   → Who did it? *I*. (Not *Myself*.)
   → *I* am Mr. Karan Lal. (Not 'Myself, Mr. Karan Lal.')
3. The noun 'people' is plural in number. The pronoun used for it should be plural in number:
   → *People* starve when *they* have (Not he has) no money.
4. While comparing the same part of two things we should be careful in making the correct comparison and should use 'that of,' 'these of' and 'those of' which are often omitted by the students:
   → My car is better than *that of* my friend. (Not…better than my friend.)
   → The size of the dress should be the same *as that of* this one. (Not…as this one.)
   → His teaching was like *that of* Buddha. (Not …like Buddha.)
5. The pronouns—its, yours, ours, hers, theirs—should not be used with apostrophe ('). '*It's*' means '*it is*,' but, '*her's*,' '*your's*' and '*their's*' *are wrong expressions*:
   → I am *yours* sincerely. (Not your's sincerely)
6. A relative pronoun is a conjunction. No other conjunction should be used with it:
   → He gave me a present *which* (Not 'but which') I did not like it.
7. Pronouns of the third person plural number are not used as antecedents of a relative pronoun:
   → *Those* (Not 'they') who are wise do not waste their time in gossiping.
8. 'How' is an adverb and it cannot function as a relative pronoun:
   → This is the principle *on which* we solved this sum. (Not…how we have solved the sum.)
9. Objective form of a pronoun should not be used in place of possessive form:
   → I don't like your coming late. (Not …you coming late.)
10. 'Whose' cannot refer to inanimate objects:
    → This is the decision the wisdom of which is questionable. (Not…whose wisdom…)

Task

Correct the following sentences:

1. Whom do you think will be our next captain?
2. Two brothers love one another.
3. One should respect his parents.
4. Everyone did their job.
5. Every poet and every artist was in their seat.
6. This is the mobile whose price is reasonable.
7. He went there and enjoyed.
8. Radha absented from the college yesterday.
9. Let you and I go.
10. This is between you and I.
11. The man who came here this evening he was my uncle.
12. Life is such a problem which cannot be solved easily.

13. Any of these two cameras will serve the purpose.
14. None of these cameras are yours.
15. If I were him, I would not make this mistake.
16. I don't like you coming late.
17. Mohan objected to me being late.
18. Being a rainy day we decided to take rest.
19. The man is my friend who called on me yesterday.
20. You and I have received your lesson.
21. He and myself went to get the seat reserved.
22. I, you and he will go to market.
23. One should respect his elders.
24. I availed of the opportunity.
25. The boys which are found guilty will be punished.

7.4 Correct Usage: Adjectives

7.4.1 What are Adjectives?

Adjectives are the describing words. They modify a noun or a pronoun, give more information and observation about it, describe its colour, material, shape, size, amount, price, quality, origin, personality, weight, temperature, age, direction, etc., and clarify the subject that is doing it. Adjectives don't have a singular and plural form or a masculine, feminine or neuter gender.

7.4.2 Classification of Adjectives

There are mainly *six* types of adjectives:

→ Numeric: *six, one, hundred, first, second, several*
→ Quantitative: *more, all, some, half, much, less, little, some, enough, great*
→ Qualitative: *colour, size, smell, weary, worn, etc*
→ Distributive: *each, every, either, neither*
→ Interrogative: *which, whose, what*
→ Demonstrative: *this, that, those, these, yonder*

Remember: The articles—*a, an* and *the*—and the possessives—*my, our, your* and *their*— are also adjectives. Present participles and past participles are also used as adjectives: *tiring journey, irritating habit, loaded goods, outdated customs*, etc.

7.4.3 Degrees of Comparison

7.4.3.1 There are *three* degrees of comparison: *positive, comparative* and *superlative:*

→ All monosyllabic and some disyllabic words may be changed into comparative and superlative degrees by adding '-er' or '-est', respectively: *soft-softer-softest, high-higher-highest, wise-wiser-wisest, thin-thinner-thinnest*, etc.
→ Adjectives ending in 'y' preceded by a consonant change into comparatives and superlatives by adding '-ier' or '-iest', respectively: *Holy-holier-holiest, ugly-uglier-ugliest, silly-sillier-silliest, lovely-lovelier-loveliest*, etc.
→ Adjectives ending in 'y' preceded by a vowel change into comparatives and superlatives by adding '-er' and '-est': *gray-grayer-grayest.*

→ Most of the disyllabic and all the words with more than two syllables use 'more' and 'most' in comparative and superlative forms: intelligent-more intelligent-most intelligent, honest-more honest-most honest.

7.4.3.2 Uses of the Degrees of Comparison:

1. Positive Degree is Used:
   → To talk about one person or object: He is a *good* boy. This is a *useful* book.
   → To show equality using 'as'—adjective—'as': That book is *as expensive as* the other one.
   → To show inequality using 'not as'—adjective—'as': Hari is *not as intelligent as* his brother.
   → To show comparison between two actions: *Walking* is *as difficult as running* in this weather. It is as difficult *to read as to write* in dim light.
2. Comparative Degree is Used:
   → To compare one object or person with another using 'than': He is *wiser than* his sister.
   → To show parallel increase or decrease using 'the': *The* higher you go *the* colder it gets. The more we earn, the more we spend.
   → To denote gradual decrease or increase using 'and': He is working *harder and harder*. The patient was becoming weaker and weaker.
3. Superlative Degree is Used:
   → To express the highest degree of something or someone using the + superlative + of/in: She is *the most beautiful girl of/in* her class.

7.4.4 Correct Use of Some Adjectives

1. Some, Any:

Both 'some' and 'any' may be used to talk about degree or quantity. 'Some' is used in affirmative sentences and 'any' is used in negative and interrogative sentences:

→ I need *some* water.
→ Is there *any* juice in the mug?
→ No, I don't have *any* books.

Remember: 'Some' may be used in questions expressing commands or requests:
→ Will you get me *some* milk?

2. Each, Every:

'Each' is used when we talk about two or more persons or objects and 'every' is used for more than two persons or objects. 'Each' is preferred when the group consists of a definite number of people or things and 'every' when the group consists of an indefinite number:

→ Last week I practiced vocabulary *each day*.
→ *Every member* gave his best to the institution.

'Every' may be used with abstract nouns while 'each' is not used with abstract nouns.
→ We have *every chance* of attaining success. (Not …each chance of attaining success.)
'Every' is be used with numbers. 'Each' is not used with numbers.
→ The bus for Delhi leaves *every 15* minutes.

3. Either, Neither:

'Either' means 'one or the other of two.' 'Neither' means 'not one nor the other of two.'
'Neither' means 'not either':

→ I *don't* like *either* dress. = I like *neither* dress.
'Either' can also mean 'each of the two':
→ The road was covered with green trees on the *either side*.

4. Either, One:

'Either' is used to refer to two persons or objects and 'one' is used for more than two persons or objects:

→ You may choose *either* of the *two* options.
→ *One* of my friends lives in Bangalore.

5. Neither, None:

We use 'neither' to refer to two persons or objects and 'none' to talk about more than two persons or objects:

→ You can have *neither* of the two prizes.
→ You can have *none* of the three prizes.

6. Nearest, Next:

'Nearest' indicates distance or space while 'next' indicates position or order. 'Next' can also mean 'immediately following':

→ The *nearest* hospital in this area is about five kilometres away.
→ I was waiting for the *next* candidate to come.
→ The *next* lecture is on Monday.

7. Elder, Eldest; Older, Oldest:

'Elder' and 'eldest' are used to refer to the members of the same family. 'Older' and 'oldest' may be used to refer to people, in general, as well as objects:

→ She is my *elder sister*.
→ My *eldest son* is an engineer.
→ This is the *oldest tree* in the garden.
→ He is the *oldest person* in the village.

Remember: 'Elder' is not followed by 'than'; it is followed by 'to' while 'older' is followed by than:

→ He is *older than* his sister.
→ This building is *older than* the other one.

8. Later, Latter, Latest, Last:

'Later' and 'latest' refer to time; 'latter' and 'last' denote position.
'Later' means 'afterwards' or 'soon after':
→ We decided to discuss the issue *later*.
'Latest' means 'newest':
→ I have bought the *latest edition* of the book.
'Latter' means 'second of the two.'
→ Of singing and dancing, I like the *latter*.
'Last' means 'final' or 'the most recent one':
→ He was the *last* one to enter the hall.

9. A little, Little, the Little:

'A little,' 'little' and 'the little' are used with uncountable nouns. 'A little' means 'some'; 'little' means 'hardly any' and 'the little' means 'not much but all of that much'.

→ There is *a little water* in the bottle. (some water)
→ There is *little water* in the bottle. (hardly any water)
→ He drank *the little* water left in the bottle. (not much water was left in the bottle, but he drank the whole of it)

10. A few, Few, the Few:
'A few', 'few' and 'the few' are used with countable nouns. 'A few' means 'some'; 'few' means 'hardly any'; 'the few' means 'not many, but all of them':

→ I have *a few* friends. (some friends)
→ I have *few* friends. (hardly any friends)
→ I have lost touch with *the few friends* I had. (I didn't have a lot of friends, but I have lost touch with all of them)

11. Much, Many:
'Much' is used with uncountable nouns and 'many' with countable nouns:

→ I have *many* friends.
→ There isn't *much food* left.

12. Many, Many a, A Great Many:
'Many' means 'numerous'; 'many a' is singular in use but plural in sense while 'a great many' means 'in large numbers':

→ I have read *many books* on this subject.
→ *Many a girl* has cleared IIT entrance this year.
→ *A great many people* attended the function.

13. First, Foremost:
'First' indicates 'order' while 'foremost' indicates 'prominence':

→ Mrs. Pratibha Patil is the *first* woman President of India.
→ The problem of female foeticide has been *foremost* in our minds recently.

14. Further, Farther:
'Further' means 'additional' while 'farther' means 'at a greater distance in space, direction or time':

→ Have you any *further* questions?
→ Let us walk a little *farther*.

15. Utmost, Uttermost, Outermost:
'Utmost' means 'extreme in highest degree'; 'uttermost' means 'remote or the most distant' while 'outermost' means 'farthest from the centre':

→ Ragging in the colleges is a matter of *utmost importance*.
→ With a telescope we can see the *uttermost stars of the galaxy*.
→ *The outermost wall of the house* was beautifully decorated.

16. Less, Lesser:
'Less' and 'lesser' mean 'not as great as the other in size number, duration, measurement', etc. However, 'less' is followed by 'than' while 'lesser' is not followed by 'than:'

→ People *of lesser importance* have no say in decision taking.
→ We will be there in *less than* thirty minutes. (Not ... lesser than thirty minutes)

17. Less, Fewer:
We use 'fewer' when talk about the countable and 'less' to talk about the measurable quantity or the uncountable. However, we use 'less' while referring to statistical or numerical expressions too:

→ No *fewer* than five hundred people were present at the ceremony.
→ It is *less* than two hundred kilometres to Delhi.
→ He is *less* than six feet tall.
→ The price of English book is *less* than that of chemistry.

18. All, Whole:

'All' refers to 'the whole number of' or 'the whole amount of' whereas, 'whole' refers to quantity or amount:

→ *The whole* milk was wasted.
→ *All* his *friends* helped him in times of need.
→ *All* his *money* was utilized properly.

19. Mutual, Common:

'Mutual' means 'reciprocal' while 'common' means 'belonging to two or more people in a group:'

→ Husband and wife share *mutual* understanding, love and respect.
→ All the members of my family share a *common* interest in photography.

20. Oral, Verbal:

'Oral' means 'spoken or delivered by mouth' rather written while 'verbal' means 'related to words':

→ An *oral* message is not given much importance.
→ There is no *verbal* difference between the two statements.

21. Due to, Owing to:

'Due to' is an adverbial complement which means 'caused by' while 'owing to' is a prepositional phrase which means, 'because of' and is used in the beginning of a sentence:

→ The team's success was largely *due to* her efforts.
→ *Owing to* his poor health, he could not qualify athletics trials.

7.4.5.   Common Errors in the Use of Adjectives

1. The adjectives ending in 'or'—*inferior, superior, junior, senior, exterior, interior, prior, major, minor*—are already in the comparative form, hence, they cannot be changed into comparative degree and are not followed by 'than':
   → This cloth is *inferior to* that in quality. (Not…inferior than…)
   → I am *senior to* you. (Not…senior than you)
   → There were calls for *major changes* to the welfare system. (Not…more major changes…)

2. The adjectives—*elder, former, likely, preferably, certain, sure, next, inner, utter*—are also not followed by 'than' rather they are followed by 'to':
   → Tea is *preferable to* coffee. (Not preferable than…)
   → He is *elder to* me. (Not elder than…)

3. If comparison is made by using 'other' we use 'than' instead of 'but':
   → He turned out to be none *other than* my old colleague. (…not none other but…)

4. The adjectives—*ideal, perfect, unique, supreme, extreme, chief, complete, universal, entire, eternal, unanimous, infinite, round, impossible, perpetual*—are not used in comparative/superlative degree:
   → Ms Gulati is an *ideal* teacher. (Not …the most ideal teacher)
   → This is a *unique* occasion. (Not…the most unique occasion)

5. Double comparatives should not be used:
   → An elephant is *stronger than* any other animal. (Not more stronger than…)
   → He is *happier* today. (Not more happier…)

6. While comparing two qualities of the same person, the adjectives should be used in 'more/less forms' and adjectives in '-er/-est forms' should not be used even if they can be changed into comparatives and superlatives using the said forms:
   → He is *more wise* than *good*.
   → She is *more smart* than *lovely*.

7. While using the comparative form to express selection from the two of the same kind or class, the comparative adjective is preceded by 'the' and is followed by 'of the' instead of 'than':
   → Ramesh is the *stronger of the* two boys. (Not… stronger than…)
   → Kalyani is *the more beautiful of the* two girls. (Not…more beautiful than…)

8. Never use 'the both pens', or 'your both eyes' because the correct word order is 'both the pens' or 'both your eyes':
   → Ram was present on *both the occasions*. (Not ….on the both occasions.)
   → *Both of my friends* came to attend my birthday. (Not My both friend…)

9. While using two adjectives—one of which is changed into comparative and superlative adding '-er/-est form' and the other one by adding 'more/most form'—in comparative or superlative degree, the adjective in '-er/-est form' should be used first and the adjective with 'more/ most form' should be used later:
   → She is *wiser* and *more beautiful* than her sister. (Not …more beautiful and wiser…)
   → He is *kinder* and *more honest* than any other person in the family. (Not …more honest and kinder…)

10. If two qualities of the same person or object are compared with something or somebody, both the adjectives should be used either in comparative or superlative degree:
    → This is the *safest and shortest* of all the routes. (Not safest and shorter…)
    → She is *more beautiful and more intelligent* than her friends. (Not more beautiful and intelligent…)

11. Comparative form + than + any should be followed by other + singular noun:
    → He is *smarter than* any other boy in the class. (Not…smarter than any boys…)
    → She speaks *more fluently than* any other girl in her group. (Not…more fluently than any other girls…)

12. Comparative form + than+ all/ most should be followed by other + plural nouns:
    → Rohit writes *more clearly than all/most other girls* in her family. (Not …most/all other girl…)
    → This idea is *more useful than all/most other ideas* expressed in the book. (Not …all/most other idea…)

13. Adjective 'worth' is used after the word it qualifies:
    → This is a *book worth reading*. (Not …worth reading book…)
    → The Taj is a *building worth seeing*. (Not …worth seeing building…)

14. In some cases, comparison is very subtle. One should use it carefully:
    → The climate of Indore is *better than that of* Delhi. (Not …better than Delhi…)
    → The roads of Haryana are *better than those of* Madhya Pradesh. (…Not better than Madhya Pradesh…)
    → My book is *less expensive than yours*. (Not less expensive than you.)

Task

Correct the following sentences:

1. He left the college latest of all.
2. No less than 60 students attended the class.
3. He is wiser than kind.
4. Tea is more preferable than coffee.
5. This is the most ideal couple.
6. He is the oldest of my uncle's 3 sons.

7. He is so cunning as his sister.
8. She is weaker than any girl in the class.
9. He is more cleverer than any other boy.
10. She is comparatively weaker in English.
11. We met him prior than his departure.
12. He is the ablest and kind person in the village.
13. Mr. Gupta is the most ideal professor.
14. Put a few fuel on the fire.
15. Many a boys were present there.
16. He came latter than I.
17. What is the last score.
18. I work whole day.
19. He has a strong headache.
20. He works on a less salary.
21. I have not any friends.
22. The 2 first chapters of the book are very difficult.
23. Mohit is my fast enemy.
24. The enemy is becoming weak day by day.
25. Gold, silver or lead which is more precious?
26. Give me six and a half rupees.
27. Of the two prices buy the least expensive.
28. Choose the least of the two evils.

7.5   Correct Usage: Articles

The demonstrative adjectives—*a, an* and *the*—are called articles. 'A/an' is the mild form of 'any' while 'the' is that of 'this.'

There are two types of articles: indefinite articles: 'a' and 'an'; and definite article: 'the.' The indefinite articles 'a/an' points out some indefinite person, place or object while the definite article 'the' points out some particular person, place or object. For example: '*A boy* came to me yesterday'—means 'any boy.' '*The boy* gave me a book'—here the boy is specific, that is, 'The same boy who came to me yesterday.'

A or an: 'A' is used before the words beginning with consonant sounds while 'an' is used before the words and abbreviations beginning with vowel sounds: *a* book, *a* pen, *a* woman, *a* university, *a* one-rupee note, *a* European, *a* yard, *an* orange, *an* apple, *an* enemy, *an* ass, *an* MLA., *an* SO., *an* heir, *an* honest man, *an* hour, etc.

7.5.1   Use of Indefinite Article

The indefinite article 'a/an' is used:

1. In the numeric sense of 'one': He has *a book* in his hand.
2. In the sense of 'any': A *degree* can't help a man these days.
3. In the vague sense of 'someone': One evening *a girl* came to me.
4. Before a proper noun used as a common noun: Today *a Shakespeare* has come to our college.
5. In the sense of 'per/every': He is getting 20,000/*a month*.
6. In the sense of 'the same': The birds of *a feather* flock together.
7. With 'few' and 'little' to refer to small amount or small number, respectively: A few books, a little milk, etc.
8. Between an adjective and a noun if the adjective is preceded by an adverb like, *so, how, too, such, quite,* etc.: *so good a* boy, *too clever a* man, *how nice a* picture, *such a great* person, *quite a few* mistakes, etc.

7.5.2 Use of Definite Articles

7.5.2.1 The definite article 'the' is used before nouns if they are:

1. Names of seas, oceans, gulfs, rivers, bays and canals: *The Arabian Sea, The Indian Ocean, The Persian Gulf, The Ganges, The Thames, The Bay of Bengal, The Sahara Canal,* etc.
2. Names of dates and seasons: *The 15th August, the 26th January, March the first, the winter, the autumn, the spring,* etc.
3. Names of famous buildings, deserts, plains, group of islands, mountain ranges: *The Town Hall, The Kutub Minar, The Thar Desert, The Indo-Gangetic Plain, The West Indies, The Himalayas,* etc.
4. Names of well-known historical events: *The Battle of Panipat, The Renaissance,* etc.
5. Names of countries and provinces if they are descriptive, that is, include words such as republic, nations and kingdom: *The United States, The United Kingdom, The Irish Republic, the Uttar Pradesh,* etc.
6. Names of famous newspapers, journals, magazines and religious books: *The Hindustan Times, The Times of India, The Illustrated Weekly, The Indian Review, The Vedas, The Bhagwat Geeta, The Bible,* etc.
7. Names of posts or titles of honour and rank: *The Principal, the Director, the Honourable Mr. Ghosh, The Rev Mr. Patil,* etc.
8. Names of ships, airplanes, community or party: *The Titanic, The Carpathian, The Boeing 707, The Hindu, The English, The Congress, the Republican Party,* etc.
9. Names of planets and things unique of their kind: *The earth, the mars, the sun, the sea, the sky, the ocean,* etc.
10. Names of musical instruments: *The flute, the sitar,* etc.
11. A common noun used in the sense of an abstract idea: He felt *the poet* rise within him. (poet-like feelings)
12. A singular noun which refers to a particular person, place or thing: I have lost *the book* you gave me yesterday.
13. A proper, material or abstract noun if emphasis is laid upon it:
    → I have invited *the Guptas* to dinner.
    → He is *the Banerji,* I was talking about.
    → This is *the proper time* to do it.
    → This is *the right occasion* to help the victims.
14. Proper nouns in metaphorical sense:
    → Kalidas is *the Shakespeare* of India.
    → Mumbai is *the Manchester* of India.
15. Before the names of directions when a preposition is added:
    → We were going *to the north.*
    → They started their journey *to the west.*
    However, 'the' should not be used if there is no preposition.

7.5.2.2 The definite article 'the' is used for adjectives:

1. To make them plural nouns: *The weak, the noble, the strong, the wicked.*
2. To represent an abstraction: *The good, the unknown, the unbelievable, the beauty,* etc.
3. To denote a nationality: *The Irish, the French, The German, The Greek,* etc.
4. Before ordinal numbers: *The first, the second, the last, the ninth,* etc.
5. Before comparative form of adjectives expressing a proportion between two states of mind or two circumstances:
    → *The sooner* a thing is done, *the better* it is.
    → *The more* they get *the more* they demand.
    → *The more, the merrier.*

6. Before the adjectives in superlative degree:
   → Nivedita is *the best singer* of her college.
   → Kushal is *the best player* of his class.

7.5.3   Omission of the Articles

No article should be used before:

1. Material and abstract nouns: *wisdom, kindness, health, sugar, rice, oil, tea, coffee*, etc.
2. Plural countable nouns used in general sense:
   → *People* love children.
   → *Computers* are used in many offices.
3. Proper nouns: names of people, cities, countries, individual mountains/hills, islands and lakes, etc.: *Rini, Rakhi, Delhi, Agra, India, America, Mount Everest, Mount Abu, Cylone, Java, lake Sambhar, lake Chilka*, etc.
4. Names of months and days: *Monday, Tuesday, January, February*, etc.
5. Names of the meals used in general sense: *lunch, dinner, breakfast, tea*, etc.
6. Names of certain places visited for their primary purpose: *school, college, church, bed, table, hospital, market, prison*, etc.
7. Names of languages: *Hindi, English, Sanskrit, Punjabi*, etc.
   Please note: English = English language; The English = English people.
8. Names of relations: *father, mother, uncle, aunt, cook, nurse*, etc.
9. Name of a famous/religious book preceded by the name of its author: *Valmiki's' Ramayan, Homer's Odyssey, Shakespeare's Twelfth Night, Milton's Paradise Lost*, etc.
10. Names of subjects: *biology, physical education, painting, drawing, history*, etc.
11. Names of title/rank/profession used as a complements or in apposition to the person holding them:
    → Mr. T. K. Singh was *chosen Chairman* of the trust.
    → Ms. Sharma *became Principal* of this school in 2002.
    → Mr. Gupta, *Principal of the college* met me yesterday.
    → Dr. Manmohan Singh, *Prime Minister of India* is very popular among the people.
12. Common nouns used in pairs in a sentence:
    → The old man had to go *door to door* asking for help.
    → *Husband and wife* complement each other.
13. Common noun after 'kind of' or 'species of': *worst kind of teacher, best kind of woman, rare species of bird*, etc.
14. Common nouns used as nominative address: *Ladies and gentlemen*, Come here, *boy*. Listen *girls*!
15. Superlative form preceded by a possessive adjective or used for address: *My best* friend, *my loveliest* gift, O, *my dearest* son, O, *kindest creature*, etc.

7.5.4   Repetition of Articles

1. When two adjectives qualify two different nouns, article should be used before both of them. However, it should be used before the first one only if two adjectives qualify the same noun:
   → I bought *a yellow and a black clock*. (Two clocks, one yellow and the other black)
   → I bought *a yellow and black clock* yesterday. (One clock which is partly yellow and partly black.)
2. When two nouns joined by 'and' denote two different individuals or objects, article should be used before both of them and before the first one only when they refer to the same one:
   → *The horse and carriage* is ready.
   → *The poet and the orator* have arrived.

3. When nouns are given in a series and some of them require 'a' and some require 'an' article should be repeated: *An M.P., an S.D.M., an artist, a dancer, a musician* were present at the occasion.

Task

Insert articles wherever required:

1. Elephant is largest of all animals.
2. We shall see him after dinner.
3. I came across a tiger in forest.
4. Don't make noise.
5. Aeroplane has conquered time and space.
6. You have too high opinion about him.
7. It is not easy to become Kalidas in India.
8. Taj Mahal was built at great expense.
9. I am certain that he is in right.
10. Both thieves were taken into custody.
11. Sun rises in the east and sets in west.
12. She has useless pen.
13. We arrived quarter of an hour earlier.
14. Whole India is protesting against inflation.
15. Principal of this college is coming.

Correct the following sentences:

1. He is an university student.
2. What type of a boy is he?
3. The book is in a good condition.
4. It was worth ten and half rupees.
5. Wheat is sold by quintals.
6. He made a mention of this in his letter.
7. Ramesh, the goldsmith of this town, is coming.
8. I want to go to cinema.
9. Men were free in past.
10. The student fell sick at the school and is now in the bed.
11. O, the dearest one, when shall I see you again?
12. I caught him by his neck.
13. I remember kindness with which he treated us.
14. He got the rank of a captain.
15. Look here, cows are grazing grass.

7.6 Correct Usage: Adverb

7.6.1 What are Adverbs?

Adverbs are the words, which modify a verb, adjective or another adverb. For example: Joy drives *slowly*. She writes *neatly*. He runs very *fast*. In these sentences the words, 'slowly,' 'neatly,' and 'fast' are adverbs and they show how the actions are done.

7.6.2 Kinds of Adverbs

	Kind	Shows	Examples
1.	Time	Shows when something happens	now, then, before, ago, soon, since, presently, never, already, when, ever, lately, early, late, daily, today, tomorrow, yesterday
2.	Frequency	Shows how often something happens	twice, often, again, once, always, frequently, seldom, doubly, usually
3.	Place	Shows where something happens	here, there, everywhere, away, backward, forward, above, below, under, in, out, far, near, away, aboard, inside, outside, whence, thence
4.	Manner	Shows how something happens	clearly, well, good, soundly, slowly, bravely, boldly, hard, agreeably, beautifully, skilfully, seriously, nicely, happily, fast, hard
5.	Degree or quantity	Shows how much or in what degree or to what extent	very, fully, almost, enough, partly, quite, too, any, altogether, much, exactly, hardly, rather, about, nearly, scarcely, utterly, wholly
6.	Affirmation and negation	Shows affirmation or negation	surely, certainly, surely not, probably, indeed, yes, not
7.	Reason	Shows why something happens	consequently, therefore, hence, owing to, because, thus, so

7.6.3 Position of Adverbs

The position of adverb affects the meaning of a sentence; hence, the adverb should be placed in the right place in a sentence:

1. The adverbs of manner, place and time and the adverb phrases of time are generally used after the verb or the direct object:
   → He speaks *fluently*.
   → I looked for my book *everywhere*.
   → I will come *soon*.
   → They are leaving for Delhi *tomorrow*.

2. The adverbs of frequency are usually placed between the subject and the verb if the verb has only one word:
   → We *usually* play tennis.
   → We *never* cook.
   However, these adverbs are placed between the auxiliary verb and the main verb if the verb has two words:
   → He has *already* finished his project.
   → I have *often* told you to write neatly.
   These adverbs are placed after the auxiliary verbs:
   → I am *never* late for the college.
   → We are *always* at home on Sundays.
   In short, responses if an auxiliary is stressed, the adverb comes before it:
   → Do you come late? No, I *always do* come on time.
   → When will you submit your assignment? I *already have* submitted it.

3. If there are more than two adverbs after a verb or its object, the adverb of manner comes first, the adverb of place comes second and the adverb of time comes last:
   → She comes *regularly at the shop every morning.*
   → He spoke *well at the meeting last Sunday.*
   → I go for jogging *in the park every day.*

4. Adverb is placed before the auxiliaries, 'have to' and 'used to':
   → He *always used to* speak politely.
   → We *hardly have to* go to college on foot.

5. Adverb is placed before the adjective or another adverb it modifies:
   → The room was *quite* cold.
   → This game is *very* interesting.

6. The adverb, 'enough' is used after the word it qualifies:
   → He is *strong enough* to lift this weight.
   → The teacher spoke *loud enough* to be heard.

7. The adverb, 'Only' modifies the word that comes directly after it:
   → It *only* rained on Wednesday. (It only rained, it didn't thunder.)
   → It rained *only* on Wednesday. (It rained on that day, not on Monday or Tuesday, etc.)
   → I solved *only* two sums. (not more than two sums)
   → I *only* solved two sums. (did not do anything else)

7.6.4   Correct Use of Adverbs

1. No preposition is used before time showing words—'morning,' 'evening,' 'night,' 'month,' 'year'—when they are preceded by the qualifying words—'this,' 'that,' 'tomorrow,' 'last,' 'next,' etc:
   → He is coming *tomorrow morning.*
   → My father left for Delhi *last Sunday.*
   If time showing words are used without the qualifying words, preposition is used:
   → I will go to market *in the evening.*
   → We will play football *in the morning.*

2. No adverb should be used between the infinitive, that is, to + verb:
   → I request you to call the doctor *immediately.* (Not ... to immediately call the doctor...)

3. Introductory 'there' has no significance as an adverb of place. In such sentences 'there' comes before an intransitive verb or the verb 'to be':
   → *There came* a tiger from the bush.
   → *There was* a large gathering in the park.

4. The verbs—'smell,' 'look,' 'taste,' 'sound,' 'feel'—etc., take an adjective not an adverb:
   → The rose smells *sweet*. (not sweetly)
   → She looks *angry*. (not angrily)

5. 'Home' is a noun. It is used as an adverb also. No preposition or relative adjective should be used before it:
   → I am *going home*.
   → They are *coming home*.

6. The adverb, 'too' usually used with the preposition 'to' means 'more than enough/desirable/required' for a specific purpose. It is used in negative sense:
   → It is *too* hot *to* go outside.
   → The news is *too* good *to* be true.
   'Too' is used in the sense of 'also':
   → He, *too*, went there.
   → We, *too*, did it.
   'Too' is also used in the sense of 'very':
   → I'm not *too* sure if this is right.
   → I'm just going out—I won't be *too* long.

7. Ago, Before: 'Ago' is used when we refer to the past from the time of speaking and 'before' when we refer to the past from any specific point of time:
   → I saw him *two years ago*.
   → I saw him *before I left* for Delhi.

8. As and So: Both 'as' and 'so' are used in comparative degree. 'As' is used in affirmative sentences while 'so' is used in negative ones:
   → This book is *as* useful *as* the other one.
   → He is not *so* good at English *as* his brother is.

9. 'Sometimes' is one word. It is used as an adverb:
   → *Sometimes* he becomes furious.

10. 'Quite' means 'perfectly,' 'entirely' or 'fully,' hence, it should not be used in the sense of 'very':
    → This is *quite a different* problem.
    → I'm *quite happy* to wait for you here.

11. 'Now and then' means 'occasionally'; 'off and on' means 'regularly':
    → He goes to the theatre *now and then*.
    → He has been learning English *off and on*.

12. Very and much:
    'Very' is used with 'different' when it is not preceded by 'not' and 'much' is used with 'different' when it is preceded by 'not':
    → Delhi is *very different* from Chennai.
    → Delhi is *not much different* from Chandigarh.
    'Very' is used with present participle while 'much' is used with past participle:
    → This news is *very surprising*.
    → He was *much upset* with the results.
    'Very' is used with adjectives in positive degree while much is used with adjectives in comparative degree:
    → This gift is *very expensive*.
    → This toy is *much more expensive* than the other one.
    Both 'very' and 'much' are used for adjectives in superlative degree but the word order is different: the + very + superlative ; much + the + superlative:
    → He is *the very best* runner of the college.
    → He is *much the fastest* runner.

13. 'Comparatively' is followed by an adjective in positive degree:
    → He died *comparatively young*. (not ...comparatively younger...)
    → This exercise is *comparatively easy*. (not ...comparatively easier...)

14. 'Rather' means 'fairly' or 'to some degree.' It has a force of comparison in it so it should not be used with the adjectives in comparative degree:
    → The instructions were *rather complicated*. (not…rather more complicated)
    → The book is *rather expensive*. (not…rather more expensive)

15. The adverbial phrase 'by and by' means 'gradually:
    → He will recover from the shock *by and by*.
    → You will feel better *by and by*.

16. 'Of course' means 'admittedly.' It should be used to emphasize something you are saying is true or correct:
    → 'Don't you like my painting?' '*Of course* I do!
    → 'Can I use your pen?' '*Of course* you can.'

17. 'Badly' when used with 'want' and 'need' has the meaning of 'urgently' and is placed before these verbs:
    → I *badly* want this job.
    → Your suit *badly* needs ironing.

18. 'Hardly' and 'scarcely' have a negative meaning and they should not be used with a negative verb:
    → I *hardly* know her. (not.. hardly don't know her)
    → He can *scarcely* see in this light. (not… can scarcely not see…)

19. 'Far and away' means 'decidedly'; 'far and wide' or 'far and near' means 'in all directions':
    → She is *far and away* the best player.
    → They searched *far and near* for the missing child.

20. Yet, still: 'Yet' shows that we are expecting something and it is placed at the end of a negative statement or a question whereas, 'still' means 'going longer than expected' and it is placed in the middle of a sentence:
    → It is *still* raining.
    → The mail hasn't arrived *yet*.

Task

Correct the following sentences:

1. Firstly I want a pen.
2. He speaks very fluent.
3. I could not find it nowhere.
4. He goes to Delhi often.
5. She is enough smart to tackle this problem.
6. She is much intelligent.
7. He paid dear for his mistake.
8. It is bitter cold today.
9. I feel so lonely without my kids.
10. He is very poorer than all of his friends.
11. He is presently in Chandigarh.
12. Last night you returned lately.
13. I only engaged this servant for a week.
14. She was even blamed by her parents.
15. No excuse is too slight not to be seized upon.
16. Drinking is quite harmful for one's health.
17. Did you do it? Yes I didn't.
18. It is nothing else than pride.
19. I have not been here too long to have many friends.
20. They haven't still spent their money.
21. We yet have time to catch the train.

22. Home made sweets are generally too wholesome.
23. Not to talk of English, he can't even talk Hindi correctly.
24. Call him anything else than a fool.
25. He behaved friendly.

7.7   Correct Usage: Preposition

7.7.1   What is a Preposition?

A preposition is a word or group of words, such as *in, from, to, out of, on behalf of*, used before a noun or pronoun to show relationships between nouns, pronouns and other words in a sentence.

7.7.2   Kinds of Prepositions

There are basically four types of prepositions:

1. Simple Prepositions: Simple prepositions are single word prepositions, for example, *at, as, at, but, by, down, except, for, from, in, like, near, of, off, on , over, since, than, to, under, up, with*, etc.

2. Compound Prepositions: Compound prepositions are the combination of a preposition with a noun, an adjective or an adverb, for example, *across, around, beside, beneath, within, without, outside, inside, into, onto, upon, underneath*, etc.

3. Participial Prepositions: Participial prepositions are, in fact, present participle forms of verbs used as prepositions, for example, *regarding, concerning, excepting, excluding, barring, notwithstanding, considering, following, during*, etc.

4. Phrase Prepositions or Conglomerate Prepositions: Phrase prepositions are the group of words used as prepositions, that is, *in accordance with, according to, with reference to, along with, owing to, due to, in lieu of, in spite of, instead of, on account of, for the sake of, on behalf of, with regards to, in order to, in the course of*, etc.

7.7.3   Position of Prepositions

1. Prepositions are generally placed before the noun/pronoun:
   → I saw him *in the park.*
   → The cat is sitting *under the table.*
2. When the object is an interrogative pronoun or a relative pronoun understood, the preposition is placed at the end of a sentence:
   → What are you *looking for?*
   → Which of these benches did you *sit on?*
   → This is the place I was *talking about.*
   → Here is the sum you *asked for.*
3. When the object is a relative pronoun, the preposition is placed at the end of a sentence:
   → These are the words that I was *referring to.*
   → Here is the girl whom I was *speaking of.*
4. Sometimes when the object is placed first, for the sake of emphasis, preposition is placed at the end of a sentence:
   → *This* I insisted *on.*
   → *The Taj Mahal* is known the world *over.*

7.7.4   Major Relations Indicated by Prepositions

Relation	Preposition	Usage	Examples
Time	In	• months/seasons • part of day • year • after a certain period of time	• *in* January/*in* winter • *in* the evening • *in* 2009 • *in* an hour
	Within	• before the end of	• *within* two hours
	At	• for night • for weekend • for festival • for mealtime • a certain point of time	• *at* night • *at* the weekend • *at* Christmas • *at* lunch • *at* six o'clock
	On	• for day • for date • day + morning, evening, etc.	• *on* Monday/Tuesday, etc. • *on* 17th October • *on* Friday night
	Since	• from a certain point of time in the past till now	• *since* 1986
	For	• over a certain period of time in the past till now	• *for* two years
	Ago	• a certain time in the past from the time of speaking	• five years *ago*
	Before	• earlier than a certain point of time	• *before* 2008
	To	• telling the time (before)	• five *to* two (1.55)
	Past	• telling the time (after)	• five *past* eleven (11.05)
	Till/until	• marking the beginning and end of a period of time • how long something is going to last	• from Monday, *till* Friday • *until* he comes
	By	• at the latest • up to a certain time	• *by* 6 o'clock. • *by* tomorrow morning
	From	• one point of time to another	• *From* 5 a.m. to 6 p.m.
Place	In	• room, building, city, country • book, paper, etc. • car, taxi • picture, world	• *in* the room, *in* Delhi • *in* the notebook, *in* the news paper • *in* the bus, *in* a car • *in* the picture, *in* the world

(Continued)

Relation	Preposition	Usage	Examples
	At	• by an object • next to • for table • for events • place where you do something typical (watch a film, study, work, etc.)	• *at* the door • *at* the end of the queue • *at* the table • *at* a concert, *at* the party • *at* the traffic lights, at school, *at* work
	On	• where something is attached • for a place with a river • being on a surface • for a certain side (left, right) • for a floor in a house • for public transport • for television, radio	• a picture *on* the wall • Agra lies *on* the Yamuna • *on* the shelf • *on* the left • *on* the first floor • *on* the bus, *on* a plane • *on* TV, *on* the radio
	By, next to, beside	• left or right of somebody or something	• *by/next to/beside* the car/fireplace/bed
	Under	• on the ground but lower than something else	• the bag is *under* the table
	Below	• lower than something else but above ground	• the fish are *below* the surface
	Behind	• at the back of something or someone	• *behind* the house • *behind* the girl
	Over	• covered by something else • meaning more than • getting to the other • overcoming an obstacle	• a jacket *over* your T-shirt • *over* 90 years of age • walk *over* the bridge • climb *over* the tree
	Above	• higher than something else, but not directly over it	• a road *above* the river
	Across	• getting to the other side of a bridge, road, water body, etc.	• walk *across* the bridge • swim *across* the pool
	Through	• something with limits on top, bottom and the sides	• drive *through* the tunnel
	To	movement to: • a person, object or building • a place or country • for bed	• go *to* the cinema • go *to* Mumbai/America • go *to* bed
Agency and Possession	*Through*	• by the means of something or someone	• *through* him/her

(*Continued*)

Relation	Preposition	Usage	Examples
	By	• who (somebody) • which (something) • means of travelling • what somebody does	• done *by* me • cut *by* knife • a journey *by* train • doctors *by* profession
	From	• a source of someone/ something	• *from* my uncle/father
	Of	belonging to: • some object • rank • person • place	• a lesson *of* the book • the picture *of* a palace • man *of* character • a book *of* my friend • Director *of* the college
	With	• belonging to someone/ something • with something/ someone	• *with* sweet voice • *with* my father • write *with* a pen
Cause and Purpose	Of	• related to something/ someone	• died *of* cholera/fever • left place because *of* her
	From	• for the reason	• died *from* fatigue
	Through	• by the means of	• concealed truth *through* shame
	For	• for the cause of	• fought *for* freedom
	With	• due to something	• trembled *with* fear
Manner and Method	By	• the way, approach, behaviour, style, conduct • how or what way something is done	• a letter *by* mail • *by* good nature/positive attitude • *by* hard work • *by* pressing the button
	With	• using something	• clean *with* a brush • fought *with* courage • treated *with* acid
Direction and Motion	Into	• movement towards the interior of a volume	• paper ball went *into* the garbage can
	Towards	• in the direction of something or someone	• heading *towards* the aim • back *towards* me
	Up	• in a higher position	• the sun was *up* • go *up*
	Round	• in a circle	• *round* the world • *round* the sun

(Continued)

Relation	Preposition	Usage	Examples
	To	• orientation towards a goal	• *to* market, *to* the office, *to* Delhi
	onto	• movement towards a surface	• Fell *onto* the floor
	Into	• movement inside something	• *into* the well • *into* the water

7.7.5   Correct Use of Prepositions

1. Beside/Besides: 'Beside' means 'at the side of' and 'besides' means 'in addition to':

→ My school is *beside* the lake.
→ He is learning English *besides* French and German.

2. Below/Under: 'Below' means 'lower than,' 'less than' and 'inferior to' and 'Under' means 'according to,' 'in the course of time' and 'lower in rank':

→ Raju is *below* fourteen, so he cannot play this game.
→ Take any number *below* hundred.
→ No one *below* the officer's rank can apply for the post.
→ Neelam inherited a large property *under* the will of her father.
→ The issue is *under* discussion.
→ The Assistant Manager is *under* the General Manager.

3. Since/For: 'Since' is used for 'a point of time from the past' while 'for' indicates 'duration of time':

→ We have been doing it *since* morning.
→ They have been learning English *for* many years.

4. Between/Among: 'Between' is used for two persons or things while 'among' is used for more than two:

→ I stood *between* Vandana and Jyoti.
→ This is a custom, which exists *among* the tribals.

5. By/With: 'By' is used for the agent or the doer while 'with' is used for the instruments:

→ He was killed *by* a terrorist.
→ The terrorist killed the lady *with* an axe.

6. In/At/On (Place):   'In' is used for bigger places, districts, countries, etc., 'at' is used for smaller towns, villages or places while 'on' is used for streets, floor, road, etc.:

→ He lives *at* 36, Geeta Marg *in* Lucknow.
→ The show was organized *at* the Art Club *in* Delhi.
→ There is a village *on* this road.
→ His house is *on* the first floor.

7. On/In/At/By (time): 'On' is used for days, 'in' is used for months or years, 'at' for 'time' and 'by' indicates the latest time by which the action will be finished:

→ We should have vacation *at* the right time.
→ We will be there *at* 6.30 p.m. *on* Monday.
→ They will visit hill station *in* summer.
→ I hope to finish it *by* 15 January.

8. In/Into: 'In' is used to show the state of being inside something, whereas 'into' shows movement to the inside of something:

→ He is sleeping *in* the room.
→ The ball fell *into* the tank.

9. On/Upon: 'On' is used for objects in a position while 'upon' presents things in motion:

→ Put it down *on* the table.
→ The boy jumped *upon* the horse.

10. In/Within: While referring to time 'in' indicates the end of a certain period and 'within' means before the certain period of time:

→ We will be back *in* three days.
→ They will repay the loan *within* three years.

11. By/Until: 'By' means 'not later than the time mentioned' and 'until' means 'up to the point in time or the event mentioned not before that':

→ We hope to finish it *by* Sunday.
→ He will be in his office *until* 5 p.m.

12. Differ from/Differ with: 'Differ from' means 'dissimilar' whereas 'differ with' means 'to disagree with someone':

→ This picture *differs from* that one.
→ I *differ with* my father on this issue.

13. Agree with/Agree to: We 'agree with a person on some point' and 'agree to' a proposal:

→ I know he will not *agree with* us on that point.
→ The members of the Council did not *agree to* the proposal.

14. Compare with/Compare to: 'Compare with' is used to compare two persons or things of the same kind while 'compare to' is used to compare a particular quality of two dissimilar objects or persons:

→ This house doesn't *compare with* our previous one.
→ I had some difficulties but they were nothing *compared to* yours.

15. During/While: 'During' is a preposition which is used before the phrases. 'While' is a conjunction that is used before a clause:

→ I usually read *during* lunch.
→ I often sing *while* I am cooking.

16. As/Like: We use 'as' to talk about a job or a function while we use 'like' to talk about things being similar:

→ You can use this bucket *as* a dustbin.
→ You look *like* your mother.

Task

Fill in the blanks with suitable prepositions:

1. He was standing — her.
2. The police have arrested the criminal — the warrant of the court.
3. He is an authority — this subject.
4. There was a long discussion — this issue.
5. What are you looking — ?
6. She was standing — the mirror.
7. He walked across the road — the flower beds.
8. He will go to school — foot.
9. The reasons — his failure are not known yet.
10. They left the room one — one.
11. The lion was shot — me — a gun.
12. The cat pounced — the rat.
13. One must learn — distinguish — the good and the bad.
14. She is — leave.
15. She is married — a rich merchant.
16. He is working — computer.
17. He prevented me — telling lies.
18. Team has lost the match — its rival.
19. I am looking — my lost pen.
20. What is the time — your watch?

7.8 Correct Usage: Conjunctions

7.8.1 What is a Conjunction?

A conjunction is a word that links words, phrases or clauses. For example:

→ He *and* his friends have come.
→ Rajasthan is famous for its rich culture *and* hospitality of its people.
→ I was upset, *still* I kept quiet.
→ You must pay the dues *or* you will not be allowed to appear at the test.

In these sentences 'and,' 'still' and 'or' are conjunctions connecting different words, phrases and clauses.

7.8.2 Types of Conjunctions

There are mainly four types of conjunctions: *coordinating* conjunctions, *correlative* conjunctions, *subordinating* conjunctions and connecting *adverbs*.

7.8.2.1 Coordinating Conjunctions

Coordinating conjunctions are used to link two grammatical constructions or statements of equal rank, that is, nouns with nouns, adverbs with adverbs, phrases with phrases and clauses with clauses. When a coordinating conjunction links two verbs, which have the same subject, the subject need not be repeated. If a coordinating conjunction links two verbs, which do not have the same subject, the two coordinate clauses may be separated by a comma or semicolon, to make the meaning clear. The following coordinating conjunctions provide additional information:

→ And: Along with: The team played well *and* won the match.
→ As well as: In addition to: Tina *as well as* Sheena has qualified for the finals.
→ Both … and: Together: Anil is *both* smart *and* clever.
→ Not only … but also: Both the things or qualities: She is *not only* clever, *but also* hard working.
→ No less than: Both equally: He is *no less than* you responsible for the job.

The following coordinating conjunctions convey opposition or contrast:

→ But Nevertheless: The workers are poor *but* they are diligent.
→ Yet/Still: However: He is very rich *yet/still* he is unhappy.
→ Whereas/While: But: He is reserved *whereas/while* his brother is outspoken.
→ Nevertheless: On the other hand: He was threatened *nevertheless* he decided to speak truth.
→ However: But: Everybody was against him; *however,* he did not leave his stand.
→ Only: In no other condition: Children are admitted *only* if they are accompanied by an adult.

The following coordinating conjunctions present two alternatives or choices:

→ Or: Alternatively: Sit quietly *or* leave the room.
→ Either … or: One or the other of two: He is *either* a fool *or* a dupe.
→ Nor: And neither: You haven't seen him *nor* have I.
→ Neither … nor: Not one nor the other of two: Their house is *neither* big *nor* small.
→ Otherwise, else: If not: The students should apologize for the misbehaviour *otherwise* (or else) they will be punished.

The following coordinating conjunctions present something inferred from another statement:

→ For: Because: He must be very hungry *for* he has not eaten anything.
→ So: Consequently: He is very hard working *so* he will definitely do it.

7.8.2.2 Correlative Conjunctions

Correlative conjunctions are used in pairs. They join similar elements to show the relationship between the ideas expressed in different parts of a sentence. While joining singular and plural subjects or the subjects of different persons, the subject closest to the verb determines whether the verb is singular or plural. Most of the correlative conjunctions are coordinate conjunctions such as 'not only…but also,' 'either…or,' 'neither…nor,' 'both…and.' The rest are as follows:

→ Not … but: He was *not* a student *but* a teacher.
→ Though … yet: *Though* he tried his best *yet* he could not succeed. 'Yet' may be omitted but it is wrong to use 'but' in its place.
→ Whether … or: I am not able to decide *whether* I should do it *or* not.
→ As … so: *As* you do *so* you will you face.

- → So … as: This question is not *so* difficult *as* you think.
- → So … that: It is *so* heavy *that* no one can lift it.
- → Such … that: He has *such* pleasant manners *that* everyone loves him.
- → Such … as: He offered *such* help *as* I could not refuse.
- → No sooner … than: *No sooner* did he reach the station *than* the train started. *No sooner* had he seen the tiger *than* he fired a shot.
- → Scarcely … when: *Scarcely* had we left home, *when* it started raining.

7.8.2.3   Subordinating Conjunctions

A subordinating conjunction links a clause to another on which it depends for its full meaning. In other words, it connects two dependent clauses. It may begin with relative pronouns such as 'that'/ 'what'/'whatever'/'which'/'who' and 'whom' as well as with the words such as 'how'/'when'/'where'/'wherever' and 'why' or with the words which are commonly referred to as subordinating conjunctions:

- → As: Because: *As* it is cold, you should take a sweater. When: We'll decide on the team *as* and when we qualify.
- → After: Later in time: You may leave, *after* you have finished your work.
- → Although or though: Despite the fact that: *Although* we worked hard, we could not succeed.
- → Before: Prior to: I had arrived *before* the train came.
- → Because: For the reason that: We were shivering *because* it was very cold.
- → For: Because: He is happy *for* he enjoys his work.
- → If: On condition that: *If* she is here, I will definitely see her.
- → Lest: For fear that: We started early *lest* we should miss the train. (The conjunction, 'lest' is always used with the verb, 'should.')
- → That: So as to: Work hard *that* you may pass.
- → In order that: So that: We should play games *in order that* our health may improve.
- → Provided: On condition that: You will do well in exams *provided* you work hard.
- → Provided that: If: *Provided that* you have the money in your account, you can withdraw up to fifty thousand a day.
- → Since: From a past time: It is twenty years *since* I have seen her. As, because: *Since* you are here, you can help me.
- → So: Consequently: It was raining, *so* we did not go out.
- → So … that: In such a way that: The programme has been *so* organized *that* none of us felt bored.
- → So that: In order that: She worked hard *so that* everything would be ready in time.
- → Supposing (that): If: Supposing (that) you are wrong, what will you do then?
- → Than: Used in comparisons: She is smarter *than* you think.
- → Unless: Except, if not: *Unless* he helps us, we cannot succeed.
- → Until or till: Up to the time when: I will wait *until/till* you come.
- → Whereas: Because: *Whereas* this is a public building, it is open to everyone. On the other hand: Some of the students are diligent, *whereas* others are not.
- → Whether: If: I did not know *whether* I had to do it.
- → Whether or not: Either of the two cases: *Whether or not* we are successful, we are sure that we have done our best.
- → While: At the same time: *While* it was snowing, we were playing games. On the other hand: He is honest *while* his brother is a cheat. Even though: *While* I have no experience in writing, I will do my best.
- → As if: In a similar way: He behaves *as if* he knows everything.
- → As long as: If: *As long as* we are together, I am not scared of anything. Since: He has been doing this job *as long as* I have known him.
- → As soon as: Immediately when: *As soon as* you finish your assignment, submit it to me.

→ As though: In a similar way: It seems *as though* it is going to rain.
→ Even if: In spite of: I am going out *even if* it rains.
→ In case: For the fear that: Take some sandwiches *in case* you feel hungry.
→ Or else: Otherwise: Hurry up, *or else* you will be late for your classes.
→ So as to: In order to: I hurried *so as to* be on time.

7.8.2.4. Connecting Adverbs

Connecting adverbs are similar to conjunctions because they may be used to introduce clauses. They are often used to show the relationship between the ideas expressed in a clause and the ideas expressed in a preceding clause, sentence or paragraph. The following are examples of words used as connecting adverbs:

→ Accordingly: Therefore: We have to discover his plans and act *accordingly*.
→ Also: In addition: She's fluent in French; she *also* speaks a little Italian.
→ Too: Also: He is an actor and his brother is a dancer *too*.
→ Besides: In addition: *Besides* working as an engineer, he writes novels in his free time.
→ Consequently: As a result: Deforestation poses a big threat to the food chain and *consequently* to human survival.
→ Furthermore: Additionally: He said that he had not discussed the matter with her. *Furthermore*, he had not even contacted her.
→ So far as: To the degree that: That's the truth, in *so far as* I know it.
→ Hence: For that reason: We suspect they are trying to hide something, *hence* the need for an independent inquiry.
→ However: But: We wanted to arrive on time; *however*, we were delayed by traffic.
→ Likewise: Similarly: The place is good; *likewise*, the climate is excellent.
→ Moreover: Furthermore: He is a talented artist; *moreover*, he is a good writer.
→ Nevertheless: But: The task was challenging; *nevertheless*, I liked it.
→ Nonetheless: But: The book is very long, *nonetheless*, informative and entertaining.
→ Notwithstanding: Despite this: *Notwithstanding* some major problems, the event was a grand success.
→ Otherwise: If not: You should be in time *otherwise* you will be punished.
→ Still: But: We tried our best *still* we couldn't find it.
→ Then: Next: We finished our work *then* we went shopping.
→ Therefore: For that reason: I was upset, *therefore*, I could not concentrate on my work.
→ Thus: In this way: He got his vehicle repaired, *thus* he was able to reach office on time.

Task

Fill in the blanks using the correct conjunctions:

1. ... you work hard, you will not succeed.
2. I doubt...he will get the tickets for the show.
3. He is very dull...his brother is very sharp.
4. The train had...started... I reached the station.
5. Start early...you should miss the class.
6. He continued to be lazy... he was fourteen.
7. I do not doubt...he was there.
8. ...you win the lottery, what will you do?
9. Men work... they may earn a living.
10. The lion lay down...he were dead.
11. ... any other job, teaching has many challenges.

12. …you stop here, you will get no time for work.
13. …you sow…you will reap.
14. …fast you go, I shall follow you.
15. He had gone away…I came.
16. He…I is bold.
17. …Ram…his brother came to attend the meeting.
18. We should get our house insured… there is an accident.
19. I enjoy the songs… this one.
20. …he came here, he didn't say anything.

7.9 Correct Usage: Tenses

7.9.1 Introduction

In some languages, verb tenses are not very important or do not even exist. In English, the concept of tense is very important. The word, 'tense' (noun) has been derived from Latin word *'tempus'* which means *'time.'* It is a form of a verb, which is used to indicate the time, and sometimes the continuation or completeness of an action in relation to the time of speaking. In other words, tense is a method that we use in English to refer to time—past, present and future.

Nevertheless, we can also talk about time without using tenses. For example, 'going to' is a special construction which is used to talk about the future but it is not a tense. One tense does not always talk about one time; for instance, a present tense does not always refer to present time: 'I hope it rains tomorrow'—'rains' is simple present tense but here it refers to future time (tomorrow). In the same way, a past tense does not always refer to past time: 'If I had some money now, I could buy it'—here, 'had' is simple past but it refers to present time.

7.9.2 Table of Tenses

Tense and verb pattern	Sentences: Affirmative/negative and interrogative	Uses	Signal words
Simple Present: *1st form of the verb* *'s/es' with 3rd person singular number*	Affirmative: I/we/you/they write. He/she/it writes. Negative: I/we/you/they do not write. He/she/it does not write. Interrogative: Do we/you/they/I write? Does he/she/it write?	• Hobbies, routine and habitual actions: I *like* coffee. • Things those are always true/general statements: The sun *rises* in the east. • Running commentary: Ajay *passes* the ball to Mahesh who *kicks* it off. • Facts, opinions and beliefs: I *think* you are right. • Exclamatory sentences: Here *comes* Mr. Yadav!	Every …, never, normally, often, seldom, sometimes, usually, generally, occasionally, rarely, frequently

(Continued)

Tense and verb pattern	Sentences: Affirmative/negative and interrogative	Uses	Signal words
Present Continuous/ Progressive: *Is/are/am + 'ing' in the first form of the verb*	Affirmative: I am writing. We/you/they are writing. He/she/it is writing. Negative: I am not writing. We/you/they are not writing. He/she/it is not writing. Interrogative: Am I writing? Are we/you/they writing? Is he/she/it writing?	• An action or an event that is developing now: The patient *is getting* better and better. • Action happening at the time of speaking: I *am reading* a book. • Action in progress not necessarily at the time of speaking: I *am teaching* in a college. • Definite future plans: I *am leaving* for Delhi tomorrow. • Repeated undesirable/ annoying habits: You *are* always *coming* late.	at the moment, at present, for the time being, just, just now, Listen!, Look!, now, right now
Present Perfect: *Has/have + 3rd form of the verb*	Affirmative: I /we/you/they have written. He/she/it has written. Negative: I /we/you/they have not written. He/she/it has not written. Interrogative: Have I/we/you/they written? Has he/she/it written?	• A recently completed action: I *have* just *finished* my work. • Past action when time given is not definite: I *have read* this article. • Past events, which have a link with the present: The workers *have called* off the strike. • An action that began in the past but is still continued in the present: We *have lived* here for five years.	Already, ever, just, never, yet, recently, lately, today, till now, up to now, for, since, today, first time, second time, this week/year/ month/year, etc.
Present Perfect Progressive: *Has/ have+ been + 'ing' in the first form of the verb + since/for to denote time*	Affirmative: I/we/you/they have been writing since 8 p.m. He/she/it has been writing for two hours. Negative: I/we/you/they have not been writing since 8 p.m. He/she/it has not been writing for two hours. Interrogative: Have I/we/you/they been writing since 8 p.m.? Has he/she/it been writing for two hours?	• An action that began in the past but is still continued in the present: It *has been raining* since two o'clock. • An action that is finished but its result or effect still persists: The children *have been playing* the whole day and are now very tired.	All day, for 4 years, since 1993, how long, recently, the whole week/day/ year, for a long time, many hours

(Continued)

Tense and verb pattern	Sentences: Affirmative/negative and interrogative	Uses	Signal words
Simple Past: *2nd form of the verb*	Affirmative: I/we/you/they/he/she/it wrote. Negative: I/we/you/they/he/she/it did not write. Affirmative: Did/I/we/you/they/he/she/it write?	• A past event or action not related to the present: I *visited* my uncle's place yesterday. • A past habit or regular action in the past: In school days he never *spoke* a lie. • An action that lasted for a period of time in the past: He *worked* in this office for five years. • Past events in the order in which they occurred: I *got up* early, *had* my breakfast and *studied* for two hours.	Yesterday, 2 minutes ago, in 1990, the other day, last Friday/Sunday/night/morning/week/year
Past Continuous/Progressive: *Was/were + 'ing' in the first form of the verb*	Affirmative: We/you/they were writing. He/she/I/it was writing. Negative: We/you/they were not writing. He/she/I/it was not writing. Interrogative: Were I/we/you/they writing? Was he/she/it writing?	• An action that was in progress at sometime in the past: I *was working* on internet at 10 p.m. • Two or more actions in progress at the same time: I *was doing* my homework while my brother *was playing*. The students *were talking* when the teacher *was teaching*. • Often repeated annoying past habits: He *was* always *coming* to my place at odd hours.	When, while, as long as, as, on…, at…, whereas
Past Perfect: *Had + third form of the verb*	Affirmative: I/we/you/they/he/she/it had written. Negative: I/we/you/they/he/she/it had not written. Interrogative: Had I/we/you/they/he/she/it written?	• An action completed before a certain moment in the past: At 7.30 a.m. I *had reached* college. • An action that was completed before another action: We *had checked* the bag before we *left*. • An unfulfilled desire: I wish I *had followed* my father's advice.	Already, just, never, not yet, once, until that day

(Continued)

Tense and verb pattern	Sentences: Affirmative/negative and interrogative	Uses	Signal words
Past Perfect Progressive: *Had been + 'ing' in the first form of the verb + since/for to denote time*	Affirmative: I/we/you/they/he/she/it had been writing since 8 o'clock/for two hours. Negative: I/we/you/they/he/she/it had not been writing since 8 o' clock/for two hours. Interrogative: Had I/we/you/they/he/she/it been writing since 8 o' clock, for two hours?	• An action that began before a certain time in the past and continued up to that time or stopped just before that: The baby *had been crying* for sometime before I attended to it. • A repeated action in the past on a continuous basis: I *had been trying* to contact him.	For, since, the whole day, all day
Simple Future: *Will/Shall + first form of the verb*	Affirmative: You/they/he/she/it/I/ we will/shall write. Negative: You/they/he/she/it/ I/we will/shall not write. Interrogative: Will/shall I/we/you/ they/he/she/it write?	• Actions scheduled to take place in future: We *will do* our work. • Instant decisions: Oh, I*'ll go* and switch it off. • Strong determination, will, warning, order or command: I *will* not *allow* you to do it. • Advice, suggestion, request or proposal: *Shall* we *start* our work? *Will* you *have* coffee? • Universal truth or habit: Christmas *will come* in December. A gambler *will gamble*.	… in a year, next …, tomorrow, perhaps in one year, next week, tomorrow
Future Continuous/ Progressive: *Will/shall + be + 'ing' in the first form of the verb*	Affirmative: You/they/he/she/it/I/ we will/shall be writing. Negative: You/they/he/she/it/I/ we will/shall not be writing. Interrogative: Will/shall I/we/you/ they/he/she/it be writing?	• An action that will occur in the normal course: I *shall be staying* with my uncle. • An action that will be in progress at a given time in the future: *At 3.30 p.m.,* I *will be attending* a lecture. • Future planning or intentions: I *will be* in Delhi on Monday. • Polite request: *Will* you *be going* to market?	At 9 a.m., on Monday/Tuesday… in a year, next …, tomorrow, perhaps in one year, next week,

(Continued)

Tense and verb pattern	Sentences: Affirmative/negative and interrogative	Uses	Signal words
Future Perfect: *Will/shall + have + 3rd form of verb*	Affirmative: You/they/he/she/it/I/we will/shall have written. Negative: You/they/he/she/it/I/we will/shall not have written. Interrogative: Will/shall I/we/you/they/he/she/it have written?	• An action that is expected to be completed by a certain time in future: I *will have finished* my project by the end of this week. • The speaker's belief that something has taken place: You *will have heard* about this.	By the time, before, by the end of this week/year/month..., on..., at...
Future Perfect Continuous: *Will/shall + have been +'ing' in the first form of the verb + since/for to denote time*	Affirmative: You/they/he/she/it/I/we will have been writing since 2 o'clock/for two hours. Negative: You/they/he/she/it/I/we will/shall have not been writing since 2 o'clock/for two hours. Interrogative: Will/shall/we/you/they/he/she/it have not been writing since 2 o'clock/for two hours?	• An action that will be in progress over a period of time in future: I *will have been teaching* for 5 years next September.	Since, for, next year/month/January...

7.9.3 Common Errors in the Use of Tenses

1. Will or shall: We use 'shall' for future only with the first person, that is, after *I* and *we*:
   → I *will/shall finish* college in June.
   → We *will/shall know* the result soon. (Not everyone shall know the results soon.)
   → They *will finish* the work today. (Not they shall...)
2. 'I/we will' and 'I/we shall' have the same meaning but 'shall' is a little formal.
3. Present perfect tense should not be used with the time expressions of the past tense:
   → I *bought* this watch *yesterday*. (Not ... have bought ...yesterday)
   → I *finished* my letter *last night*. (Not ... have finished ... last night...)
4. Past tense in the principal clause is followed by the past tense in the subordinate clause:
   → I *asked* him what he *had done*. (Not ...what he has done.)
   → Children *ran* outside to see what *was happening*. (Not ...what is happening.)
5. Past tense in the principal clause is followed by the present tense in the subordinate clause to denote universal truth or facts:
   → I *learnt* at school that the *earth is* round like a ball. (Not ...was round like...)
   → My father *taught* me that honesty *is* the best policy. (Not...honesty was...)

6. Simple present tense is used for states or permanent facts while present continuous tense is used for temporary actions:
   → A photographer *takes photographs*. Smile please; I *am taking* your photograph.
   → They *live* in a nice flat. They *are living* in a small flat for the time being.
   → It *usually rains* at weekends. It *is raining* at the moment.
   → Paper *burns* easily. See how the paper *is burning*.

7. Verbs of senses—*see, hear, smell, notice, seem, appear, recognize*; verbs of emotions—*want, like, desire, love, hate, forgive, forget, wish, prefer*; verbs of thinking—*think, suppose, know, mean, realize, understand, suppose, believe, remember, expect, agree, consider, trust, imagine, mind* and the verbs showing possession—*have, has, own, belong, possess, contain, consist, keep*—are used in simple tenses not in continuous tenses when they refer to states, permanent quality or facts. However, they may be used in continuous tenses when they refer to actions, temporary behaviour or short-lived feelings, etc.:
   → The house *is clean*. The sweeper *is cleaning* the house.
   → I *see* your problem. I *am seeing* your problem.
   → I *like* my school. I *am liking* school much better now.
   → I *think* you are right. I *am thinking* about your problem.
   → We *have* a big car. We *are having* lunch.
   → We all *enjoy* parties. We *are enjoying* this party.

8. For interrupted actions we use present perfect tense not present perfect continuous:
   → I *have written* five letters *since morning*. (Not … have been writing…)
   → They *have played* four games *since afternoon*. (Not … have been playing…)

9. The adverbials—*just, already, never, ever, so far, till now, lately, recently, yet, before, today, this week/month/year*—are generally used in the present perfect tense when they show finished actions in the present state of completion:
   → I *have just finished* writing it. (Not I just received…)
   → They *have already received* your message. (Not They already received…)

10. 'Since' and 'for' denote time. Both of them are used as prepositions. 'Since' is used for 'a point of time' while 'for' is used for 'the duration or length of time':
    → I *have been learning* English *since* class II. (Not …for class II)
    → We *have been reading* this book *for* two hours. (Not since…two hours)

11. When 'since' is used as a preposition, it is always preceded by a verb in the present perfect or past perfect tense:
    → The college *had been closed since* Monday. (Not … was closed…)
    → He *has been* irregular in classes *since* July. (… Not was irregular…)

12. When 'since' is used as a conjunction, it is followed by a verb in the simple past tense and preceded by a verb in the simple present or present perfect tense:
    → A month *has passed* since I *came* here.
    → Two hours *have passed* since he *fell* asleep.
    → Hours *pass* quickly since I *have got* this job.

13. Two or more actions, given in a sequence are described in the simple past tense. If the sequence is not given, the first action is described in simple present tense and the second one is described in the past perfect tense:
    → He *got up, looked* here and there and *went* away.
    → The train *had left* before I *reached* station.

14. Future tense is not used after the temporal conjunctions—*until, when, before, after, as soon as, as*, etc.:
    → He *will come* when he *is* ready. (Not …when he will be ready)
    → I *will be* here till you *come*. (Not…till you will come)

15. When 'were' is used to refer to the future, subordinate clause cannot express a completed action:
    → *Were* I in her place, I *would enjoy* a lot. (Not…I would have enjoyed a lot.)
    → *Were* you in my place you *would feel* sick. (Not…you would have felt sick.)

7.9.4. Conditionals

When we talk of the future, we think about a particular condition or situation and the result of this condition. Sentences describing such situations are called conditionals. There are several structures of conditionals used for different purposes:

1. The structure, 'If/when + simple present + simple present' is used for the result of a condition that is always true like a scientific fact. One thing follows the other automatically:
   → If you *heat* water, it *boils.*
   → When I *get up* late, I *get* late for the office.

2. The structure, 'If + simple present + will/can/shall + main verb,' shows a real possibility that the condition will happen:
   → If it *rains*, I *will stay* at home.
   → If they *don't pass* the exams, their parents *will be* unhappy.
   We can use present perfect or present continuous tense also in the 'if clause' and a modal in the main clause:
   → If you *are going* for a job interview, you *should* wear a tie.
   → If you *haven't got* a television, you *can't* see the match.

3. The structure, 'If + simple past + would/past form of a modal + main verb' shows unreal possibility or dream:
   → If we *took* a car, we *would reach* early.
   → If I *won* a lottery, I *would buy* a huge bungalow.

4. The structure, 'If + past perfect + would have + past participle' shows no possibility. In such conditionals, the condition as well as result is impossible now:
   → If you *had been* more careful, you *would* not *have fallen.*
   → If you *had called* me, I *would have come* to see you.

5. The 'if clause' usually comes first but it can come after the main clause too:
   → The ice *melts,* if you *heat* it.
   → We *will miss* the bus, if we *don't hurry.*
   → I *could do* it faster, if I *had* a calculator.
   → He *would have passed* the test, if he *had* not *made* that mistake.

7.9.5   Question Tags

A tag is something small that is added to something larger. For example, when you buy a dress, the little piece of cloth or a tag attached to it shows size, washing instructions or price. A question tag is a mini-question that follows a statement. The whole sentence is a 'tag question,' and the mini-question at the end of it is called a 'question tag.' Question tags are commonly used in spoken English to ask for confirmation or to make polite and friendly requests or to give orders.

The question tag should have the same verb or tense as that of the tag question. If the sentence is in negative, the tag should be in affirmative and if the sentence is in affirmative, the tag should be in negative. Contractions—*can't/don't/doesn't/won't/shan't/aren't/isn't/wasn't/weren't/hasn't/haven't/hadn't/shouldn't/wouldn't/couldn't/mustn't*—should be used. For example:

→ The rose is beautiful. *Isn't it?*
→ Honey tastes sweet. *Doesn't it?*
→ I could do it well. *Couldn't I?*
→ You can't climb mountains. *Can you?*
→ You don't know him. *Do You?*
→ They will not help us. *Will they?*
→ We must not give her the news. *Must we?*

Task

Correct the following sentences:

1. We have written to you yesterday about this matter.
2. He ran outside to see what is happening.
3. He would come, if you wished it.
4. Were I in his place I should have paid the money.
5. I am here since 1992.
6. She didn't see the President yet.
7. Two years passed since his father died.
8. He is long known to me.
9. Boys are to go to school daily.
10. He might have come to see me now.
11. He will come when he will be ready.
12. She sang very well. Isn't it?
13. He saw the Taj Mahal.
14. Kindly see my testimonials.
15. He asked me where was I going.
16. I did nothing but cried.
17. I want to realize the consequences of your actions.
18. We shall start for picnic as soon as you will come.
19. Let us purchase a radio before the price will go up.
20. If only I met her earlier, I would have given you the invitation for the party.

7.10 Correct Usage: Subject–Verb Agreement

The verb must agree with the subject in number and person. The basic principle is: singular subjects need singular verbs; plural subjects need plural verbs. For example:

→ My *brother is* a doctor.
→ My *sisters are* teachers.

1. Two or more singular subjects joined by 'and' take a plural verb:
   → *Oil* and *water do* not mix.
   → A *car* and a *bike are* the popular means of transportation.

2. When two singular nouns joined by 'and' together express one idea, a singular verb is used:
   → *Slow* and *steady wins* the race.
   → *Rice* and *curry is* my favourite dish.

3. If two subjects are joined with—'as well as', 'in addition to', 'besides', 'not', 'with', 'along with', or 'together with'—the verb agrees with the first subject:
   → The owner *as well as* his servants *is* honest.
   → The players *as well as* their captain *are* happy.
   → Diseases *in addition to* poverty and illiteracy *pose* a big challenge in slums.
   → You *not he have* been fined.
   → Several other activities *besides* writing *keep* me busy.
   → The teacher *with/ along with* his students *was* present in the programme.
   → The leader *together with* his friends *is* going to prison.

4. When two subjects are joined with 'not only – but also' the verb agrees with the latter subject:
   → *Not only* the students *but also* the teacher *was* asked to give a presentation.
   → *Not only* the master *but* his attendants *were also* praised.

5. Two singular subjects connected with – 'or,' 'nor,' 'either – or,' 'neither – nor' – take a singular verb: For example:
   → *Neither* Joy *nor* Sam *is* available.
   → *Either* Vandana *or* Jyoti *is* helping with stage decorations.

6. When the subjects of different numbers are connected by 'or,' 'nor,' 'either – or,' 'neither – nor' the plural subject is placed the last and verb is used according to it:
   → *Neither* Aarti *nor* her friends *like* coffee.
   → The minister *or* his officials *have* to take responsibility of the accident.

7. When subjects of different persons are connected by 'or,' 'nor,' 'either – or,' 'neither – nor', the second person comes first, the third person comes second and the first person comes last. The verb agrees with the subject nearest it:
   → *Neither* she *nor* I *am* going to the festival.
   → *Either* you *or* Tinkle *has* to do the job.

8. The expressions, 'many a,' 'a great deal of,' 'one of the + (plural noun),' 'the number of,' 'a majority of,' 'pair of' take a singular verb:
   → *Many a* new idea *has* come to my mind.
   → *A great deal of* patience *is* required to do this job.
   → *One of the* boys *has* broken the flask.
   → *The number of* books on this subject *is* very small.
   → *A majority of* people *was* in favour of banning smoking.
   → *A pair of* shoes *was* lying on the floor.

9. Some plural nouns showing an amount, a fraction or an element of time are considered singular and take a singular verb:
   → *Sixty minutes is* enough to finish this task.
   → *Ten dollars is* a high price to pay.
   → *Two weeks is a* good holiday.
   → *Three fourths* of land *is* barren.

10. The pronouns, 'anyone', 'anybody', 'everyone', 'everybody', 'someone', 'no one', 'nobody', 'each', 'every', 'neither' and 'either,' are singular and take a singular verb:
    → *Does anyone* else *want* to come?
    → *Is* there *anybody* in the room?
    → *Everybody has done* his or her homework.
    → *Someone has left* her book.
    → There *is no one* in the room.
    → *Each of* these shops *is doing* good business.
    → *Every* boy and *every* girl *was given* a sweet.
    → *Neither* of the traffic lights *is working*.

11. Indefinite pronouns—'several', 'few', 'both', 'many'—are used with plural verbs:
    → *Several* books *were lying* on the table.
    → *Both* the books *require* careful reading.
    → *Few* people *were* present on the occasion.
    → *Many* mistakes *were found* in the article.

12. The words 'here' and 'there' are generally used as adverbs even though they indicate place. In sentences beginning with 'here' or 'there', the verb is used according to the real subject that follows it:
    → There *are* many difficulties to overcome.
    → There *is* a big problem in his way.
    → *Here are* two apples.
    → *Here comes* Mr. Smith.

13. While using the words indicating portions—'half of', 'a part of', 'percentage of', a variety of', 'plenty of', 'a lot of', 'remainder', 'fraction of', 'all', 'any', 'more', 'most of', 'none of' and 'some of'—take a singular verb when they refer to amount or quantity as a whole and a plural verb when they refer to a number. For example:
   → *Half of* the money *was* mine. *Half of* the students *have passed.*
   → *A large part of* the population *is* voting against her. /*A large part of* students *enjoy* doing mischief.
   → *Forty percent of* the students *are* in favour of changing the examination system./ *Forty percent of* the student body *is* in favour of changing the policy.
   → *A variety of* questions *were selected* for the test. /*This is a* rare *variety of* rose.
   → *Plenty of* books *are* available on this topic. /*Plenty of* money *was spent* on decorations.
   → *All* five men *are* hard workers. *All* wood *tends* to shrink.
   → *Are* there *any* stamps? *Is* there *any* water?
   → *Some of* the books *have been stolen. Some of* the milk *is missing.*
   → *More* work *remains* to be done. /*More* people *are* expected to visit this place.
   → *Most* of the classical music *sends* me to sleep. /*Most* of the stories about him *are* false.

14. Adjectives—'much', 'less', 'little'—are used with uncountable nouns and take a singular verb:
   → *Much* of the work *has been done.*
   → It *is less* of a problem than I had expected.
   → A *little* knowledge *is* a dangerous thing.

15. When subjects and verbs are separated by a comma, a clause or a longer phrase, use the verb according to the actual subject:
   → *The dress*, I bought on my birthday, *is* really good.
   → *All the songs*, recorded by him, *are* really entertaining.

16. Similarly, when the subject of the verb is a relative pronoun, use the verb according to the antecedent of the relative pronoun:
   → I am *the person who has* always stood by you.
   → *I who am* your friend should have been told about it.

For the correct usage of verb with collective nouns, nouns singular in form and plural in sense, nouns plural in form but singular is usage, nouns used in singular only, nouns used in plural only, nouns used in the same form in plural as well as in plural and nouns indicating length, weight, measurement, money or number, please refer to 'Correct Usage: Nouns'-7.2.6.

Task

Correct the following sentences:

1. This is one of the most difficult papers that has ever been set.
2. I am one who have always prayed for your well being.
3. Not only boys but their teacher also deserve praise.
4. Each of the suspected men was arrested.
5. A pair of spectacles are lying on the table.
6. None of his speeches have been appreciated.
7. Neither praise nor blame seem to affect him.
8. A series of lectures were delivered by him.
9. A lot of time have been wasted.
10. Every boy and every girl were given a prize.
11. Hard work as well as luck are necessary for success.
12. Gulliver's Travels are a captivating book.

13. A great deal of work remain to be done.
14. Everyone in the class read their book.
15. Students together with their teacher was watching the match.
16. Three miles are not a long distance.
17. Soup and salad are too light a breakfast.
18. Neither he nor you is allowed to go there.
19. My friend who lives with his aunt come to meet daily.
20. The cows as well the dog is a faithful animal.
21. The teacher and the student goes there.
22. The majority of students was satisfied with the decision.
23. Any body who are a student of the college can take part in this contest.
24. She or her friend have stolen my book.
25. There was no windows in our room.
26. The owner of these houses are very clever.
27. There is 11 players in the team.
28. Rice and curry are his favourite dish.
29. Both of the books requires careful reading.
30. Neither Tina nor her friends is going there.
31. A number of books is missing.
32. A doctor and a nurse is working in this hospital.

"Every man who knows how to read has it in his power to magnify himself, to multiply the ways in which he exists, to make his life full significant and interesting."

–Aldous Huxley

8.1 Introduction

Reading, basically, is a physical process of comprehending a text using our eyes. However, reading becomes studying when it is done with the involvement of all the mental faculties of concentration, comprehension and analysis. Studying involves the practices of answering questions, note taking, note making, summarizing, reading the text more than once and analyzing the written words thoroughly. The purpose of reading is to understand the material as effectively as possible to retain the information for a long time. When we study, we spend some time learning about a particular subject or subjects, for example: *He went to the university, where he studied History and Economics.* However, we have to understand that we may only read and not study as we do while reading a newspaper, a magazine or a novel, which we read to pass time, for enjoyment or as a hobby. Nevertheless, we cannot study something without reading or observing it. You read your course books as well as study them. The weather department observes the weather and studies it, but it cannot read the weather. In short, we can say to study is to read, to observe or to know the information in-depth. To strengthen reading as well as study skills, reading comprehension, note taking, note making and précis writing skills should be nurtured carefully.

8.2 Reading Comprehension

Reading is an interactive process between the reader and the text, resulting in comprehension of the text read. Reading comprehension is the ability to understand fully the sense and the meaning of a written or a printed matter. Linguists have shown that the four language skills—listening, speaking, reading and writing—are interrelated. Good listening generates good speaking and good reading generates good writing. Reading is an activity that involves greater level of mental as well as physical concentration. As eye muscles are actively involved in the process, reading stimulates them. The habit of reading also helps readers interpret new words and phrases that they come across in day-to-day conversation. Reading affects our mind; so, whatever we read should be a quality material. A systematic audible reading can improve oral communication too. Above all, reading enhances knowledge and information, entertains us and helps us pass our leisure time. Reading is, undoubtedly, a paramount skill of language.

8.2.1 Mechanics of Reading

Reading is a complex process in which a reader receives inputs through the physical process of reading, followed by decoding and understanding the text, analyzing it and finally giving a proper response. You should be able to identify the written symbols of letters, which make up the words that in turn give rise to sentences. One has to be familiar with the language being used, the visual shapes of words, sound and pronunciation of each word, its meaning and should have the knowledge of grammar of that particular language. Apart from these skills, you as a reader should develop the ability to read at different speeds, skip and skim the text when required, anticipate and read between the lines. These skills are required for loud as well as for silent reading. However, there are certain practices that you should avoid while reading. These undesirable habits are:

→ Moving head from side to side instead of eyes.
→ Indicating words with a finger or something like a pen or a pencil.
→ Reading words inaudibly or too loudly.
→ Noticing one word at a time while reading.

These actions obstruct the process of reading. Instead of reading words individually, develop the habit of perceiving word groups.

8.2.2 Types of Reading Skills

A study of the major types of reading skills may assist you in improving your reading comprehension as well as in employing the required skill for different reading situations. It has been found that these skills are used naturally when we read something in our native language but are often forgotten while reading a foreign language. Such types can be categorized into the following headings:

Scanning: Scanning is reading something rapidly for some specific piece of information. You can use this skill when you are in search of key words, for example, scanning a telephone book or a dictionary to look for a name or a word. You 'see' every item on the page but you do not necessarily read all the pages—you skip anything you are not looking for. You just have to concentrate on the key word and need not recall the exact content of the page. Scanning saves time but it has to be done with accuracy. This skill develops with practice.

Skimming: Skimming is reading a text quickly to gain a general impression whether the text is of any use to you or not. You can see people skimming through books in a bookstore before they decide to buy them. You need not necessarily search for a specific item or a key word and many parts of the material may be left unread. The purpose of skimming is to get an 'overview' of the text that is to check its relevance, grasp its central theme and the main points. It prepares you for the more concentrated effort of detailed reading, which is to follow, if the text is useful.

Intensive Reading: Reading intensively is to read for detailed information when the aim is to understand the material in-depth. The techniques of scanning and skimming are good launching pads for an in-depth reading.

Extensive Reading: Extensive reading is another device often used when we read for pleasure with emphasis on understanding the overall meaning. It is a lighter type of reading, and it may be used at the time of leisure. This form does not generally require detailed concentration, but it should be done with proper understanding. Extensive reading may involve a lot of skimming like skipping boring and irrelevant passages. An average light reading speed is 100–200 words per minute (WPM); however, you can read at a pace in which you feel comfortable.

Word for Word Reading: This type of reading is generally not recommended but sometimes its use becomes indispensable, when some textual material is not readily understood and it requires a slow, careful and analytical reading. People use this type of reading to understand unfamiliar words, concepts, scientific formulae, etc. For example, going through a legal document, analyzing a written contract or reading a passage for writing a précis, may require such kind of reading. This sort of reading is time consuming and it demands a high level of concentration.

Speed Reading: Speed reading is a skill that is acquired after much reading practice. In skimming and extensive reading you skip some points and items to gain speed, whereas in this type of reading, speed has to be attained without skipping. You read everything, taking into each detail, but develop speed simultaneously through practice. The more you read, the more your mind adapts itself to this sort. Students appearing for entrance tests for various professional courses have to speed read passages for comprehension. It is a test of their effective grasping of information with time constraints. A good way to increase your reading speed is to adjust the focus of your eyes at one particular word and then zoom at it in a way that you are able to see the whole text. Using this process, you may increase your reading speed by increasing the number of words you take in at each eye stop.

8.2.3   Reading Speed

Edward Fry, in his book, *Teaching Faster Reading*, talks about three reading speeds. The first is the 'study reading speed' which is generally used for total understanding and retention. The second is the 'average speed' which is helpful for everyday reading like that of reading newspapers, magazines, etc., and the third is 'skimming', as you have seen above, it is the fastest mode of reading. Reading speed is measured in WPM. You should be able to vary your speed as per the requirement of the text. A casual reading is normally faster than a serious one. A newspaper may be read at a fast rate for general news, but you may have to slow down your pace for reading an editorial in the same paper. Technical reports, proposals, agreements also need a slower speed.

8.2.4   Reading Comprehension Skills

Reading comprehension means understanding an idea of a text in its wholeness. It involves interpreting the meaning of words in the prevailing context. When you read a passage closely, make an effort to follow its idea and purpose and at the same time try to understand the writer's thought process. Students are made to practice comprehension in classes to develop their reading as well as understanding skills. How well you understand a comprehension passage depends on how well you read. By solving such exercises you are, in fact, preparing yourself for a good professional environment, where you will be required not only to grasp messages of written texts but also to respond to them. A good comprehension helps you interpret things in the right context. On the other hand, a poor comprehension may cause misinterpretations. The following are some practical hints to help you inculcate reading comprehension skills:

→ Skim the passage cautiously for overall understanding and to grasp the main idea.

→ Read it for the second time for intensive reading to get the contextual meaning of words, phrases, sentences and writer's thought process. Read silently and do not mutter or hum words aloud.

→ Use the 'study reading speed' of about 200–300 WPM. However, you may increase it with practice, which is surely a good sign, but it should not be at the cost of understanding.

→ Go through the questions carefully.

→ Read the passage for the third time looking for the answers of the given questions.

→ Answer the questions in the given order. Come back to the unanswered questions later on.

→ Answer to the point even if the answer is in a few or just one word. Follow the given word limit.

→ Check your answers for correctness, grammar, spelling and relevance.

Apart from using the above hints, you need to have a good vocabulary for an effective comprehension. As it is not possible to know each and every word, the use of contextual clues can be one of the best ways to improve reading skills. Do not insist on understanding each word while reading. A text can be understood in a general sense by using contextual clues. At the same time, the use of contextual clues can provide a means by which you may increase your existing vocabulary base. You can get such clues by asking these questions to yourself: What does the sentence refers to? What is the part of speech of the unknown word? Is it a verb, a noun, a preposition, an adjective or something else? What do the words around the unknown word mean? How is the unknown word related to those words? In addition to this, use the do's and don'ts of an effective reading discussed above in Section 8.2.1.

Task

1. Read the passage carefully and answer the following questions:

   Globalization is gradually creeping into every nook and corner of the world, but the ghost of brain drain still continues to haunt India as talented young students continue to go abroad every year for education, as well as for employment opportunities. UNESCO report in 1969, defined brain drain as, 'an abnormal form of scientific exchange between countries, characterized by a one-way flow in favour of the most highly developed countries'. Even after many years, the definition of brain drain has not changed much as the talented students are still leaving developing countries in pursuit of greener pastures in the developed nations. India has become the outsourcing hub of the world, where all international companies are setting their shops. But this outsourcing is, more or less, a kind of brain drain for those who cannot find good job opportunities in India and have to travel abroad in search of better job profiles. More than 25 per cent of the medical staff in America and Britain consists of doctors, who attended medical school elsewhere. These are the same students who got trained in India, Pakistan or China and have now moved abroad for better opportunities. In the year 2008, maximum students going to the United States of America to study were from India. Most of these students, after finishing their education, get recruited and more often than not settle in abroad. But still brain drain continues to be a cause of worry for India, for we are getting used to thousands of students going abroad every year for education. Former Indian President, Dr. APJ Abdul Kalam said that reverse brain drain will have to begin if India is to become a developed nation in the future.

   (Source: www.merynews.com)

   1. What is brain drain?
   2. Is brain drain still affecting India?
   3. In what way has the definition of brain drain not changed for India?
   4. What major step has to be taken to stop brain drain?
   5. (a) Give meanings of the following words/phrases used in the passage and use them in sentences:
      haunt; hub; outsourcing; one-way flow; greener pastures

8.3 Note Taking and Note Making

8.3.1 Note Taking

Note taking is a method of writing down the crucial items of a lecture, a meeting or a reading text rapidly, briefly and clearly. Studies show that we tend to forget a good part of a lecture within 24 hours. Unless one has an excellent memory, one should take notes for future references. In the current scenario when information is flooding from every quarter, note taking has got an added importance. Whether you are a high school student or a university scholar or a professional, the ability to take effective, meaningful and comprehensive notes is an important skill. Good notes save our study time as they facilitate us review them for reuse during test preparations, assignments and meetings. At the same time, taking notes helps you concentrate in class and moulds you for the better understanding of a topic. While taking notes, two major questions related to note taking—what to write and how to write—should be kept in mind.

8.3.1.1 What to Write

One has to be a bit choosy at the time of taking notes. Only the most important items should be included. Your notes need not contain everything. If you try to take elaborate notes, then at the time of a test or term paper, you will have to go through all those extra things to get some important information. Your focus, while taking notes, should be twofold. First, 'what is new to you?' There is no use in writing down facts you already know. Second, 'what is relevant?', that is, what information is most likely to be of use later. Focus on the points, which are directly related to your reading. The details on which you should pay special attention are—dates, numbers, titles, names of people and books, theories, concepts, definitions, arguments, diagrams, exercises, speaker's conclusion, comments of the other listeners as well as your own interpretation, doubts or questions. Examples, idiomatic expressions and minute details should be excluded.

8.3.1.2 How to Write

The five R's of note taking are record, reduce, recite, reflect and review. Use them for a holistic approach. You may use either a linear or a patterned format to note down the main points, key words and phrases. Use abbreviations wherever possible; leave out the short words such as 'the', 'is', 'to', etc. However, remember that 'no' and 'not' are important words. Although note-taking techniques should be user specific, you may use the following guidelines for an effective note taking:

1. **Outlining:** Outlining is an effective way to take notes in a hierarchical structure. You may use alphabet, numbers, Roman numerals or bullets/dots to indicate the structure. Outlining can be very useful while taking notes from books and presentations because the authors usually organize the material in a fairly effective way. For lectures, however, outlining has some limitations. The speaker does not necessarily maintain connection between ideas, consequently, there is a risk of losing the relationship between what the speaker just said and what he/she said before.

2. **Mind Mapping:** For lectures, a mind mapping may be a better option to keep track of the connections between ideas. Write the main topic of the lecture in the centre of a blank sheet of paper. As a new subtopic is introduced, draw a branch outward from the centre and write the subtopic at the end of the branch. Then each point under that heading gets its own, smaller branch off the main one. When another new subtopic is mentioned, draw a new main branch from the centre and so on. If a point is under the first heading but you are on the fourth one, you can easily draw it in on the first branch. Similarly, if a point connects to two different ideas, you can connect it to two different branches.

3. The Cornell System: The Cornell System is a simple but effective system of note taking. It was devised in the 1950s by Walter Pauk, professor of Education at Cornell University, New York. In this system, we have to leave about 3½ inches space from the bottom of a sheet of paper and draw a line across the width of the page to mark this space. Draw another line from that line to the top, about 2½ inches from the left-hand edge of the sheet. Now you have divided your sheet into three sections, the largest section is the 'notes column'. Take down notes in this space—you can outline or mind map or whatever is suitable to you. Write legibly. The column on the left is the 'recall column', wherein you write a series of cues, hints or questions about the corresponding item you have just taken down in the notes. Now cover the 'notes column' and use the 'recall column' to help you remember facts, ideas and information of the lecture as completely as you can. Then, uncover your notes and verify what you have recalled. Then in the bottom section write a short, 2–3-line summary in your words of the notes you have taken down. This helps you process the information, provide a useful reference when you are trying to find something in your notes later and transfer facts and ideas to your long-term memory. The following illustration gives you the format of the 'The Cornell System' of note taking.

The Cornell Note-Taking System

Recall Column	Note-Taking Column
	Summary Column

8.3.2   Note Making

Note making is another study skill to write down relevant key points of a written material to use them at a later date. This is a more serious and organized method of recording notes than note taking. Notes are taken down rapidly and hence, they may lack proper planning and structure. Note taking is usually followed by note making, where you devote some time to your earlier jottings to systematize them and preserve them for future use. Note taking is more suitable while listening to lectures, presentations or for meetings, while note making is more appropriate for a written text.

8.3.2.1   Purpose

We generally make notes to read a book or to write an article, a research paper or to prepare an essay. We put things into your own words or summarize them as well as highlight the key points. Note making is highly useful at work places too, as it helps not only in writing reports but also in recording the main points of an already written report. At the same time, notes can be preserved for future use like revising, forwarding or recalling information. Note making is, thus, a crucial exercise that is performed not only for others but also for self.

8.3.2.2   Mechanism

When one starts with note making, the two most important aspects that one has to consider are—which points should be included and which should be excluded. These aspects have already been discussed in this chapter under Section **8.3.1.1.** While making notes keep the following points in mind:

A Diagrammatic Summary of Note Making:

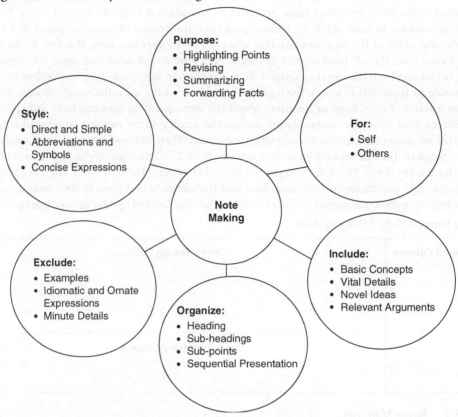

→ Skim the text briskly to grasp its gist, purpose and key points. At the same time take notes (techniques of note taking are given under Section 8.3.1.2 for further use.)

→ Read it again, this time more carefully, to find out the development of idea, the main divisions/chapters/sections of the text and their mutual relationships.

→ Write down the main points and the subpoints in the order as they appear in the text.

→ Rephrase the main points and subpoints into shorter phrases or may be into single words.

→ Use schematizing—using tables, charts or diagrams—for organizing scientific and technical material, which may be in the form of classification, figures, etc.

→ Use standard abbreviations to save time. First few letters of words and phrases can be the functional abbreviations that may be easily understood later also. For example volume: vol; usually: usu; approximately: approx; somebody: sb; especially: esp; secretary: secy; that is: i.e.; compare and contrast: cf; namely: viz; west: w; joul: j; oxygen: O; pages: pp; with effect from: wef; kilogram: kg; computer: comp; month: mth; magnesium: mg; specific gravity: sg.

→ Signs and symbols are useful tools for making notes. Some of them are: dollar: $; at the rate of: @; a number: #; and: &; percentage: %; key point: *; euro: €; copyright: ©; trade mark: ™; not equal to: ≠; infinity: ∞; registered: ®; ohm: Ω; plus or minus: ±; less than or equal to: ≤; greater than or equal to: ≥; almost equal to: ≈, identical to: ≡; house: ⌂; female: ♀; male: ♂; increase: ↑; decrease: ↓; cause: →; results: ←; less than <; greater than: >.

→ Don't forget to give the key with full forms of the abbreviations and symbols.

→ Give the notes a proper title to help you recall the main theme as well as the gist.

→ Structure your notes in a hierarchical order by inserting headings followed by sub headings, supporting points and may be supporting sub-points. The order of the headings should be logical so as to convey the right attitude of the author. Avoid including more than 3–4 sub-points under a subheading to make the details as simple as possible. If there are more sub-points give them a separate subheading.

→ Provide a proper sequencing to the points. You may use capital letters—A B C—for headings, small letters—a b c—for subheadings and Roman numerals—I II III—for supporting points and so on. The arrangement may be altered or reversed as per the need of the text.

→ Decimal system of sequencing is another method of arranging the points systematically. Study illustration given as under:

1_____
  1.1_____
  1.2_____
    1.2.1_____
    1.2.2_____

2_____
  2.1_____
  2.2_____
    2.2.1_____
    2.2.2_____

The numbering 1 and 2 comes in the margin and subsequent number in decimals outside but along the margin.

8.3.3 A Sample Note Making

Read the follow passage carefully and make notes on it. Further, supply a suitable title to it:

A robot can be defined as a mechanical gadget that performs functions normally ascribed to human beings. Karel Capek introduced the word robot while Sir Issac Assimov coined the word robotics, which is a science of dealing with robots.

The study of robotics includes, selection of material of proper quality for the components, design, fabrication, design of electronic circuits, computers and computer programming and its control. The science of robots is still in developing stage and a lot of research is being pursued for making robots more suitable for working.

Depending upon the area in which robots are to be used, robotics is a multidimensional field that includes disciplines such as biology, medical science, psychology, agriculture, mining, various branches of engineering, outer space, etc. At present, robots are mainly used in industries. These industrial robots are reprogrammable and perform a variety of jobs through programmed motions.

Basically, there are two types of robots: fixed and mobile. A fixed robot is attached to an immovable platform. It is similar to a human being standing or sitting in a fixed position while doing the work with hands. On the other hand, a mobile robot moves from place to place. The mobility of a robot is due to wheels or legs or other crawling material provided to it. A mobile robot can be given a human shape. However, the actual shape has nothing to do with the real functioning of the robot.

Title: Robot: A Human Machine

Notes

A. **What is a robot?**
    (a) Definition of a robot
        (i) a mechanical gadget
        (ii) performs functions ascribed to human beings
    (b) Words 'robot' and 'robotics'
        (i) robot by Karel Capek
        (ii) robotics by Sir Issac Assimov

B. **Study of Robotics**
    (a) matl. for components; circuits; fabri.; design; comp. prog.
    (b) research
        (i) study in development stage
        (ii) research—pursued for better robots

C. **Uses of a Robot**
    (a) multidimensional uses
        (i) biology, medical science, psychology, agriculture, mining, various branches of engineering, outer space
        (ii) At present mainly used in industries

D. **Types of Robots**
    (a) fixed
        (i) immovable
        (ii) similar to a human a fixed position
    (b) mobile
        (i) mobility due to wheels, legs or other crawling material
        (ii) can be given a human shape

Task

Take any article, biography, report or story, and read it carefully and make notes on it.

8.4   Précis Writing

Précis writing is another important productive study technique. A précis (*pronounced pray-see/pl. pray-seez;* comes from *French word '**Precis**' that literally means 'precise'*) is a shortening of the text of a written work, in your own words. The Oxford Dictionary defines it as "a short version of a speech or a piece of writing that gives the main points or ideas". The time constraints of the professional life and the conciseness of the technical language, require a description that is as accurate, brief and to the point as possible. However, one has to keep in mind that it is not just paraphrasing, which merely represents the original text in different and simple words nor is it listing the main points. The basic idea in précis writing is reproduced in miniature form, retaining the mood and tone of the author. It is a type of summarizing that insists on the economy of words or an exact reproduction of the facts with logic, organization and emphasis of the original material. A précis is useful while dealing with lengthy passages that demand careful attention to the logic and organization of an argument.

8.4.1 Advantages of Learning Précis Writing

Précis writing is a rewarding intellectual exercise. The skill is necessary to develop one's critical thinking, reading and writing abilities, along with condensing and synthesizing techniques. Students need summarizing to write a synopsis or an abstract, to remember the essential details of a long written material and to gain an insight into the underlying meaning of a text. It helps them save time and energy that can be utilized for other fruitful activities. It assists them to develop grammatical skills and vocabulary, as the use of synonyms and one-word substitutions is a great help in the art of condensing. At workplace, it is an immense help in writing the 'executive summary' of a technical report.

8.4.2 Qualities of a Good Précis

A good précis has the characteristics of the 5Cs, that is, completeness, conciseness, coherence, correctness and clarity. Completeness: A précis contains all the major points of the original text. Conciseness: It is brief and precise and its length is approximately one-third of the original passage, but one should be very careful not to lose or distort the original meaning. Coherence: (unity of thought) The ideas and the sentences are well knit and well linked to one another. Presentation of ideas in a précis should not be done through disjointed or unlinked sentences. Correctness: It is grammatically correct with right spellings. Clarity: The ideas are expressed distinctly so that even a reader who does not have enough time to read the original text has no trouble getting the message.

8.4.3 Skills Required to Write a Good Précis

Précis writing is not as creative as other types of writing skills. Nevertheless, drafting a précis is not a mechanical process as it does call for certain talents on the part of the writer. These desirable qualities are:

→ Good concentration
→ Good reading ability
→ Good comprehension
→ Good analyzing skills
→ Good summarizing skills
→ Good command on language

8.4.4 How to Write a Précis?

To write a précis effectively, the above stated skills are essential. Along with these, practice is utmost necessary to draft a good brief. Here are some steps that may be followed to write a useful summary:

→ Keep a blank sheet ready to take down notes to be used for compiling the précis.
→ Skim the text carefully in the first reading to get a general idea. Note down the main topic and the author's purpose of writing the passage.
→ The main topic or the central idea, that may be traced from the first few or the last few lines, can be in the form of a short phrase or a word.
→ Give a second or a third reading and read word for word to select and underline the important supporting ideas. Each paragraph should have one key point. The supporting points should be marked differently. Look up in the dictionary for any words whose meaning is not very clear. Eliminate the non-essential items.
→ Only relevant details should be included and all the non-essentials should be struck off such as: (a) unnecessary or irrelevant ideas, (b) repetitions, (c) examples and illustrations, (d) anecdotes, stories, etc., (e) adjectives, (f) abbreviations, contractions and slangs, (g) clichés, (h) proverbs, quotations and idiomatic phrases, (i) comparisons, (j) rhetorical and flowery expressions.

→ As you read, list the key ideas and the subpoints separately on the note sheet. Take notes and write an outline summary containing all the points, possibly in the same sequence as you have marked them in the passage. (For details refer to note taking, Section 8.3.1.2 of this chapter.) If you have left out some points, add them and if the outline contains unnecessary details, strike them out. Keep supporting points as your reserve material.

→ Always give the name of the article/document, the author and the source (whether it is from a magazine, a book, an encyclopaedia, or a technical report, etc.).Students while writing a précis may state: 'The following is the précis of the passage given in question no.___.'

→ Exhibit unity and coherence by arranging the key ideas of the outline notes in a logical order. Now, get ready to write a rough draft of the précis.

→ Prepare the rough draft with the help of your notes. Combine the key ideas into one or more smooth paragraphs, maintaining the unity of thought. Make sure that you retain the order of the original points in your précis but sometimes, you may have to change the order for the sake of unity and logicality. However, as the author's view point and attitude are the most important aspects, see that they are conveyed in the right spirit.

→ Write the rough draft in your own words and not in the words of the original text. Avoid using the vocabulary used in the original except for certain key words, which you may find indispensable. After careful second and third reading, put the work aside, and then start writing. This will force you to use your own words without the temptation of borrowing directly from the original.

→ Do not refer to the original text or begin with the expressions as 'In this article.'; 'The author says' or 'The paragraph means.' Begin as though you were summarizing your own writing.

→ A précis is written from the point of view of the author whose work is being summarized. So, you should not use phrases such as 'I think' or 'in my opinion'.

→ Use simple and direct language, short and crisp sentences and familiar and unambiguous words. This will bring clarity as well as economy of words to the précis.

→ The sentences should be grammatically correct. It is best to write summary in the same tense as the original.

→ If the text is subjective in nature and the writer has used the first person 'I' for himself or herself, it has to be changed into third person he/she, only if the gender is known, otherwise use the term 'the author'.

→ All the sentences given in the direct speech should be changed into indirect narration.

→ Note that the summary should not contain anything that is not given in the text. You should not make any interpretation nor should give personal opinions or any introduction/conclusion about the original text.

→ Capture the tone or feeling of the original, particularly if it is humorous, satirical, aggressive or moralistic.

→ As stated earlier, the length of the précis should be around one-third of the original passage. Check the length. If it is more than the limit, edit it. You can also borrow a supporting idea kept in reserve, in case the length is shorter than the limit.

→ Review the rough draft for completeness, clarity, conciseness, coherence and correctness of grammar, spelling and punctuation.

→ Check all important points for irrelevancy.

→ Write down the fair draft of the précis of the original text.

8.4.5 Methods for Editing Long Sentences

Long sentences can be extremely effective for elaboration but for summarizing they may be quite wordy. The following strategies may be useful for condensing them:

1. Avoid using passive constructions as they create wordiness. Compare 'The boy was stuck by the driver who was driving a red car', with 'The red car hit the boy'.

2. Avoid using too many prepositional phrases, for example, 'the bank account of Mr. Deshpal' rather than 'Mr. Deshpal's bank account'.

3. Use connectors—that, unless, and, which, whereas, but, so that, etc.—intelligently to check repetitions, to reduce the number of words and to link ideas. For example, 'The crowd would disperse. It was our wish.

Our wish was encouraging,' can be reduced to *'Our wish that the crowd would scatter, was heartening'.* However, be careful and don't use too many of them.

4. Use word substitution for conciseness. *'He came and offered his services',* may be replaced by *'He volunteered his help'.* (Refer to Section 4.7 in 'One-Word Substitution' for more examples).

5. Learn the art of reducing a clause to a phrase, for example, *'He confessed that he was guilty'—'He admitted his guilt'./ 'The master was as bad as he could be'—'The master was altogether bad'.*

6. Trim down a list of same category words to a common term—*'taps, pipes, bends, joints and water seal'*—can be condensed to *'plumbing material'.*

8.4.6   A Sample Précis

Write down a précis of the following passage and give it a suitable title.

In the realm of human conduct and behaviour, Indian movies are an infinite source of ingenuity. All our new fashions related to, the style of our hair, the design of our footwear, cut of clothes we wear, interior decoration of our houses, and even our body language, manners and habits at social and public gatherings, somehow have originated from the film industry. It is there that they first appeared with all the glamour of their freshness and the appeal of their intense charisma. Nothing ever grows dreary and stale there. Even the most ordinary things are provided with a halo that changes them into objects of exquisite appeal. Dress designers, photographers, hair stylers, shoe companies, manufacturers of articles and of a thousand other varieties of luxury goods, interior designers and other men in different trades look to this industry for direction and inspiration. The science of make-up, is the product of the cinema industry without which it would lose much of its fascination. All such new and wonderful ideas enhance the professional knowledge of the traders and manufacturers and help them meet their customer's demand for newness. (Words 184)

The précis of the given passage is as under:

The Influence of the Indian Cinema

The Indian cinema is the source of many original ideas which get circulated in Indian society, in the form of fashions, decorations and even the mannerisms of people. The allure of the films changes the most ordinary into something glamorous. Traders and manufacturers capture the public demand by using them as profitable tips to maintain freshness in their up-coming products. (Words 60)

Task

Write down a précis of the following passage and give it a suitable title:

Global warming appears to have taken a toll on the climate patterns in Kashmir valley, which has been experiencing a decline in snowfall and rise in temperature, weather scientists have found. Analysing the snow accumulation and ablation patterns in Pir Panjal and Shamshawari regions of the valley during the winters of 2004–05 to 2006–07, scientists have shown that the seasonal snow cover has reduced while the maximum temperature is increasing steadily. The senior scientists of Snow and Avalanche Study Establishment have reported that this decreasing trend in areal extent of snow cover, rise in maximum temperature and reducing rate of total snowfall may be the indicators of global warming or climate change. The total snowfall in the winter of 2004–05 was 1082 centimetres across the valley that declined to 968 centimetres in 2005–06 and further to 961 centimetres in 2006–07. February, the second month of maximum snowfall, showed rapid fluctuation with 585 centimetres in 2004–05 compared to 207 centimetres in 2005–06 and 221 centimetres in 2006–07. (Words 166)

(Source: *The Times of India*)

Written Communication

9

In this unit

- ✓ Introduction
- ✓ Paragraph Writing
- ✓ Developing Outlines, Key Expressions and Situation
- ✓ Slogan Writing
- ✓ Dialogue Writing
- ✓ Interpreting Pictures and Cartoons

"Practice, practice, practice writing. Writing is a craft that requires both talent and acquired skills. You learn by doing, by making mistakes and then seeing where you went wrong."

–Jeffrey A. Carver

9.1 Introduction

Humans are social creatures. They crave for communication with their fellow beings and have been interacting with one another since ages. Communication started with oral interaction. Writing as a skill developed at a later stage as man took time to get mature enough to express himself/herself using the written channel of communication. Hence, writing is a skill that requires growth, which comes with training, experience and practice. William Faulkner has rightly asserted "A writer needs three things, experience, observation, and imagination, any two of which, at times any one of which, can supply the lack of the others."

In the present age where communication is considered as key to success in personal, social and professional life, writing is the major skill one should master. Writing requires all the language skills— listening, speaking and reading—to get used to it. It is the most interesting job that you could do in your lifetime. Writing exams, assignments and articles, poems, stories, novels, writing about yourself, your routine activities and writing a personal dairy—are all writing activities you regularly use as a student to pass the examination or to create interest in people. In your day-to-day working you communicate through writing letters, applications, reports, e-mails, SMS, etc. All these types of writings require a certain amount of qualities, which you should possess as a writer.

If you want to be a good writer or would like to become a better one, there are plenty of things you can do to improve and become better at communicating via the written medium. To achieve this aim you should read a lot, write every day, and interact with people to broaden your horizon by knowing their ideas, learn some rules of writing, use imagination, enrich your expression and brainstorm yourself to develop creative writing. At the same time, you should be aware that the style of writing changes with time, although it may not change as frequently as fashions. The Victorian verbosity and formal

English of the earlier days has given way to the current trend of plain English, which is clear, concise, direct, unambiguous and fluent. The wallpaper English overloaded with official jargons is not the call of the day. Even among the native users of English, plain and direct language is regarded as a virtue in communication. "Good writing can be defined as having something to say and saying it well" says Edward Abbey. A good piece of writing should take into account the following points:

1. Getting the grammar right
2. Having a range of vocabulary
3. Punctuating meaningfully
4. Using a variety of sentence structures
5. Employing imagination and creativity
6. Developing and organizing the content clearly
7. Linking ideas and information to develop a topic
8. Implementing a suitable style and using a correct layout
9. Containing a sense of purpose, sense of audience and sense of direction
10. Encompassing directness, conciseness, plainness and fluency

While writing, be mindful of the fact that once something is in written form, it cannot be taken back. Communicating in this way is more concrete than verbal communications, with less room for errors.

9.2 Paragraph Writing

A paragraph is one of the central components of writing. The Oxford Advanced Learners' Dictionary defines it as "a section of a piece of writing, usually consisting of several sentences dealing with a single subject." The word 'paragraph' has been derived from the French word—*paragraphe*—and the Greek word—*paragraphos*—which mean "short strokes marking break in sense." A paragraph, however, is "a group of sentences or a single sentence that forms a unit". Ultimately, good paragraphs contain a sentence or sentences unified around one central, controlling idea.

A paragraph is a separate section of a piece of writing. It provides a break to the reader. Each paragraph tells the reader that one topic is over and now he/she is going to read the next one. There are no fixed rules about the ideal length of a paragraph. For instance, in some light journalism and advertising a paragraph can be one sentence. In serious writing, a paragraph can last for a page or more. In fact, it is not the number of sentences that construct a paragraph rather the unity and coherence of ideas among those sentences. Most of the paragraphs contain at least three sentences but occasionally a one-sentenced paragraph is refreshing to the reader. Nevertheless, two unlinked topics require two paragraphs.

A paragraph begins on a new line even if you have to leave most of the previous line empty. It is often 'indented' from the edge of the page or 'blocked' leaving one word space from the edge. In typing one extra line may be left in 'indented' style. When a paragraph reaches its completion, it should summarize what has been read.

9.2.1 Parts of a Paragraph

A paragraph is divided into three basic parts as listed below:

1. Topic Sentence: This is the first sentence of the paragraph. It conveys the main idea of the paragraph to the readers and helps them focus on the theme as well as enables him/her to know what is going to be conveyed in it. You should summarize the main points of your paragraph in the first sentence.

2. Supporting Details: The rest of the paragraph consists of a series of sentences that develop, support or explain the main idea. They come after the topic sentence, forming the supporting details or the body of a paragraph. They give detailed information about the main idea through examples, illustrations, facts or stories. The information given in this part should be reliable, convincing and trustworthy.

3. The Concluding Sentence: The concluding or closing sentence is the last sentence of a paragraph. It sums up and restates the main idea as well as the details supported in the paragraph. It is the closing sentence that reminds the readers what they should value. You should restate the main idea of the paragraph as well as summarize it using different words.

9.2.2 Writing a Good Paragraph

While writing a paragraph certain basic elements, such as those listed below, should be considered before, while and after writing the paragraph:

(i) Pre-writing Stage: At the pre-writing stage think carefully and organize your ideas for your paragraph before you begin writing:

1. Consider the topic carefully: Before writing specify your topic, ask yourself: What questions are you going to answer in the paragraph? How can you best answer those questions? What is the most important point you want to make? How can you make an introductory sentence? What facts, ideas or details can you use to support your topic sentence? How can you make your paragraph interesting? Where can you find more facts on this topic?

2. Collect facts related to your topic: Look for the facts that will help you answer your questions. To save time, make sure that the facts you are writing are related directly to the questions you are going to answer. Take a sheet of paper and start jotting down the points that come to your mind. You should not spend a lot of time doing this; just write enough to help you remember why and how you are going to write your paragraph. At this stage, word order or grammatical mistakes may be overlooked.

4. Choose relevant and interesting points: Think carefully on the points you have noted down. What else do you want to say about this topic? Why should people be interested in this topic? Why is this topic significant? Choose the most important point you are going to present. If you are not able to decide which point is most important or stimulating, just choose one point and stick to it throughout the paragraph.

6. Organize your facts to develop your main idea: Once you have chosen the most important point of your paragraph, you must find the best way to tell your readers about it. Look at the facts you have written and the most important point you have chosen. Decide which facts and ideas will best support the main idea. Once you have collected all relevant details, arrange the points in the order you want to present them in the paragraph. You may write them down on a piece of paper to guide yourself as you write your paragraph.

(ii) Writing Stage: This stage is when you turn your ideas into sentences. The topic sentence should be a tempting sentence that catches readers' attention and attract them to carry on with the reading of the paragraph. It will help the readers as well as the writer focus on the main points and not drift away from them. Supporting details should give information that reinforces or supports the main idea.

One should use all the techniques such as descriptions, elaborations, definitions, examples, quotations, etc to make the paragraph sustainable and eligible. The last sentence should sum up your paragraph and should echo your topic sentence in a way or another. Write clear and simple sentences to express your meaning. Focus on the main idea of your paragraph. Use dictionary to help you find additional words to express your ideas.

(iii) Post Writing or Editing Stage: The editing stage is when you check your paragraph for mistakes and correct them. At this stage, check all the words, spellings, grammar, punctuation, handwriting and form. There should be no long unwinding sentences, no repetitions, no complex examples or difficult terms. Instead of definitions, give examples and supporting details should not be excessive. No irrelevant information should be given. Read your paragraph again. Make sure each sentence has a subject. See if your subjects and verbs agree with each other. Check the verb tenses of each sentence. Make sure that each sentence makes sense, your paragraph has a topic sentence and your supporting sentences focus on the main idea. Be assured that you have a closing sentence. Finally see if your paragraph is interesting.

9.2.3 Characteristics of a Good Paragraph

A good paragraph is:

→ **Unified**—A good paragraph should be unified. All of the sentences in a paragraph should be related to a single main idea expressed in the topic sentence of the paragraph. Anything that can distract the reader should not be included. The writer should focus on the central idea to unfold the theme logically.

→ **Coherent**—Coherence means logical relationship between the ideas and the presentation. Unity means dealing with the single idea while coherence means linking them in an appropriate manner. The sentences should be arranged in a logical manner and should follow a definite plan for development. To achieve coherence in a paragraph, one should use the given pronouns and linking words appropriately:
Pronouns – *this/that/these/those* – should be used carefully to maintain continuity otherwise they will confuse the readers. Sentence linkers such as *first/meanwhile/later/afterwards/finally/at that time/ at that very moment/next to/in front of/besides* and sequence words, *between/behind/after/then/now* are used to show chronological order or sequence. In the same way linking words – *thus/therefore/hence/ however/as a result of/accordingly/due to/owing to/consequently/similarly/likewise/yet/nevertheless/on the other hand/on the contrary,* etc. – present the objects or situations in comparison or contrast to one another as well as explain them. Transition words – furthermore/*in fact/in addition to/for an example/ as an illustration/for instance/in other words,* etc. – help the writer exemplify ideas or objects. While the use of words like *to conclude/to sum up/to summarize/in short/in a nut shell* concludes or summarizes the piece and words such as *definitely/certainly/of course/no doubt/undoubtedly* restate or reaffirm the ideas.

→ **Well Developed**—A good paragraph should be well developed in a logical manner. Every idea discussed in the Paragraph should be adequately explained and supported through evidence and details. Ideas should be organized in such a way that one sentence leads to the next one naturally.

9.2.4 Sample Paragraphs

1. Reading Books: Books are the most lasting product of human thought. They are the best friends of a man in all circumstances. Man being a social animal depends upon others for his development, fulfilment as well as entertainment. For this purpose, he needs guidance, company and support at various stages of life. Books are the best philosophers, associates and guides of man at every stage of life. Children enjoy them by colouring, solving puzzles and reading comics; young people find best companions in them while elderly persons pass their free time with them. Like true friends they remind us of our weaknesses and help us review our personality. In times of need, they directly talk to our mind and keep us fit. At the same time they are a vast storehouse of knowledge and learning. They supply us information, which can be stored in our memory for a long time and help us in mental as well as physical growth. We learn new words, ideas and expressions from them. Through books, we can share many things, which we cannot experience in reality. For instance, we can participate in sports events, beauty contests, quizzes, witness historical events, experience distant happenings, etc. They accompany us when we are alone. We can pass hours together reading, enjoying and learning them without getting tired of their company. They give us pleasure and joy for a long time. Therefore, it is rightly said, 'A world without books cannot be considered.'

2. The Art of Conversation: A good conversation is one of the greatest pleasures of mankind as well as an art. If we look at it seriously, we'll find that most of the people are lacking in this art. People are generally well versed in the art of speaking but they lack the initiative and deliberate purpose. It does not mean that people should converse seriously rather they should make their conversation more interesting and amusing. They should think over their mistakes and should try to improve them. They should practice conversation and should try to make it livelier like a game of cricket, hockey, football, shooting, etc. The ability to converse can be cultivated very well. To make our conversation meaningful, we should show genuine interest in the subject being discussed or the person we are talking to. We should not be too forceful or emphatic in asserting our feelings nor should we contradict or oppose the other person flatly. Even while giving advice, we should do it without imposing our wish on the listeners. On the whole, our conversation should generate positive feelings, it should not hurt anyone and people should enjoy it. Many people want to improve it but they keep on speaking and they hate listening. Silence plays an important role in a conversation. One can participate in a conversation effectively through listening as well as speaking. It must be done with natural zest and enjoyment; otherwise, it will not yield desired results. If learnt and practiced well, the art of conversation can be proved to be significant in winning the heart of the people.

3. Examination Fever: Examination fever is a common phenomenon among youngsters. Examinations are an essential part of the present education system. No one can pass a class in a school or a college or get admission in a reputed institute without appearing at the examination. Indispensability of the examinations has made it the most fearful aspect of a student's life. Dreams of failure keep haunting not only the students but also their parents and teachers. At the time of exams, young people and their parents have to postpone their engagements, give up pleasure loving activities— TV, computers, games, picnics, functions—and have to focus only on exams. This situation causes examination fever, which reaches at its peak one night before the exams. Students keep awake the whole night and revise the syllabus in a hurry. In the morning, they feel nervous and pray to God. If the paper is difficult, this nervousness leads to sickness. No doctor can cure this sickness. Rather, it can be cured through a thorough study of a subject. One should remain regular in his/her studies not only at the end of the session but also throughout the session. One day before the exams, he/she should revise the syllabus and should have sound sleep, nutritious food and good exercise. After receiving the question paper, he/she should read it carefully and answer appropriately. Before handing it to the teacher, one should revise it thoroughly. He/she will come out of the examination room relaxed not feverish. In fact, examination is an art. It teaches us to face challenges of life. No doubt, it causes anxiety; it is the landmark of success. One should learn how to face it confidently instead of fearing it.

4. Co-Curricular Activities: Co-curricular activities previously known as extracurricular activities are the backbone of the education system. Schools and colleges offer a variety of activities, which all the students must attend along with the standard study curriculum. Academic activities in the classroom education of an institute adhere to the requirements of global standard. On the other hand, co-curricular activities, which are meant for synchronizing and developing the mind as well as the body, also form an integral part of the curriculum. These activities are held outside the standard curriculum hours and participation in these activities depends upon the nature as well as the participants of the particular activity. Student groups do foot drills and team-building exercises, while with painting tools, children, are found busy in painting, drawing, sketching in the art rooms or learning dancing, singing, acting, etc. with musical instruments. Moreover, competitive sportspersons spend most of their time training and learning their respective sport techniques. A whole range of indoor and outdoor activities accompanying the course studies serves a twofold purpose in furthering the development of a student as well as in character building. 'All work and no play, makes Jack a dull boy' is an old saying. Recreation, is an essential part of a student's life and co-curricular activities help them in refreshing and rejuvenating young minds. Secondly, they pave way for nurturing the hidden talents. The students who do not excel in academics feel a sense of fulfillment, satisfaction and achievement through excelling in them. Besides this, co-curricular activities develop leadership, time management, teamwork, interpersonal communication and other useful skills which employers value the most when making hiring choices. To achieve the desired purpose, they should be planned, chosen and conducted fruitfully. No one can deny the fact that the activities outside the classroom are directly related to the career, personality and all round development of the students.

5. All that glitters is not gold: 'All that glitters is not gold' is an old proverb. It implies that appearances are often deceptive or in other words, the outward pomp, show, external glory and luxury may not be a true expression of one's personality, an object, a place or even one's personal life. A man may enjoy sunshine of wealth and prosperity but he may not be inwardly contended. For instance, a wealthy man may enjoy a lot of wealth, comforts and riches or all the possible luxuries but when he sleeps, in his unconscious mind he keeps brooding over how to accumulate more and more wealth the next day. He is always dissatisfied and mentally disturbed in planning ways to have more and more. He, therefore, proves the statement that things are different from how they appear to be. Similarly, a person may be very beautiful, handsome, smart or good looking but if he is not physically fit, mentally alert or socially respectable, his outward charms have no value. An object may be very attractive; however, its attractiveness has no value unless it has utility. In short, the proverb, 'All that glitters is not gold' enlivens us to the truth that only outward beauty or charms are not sufficient. The importance of outward glitter may be short-lived or temporary. We should care more for inward perfection, beauty of the soul and moral values, which have a lasting effect on mankind and society.

6. Health is Wealth: A healthy mind resides in a healthy body. Health is the basic source of human happiness. A man who is suffering from an ailment cannot enjoy anything in his life. He can have all the comforts in his life—a bungalow, car, good furniture, air conditioner, and expensive dresses but he can use them only if he is physically fit. His friends, neighbours and relatives can be very good but he can share his joys and grief with them only if he is in good health. There can be numerous opportunities in life but he can avail them with hard work and wisdom, which are not possible without health. One thing should be kept in mind: health is not just the physical aspect because man is not made of only flesh and blood but also with various organs forming different systems in a body. He/she also has a mental, social, and moral outlook. However, physical health is the base of human personality because a sick and poor person cannot be expected to follow any social norms. A physically fit man can do nothing without his mind.

Man is a social animal as no man can be an island in himself. A person should live peacefully in society and should cooperate with others. However, the most important thing, which makes a man human, is his moral outlook. Major evils like terrorism, corruption, anarchism exist in society because of lack of human values. Everybody talks of falling standard of education, students, losing interest in studies and growing materialism but no one thinks of providing a healthy moral atmosphere to the young generation or developing a sense of right and wrong. In this way a physically fit, mentally sound, socially healthy and morally strong people can be a real asset to a nation or in other words the real wealth of a nation.

Task

Write a paragraph on the following topics:

1. Role of children in TV advertisements
2. Computer as a classroom teacher
3. Might is right
4. TV serials
5. Life in a college hostel
6. Brain drain
7. Mobile phones
8. Increasing crime in Indian society
9. Newspaper
10. My favourite TV show

9.3 Developing Outlines, Key Expressions and Situations

Words are the symbols of ideas and images in our mind. They are verbal clues that can be used in the form of outlines, key expressions, situations and themes. First of all, we should understand what do they mean? How can we utilize them as guidelines to achieve our goal? How can they be used to develop written communication? Writing through outlines, key expressions and situations, undoubtedly, improves the speed and the quality of writing and the results simultaneously. Many writers use an outline to help them think through the various stages of the writing process. It is a kind of designing scheme or making a skeletal sketch of the organization of a written piece.

9.3.1 Advantages

Preparing an outline will help you refer to your notes, think over them from several perspectives, and chalk out an organizational plan according to your topic, audience and assignment. It will keep you precise and help you stick to the topic along with imparting unity of thoughts as well as compactness to your composition. An outline accompanying the final draft of a report or a research paper also functions as a table of contents for the readers. You may prepare an outline when you want to show the hierarchical relationship or logical ordering of information. For research papers, an outline may help you keep track of large amounts of information. For creative writing, an outline may help organize the various plot threads and help keep track of character traits. Many people find that organizing an oral report or presentation in the form of an outline helps them speak more effectively in front of a crowd. In a nutshell, outlines aid us in the process of writing by organizing our ideas and material in a logical form, showing relationships among thoughts, constructing an ordered overview of the piece and defining boundaries and groups.

9.3.2   Generating Outlines

Outlines can be generated from "bull's eye outward" that is following inside to outside direction. With a single topic, sentence or idea, start writing down clues about what you might include in your presentation, paragraph or any other composition. Don't think about this too much—just jot down any idea which comes to you, even if you are not sure how or where it will fit into your writing. As you get fresh ideas, include them. This method is called brainstorming. You can capture the ideas you generate in a number of ways—using a sketchpad, a sheet of paper or memory cards. However, start with noting them down in a random order, then arrange them in a logical sequence. The stages of writing, revising and rewriting the final piece should follow. Another method can be brain mapping, that is, noting down the points systematically. This method can be useful in narrating events like description of cricket match, scene of a technical fair or discussing problems. While using the given outlines try to read between the lines, provide the missing links and shape the twists and turns. In short, the writer has to give a finish to the incomplete picture.

Formal outlines can be prepared in two ways. The ideas can be expressed in parallel phrases or in other words, they can be expressed in the same grammatical form—as noun phrases, verb phrases or adverbial phrases. Topic outlines are useful for the writer as they are brief and to the point. In sentence outlines, on the other hand, the ideas are expressed in complete, though not necessarily parallel, sentences. Sentence outlines give the reader a clearer idea of what you are going to say. For shorter and simpler compositions, a few informal notes may be enough but for the longer ones, which are a bit difficult, you need a systematic plan.

9.3.3   Key Expressions and Situations

Key expressions and situations can also be used as clues to write essays, articles or other compositions. Sometimes key expressions appear in the form of outlines and give us a complete sketch of the picture. However, they may be given in the form of a sentence, a key statement or a topic sentence and we have to develop them into a write up. In such a case, we have to complete the work of an artist who began it but left it just after starting it. Key expressions can be a purely fictitious event, a deep-rooted desire, a reflection or a thought based on facts observed. We should use our brain to analyze the situation, our imagination to produce details and expressions to develop them into a composition. We should place ourselves, imaginatively in the situation and should empathize effectively with it. Although it is a non-verbal clue, it is very much like a picture clue. It is an actual translation of visual input as it inspires our imagination to draw a picture in our mind. By identifying ourselves with the characters, situations or events we provide the missing link and complete the picture.

9.3.4   Sample Outlines

Sample 1   Developing Outlines for Presentation

Importance of Discipline
Meaning of discipline _____ its requirement _____ discipline in nature _____ usually misunderstood as restriction _____ a virtue for the people of different professions _____the best discipline is self discipline _____

Discipline is the guideline to do any task in a proper manner. It means training according to rules. Without discipline nothing can be done as there will be only chaos and confusion. Discipline is indispensable in every walk of life. It is, in fact, the way of life.

Life requires discipline at every step. The world can be really difficult for those who don't have it and don't get it. Nature is the base of all discipline. The rules of gravity, hunger, temperature, danger, curiosity and even aggression teach us a lot about discipline. Nature has been rightly called as the mother of all discipline. It provides all of us with an experience of challenges, problems and consequences, as well as parents who nurture, protect, teach and guide us. Nature offers a real-world experience that parents can use to teach discipline to children. Some of these include making children aware of their surroundings as well as showing concern, cooperation and understanding among the people of the society.

Many of us feel that discipline restricts us but this is wrong because discipline opens our mind and supports us to move in the right way. It makes our life systematic and organized, hence, instead of restricting our freedom it gives us better opportunities to succeed. It directs us to fight every problem. A disciplined person succeeds in each and every field of life. Discipline helps a person get rid of doubts when his mind is divided between duty and self-interest or fear.

Discipline is a virtue not only for the students but also for the people of all the professions and keeps them charged, agile and alert. Disciplined people make a disciplined society and a powerful country. It is a great source of unity. A disciplined nation is a strong nation. Discipline is surety of safety and guarantee of security from the enemies and unfriendly countries. It is the only cure of our social problems.

Discipline should not be imposed upon the people rather it should come from within. One should practice self-discipline because self-discipline is the best discipline. Part of growing up involves the ability to identify our needs, think about our options and to make choices that meet our needs and protect our long-term well-being. Parents who rely on this approach create opportunities for their children and let them experience nature and society. They allow their children to make choices and to learn from the consequences that follow. Children make choices and learn from the consequences that follow. In this way, self-discipline leads to the successful growth of an individual.

Sample 2   Developing Outlines for Writing a Paragraph

Reality Shows on TV

Success of reality shows _____a few successful shows_____ provide a platform to the budding talents, amuse us, enhance our knowledge_____ increase the burden _____ involve politics _____ game of power

Reality shows are gaining a lot of popularity these days. In 1995, India's first TV show 'SA-RE-GA-MA' was shown on the national channel. As far as TRP (Television Rating Points) is concerned, it was a great success. The show not only had a large viewership but earned a lot of name and fame for its makers. Since then, the reality shows have become a usual practice to gain more and more popularity. Many shows such as, *sa-re-ga-ma-pa*, *Close Up Antakshari*, *Meri Aawaz Suno*, *Indian Idol*, *Kaun Banega Crorepati*?, *Bigg Boss*, *Dus Ka Dum*, *Star Voice of India*, *Boggie Woggie* and many more have attained a huge popularity. Reality shows are planned according to the taste of the people. These shows are liked as they showcase the talent of the budding artists, provide the audience with healthy entertainment and guide the viewers in the right direction. Shreya Ghoshal, Kunal Ganjawala and Sunidhi Chauhan, the famous singers of the music industry have come from reality shows. Shilpa Shetty gained a lot of popularity as an international artist because of such a show named 'Big Brother.' Some shows give us an opportunity to know the life of the film stars. While laughter shows contribute to the national health by relieving people of their day-to-day stress, the other shows like KBC, Bournvita Quiz Contest enhance our knowledge. Dance and musical shows provide us with sheer amusement, keep us in touch with the latest trends and at the same time provide us an opportunity to give our judgement. Nevertheless, these shows have many shortcomings too. Such shows have increased burden on children. Not only do their studies suffer but also the pressure of competition gets accumulated them. Besides this, they take us away from our culture. To gain popularity, the show owners include gossips, controversies and fights. It is shown that the people win due to public opinion but it is, in fact, the game of power and money. To conclude, the reality shows are not always real.

Sample 3   Developing Outlines to Write a Story

Sir Gobble (A fairy tale)

Bessie Curtis spent a year with her aunt and uncle _____happy in the country _____ her uncle gave her a turkey _____it was to be brought on the dinner table on thanksgiving day_____ Bessie and turkey grew fond of each other _____she was sad _____ was afraid at dinner time on the thanksgiving day_____ turkey was brought on the table alive_____ astonished_____ uncle named turkey as "Sir Gobble"

Bessie Curtis was in a great deal of trouble. She was staying in the country while her parents were in Europe. She liked the country, she loved her uncle and aunt with whom she lived, and she heard every week from her father and mother. But something kept disturbing her. As the summer passed, and the autumn came, she had moments when she looked very dull. Early in the spring, her uncle had given her a young turkey. "There, Bessie," he had said, "that is one of the prettiest turkeys I have ever seen. I will give him into your care, and on Thanksgiving Day we will have him on the dinner-table."

For some time, Bessie fed the turkey every day without feeling particularly fond of him. Very soon, however, he began to know her. He not only ran to meet her when she brought him his corn and meal, but he also would follow her about just the way Mary's little lamb followed her about. Her uncle often called after her: "And everywhere that Bessie goes, the turkey's sure to go." Yes, round the garden, up and down the avenue, and even into the house itself the turkey followed Bessie. Alas! She remembered her uncle's words when he gave her the turkey, "On Thanksgiving Day we will have him on the table." Thanksgiving Day would be here in a week. Now, if Bessie had been like some little girls, she would have told her trouble to her uncle. But she never mentioned it to any one, although she cried herself to sleep several nights before Thanksgiving Day.

At last the day came, and Bessie, instead of going out to the fowl yard as usual, kept in the house all the morning. She was afraid that, if she went, she would not find her beloved friend. Dinner time came, and, with a heavy heart, she seated herself at the table. Her uncle and aunt noticed her sober face, and thought that she missed her father and mother. "Come, come, said her uncle, "we must cheer up; no sad looks on Thanksgiving Day. Maria, bring in the turkey." Poor Bessie! She could not look up as the door opened, and something was brought in on a big platter. But, as the platter was placed on the table, she saw that it did indeed hold her turkey, but he was alive and well. She looked so astonished that suddenly her uncle understood all her past troubles. "Why, Bessie," he said, "Did you think I would kill your pet? No, indeed, but I told you he should be on the table on Thanksgiving Day, so here he is."

Then Bessie's uncle struck the turkey gently with his carving knife, the way the queen strikes a man with a sword when she makes him a knight. "Behold!" said Bessie's uncle, "I dub you 'Sir Gobble;' you shall never be killed, but die a natural death, and never be parted from Bessie."

Sample 4   Developing Key Expressions

Where there is a will there is a way

Great souls have strong will_____ with firm will man can do the unexpected _____once he decides he should not waver _____great people achieved success with determination _____ Curies, Napoleon, Amitabh and Tendulkar – a few examples to quote _____nothing is impossible for the strong willed

It is truly said, "Great souls have will: feeble have only wishes." He, who has a firm will, moulds the world to himself. A man can achieve everything in life if he has a strong will power. A successful man rises from the lowest ebb of life and attains great heights because once the goal is set before him, he does not waver or hesitate. Strong will power accompanied with practice, patience and perseverance can move even mountains. To achieve success one should have firm resolve and put his heart and soul into work. The person who is irresolute cannot make any headway in life. There are people who aspire for great ends but lack self-confidence and suffer hardships. Curies had to work in extreme poverty and in the shabbiest and most ill-equipped laboratory. Even then, they discovered radium. Napoleon crossed Alps in winter. Even in the recent times we have examples of Sachin Tendulkar and Amitabh Bachchan. These people too confronted many setbacks, frustrations and struggles. Still, with their strong will and determination, they could achieve success, which could be a dream for others. Whether it is the field of sports, education, business or entertainment, victory comes to those who have undefeatable will. In this way, man is the master of his own fate. With determination and indomitable courage, he can cross oceans or move mountains to achieve his goals. So, every problem has a solution, provided one has a strong will.

Sample 5   Developing Outlines to Write an Article

Environmental Pollution
Threatens man's survival_____universal problem _____dangerous for health _____ adversely affecting flora and fauna _____ collective effort is required _____strong measures are needed to check its menace

In recent years, environmental pollution has increased so much that it threatens human survival. It has become a global problem. Almost all the countries are facing this problem. The causes of pollution are quite evident. Vehicles burn smoke and emit toxic gases containing carbon dioxide and monoxide. Chemical wastes from the factories pollute air as well as water. Contaminated water causes death and destruction of both marine and organic life. Man is cutting trees and forests at a fast rate, which is causing global warming.

Pollution has started showing its bad effects on human health and life. Breathing has become very difficult and it has given rise to many diseases like asthma, bronchitis, etc. School children are easy victims of the pollution problems because they are directly in contact with fumes from the exhaust pipes of the vehicles. Due to global warming, ozone layer has developed a big hole. Rainfall is scanty and crop fails in many places. Flora and fauna have been adversely affected. Global warming may cause rise in the level of seawater which may be disastrous.

All the countries should come together and fight against pollution, which poses a threat to human survival. More and more trees should be planted at every possible place. Fuming vehicles should be strictly banned in the cities as they cause maximum pollution. An awareness should be created among the people of the world towards environmental degradation and every human should fight this man-made menace. Protecting environment is every body's pious duty and all of us should come forward for this noble task.

Task

Develop the outlines of the following presentations:

1. Growing aggressions among the students
2. Female foeticide—A bane on Indian society
3. Importance of technical education
4. Engineers: The builders of the nation

5. Developing communication skills
6. Free periods in college
7. Women sports
8. My favourite pastime
9. Old is gold but new is gem
10. Fighting terrorism

9.4 Slogan Writing

Slogans, when used properly, can build and sustain name and recognition of a firm and can possibly become a symbol that really means something for it. When used badly or irrelevantly, they are little more than nonsense. What is a slogan, after all? It is a statement that asserts to characterize a firm or a product and sums up its spirit, aim or the main theme in a few words. Slogans are, therefore, short and memorable words or phrases. They are mostly used in political, social, commercial and religious fields for propaganda, attracting the attention of the masses, suggesting an idea quickly or creating awareness among people on social issues. The following are some examples of slogans:

1. 'Quit India!' (political)
2. 'Ganpati Bappa Moriya!' (religious)
3. Sony Max – 'Deewana bana de!' (commercial)
4. 'Cleanliness is next to Godliness!' (social)

9.4.1 Types of Slogans

There are mainly four types of slogans:

1. **Imperative**—An imperative slogan commands to do something: "Define Your Body Inspire Your Mind!"
2. **Descriptive**—A descriptive slogan describes the key feature or benefit of an organization or a person: "GNI—Exploring Futuristic Education!"
3. **Superlative**—A superlative slogan exaggerates ideas in such a way that they appear to be rather true: "Saving the Planet!", "Give the Gift of Life!"
4. **Provocative**—A provocative slogan makes the listener or viewer think or reflect on their situation: "What's the Best for You?

9.4.2 Attributes of a Good Slogan

1. It should be short, for example, 'Just do it!'
2. It should be memorable, for example, 'Get listed. Get sold!'
3. It should reflect your business philosophy and target markets, for example, 'Work is worship!'
4. It should appeal to your customer's emotions, for example, 'A Diamond Forever!'
5. It should have an urge, for example, 'Don't Shed Blood; Donate It!'
6. It should emphasize the superiority of the product in the market, for example, 'King of Good Times— King Fisher!'
7. It should be specific, for example: "(Name) Stands for Excellence!"
8. It should be believable, for example: "The pause that refreshes!"
9. It should impart positive thoughts, for example, 'Because you are worth it!'
10. It should be trendy, for example: "Gimme (give me) a Break, Gimme a Break!"

9.4.3 How to Write Slogans?

"*Good ideas are a dime a dozen, but implementation is priceless!*" While writing slogans, we should remember that slogans should have rhyme, rhythm and pun. Catchy, simple and short words, phrases and expressions should be used to inspire the mind of the masses. A little research, humour, hard work and insight will help the writer make it impressive and memorable. Some well-known quotations may also be used to attract the attention of the people as well as to create a lasting impression on the mind of the people. A good slogan rarely has a life of its own unless it is created carefully and used appropriately. If you think you have simply come up with a catchy phrase, put it on a business card or a letterhead and practice it. Then, you have built a castle in the air and moved in. To be successful, a slogan, no matter how good it is as a piece of marketing writing, has to have a strong body of explanation behind it. It should sum up the essence of an advertisement or a brochure, or else it is meaningless. Credibility is important in slogans. They appeal to those who like to think and it is purely emotional rather rational. If you were to say, "We do better audits," or "We write better briefs", you could say it but ethically and realistically you may not. It is a major difference between a product and professional service marketing.

9.4.4 Sample Slogans

Sample 1

Reading is to Mind What Exercise is to Body

Books Are:
→ A warehouse of knowledge
→ A source of entertainment forever
→ A food for thought and mental health
→ Our best friends, philosophers and guides

Remember
■ Do regular reading and broaden your horizon and experience

Sample 2

Drug Addiction—An Endless Destruction

Drugs:
→ Never thrill but only kill
→ Cause death and doom
→ Lead man to living hell
→ Spoil family and social life

Remember
■ Drugs merely rot the body and anaesthetize the mind
■ Say 'NO' to DRUGS forever – for yourself and your loved ones

Sample 3

Check Pollution—Save Humanity

The Monster of Pollution
→ Pollutes air, water and land
→ Depletes ozone layer and melts polar ice

→ Decreases forests and chokes earth
→ Causes deadly diseases and acid rains

So
→ Grow more and more trees
→ Adopt eco-friendly ways
→ Spread awareness towards environment
→ Preserve natural resources

Come together and make the earth beautiful, lovable and healthy

SAVE ENVIRONMENT – SAVE YOURSELF

Sample 4

**Enjoy Exercise Year Around and be
a Happier, Healthier and Livelier Human Being**

HAVE
→ Regular walk, jogging and yoga
→ Cycling, skating and skipping
→ Dancing, playing and swimming

AND
→ Keep yourself healthy and energized
→ Remove stress and burden
→ Control weight and fats
→ Improve stamina, build muscles, bones and joints

Consider: Those who do not find time for exercise will have to find time for illness.

Sample 5

Female Foeticide – A Crime Against God

Girls are:
→ MOTHERS
→ SISTERS
→ FRIENDS
→ WIVES
→ TEACHERS

Murdering them in the womb means:
→ Destroying happiness and brightness of homes
→ Killing love and affection in life
→ Disturbing male–female ratio
→ Hindering country's progress

Remember:
■ No society or country can progress if girls are killed before they are born!
■ Girls are mothers and mother is the name of God!

Sample 6

Better Late Than Never – Drive Safe

DO'S:

→ Use seat belts and helmets
→ Drive in your lanes
→ Follow traffic signals
→ Keep your speed in limits

DON'TS:

→ Jump red lights
→ Mix driving and drinking
→ Park at the wrong sites
→ Use mobiles while driving

Remember:

■ Safety – It is in your hand!
■ Your first mistake could be your last!

Task

Write out slogans with supporting text on the following topics:

1. Donate blood
2. Deforestation control
3. Animal protection
4. Stop ragging
5. Preserve natural resources
6. Illiteracy: A curse

9.5   Dialogue Writing

"Conversation is the laboratory and workshop of the students."

–Ralph W Emerson

Man is a social animal and to converse with others is one of his natural desires. Conversation links people with one another and makes social and professional interactions possible. Writing a dialogue is, in fact, writing a conversation, which enriches understanding. As compared to other writing skills, dialogue writing may be difficult. It is true that the idea of dialogues is simple and the writer creates or retells a conversation between characters or real people, but experienced people know that dialogue writing is an art. Writing realistic dialogue does not come easily to everyone. If it is written well, dialogue helps in advancing the story and unfolds the characters. As for learners, it helps in improving communication.

9.5.1   Writing a Good Dialogue

A good dialogue has a desired effect only if it is realistic and meaningful. The readers, at some point of time, may come across a bad dialogue, which may be grammatically correct but fails to attract the readers. Why is this? One of the most common mistakes a writer may commit with dialogue writing is pushing his/her own views into it. The author, working in the background, is concerned about creating a story or advancing the theme, so the natural conversation between the characters is sacrificed. A dialogue writer should have an ability to empathize with the characters, that is, he/she should keep himself/herself in the shoes of the characters. They should proceed in a natural and realistic way to make it meaningful. The art of dialogue writing needs practice, knowledge and patience to provide satisfaction to the readers or listeners.

9.5.2   Mechanics of Writing Good Dialogues

1. Use a conversational tone: When dialogues are written in a conversational tone, we feel that they are real conversations. Researchers have proved if we are involved in a conversation, our brain responds accordingly and pays more attention to it. Use a conversational tone and help the readers understand the interaction.

2. Pay attention to day-to-day conversations: It is essential to have a sense of natural speech patterns to write a good dialogue. One should pay attention to the expressions and the techniques of day-to-day conversation. This exercise will help us not only write dialogues in an appropriate manner, but also start developing an ear to the way people talk.

3. Write the way you talk: You may ignore what you may have learnt about writing and write the way you talk to help your readers understand your material. What this really means is to write in a direct and friendly manner—it is more appealing to our brain than formal writing. Dialogues should read like real conversations. How do we accomplish it? Alfred Hitchcock said that a good story is "life, with the dull parts taken out." This very much applies to a dialogue. Edit out the filler words and irrelevant dialogue—that is, dialogue that doesn't contribute to the theme in any way.

4. Don't provide too much information at once: It should not be obvious to the reader that they are being fed important facts. Let the conversation unfold naturally. One doesn't have to tell the reader everything up front; rather one should help him or her remember details from the background.

5. Don't overdo dialogue tags: Using too much beyond "he said/she said" only draws attention to the tags. One should try to draw the reader's attention towards the brilliant dialogue, not towards the ability to think of synonyms for "said."

6. Punctuate the dialogue correctly: The rules for punctuating dialogues can be confusing. Take some time to learn the basics. A reader should get the content of your dialogue and should not feel distracted by wrong punctuation marks.

7. Use contractions: Contrary to what you may have learned, it is ok to use contractions such as *I'll, you'll, won't, shan't*, etc., in dialogue writing. You will grab your reader's attention and engage their brain without making them aware of it.

8. You may begin a sentence with 'and' and 'but':   Although starting a sentence with 'and' and 'but' is grammatically incorrect, in dialogue writing, this is permissible occasionally. It makes your dialogue sound authentic.

9. Use ellipsis: Ellipsis is an important feature of informal talk. Use it to make your dialogues true to life and colloquially correct. For example, instead of saying, 'Do you want a drink?' say 'Want a drink?'

10. Read out the dialogue loudly: If you are not sure about your dialogue, read it out loud to yourself. If it doesn't sound right, change it. Reading your dialogue out loudly gives it a new meaning.

11. Don't use jargon, slangs or difficult words: If you are really concerned about your readers, don't use words that show off your intelligence. The use of jargons and slangs makes your dialogues difficult to understand and at the same time gives an impression that the writer either lacks seriousness or is not aware of the technique of creating a rapport with the reader.

12. Remain organized and don't ramble: Writing dialogue does not give you permission to write like you are sending a text message or to ramble using long sentences. Your writing should be well organized and should have thoughts that flow together. Dialogues should be well linked and each following dialogue should be the by-product of the previous one.

13. Paraphrase back what you have heard, using your own words: This seems like an easy skill but needs some practice to master. A dialogue occurs in turns, each person taking a turn to listen and a turn to speak or to respond. Paraphrasing the speaker's ideas in your own words shows respect to the speaker and when you have your "speaking turn" you indicate that you have been listening carefully. Moreover, you have a chance to correct your understanding, affirm it, restate it, oppose it or say something new about it.

14. Start conversation with greetings: Start your dialogue with proper greetings to establish contact with the other person and to show friendliness. For example—Good morning! Good afternoon! Hello! How are you? Hi Radha!

15. Don't end your conversation in confusion or abruptly: Ending should include the phrases which signal the end of conversation in a polite manner. Like greetings, end it with the phrases such as see you/good bye/have a nice day!

16. Make it realistic: In a real conversation, people often ask a question to answer another or sometimes they answer a question before it is asked. For example – A – What will you do if you win 10 thousand rupees? B – Well, what will you do?

17. Be careful about formal and informal situations: You should know whether the situation is formal or informal. Use your sentences, vocabulary, style and techniques accordingly. In a formal situation a senior person ends the conversation and in informal situation either person can signal the end of conversation. In telephonic conversation, the caller ends the dialogue.

18. Think over the topic and the situation: Note down the points you are going to use. Arrange your ideas in a logical manner. Think positively about your audience and about what you have to say.

9.5.3   Some Useful Phrases

Greetings: (**starting**) Hallo!/Hello!/Hi/Good morning/Cheerio/How nice to see you!/What's a pleasant surprise! (**ending**) Bye!/Have a nice day!/Good day!/See you!/ Come again!/It's good to see you!/Thanks for coming!/See you again!/Good bye!/It was really good to see you here!

Salutations: Mr. Sharma/Mrs. Mathur/Miss Gulati/Madam/Ma'am/Sir/Ladies and gentlemen/Yes, Mr. Smith, Yes/madam/No, sir/No ma'am.

Introduction: Let me introduce Mr. Garg (to you)/I would like you to meet Mr. Sharma/Let me introduce myself/I'm/My name is Nivedita/Meet my friend Jasmine/How do you do?- How do you do?/I'm very pleased to meet you/Could you introduce me to Mrs. Chopra?/Excuse me, are you Mr. Bhatnagar?/Yes, that's my name/Nice to meet you.

Thanks: Thank you/Thanks/Thank you very much/I'm most grateful to you/Thanks a lot/I'm much obliged to you/It's good of you/You've been very helpful/Not at all/It's all right/You're welcome!

How to say "yes"/"no": Yes, good/OK/All right/That's it!/Certainly!/Of course!/Sure!/By all means/I think so/Yes, you're right/Oh, no/I don't think so/Not at all/ Certainly not/Not yet/It's no use/Never/No, on the contrary/No, but thanks anyway/May be next time/I'm sorry but I can't accept that.

Requests: Will you please pass me/help me?/Here you are/With pleasure/I'd like .../Could you...?/Would you help me?/Will you come ..., please?/Stop it/Go ahead/Look here/May I ask you to do me a favour?/I wonder.

Excuses: I'm sorry/Excuse me, please/Sorry, I cannot help it/It's ok/That's all right/Will you excuse me for a moment?/So sorry to trouble you/Sorry to disturb/bother you/Never mind/It's all right/It's no trouble at all/I beg your pardon/Pardon me!

Courtesy: How are you?/I'm well, thank you, and you?/Have a good time/Quite well, thanks/This way, please/May I come in?/After you/Excuse me, I'll lead the way/Will you come in, please?/Give them my kind regards/I'm sorry to hear that.

Satisfaction: Very good/Great/Splendid/Amazing/That's fine/That's OK. That's all right/It's good to see you again/I'm glad about that/He's lucky!/I'm glad to hear that.

Dissatisfaction: Stop it!/How can he be so silly!/It's stupid!/It's unbelievable!/I'm sick of it!/I'm fed up with it!/It's impossible!/Leave her alone!

Regret: I'm afraid it's true/I'm very sorry about that/What a shame!/That's bad luck!/I'm afraid I can't be of any help/I'm deeply sorry/What a pity!

Weather: What's the weather forecast?/It's awfully hot/It's sultry/It's getting warm/It's sunny/It's raining/It's damp/It's overcast/It's cloudy/It's breezy/It looks like rain/The dew's falling/It's a cloudburst/There's rainbow in the sky/It's drizzling/It's foggy/It's pouring rain/It's going to snow/It's snowing/It's chilly/cool/It's cold/It's freezing/I'm freezing/It's slippery/It's windy/It's dusty/A wind is rising/The storm is drawing near/It's hailing.

Health: How are you?/Are you (feeling) better now?/You look/don't look well/You look (are) pale/I'm very well/I'm not well/I feel tired/You should go to the doctor's/It's nothing; I'll soon get over it/What's the matter with you?/What's the trouble?/I'm sick/I feel faint/ I'm sick/I fell and bruised my leg/I hurt my knee/I sprained my ankle/I've broken my arm/I've cut my finger/I've got a blister on my heel/I've burnt my back (in the sun)/Something's fallen in my eye/I was bitten by some insect/My arm's swollen/Send for a doctor/Fetch a doctor at once/Where's the health centre?/What are the surgery hours?

Sympathy: Please accept my condolences/I share your distress/Accept my deepest condolences/I'm so sorry for him.

Making Suggestions: How/what about (+ gerund)?/Why don't you/we…?/You should/ought to…/If I were you, I'd…/I suggest/propose (+ gerund)…That's a good idea!/Yes, let's do that/Yes, why not?/That isn't possible/practicable/feasible.

Agreeing: Absolutely/Precisely/Exactly/I totally agree/So do I/Nor do I/I can go along with that/I think you're right up to a point.

Disagreeing: You're quite wrong there/I'm sorry, but I don't agree at all/That's an exaggeration/Do you really think so?/It isn't as simple as that.

Checking your Understanding: Do you really mean to say…?/So, if I understand you correctly, …/What exactly do you mean by that?/I didn't follow what you said about….

Asking for Opinions: So, what do you think, (name)?/How do you feel about this/ that?/What is your view/position on…?/Do you agree with that, (name)?/Would you like to add anything, (name)?

Giving Opinions: In my opinion/view…/As far as I'm concerned…/I think/feel…/As I see it…To my mind….

Correcting Misunderstandings: That's not quite what I meant by…/Don't get me wrong. What I meant was…/You have got the wrong end of the stick/Look, to put it another way……

Interrupting: Sorry to interrupt, but…/May I interrupt you for a moment?/Can I just make a point?/Mind if I just say something?/ Excuse me!

Dealing with Interruptions: I haven't finished, if you don't mind/If I might just finish…/I haven't got to my point yet/Let me just make my point.

9.5.4 Sample Dialogues

1. Conversation between two friends discussing their college life.

Avneet: Hi Mahak!
Mahak: Hi Avneet! Nice to see you after a long time!
Avneet: Same here! How are you?
Mahak: I'm fine. Thanks. What about you?
Avneet: I am also fine.
Mahak: What are you doing these days?
Avneet: Nothing special….just enjoying holidays.
Mahak: That's great!
Avneet: What is going on at your end?
Mahak: Same here. I am at home with my family.
Avneet: How's your college life going on?
Mahak: It's very nice and relaxed. We enjoy a lot in our college. And yours?
Avneet: Not so good. There's no discipline or strictness in our college. Students bunk their classes and they don't let others also study.
Mahak: But in our college we have regular classes. The discipline part is very good. Bunking classes is not possible here.
Avneet: You must be happy. We have so many problems in studies……and have no one to discuss them.

Mahak: In our college, faculty is very good and experienced. They teach us very well and give us a lot of study material such as notes, assignments, etc. You may also refer to them if you wish.

Avneet: Thanks a lot! Of course, I'd like to use them.

Mahak: Come to my place in the evening. We'll discuss these points and will have a nice time.

Avneet: Sure! I'll definitely come.

Mahak: Ok. Bye!

Avneet: Bye! Take care!

2. A dialogue between the receptionist and the student who has come to inquire about the courses run by the institute.

Student: Good Morning, ma'am!

Receptionist: A very good morning! How can I help you?

Student: Ma'am, I'm a student of +2. I wish to seek admission in a reputed engineering college next year. I've come to inquire about the B. Tech. course run by your institute.

Receptionist: Sure! Our college runs B. Tech. course for four years in Computer Science and Engineering, Information Technology, Mechanical Engineering and Electronics and Communication Engineering.

Student: Is the course approved by AICTE or some other authorized body?

Receptionist: Of course! Our B. Tech. course is duly approved by AICTE and is affiliated to Kurukshetra University, one of the oldest and most reputed universities of India.

Student: What is the fee structure?

Receptionist: Total fee is Rs. 65,000 per annum. You've to pay it in four instalments. This is the information brochure of the college. It contains all the details about the fees.

Student: How much does it cost?

Receptionist: It's free of cost.

Student: Thank you, ma'am. What about the faculty of college?

Receptionist: Faculty of our college is very good and experienced.

Student: And co-curricular activities?

Receptionist: We have special classes for personality development. We also have a number of activities for this purpose.

Student: That's nice. Does the college offer other facilities too?

Receptionist: Yes, we offer conveyance, medical and hostel facilities too.

Student: That's absolutely fine! I would like to get myself registered.

Receptionist: The brochure, I just gave you has an application form. Fill it and submit it to me. You'll get registered. Once your result of +2 is declared you may contact us.

Student: Thank you very much.

Receptionist: You're welcome! If you need to know anything else, please feel free to ask.

Student: Sure!

Receptionist: Thanks for coming. Have a nice day!

Student: Thanks!

3. An interaction between the student and the librarian.

Student: Good Morning, sir.

Librarian: Good morning!

Student: I've come to return these books.

Librarian: Sure! But two of these books were due on last Tuesday. You're late by a week.

Student: Yes sir, I know. But....I was suffering from jaundice and have not been coming to college these days.

Librarian: Oh! But you've to pay the fine.

Student: I know students are excused from fine on medical grounds.

Librarian: Of course it is. You'll have to fill the application form and get it signed by your Head of the Department. He'll certify that you were not well ....then only you can have this exemption.

Student: Fine sir. I'll get it done. Meanwhile, please issue these books.

Librarian: Put your signature here ......and here.

Student: I want to point out something. Please see that in this book two pages are missing.

Librarian: Oh my God! Somebody has torn these pages. How mean! Wait I'll sign here, otherwise the blame will be on you or on the next borrower after you.

Student: Thanks a lot, sir.

Librarian: Thanks!

4. A dialogue between two friends discussing a TV programme

Kush: Hello Nivedita! How are you?

Nivedita: I'm fine. Thanks. And you?

Kush: I'm fine too. What are you doing these days?

Nivedita: These days? Nothing special…just surfing on the net, sleeping and watching TV….

Kush: So, you too like net surfing and watching TV.

Nivedita: Yeah! You too like watching TV?

Kush: Of course! Me too!

Nivedita: Which TV show do you like the most?

Kush: My favourite TV show is 'Sa re ga ma pa.'

Nivedita: Wow! This is my favourite TV show too. You know I'm fond of singing.

Kush: I remember very well. You used to sing in almost every programme in school.

Nivedita: Hmm. Now I'm busy with my studies so I don't get much time to practice singing. But I keep my singing updated with the help of such competitions as 'sa re ga ma pa' shown on TV.

Kush: Great! Even I love this show.

Nivedita: This programme is really wonderful because the mentors of the participants are the renowned musicians and they are experts in their field. Whatever tips they give them help all the learners.

Kush: Absolutely right. Even the participants are very good. They are from different parts of the world. They all are extremely talented.

Nivedita: Yes. Kush even you were a great singer in school days. Am I right?

Kush: Not great! I used to practice singing as a hobby. Even at present I love listening songs and whenever I get an opportunity, I sing.

Nivedita: Good! What are you doing these days?

Kush: I'm pursuing B. Tech. (Electrical) at N. I. T. Kurukshetra.

Nivedita: What a pleasant surprise! Congratulations!...... I've to go as I'm getting late for my MBA classes.

Kush: Sure! It was so nice to see you after a long time.

Nivedita: It was nice to see you too. We'll soon arrange a get together soon and will invite our old friends, Pranjal, Prakhar, Gouri, Krishna, Asmita also.

Kush: Wonderful! That will be great!

Nivedita: Good bye! Take care.

Kush: Bye! See you!

Task

1. Write a dialogue between two women who are discussing advantages and disadvantages of life in a metro.
2. Write a conversation between two friends over 'Re-mixing of Songs.'
3. Write a dialogue between two friends discussing preparations for the final exams.
4. Write a conversation between a father and a son who wants to go on a school trip and asks for money from his father.
5. Write a dialogue between a teacher and a parent discussing learning problems of the students.

9.6 Interpreting Pictures and Cartoons

"A picture paints a thousand words" is an old maxim. Pictures are the visual materials, which can be effectively used in acquiring communication skills. They offer a wide range of language learning situations providing real opportunities for students to communicate, whether they are working as a class, in groups or in pairs. A picture is a powerful medium to unlock speculations in us. It kindles a process of ideas, thoughts and imagination. Of course, we infer to the background of a picture and think: What could it be? How could such a thing happen? Who are the persons involved in it? Why does such a situation arise? How do the people in these situations feel? What could be the solution? There can be several other queries, which should be satisfied while writing a picture composition. In short, imagination, logic and creativity should be used in describing a picture. One should study the picture thoroughly, use the details given in it and should interpret them effectively in writing. Details of the pictures should be used to find points. We should try to make the piece not only meaningful but also relevant. It should have a beginning, climax and conclusion. Moreover, it should convey a message.

Cartoons and comic strips can be used from beginner level to the advanced level for a variety of language and discussion activities. A cartoonist is a writer as well as a critic. He knows the art of communicating effectively and economically. Usually a cartoon ridicules, exposes, attacks, amuses and tries to correct. While interpreting a cartoon one should find the context, recognize the characters and identify the message. One should read what the cartoonist is trying to ridicule. Cartoons can be used as powerful tools in teaching communication skills. They may be used to tell a complex story in a few images, provide comments and provoke thoughts on the events and the issues discussed in the news. They give an example of vocabulary related to the current trends and comment on them along with illustrating a whole range of issues such as racism, teenage relationships, sexism, ageism, family relationships, etc. The language used can sometimes be too colloquial and referential for lower levels to cope with; therefore, one should be careful in choosing cartoons.

9.6.1 Sample Illustrations

Sample 1

Corruption

"Corruption: an ingenious device for obtaining individual profit without individual responsibility." Corruption is one of the major problems of our country. It is, in fact, lack of integrity or an act done with the intention to gain some advantages, inconsistent with the official duty and rights of others. It is not only related to bribery but also to the abuse of power in decision making. It indicates that our behaviour deviates from ethics, morality, traditions and laws. The problem of corruption is getting

worse day by day. Earlier bribe was given to get the wrong thing done but, nowadays, it is given to get the right thing done at the right time. Corruption is seen everywhere in the world and at every step. Government announces so many schemes for the welfare of the people but corruption comes in the way of their implementation. Causes of corruption are very complex. Some of them are over population, unemployment, illiteracy, low wages of the government officials and the monopoly of the elite class. The situation gets worse because men and women are collectively and individually corrupt. However, it is not impossible to abolish the evil of corruption. It is quite possible to have a corruption-free state. The target is, no doubt, highly difficult to achieve because it requires cooperation from every citizen, every industry and every organization whether it is private or government from the grass-root level. There are some measures, which should be taken to control the increasing corruption. The Right to Information Act is one of them. Under this act, one can ask what the government is doing in a particular field. One can also use Grievance Redressal Machinery to voice his or her problems. Another potent check on corruption can be Central Vigilance Committee. Establishment of speedy courts can also be extremely beneficial in this regard. These strategies combined with strong will power and whole hearted cooperation of all the citizens as well as the officials, politicians and bureaucrats can make India a corruption-free nation.

Sample 2

Ragging

Ragging is a form of abuse on the newcomers to educational institutions. "Ragging' means the doing of any act which causes, or is likely to cause any physical, psychological or physiological harm of apprehension or shame or embarrassment to a student. It includes (1) teasing or abusing of playing a practical joke on, or causing hurt to any student or (2) asking any student to do any act, or perform anything, which he/she would not, in the ordinary course, be willing to do or perform." It has been a bane on Indian educated society. It spoils the atmosphere of educational institutions. Many education institutions have not been able to check this menace. In fact, ragging is not a new phenomenon. It has been prevalent in India for a long time. However, its nature has completely

changed over the years. Earlier it was limited to a friendly interaction or introduction among the students and helped the new comers adjust with the new atmosphere. With the passage of time, it has taken the form of a threat. Nowadays, some frustrated people try to derive sadistic pleasure out of it. In this process, they impose the beginners to a grave danger. The most touching part of ragging is that it leaves the victims emotionally, physically and mentally broken for the rest of their life. Sometimes it leads to more serious outcome, as we read in the newspapers, that the students have to pay with their life. There are various other aspects too related to this issue. All the educational institutions as well as the governing bodies have banned ragging as per the ruling of the Supreme Court. However, these efforts by the court, law, educational institutions are not enough. Of course, laws are there to check it but they have not been implemented effectively. To solve this problem, collective and concerted effort from various quarters is urgently needed. Above all, millions of students have to be convinced that they should help their juniors in the noble task of acquiring education rather discouraging them.

Sample 3

TV Viewing and the Young Generation

Television is one of the most remarkable inventions of the present time. Its advent has totally changed the life of man. It has brought about complete change in the life and attitude of man. Television is one

of the biggest inventions in the electronics field. It is a source of entertainment as well as knowledge. Many educational channels like BBC and Discovery, quiz programmes, etc., help us a lot in upgrading our knowledge. It is a very powerful medium of communication. Anything that happens in one part of the world can be seen live or known in another part of the world within seconds. Through various discussions, interviews and conferences, it creates public opinion and educates the masses. However, TV has demerits also. Too much involvement in TV makes a negative impact on the studies of the students. Moreover, it leaves a bad effect on their health as they avoid outdoor activities. Overdose of TV is ruining the gains of Indian culture and heritage. It promotes those aspects of western culture, which are against Indian traditions. It adversely affects social as well as human relations. Television has both advantages as well as disadvantages. It should be watched in limits and children should watch only good programmes so that they may make use of its merits and avoid its demerits.

Sample 4

Self-Confidence

Self-confidence is faith in oneself. It is being able to do things with a feeling that we have the ability to do them well. When we have faith in ourselves, things silently happen the way we want them to take place. Moreover, if a man has faith in himself, others will also have faith in him. Nobody trusts a person who lacks confidence. Self-confidence is the birthright of a person. Most of the people feel that their friends and colleagues have talents so they are confident. This notion is not correct because everybody is born in this world with something special to feel good about it. It is up to us to find it out for ourselves. It may take time but if we believe in ourselves, we will definitely find confidence eventually. To gain confidence we should keep telling ourselves that we can do whatever we wish to do. It happens easily when we think of it without any fear or doubt. Telling ourselves repeatedly that we can do anything we wish to do creates strength and ability in us to achieve a particular target. No two human beings are alike and we are special like no one else. We should make the best use of our talents and should feel good about them. We should keep one thing in mind that we should never compare ourselves with others. If we find only strengths of others, we may feel miserable. On the other hand, if we find only weaknesses in others, we can become arrogant. Believing in oneself is good but becoming proud is bad. Therefore, we should have confidence in ourselves in a calm and modest way otherwise self-confidence may turn into overconfidence.

Sample 5

Beggary

Beggary is a major problem, which is affecting a large population of India. There are large numbers of beggars in India who are forced into begging because our societies fail in providing any good alternative to them. For the last few centuries, India has suffered from acute poverty. Poverty, disability and unemployment are largely responsible for the problem of beggary, which is a social evil. Begging problem is getting worse day by day in India. It presents a poor image of the country. Ill-clad beggars particularly children are seen begging for alms at public places such as railway station, bus stand, temples, squares and crossings. They use emotional language to exploit people psychologically. Moreover, they use all the tricks to draw sympathy from the people as well as use different styles of begging. Some beggars use musical instruments, some sing devotional songs while some have infants in their arms. In some places, beggary has taken the shape of an organized crime with rackets working behind the curtain. Some of them are cheats too. Under the disguise of beggars they loot people, kidnap children or indulge in other unsocial activities. Many people who are strong and sturdy also keep begging. Some people have adopted begging as their profession. Even when their financial condition is good, they do not stop begging.

This problem is getting serious day by day. Forcibly vacating these public places from the beggars will not be enough. Some agency has to be there and it should encourage these beggars to live their life respectfully in a dignified way. Specially those who are physically strong should be identified and should be given some jobs. With the help of public donation beggar homes can also be constructed. If all the people unite socially, this job will not be difficult. What we need are strong-willed people who are determined to contribute to this noble cause.

Professional and Technical Communication

10

In this unit

- ✓ Introduction
- ✓ Letter Writing
- ✓ Job Applications
- ✓ Letter to the Editor
- ✓ Business Letters
- ✓ Reports
- ✓ News Reports
- ✓ E-mail Writing

"Communication becomes effective when its what, when and how have been pondered over."

–Sai Vaidyanathan

10.1 Introduction

A professional and technical communication, broadly speaking, is a formal system of writing messages to disseminate and receive useful information, within and outside an organization, following the technicalities and tools normally adopted to write such communications. A technical communication is a modern business technique or skill used as an aid to write down messages and to make them understandable. The technical aspects of business correspondence grow with time to cope up with the increasing complexity of the national and international trade.

Formal communication is the living support of an organization. It is through the written medium that a company develops and maintains its contacts and business in the outside world, as well as keeps the communication flowing within the company itself. As a person enters into the professional field, he/she has to start communicating not only orally but also through various types of formal written communication, that may be broadly grouped into letters, memos, reports, proposals and tenders. The author has to select the right type of medium according to the specific purpose. Although the basic aim of all the types of written correspondence is to communicate, their precise aims vary depending upon their use, scope and the targeted audience. Technicalities of writing may differ as each has its own format, layout and contents, but all have to be accurate, clear, factual, objective, coherent and concise They may have different finer linguistic contents, but all the types have an overall simple language, common words, short and direct sentences and correct grammar. The chapter will take you through the different varieties of professional communication, which we have earmarked as letter writing, job applications, letter to editor, business letters, reports, news reports and e-mails.

10.2 Letter Writing

A letter is an effective medium of exchange between two people, groups or parties. Letters are one of the most popular and effective means of communication in the civilized world. More than communication, letter writing is fun. Writing as well as receiving letters is a joy when they relate us with our loved ones. In earlier times, when telephone and e-mail were not available, the only means of communication between people was letter. Even today, in the recent age of advanced communication, letters have not lost their importance because they can be preserved, they are authentic and they convey emotions of the people effectively. Letter writing is a skill that has to be nurtured carefully.

10.2.1 Types of Letters

In general, there are two types of letters: 1. *Formal* or *official letters*: The letters written to various public bodies or agencies for our requirements in civic, professional or business life. 2. *Informal* or *personal letters*: The letters written to communicate with friends and family.

Usually a formal letter is written in a formal language. Its style is direct, simple and cordial. You have to be conscious that you are writing to somebody who is not your friend, boyfriend or girlfriend, but to somebody who may be a mayor, your boss, a bank officer, etc. In such cases, its language as well as structure has to be different from that of an informal letter. Informal letters are the kinds of letters that may be written in a natural, informal and communicative style.

10.2.2 General Strategy

10.2.2.1 Layout

→ 'To' and 'From' should be avoided.

→ Every letter should have your address, date, salutation, the text, conclusion and your signature. The formal letter has the recipient's address and subject line as well.

→ Write your complete address without your name in sender's address—Write one part in one line, start each word with capital letter and write the name of the post office in a separate line followed by pin code, district, state and country, if the letter is sent abroad, for example:

'Kothi Raghu Nivas'
#4258
Ambala Cantt
Haryana, India

→ Open punctuation—no punctuation marks in the sender's address, reference, date, inside address, salutation and closing section—is common with blocked style while punctuation marks are used thoroughly in semi-blocked and indented style.

→ In a formal letter complete date should be written, that is, day in figures, month in words and year in full—*14 February 1992*—while in an informal letter it can be abbreviated like—*14th Feb* or *14/02/92*.

→ In a formal letter, write the recipient's full address along with his/her name or designation:

The Vice Chancellor
M. D. University
Rohtak (Haryana)

→ Give the brief of your letter in the subject line in formal letters, for example, *Subject: Presentation on Group Discussion/Proposed Software for Language Lab.*

→ Formal letters end with signature, full name and designation of the author while informal letters may end with first/nick name omitting the pronouns.

10.2.2.2 Common Beginnings and Endings

S. No.	Relation	Salutation	Subscription
1.	Blood relation	My Dear Father/Mother/Brother/Uncle, etc., or Dear/Dearest Sister/Nivedita/Kushal, etc.	Yours, Yours affectionately/lovingly or Your loving/affectionate son/brother/sister/daughter/nephew, etc.
2.	Friend	My Dear Vishakha/Kumkum or Dearest Sushma	Your friend, Yours affectionately/ever
3.	Acquaintances	Dear Mr. Sharma/Dear Prof. Bhatnagar, etc.	Yours truly/sincerely or Yours very truly
4.	Business	Dear Sir/s, Dear Madam/s (discussed in detail in 'Business Letters' in Section 10.5 separately)	Yours truly/sincerely
5.	Editors of the newspapers	Dear Sir	Yours truly
6.	Applications	Sir/Madam	Yours faithfully
7.	Teachers/Principals	Sir/Madam	Yours faithfully/obediently
8.	High officials	Sir/Madam	Yours faithfully

10.2.2.3 Style

The standard format styles of letters are 'completely blocked,' 'semi-blocked' and 'indented.'

1. Completely Blocked Style: Every section and each line of the letter begins with the left margin of the page and paragraphs are indicated by a blank line between them.

2. Semi-blocked Style: The date, signature, and self-address (if not printed on the letter head) are aligned on the right side of the page. All the other sections are parallel to the left margin. Paragraphs in the body of the letter begin from the left margin and are divided by one space line.

3. Indented Style: The date, signature and address heading (if not printed on the letterhead) are aligned on the right side of the page. The greeting is given on the left. Paragraphs in the body of the letter are indented with no space line between them. Postscript and enclosures, if any, are given on the left.

None of the styles is superior or inferior, hence, whatever you choose, stick to it. However, completely blocked layout has become universally established as the most popular way of writing letters. As all the parts of the letter are aligned on the left it makes typing convenient and saves time.

10.2.2.4 Tone

In formal letters, tone has to be considerate, polite, pleasant and sincere and presentation should be clear and courteous. At the same time in informal letters, one has to be friendly and concerned.

In formal letters, there is no place for emotions, whereas in personal letters emotions are expressed freely and naturally. Single-word verbs, formal linking verbs and phrases are used in impersonal style while informal letters give liberty to use not only the pronouns—'I', 'we',—contractions, abbreviations, phrasal verbs, idioms, phrases but also colloquial language. However, both the types of letters should be grammatically correct, concise and complete.

10.2.2.5 Paragraphing

Introduce yourself briefly if it is the first time you are writing; refer to the earlier letter if you are responding to some letter and give your reason for writing the letter in the opening paragraph. Then, give further details and facts you want to present, explain the situation, give clarification, register a complaint or supply information whatever is applicable. Present these facts in a proper order. In the closing paragraph, urge for the action to be taken, seek information, offer assistance or state the course of action you want to be taken along with stating the response you expect from the recipient.

Keep your paragraphs short and try to give one idea in each paragraph. In formal letters single-sentence paragraphs are very common while in informal letters length may vary according to requirement.

10.2.3   Useful Phrases

Formal	Informal
Please confirm the receipt of.....	Let me know when you get...
We are pleased to confirm...	I am happy to tell you....
Please accept our apologies.....	I'm sorry....
We are writing to advise/suggest...	I am writing to let you know...
We are looking forward to hear/hearing from....	I am waiting for your letter/message...
	I'm sorry to tell you...
We regret to inform you...	I'm writing to ask...
I am writing to inquire...	We'd be really happy if...
We would appreciate if....	I want to tell you...
I would like to inform you....	I'm writing back to you...
In response to your inquiry....	I am sending it along with this letter...
We have pleasure in enclosing...	Please, could you....?
I would be grateful if....	Thank you very much...
I am grateful to you...	I promise....
I can assure you....	It seems that....
It appears that....	Let me know as soon as...
Kindly inform us at the earliest...	Why don't we postpone...?
Unfortunately, we will have to postpone...	I'm sorry, I can't attend....
I will not be able to attend the.....	Love/All my love/lots of love/All the best/With
Best wishes/warm regards/kindest regards....	love to you all/Do give my kindest regards to/
	With love and best wishes....

10.2.4 Sample Letters

1. Informal Letter (Completely Blocked Style)

231 Anand Vihar Colony
Near Railway Station
Ghaziabad (UP)

27th June, 2010

Dearest Nivi

Hi!

Thanks a lot for your letter and the lovely snaps. They really brought back the happy memories of our college days. Indeed, we all had a very nice time in college and of course in the hostel too. I can never forget those days when we used to study together, have a lot of fun and live like a family. Initially, we missed our home but after some time the hostel became our second home. Picnics, celebrations, dances—all seem to be out of the world now.

I'm glad to note that your MBA is going on well. It must be easy for you to adjust in your new routine now, though you'll take some time to be friendly with your new friends. How's your new college and its hostel? You've an annual system or semester system? How are the people in general in that place? Please do write to me.

Why don't you plan a visit to my place whenever you have holidays? We haven't met for a long time. Please do come and let me know your programme in advance. I'll inform Vandana and Amisha also. We'll have a nice time together.

The rest when we meet! I'm getting late for my classes.
Catch you later.

Bye

Yours
Nishtha

2. Formal Letters (Completely Blocked Style)

B-26, Shastri Nagar
M.G. Road
Sirsa

January 20, 2010

The Post Master
Defense Colony
Sirsa

Subject: Informing change in the address

Sir

This is to bring it to your kind notice that I have shifted to a new house and the address is given at the top of the letter. Previously, I was staying at G-36, Defense Colony, Sirsa.

I will be grateful to you, if you kindly direct all of my letters, parcels and registries to my new address.

With anticipatory thanks

Yours faithfully

Rajesh

Rajesh Kaushik

3. Formal Letters (Semi-blocked Style)

SMN Agriculture College,
65 Gandhi Colony,
Ambala.

15 March, 2010

The Manager,
S.R. Cotton Mills,
Panchkula. (Haryana)

Subject: To visit the factory

Sir,

I am a student of Agriculture Science and visiting a factory as well as preparing a project report on it is an essential part of our curriculum. For this purpose, 40 students along with 4 teachers of the Department of Agriculture Science wish to visit your factory.

We will be highly obliged, if you give us any date between 20th March and 31st March 2010 and time from 10 a.m. to 5 p.m. on a working day, convenient to you, when we can visit your factory. We would be further grateful, if you could also depute an official to show us the factory and explain its working to us.

Kindly inform us at least two days in advance so that we may make necessary arrangements. We are looking forward to receiving a favourable response from you.

Yours faithfully,

Manish

Manish Shukla
President Science Club

4. Formal (Indented Style)

56 Vasudev Nagar,
Ambala City,
Ambala.

February 20, 2010

The Director,
Guru Nanak Institute of Technology,
Mullana –Ambala.

Subject: Regarding progress report of the ward

Sir,

I am Mr. Mahesh Mehta, father of Ashok Mehta of B.Tech. II, Mechanical Engineering, of your college. I know that the college sends progress report of the students to their parents after each cycle of sessional tests. I have not received any information about the progress of my ward, may be due to postal irregularities.

I believe, even the second cycle of the test must have been over by this time. I have no idea whether my son is doing well or not.

I request you to send me his report, if it has not been sent to me and its duplicate copy in case it has already been sent.

Looking forward to hearing from you soon.

Yours sincerely
Mukesh
Mukesh Mehta

Task

1. Write a letter to your brother advising him not to neglect sports in school.
2. Write a letter to your friend requesting him to lend you his/her camera for a week.
3. Write a letter to your principal requesting him to arrange extra-curricular activities in your college.
4. Write a letter to your landlord requesting him to carry out white washing in your house.
5. Write a letter to the station house officer of the nearby police station reporting the cases of increasing theft in your locality.

10.3 Job Application

A job application is a kind of official letter (discussed in detail at 10.2) that one has to write some or the other time in one's professional career. It follows the format of an official letter but differs in its tone and phraseology. A formal letter may or may not have an enclosure, but a job application letter has a résumé or a CV attached to it.

The process of acquiring an employment starts with the first stage of job searching that one may do through different sources like newspaper advertisements, job-locating sites or personal contacts. The second stage is the process of sending of an application. This is a very significant stage because it is here that the first short listing of the prospective candidates takes place before inviting them for the third stage that is 'an interview.' Many job seekers are rejected on the basis of their applications. To get into an employment and to grow thereafter you should know how to write a good job application.

A job application constitutes of mainly two parts: 'The covering letter' and 'The résumé/CV.' Let us discuss each part separately.

10.3.1 Covering Letter

A covering letter is the opening part of an application that introduces the candidate to his/her prospective employer. It is a kind of a summary of the résumé written to convince the reader about the suitability of a candidate. The recruiters are normally burdened with applications and they do not go further unless the covering letter is convincing to them. So, this letter should be written with utmost care.

The layout of a job application cover letter is the same as that of a formal letter. Preferably, it should be written in the blocked style as it is the most popular style of writing official letters today. The body of the letter may be divided into the following four paragraphs:

First/Opening Para: Attract the attention of the reader by mentioning the post you are applying for and how you have come to know about it. Avoid using the word 'job' in place of 'post/vacancy'. You may use one of the following phrases:

→ I am writing in response to your advertisement in…, of…, for the position of…. / I am writing to apply for the post of…, advertised in the…, of…. / I would like to apply for the vacancy of…, displayed on your website…, on…. / I am interested in applying for …, the position that you have advertised in the… issue of….

→ As you can see from my résumé that I am specifically interested in the field of…; I apply for the opening of…, announced in…, of….

→ With reference to your advertisement in…, of…, for…, I want to propose my candidature for the said vacancy. (This construction has become a cliché, try to avoid it)

→ I have come to know through Mr./Ms…, of Sigma Counselors, that you need…with an experience of…, at your…. Kindly accept my application for this vacancy.

→ Your company's growth is an established phenomenon in the market and I would like to be a part of it and contribute to its growth. Do you have an opening for…in your company? If it is so, please accept my application.

Second Para: To sustain the interest of the reader in this section, describe your relevant qualification (usually the last one) and state your experience in brief, if you have. The following phrases may be useful:

→ I am currently pursuing … at …. / I am presently employed as…, at …. My total experience in this field is …. / I am a/an … in … from …, with … experience in …..

→ After graduating from the University of …, I have been working for …, since …. / I am an engineering graduate from … trade. / Since gaining the degree of …, I have been employed at … for the last ….

→ As a/an …with…experience and know how in…and a wide exposure to…, I am confident to contribute to….

Third Para: After catching the attention of the receiver, it is a crucial part of the letter as it helps generate interest of the employers in the applicant and finally guides him/her to decide if the candidate is worth hiring. Show your awareness towards the need of the company, give a brief summary of your experience, relevant skills, strengths and attitude and convey how they are integrated with the requirement of the post. Express your keenness to enhance your skills further. If you are a fresher, emphasize on the training attended, projects prepared, courses done, activities carried out, etc. In short, an experience holder should emphasize on his/her experience while a fresher should highlight his/her academic and extracurricular achievements. However, be very concise and specific. Some helpful phrases are given below:

→ The position interests me as… / I am well versed with… / My ability to…., makes me suitable for this position. / I would welcome the opportunity to contribute while enhancing my skills further.
→ The position will provide me an opening to improve my skills and…. / I have an extensive experience of….

Fourth/Final Para: This paragraph should inform the employer how you can be contacted and/or when you are available for interview. Some useful phrases are as follows:

→ If you consider me suitable… / I am available for interview (in person or on telephone) whenever convenient to you./ I would be pleased to have an interaction any time from…to…. / I am available to discuss the position in person at a time and date suitable to you.

A specimen covering letter

B/44, Krishna Nagar
The New Link Road
Sonepat (Haryana)

January 26, 2010

The Manager Human Resource
Syntel India Ltd.
Pune (Maharashtra)

Subject: Application for project engineer

Sir/Madam

I am writing in response to your advertisement in *The Times of India*, of January 20, 2010, for the position of a project engineer. Kindly find my résumé enclosed herewith.

I am a B.Tech. in Computer Engineering from NIT Kurukshetra. The position of a project engineer interests me as it requires the knowledge of C; C++; Java and other relevant languages, which I am well versed with. Further, it will also provide me a chance to work for the challenging projects. My ability to work patiently on computer for a long time and not to give up unless a task is done as well as my experience in handling unique college level projects as 'project-in-charge,' makes me suitable for this position. I believe, the on-job training, which your company provides, will help me grow, utilize my existing skills and learn more with experience.

I would be pleased to appear for an interview, in person or on telephone, at a time and date suitable to you.

Thank you

Yours faithfully

Vandana

Vandana Rana

Encl.: Résumé

10.3.2   Résumé/CV

Résumé is a French word that means 'summary'. Although in English it is used to refer to 'an account or a summary of something', its popular use is limited to mean 'a brief account of an applicant's details to procure a job.' 'Résumé', pronounced as '*razume*', should not be confused with the word 'resume', uttered as '*rizum*', which distinctly means 'to begin again'.

Professionally, a résumé is a document that contains a summary of the personal details, relevant job experience, education, skills, goals, achievements and interests of an applicant. It is the first item that an employer encounters regarding the job seeker to short list him/her for a job interview. Therefore, the primary aim of a résumé is to get a call for an interview, although securing the job is the ultimate objective.

10.3.2.1   How does it differ from a CV?

A CV is an abbreviation of 'curriculum vitae', which is defined as a written record of your education and experience that you send while applying for a job. Superficially, a CV and a résumé appear to be similar and may be considered comparable in some places but there are certain basic differences in their purposes, layouts and approaches:

1. CV is a traditional method of presenting personal data, while résumé evolved much later.
2. A résumé is normally used for seeking employment in business, finance and HR fields, especially in the private sector, whereas a CV is helpful while applying for academic, scientific, research, medical, university, fellowship and other educational positions.
3. A résumé is brief and concise—not more than a page or two. A CV is a longer version, a more detailed synopsis, extending up to four to five pages, perhaps more, in case annexure is attached.
4. By and large, a résumé has a free style and customarily enumerates a candidate's data in reverse chronological order, while a CV conveys chronologically arranged information.
5. A résumé highlights only the relevant credentials, while a CV provides a comprehensive summary of an applicant's personal, educational and career details.

In the United States, résumé is common in the business field while CV is used for academic positions. In some Asian countries such as India, the terms 'résumé' and 'CV' may be used interchangeably. Although, the use of résumé is fast gaining acceptance in the private business sector, some employers, especially government departments, may expect to receive a CV rather a résumé.

Résumés are always position specific and they cannot be identical for different posts. The best way would be to prepare a standard CV, update it regularly and use it to design different versions of résumés as and when required.

10.3.2.2   Attributes of a Good Résumé

A good résumé has the following major attributes:

→ Designed for a specific post, arouses interest in the reader.
→ Well displayed with proper formatting, spacing and sufficient white space.
→ Factual, correct and complete.
→ Information is categorized under headings and columns.
→ Uses appropriate concise style rather than using 'I' repeatedly.
→ Coherent, uniform and brief in presentation (preferably not more than one to two pages).
→ Does not make overstated assertions.
→ Highlights relevant areas starting from the recent ones.
→ Uses right words, grammar, spelling and punctuation.

10.3.2.3   Styles of Résumé

Résumés may be organized in two styles:

(a) **Reverse Chronological Résumé:**   This is the most commonly used format. It gives the data in a reverse chronological order, as the employers today are more interested in your recent achievements. Such résumés go well for both a fresher and a beginner.

(b) **Functional Résumé:**   This is basically a skill profile that is used to focus on abilities that are specific to the type of position sought for. These résumés present details skill wise. They are suitable for those who want to change their career, have a wide work experience or are applying for jobs that require clearly defined profile and personality traits.

10.3.3.4   Components of a Résumé/CV

We have seen that a CV is a comprehensive document and a résumé can be tailored from the former according to the requirement of a job. For the sake of convenience of designing, both the documents can be divided into three major parts—the opening, the middle and the closing. The following table highlights their formats, segments and techniques of writing in a comparative form:

(a) **The Beginning**

A Comparison between a Résumé and a CV

Headings	Résumé	CV
1. Headline	Begins with a headline giving: Name, address, e-mail ID, Tel, no., and fax no.	Not given
2. Desired Position	Stated	Not given
3. Career Objective	One sentence—statement of career goals—job specific and not vague, need not be in high-flown English, communicates self-motivation and interest (specimen is given after the table)	Not given

(Continued)

Headings	Résumé	CV
4. Personal Details	Comes in the closing part (see below)	• Begins with personal details: Name (capital letters), address, Tel. no., e-mail ID, fax, nationality, date of birth, marital status • All entries are listed one below the other

Some Specimen of Career Objectives:

i) To work on a suitable position in a prestigious Electrical Component Production Set-up, where I can learn with experience, utilize my existing skills and grow in my relevant field, contributing to the development of the organization. (This type of objective will be more suitable for fresh candidates.)

ii) To contribute to the growth of a prominent company by seeking a managerial opening in the recruitment division of HR department and thus explore new HR skills for such senior posts (appropriate for a senior and experienced person).

(b) The Middle:

This is the functional segment of your document and should be designed very carefully as the major part of your interview deals with the data given here (see 'Job Interviews'; in Section 6.3.8.).

Headings	Résumé	CV
5. Work Experience	Only relevant work experience	Complete work experience
6. Education	Relevant qualifications, trainings, etc., are mentioned. (Highlight your educational details if you are a new job applicant.).	• Qualifications, degrees, training, schooling, names of institutions/ university, years of passing, grades/division. • Seminars/workshops attended, research projects undertaken and publications, etc., may be given under separate headings.
7. Skills and Personality Traits	Only special skills suitable to the targeted position are listed, for example, expertise in a related computer language/data processing/knowledge of foreign languages/interpersonal skills/leadership qualities	May be listed but more broadly
8. Achievements	Only concerned achievements are listed or those that differentiate you from others and show that you are a go-getter and can take challenges	Distinctions, awards, merits, scholarships, fellowships, a prestigious research project, or anything that conveys recognition.

Employers are interested in your work experience, professional skills and achievements as such things give you an edge over the others. Support such information with relevant documents and facts.

(c) The Closing:

Headings	Résumé	CV
9. Activities and Interests	Extra/co-curricular activities/hobbies, memberships, participation in sports, seminars, exhibitions, quizzes, academic and cultural competitions (only special items briefly and in points)	• Little elaborated but in composite form • These things show that you are a multifaceted and dynamic personality
10. Personal	A résumé closes with personal details—age, nationality, driving license and passport no., married/unmarried*; children* (* optional)	A CV opens with personal details (see above).
11. References	2–3 names of referees (holding a responsible position) who can recommend your name for the concerned post. Names, designations, addresses, and telephone nos. should be given.	Same as in a résumé

A specimen résumé of an experienced applicant

Rakesh Kapoor
B/44, Garud Vihar, Karnal – 132001
E-mail: raksha_24@gmail.com
Mobile: 09997788666; Fax: 0184-234654

POSITION ASPIRED:
Chief Design Engineer

CAREER OBJECTIVE:
To contribute to the growth of a prominent electrical company by seeking a senior technical position in '*Electrical Products and Circuit Designing*' and by exploring new relevant areas.

WORK EXPERIENCE:
January 2008 to present: Assistant Electrical Engineer, Hindustan Electrical Systems, Industrial Estate, Bangalore. (A Govt. of India Undertaking)

→ Prepare electrical drawings and specification using software programmes.
→ Design and install computer-monitored voltage regulating apparatus in minimum cost.
→ Handle job time table and administer staff.

September 2006 to December 2007: Electrical Engineer, Bayer Electricals, Sector 4, Industry Zone, Faridabad.

→ One year training in (a) Electrical/electronic drawings and circuits.
        (b) Production of electrical systems and components.
→ Part of the team working on a Korean project of designing computerized motors.

EDUCATION:

→ **M.Tech**. Electrical Engineering, June, 2006 from **IIT, Mumbai**.
→ **B.Tech**. Electrical Engineering, July 2004 from **NIT Kurukshetra**.

SKILLS AND PERSONALITY TRAITS:

→ Well versed with the current versions of relevant software.
→ Skilful in computer application, designing and handling complex electrical circuits and components.
→ Experienced in problem identification and technical solutions.
→ Soft skills and leadership qualities.
→ Proficient in English; can communicate in American accent.

ACHIEVEMENTS:

→ Was awarded for the best design of **'Computer Monitored Voltage Regulating Apparatus'** by the present company, in November 2009.
→ Stood 2nd in the merit list of B.Tech. Final Year examinations.

ACTIVITIES AND INTERESTS:

→ Life member of ISTE, IIT, Delhi since 2002
→ Take active part in its programmes, attend workshops and seminars.
→ Keenly interested in music, playing volley ball and cricket

PERSONAL:

Age: 27
Nationality: Indian
Marital status: Married
A valid passport and a driving licence holder

REFERENCES:

1. Mr. Raj Chahal
   HR Manager
   Hindustan Electrical Systems, Industrial Estate, Bangalore. (A Govt. of India Undertaking)
   Contact: 080-2345432

2. Mr. Roshan Garg
   Branch Manager
   State Bank of India
   Bus Stand Road Branch, Rohtak. Contact: 01262-2567895

10.3.2.6   Résumé for a Fresh Applicant

In the absence of experience, employers would be more interested in aspects such as training, projects, education, skills and achievements. The layout of the Résumé for a new candidate is not much different. However, there is a difference in approach and may vary in its presentation as given under: (study the specimen résumé as well)

(a) Career Objective: Express your broad career goals, type of task you would like to do and willingness to learn (study the sample objective in Section 10.3.3.4).

(b) Training: Mention about your training highlighting the training field and what you have gained from it. Use sentences such as 'Received three months training, at …, from … to …, in the field of …' Gained knowledge on ….

(c) Education: Provide this information in a little detail, that is, starting from the current; you may go back to matriculation.

(d) Skills and Strengths: At this stage as you cannot be very specific, mention your general capabilities and traits relevant to the position, for example, proficient in C++, Excel, Java and MAT Lab/very good at maths and English/logical reasoning/ability to co-relate theory with practical/communication skills/leadership qualities/problem solving skills/keen to learn and so on.

(e) Achievements, Activities and Interests: These should be emphasized as companies want people who are all rounders, self-motivated, have a positive attitude and are eager to take challenges.

Task

1. Write an application with an enclosed résumé for the post of a Civil Engineer in a construction company highlighting your skills and experience.
2. You are an MBA in marketing with an Engineering graduation. Draft a covering letter and a résumé for a position of marketing manager in an automobile company.

10.4   Letter to the Editor/Media

Letters to the editor are great advocacy tools as they reach a large audience. They are monitored by trained persons such as editors and officials and create an impression of widespread support or opposition to an issue. Besides this, they are written to create public awareness and they enable us to help one another in society.

10.4.1   Purpose

The purpose of a letter to the media is to express and share one's observations and views in a public forum such as magazine, newspaper or a journal on:

1. A wide range of social issues.
2. An issue that is already raised in a letter, article, discussion, debate or a news item.
3. A particular point of view, problem or idea untouched or unnoticed by the general public or the concerned authorities.
4. A personal experience, which you have had locally and/or overseas.
5. A recently announced government policy.

10.4.2   Drafting a Media Letter

Whether you are motivated by a passionate point of view or you are responding to the views of others, you may use these guidelines to draft a letter to the editor of a newspaper or a magazine:

- → 'Letter to the Editor' is a formal letter; so, follow the layout as well as the guidelines discussed in 'Letter Writing,' in Section 10.2.2.
- → Select a topic and relate your thought to an issue very recently discussed in a publication. If you are encouraged to write a letter to the editor by somebody such as your teacher, you should start by reading a publication that is likely to contain articles of your interest.
- → While planning a letter, keep a scratch pad/sheet handy. Jot down any ideas or phrases that appeal to you before you forget them.
- → Determine your target audience and write to their level. Some readers are educated while others are very sensitive. Therefore, be considerate, clear and comprehensible.
- → If the publication has given any instructions to write a letter to the editor in the newspaper or on the website, follow them carefully.
- → Give your name, address, e-mail ID and phone number at the top of your letter. Editors often require this information to verify your identity. However, you may state that this information is not to be published.
- → Refer to the article that has raised the issue with its heading, author's name and date of publication.
- → Be precise, focused and brief because there's a lot of competition for a small amount of space. You may have to write several drafts of your letter to condense the message. Deal with one issue, article or speech in one letter.
- → Limit your letter to maximum three parts. Introduce the issue, refer to the article, news item or some happening that has generated the discussion and sum up your objections, in the first. In the second, include suitable examples, facts and relevant details to support your viewpoint. End the letter with an impressive summary and a witty punch line offering your recommendations and solutions as well as an urge for the steps to be taken.
- → Type your letter in double space between the lines. Sign it and write your name in block letters along with your designation.
- → Use spell check and then proofread your letter thoroughly to check its content, style and language.
- → Observe that your letter deals with a public issue. Be prompt in writing because even the best letter in the world won't be appreciated three or four weeks after the publication of the original article it refers to.
- → Read out your letter aloud. Does it sound good? Are the points included in it justified? How would others react when they read it? If you are satisfied, finalize it.
- → Preserve a copy of the letter. May be it gets corrupted or lost, then you will be able to resend it. If it is edited, you will have guidelines to write in future.
- → Submit your letter by e-mail, if the publication allows it. This will enable the editor to cut and paste the content of your letter. If it is not possible, fax the letter instead of posting it to ensure that the editor has plenty of time to plan for it to be printed.
- → Feel free to follow up with a phone call to make sure that the concerned person gets your letter. If your letter is not published, telephone the editor to find out why it wasn't. You may also ask him/her for suggestions to send another modified draft of the letter.

10.4.2.1   Style

- → Use bullet points, bold letters, italics or capital letters in the body of the letter to cover, organize and highlight important aspects of an issue in your letter.
- → Avoid moral statements like *'pollution is harmful and it should be checked.'* Give solid examples and arguments how and why it is so.

→ Writing in the first person is more direct. For example, instead of saying *'It has been observed...'* say *'I have noticed it many times...'*

→ Give real-life examples or analogies to demonstrate your point(s). This will support your arguments.

→ Tone should be polite. Authoritative tone is considered rude as it may hurt the readers. Respect the people you are talking about, even if you disagree with their views.

→ State your qualifications, if useful to the letter. For example you may say, "*I have been teaching in an engineering college for a long time and I have experienced.....*"

→ Wherever possible, compare and contrast. State why your point is better and why the other one is not appropriate. For example you may write, '*Government's move for quality education in private institutions is praise worthy but quality should be controlled in government set ups too.*'

→ Use humour because laughter is more effective critic than pontification. For instance, the statement, '*Thanks to the fashion world that has made saving easier to us by introducing short dresses for the models*' will have more effect than, '*The fashion is polluting the Indian culture.*'

→ Be grammatically correct. The editor will correct any minor spelling errors, but they won't edit letters in which sentences make no sense.

→ Use short punchy sentences. This makes it easier for the reader to follow your thinking and easier for the editor to edit your letter if required.

10.4.2.2 Ascertain

→ You are original and have discussed the topic in innovative ways as well as presented unique solutions to it.

→ Have a positive approach. Don't hesitate to compliment a good editorial or a story or the personalities you agree with.

→ Use facts and figures to reinforce your arguments. Quote other experts who have commented on the same subject, especially if the news article did not mention them.

→ Use statistics carefully as distorted facts often create confusion, panic or misunderstanding very quickly.

→ Remember, the letter should influence the public, not the adversary; hence, you should appear reasonable and fair.

→ Comment on actions more than personalities. For example, while criticizing a government policy, oppose the theory not the minister.

→ The first line should be captivating. Instead of writing, '*I am writing to respond to 'The Tribune' editorial of July 5th*' write, '*as an eye opener, the July 3rd editorial left me wondering whether man has stooped to such a level.*'

→ Don't mention criticism that has been levelled against you or your organization. Don't say, '*I am not a cheat, thief or a liar as reported in last week's Times.*' You may write, '*The article has left the readers wonder who's telling the truth in the controversy.*'

→ Make it legible. Your letter need not be decorative but you should use a typewriter or computer word processor if your handwriting is difficult to read.

10.4.3 Sample Media Letters

1. Sample letter to discuss a problem

88 Vijay Nagar
Sector 8
Karnal (Haryana)
E-mail: maneet@sifi.com.
Mobile: 09999765400

25 January 2010

The Editor
The Times of India
Sector 14
Chandigarh

Sir

Subject: Reckless driving

This is to draw the attention of the public and the concerned authorities towards the increasing cases of road accidents. Most of the victims in these accidents are the school-going children or the college students.

There are numerous reasons responsible for these mishaps. Children and students under 18 drive big vehicles without any license defying the traffic rules. Secondly, the rushing buses and the truck drivers drive on the busy roads regardless of the safety of the people. Not only this, overtaking from the wrong sides, stopping anywhere and violating the fixed speed limit is very common. Stray animals too, often sometimes cause serious accidents. After each mishap, we all feel sad for sometime and then forget it. We have no thought for the families who suffer the pangs of losing their dear ones.

I appeal to the concerned authorities as well as the civilians to come together to take a strong action in this regard. Speed breakers should be erected near schools and colleges and speed limit should be fixed up. Traffic police should be made vigilant and rule breakers should be penalized heavily. Moreover, parents and teachers should create awareness among the students about the traffic rules and should not allow them to drive unless they are 18 and have a license.

Road is not a place where you can rectify your mistake. Prevent the accidents by following the traffic rules instead of crying for help afterwards.

Yours truly
Maneet
Maneet Singh

Some letters published in newspapers:
  2. A letter written to create awareness:

World Red Cross Day

Tomorrow is World Red Cross Day (May 8). It is celebrated to mark the birth anniversary of Sir Jean Henri Dunant, the founding father of Red Cross. On June 24, 1859, in the fierce battle between Italy and France on the one hand and Austria at Solferino in North Italy on the other, 10,000 soldiers died and 30,000 severely wounded and maimed. Nobody cared for the respectful disposal of the bodies. The provisions for evacuation, treatment and rehabilitation of the soldiers were absolutely nonexistent.

Sir Dunant, a Swiss national, collected around 5000 local youth, motivated and trained them for the evacuation and treatment of the wounded at his own expense. Thus came into being the Red Cross. Its emblem (red cross with white background) is conspicuous so that Red Cross personnel are easily recognised and their safety is ensured in the battle zone.

Lt-Col I.J.S. CHEEMA (retd), Chandigarh

(Source: *The Tribune*, Chandigarh, Saturday, May 7, 2005)

3. A letter written to discuss a government decision:

Happiness at 50

With reference to the Times View/Counter View (May 20), happiness is just not a matter of perspective. It is related to material gains and accomplishments. Before the age of 50, an individual faces the ups and downs of career and marriage, has to secure the future and the like; all this causes stress and worry. But as the years pass and these issues are slowly resolved with careers and finances settling and children growing older, the majority of the reasons for stress and unhappiness are removed. That's when an individual often feels he has fulfilled many of the main objectives of his life. No wonder the half-century mark brings happiness.

M.C. Joshi, Lucknow

(Source: *The Times of India*, New Delhi/Chandigarh, Saturday, May 22, 2010)

4. A letter written to discuss an important issue:

Linguistic diversity is an asset

With reference to the Jugular Vein, "What are you saying?' (Jan 8) by Jug Suraiya, India is a country of many languages and these help us to understand the diversity of our culture. Often, it forms an integral component of our identity. For instance, a person speaking in Hindi is instantly labelled as someone from Uttar Pradesh or Bihar, or more generally called a 'north Indian.' On the other hand, a person speaking Telugu or Malayalam is referred to as a 'South Indian.' The various languages are an asset to our country.

Abhiskek Chaturvedi,
Mumbai

(Source: *The Times of India*, New Delhi/Chandigarh, Monday, January, 11, 2010)

Task

Write letters to the editor of your favourite news paper on the current issues like: Power cuts in your area, improvements required in examination system, Preservation of natural resources, NRI's should have a right to vote.

10.5   Business Letters

A business letter is a correspondence used for the purpose of carrying out a business or it can be called an activity related to writing letters in the business world. It is essential for many business tasks such as enquiries, orders, buying, selling, answering queries, lodging complaints and reminders of payments, etc. A business letter acts as an ambassador of the company. A well-drafted letter can help you develop and expand business along with improving and maintaining relations.

In the 21st century, where many modern channels of communication are available, traditional business letter continues to be an important means of sending messages. It enjoys a unique status because it acts as a permanent record or a document that can be stored and filed.

10.5.1 Attributes of a Good Business Letter

Although all good formal writing follows the same basic principles, a business letter is different in its purpose and approach. A good letter is:

→ Specific and accurate
→ Simple and direct
→ Clear
→ To the point
→ Polite

10.5.2 Planning a Business Letter

Writing a crisp business letter is an art in itself and it develops with regular drafting. Knowledge of its different parts, layout and style is necessary. (For details refer 'Letter Writing' at 10.2.2.). A business letter starts with proper planning. Before you begin, you should think and plan it systematically. Here are some points:

(a) **Previous Communication:** Read if there is any previous correspondence with the person you are writing to. It will guide you in drafting the new one.

(b) **Objective:** Determine your purpose—whether it is to invite proposals, give information/orders, request for payment, quote a price, calm down an irritated customer or to say 'no' to a request. When you write your letter think—what do you hope to achieve with your letter? What should your audience know? How much do they already know? How will they react after receiving your letter? This will help you write in brief, to the point, systematic and focused.

(c) **Know your Receiver:** Know your readers—who are they? How much do they know about you? What is your relationship with them? What medium of interaction do they prefer? What is their requirement? Gather a feedback on the reader if this is your first communication with him/her. Depending upon the information collect and organize your data.

(d) **Organize Information:** Collect all relevant details and organize them methodically. For this purpose, jot down points either from a written source, if it is available and useful, or note down facts/ideas as they come to your mind, that is, use mind storming. Anticipate the queries of the readers and satisfy them. Now, list these details logically to avoid any doubt and confusion in future.

(e) **Drafting:** Prepare the first draft. Review, revise and refine it by adding or deleting points. When you are satisfied, write down the final draft, which is now ready for typing.

10.5.3 Guidelines to Write a Good Business Letter

The drafting and editing of a business letter needs appropriate writing and language skills as well as knowledge of its technicalities:

1. The message should be accurate, brief and clear. Your readers have limited time in which they have to read it. Their objective is to know the bottom line: the point you are making about a situation or a problem.

2. Be direct, to the point and positive in your approach. Develop points logically.

3. Avoid clichés, jargons, foreign expressions and technical terms. Do not use slangs. To avoid any confusion do not use ambiguous terms and indirect expressions.

4. Use words and expressions of current usage in business letters—familiar, concrete and short words, small sentences, and simple expressions written in an easy and natural style.

   → Here are some illustrations of the traditional usage and their current replacements:

Expedite – speed up	*utilize – use*	*terminate – end*
Dispatch – send	*require – need*	*regarding – about*
kindly – please	*assist – help*	*commence – start*
purchase – buy	*endeavour – try*	*antiquated – old*
continually – constantly.		

   → Some long phrases which should be replaced by one word for the modern usage in business letters are as follows:

during the time that – while	*in view of the fact that – because*
at a later date – later	*in spite of the fact that – despite*
with regard to – about	*the negotiating process – negotiations*
at the present moment – now	*in large amounts – many*
in the very near future – soon	*take action on the issue – act*
was of the opinion – believed	*we would like to request you to – please*
employment on a part-time basis – part-time work	

   → Study the following words in italics which are just duplicates of the next word, hence are not required:

end product	*final* outcome	*still* continue
root cause	*proposed* plan	*past* history
joint collaboration	*original* source	*actual* facts
free gifts	*future* prospects	*advance* warning.

5. Be courteous and understanding. It does not mean that you should be naturally apologetic and use outdated elaborate expressions of politeness and compliments. For instance, in place of *'It is a humble request from…./ We hope it would not be wrong on our part if we kindly appeal you to…/May I plead your good self…'* write *'We request you to…'* Show consideration and respect to reader's feelings using expressions like *'We understand…/ we are aware of…'* To show courtesy, answer the letter the same day. If you are not able to do so, give reasons for delay. If you have to refuse an offer, do not destroy hope for future relations.

6. Use a suitable tone. It reflects the writer's personality. Business writing varies from the modern conversational style, often found in e-mail messages, to the traditional formal way of expression. The approach should be between these two extremes. Writing that is too formal can distance readers, while an over-casual approach may appear insincere or unprofessional. Choose your words carefully and try to be firm, friendly and polite.

7. Use active sentences and avoid passive voice. Passive voice is not a feature of current business usage as it indicates that the author does not want to take responsibility or wants to maintain gap with the reader. For example, the sentence, *'The product launch will be held at a time to be determined somewhere later in the month'*, is quite indirect and passive in expression. A better sentence will be, *'We will launch the product later in the month.'* Active voice is direct, focused, personal, clear and interesting. Nevertheless, passive voice may be used when you want to focus on the action and not the doer or when you want to hide facts.

8. Follow uniformity throughout the letter. Type neatly using even spacing, use uniform way of dividing paragraphs and be consistent in using language, font and style as well as presentation.

9. Favour verbs over nouns as verbs make your English direct and easy to understand, for example, instead of saying *'conduct the investigation'* say *'investigate.'*

10. Come to the conclusion naturally and state the response you expect from the readers. If there is anything that is unclear or legally or ethically incorrect, change it before you send it. Always keep copies of business letters in your record.

10.5.4 Parts of a Business Letter

Each type of business letter has the following parts:

1. Heading
2. Date
3. Reference
4. Inside Address
5. Attention Line
6. Salutation
7. Subject Line
8. Body of the Letter
9. Complimentary Close
10. Signature Block
11. Identification Mark if Required
12. Enclosures
13. Copy Line

Heading
Complete Address
Telephone Number, Fax
e-mail ID, Website

Date-----

References:-----

Inside address

Subject line: -------------------------

Salutation

--------------------------------Body of the letter--

Complimentary close

Signature Block

Identification mark

Enclosure/s

Copy line

---

1. Heading or Letter Head: Heading or letter head is usually printed on the letter head at the top in the centre of the page two spaces below the margin. It contains information about the organization's name, full address with various other details such as telephone number, telegraphic details, telex number, fax number, postal index number and e-mail id. For example:

Excel Technical Solutions
63, Vivek Vihar, Ghaziabad (U.P.)
Tel No: 0112345678, Mobile No: 99987654300
Website: www.exceltechnicalsuolutions.com E-mail: etsolutions@gmail.com

2. Date: Date is typed in full two spaces below the reference line on the right-hand side in semiblocked style and on the left-hand side in the blocked style. In British style 2/3/09 means 2 March 2009 while in the American pattern it stands for 3 February 2009. To avoid confusion caused by British or American interpretation, write day in figure, month in words and year in full. For example: *26 April 2009* or *April 26, 2009.*

3. Reference: Reference is given at the left margin two spaces below the letter head and it is followed by dateline. Even if the dateline shifts on the left-hand side due to the demand of the format, reference remains aligned along the left margin. It contains letter number, file number and other filing details and contains the reference of the sender as well as the recipient. For example:

Your Ref: GDS/ 56/S54
Our Ref: JKH/33/M24

4. Inside Address: Inside address is given at the left-hand margin usually two spaces below the dateline or the reference section. The inside address includes full name of the recipient, company's name, complete address, post office number, city, state with zip code. For example:

The District Collector
Sector 24
Madhya Marg
Chandigarh

5. Attention Line: Attention line was prominent in the past when letter was addressed to the company in general and attention line was given to ensure that the letter reaches the particular person or the title or the department in an organization. We rarely need it today. However, sometimes it is still given to ensure prompt action. It is placed between inside address and salutation, with a blank line before and after it and aligned with left margin indented with paragraphs or given in the centre in one of the following ways:

Attention: Chief Librarian
Attention: H.R. Department
For the Attention of Mr. Aggarwal, Sales Executive

6. The Salutation: The salutation is a little, polite complimentary greeting. It is given in the form of an introductory phrase and it is addressed to the firm or the person to whom the letter is sent. Though it is a formal way of beginning a letter, it gives a personal touch to the correspondence. The salutation of a business letter varies with the extent of relationship between the writer and the addressee. It is given on the left-hand side two spaces below the attention line/inside address. If you know the person it may be, '*Dear Mr. Sodhani*,' or '*Dear Ms Rachna*.' If the letter is addressed generally to an organization not a specific person, the more formal salutation, '*Dear Sir/s*' or *Dear Madam/s*' should be used. If the first line is the name of a group or a department use, '*Dear Ladies and Gentlemen,*' '*Dear Colleagues*,' '*All Sales Representatives*,' '*All Staff Members*' or '*Committee Members*.'

7. Subject Line: The subject line is given two spaces below the inside address or salutation at the left-hand margin or in the centre usually in lower case and is sometimes underlined. It saves time as it highlights the theme of the letter in brief. For example:

Dear Mr. Sharma
Subject: Inquiring about the course
or
Subject: Inquiring about the course
Dear Mr. Sharma

8. Body of the Letter: This is the main part of the letter. The message should be precise, brief, clear and pleasant. It should have four parts evenly arranged between the margins of the two sides of the page:

→ The first part should give reason for writing the letter or should refer to the previous letter, contact or document or should provide an introduction to the matter being discussed. For example: *'Thank you for your letter of…./It was nice meeting you at last week's meeting…../ As per our telephonic talk……/ I apologize/ confirm/inquire about…'*

→ The second part is the central section. It contains the main message, which includes all essential information as well as details of the letter. Information in this section should be given clearly, simply and logically.

→ Third part is the conclusion, which draws the message to a logical closing. It includes a polite request, wish, assurance, the action you expect from the recipient, the action you will take or gives a deadline as required. For example: *'Kindly give full details of the cost expected together with some sample catalogues./ If we don't receive the payment in time, we are afraid the deal stands cancelled.'*

→ The fourth part is the ending, that is, simple one-line closing sentence. For example: *'Hope to meet you soon,' 'We are waiting to receive your positive reply,' 'We look forward to receiving an encouraging reply from you/hearing from you/receiving your order/welcoming you as our guest'/ 'Waiting to receive your reply.'*

Within the message parts formatting style—bold, italics, bullets, underlining, etc., can be used to highlight the main points.

9. Complimentary Close: Complimentary close is a customary, polite way of ending a letter. It is written two spaces below the body of the letter. It has to be in harmony with the salutation. For example: salutations, '*Dear Sir/Sirs/Madam/Madams*' are followed by '*Yours faithfully*' while '*Dear Mr. Sharma/Amit/Ms Nivedita*' are followed by '*Your sincerely.*' The other forms of complimentary close are—*yours/cordially/truly*, etc. In modern communication, one-word expressions are most aptly used. The pronoun 'yours' is omitted.

10. Signature Block: Complimentary close is followed by the signature block, which includes the signature, full name, designation and address of the sender. If an organization has given power of attorney to an executive, the executive will write PP (Per Pro) before the name of the firm and will sign below it. Per Pro or PP is the short form of '*per procurationem,*' a Latin phrase which means 'on behalf of.' It means that the firm is legally bound by the commitment made to somebody else. For example:

Per Pro Bharat Products and Associates
(Signature)
K. S. Mann

However, unimportant and routine letters of the firm may be signed by their PA/PS adding the word 'for.' For example:

For Deputy Commissioner
Dept. of Environment
Govt. of Punjab
(Signature)
Adesh Kohli

11. Identification Mark: Identification mark is given one or two spaces below the signature containing initials of the person who dictated or composed the letter (always in capitals) and the one who typed it (in capital or small letter). These can be given in any of the following ways:

(1) *KPS/hs or KPS/HS*

(2) *KPS:hs or KPS:HS*

12. Enclosures: It is usually typed below the identification mark. It refers to the documents, which are attached to the letter. This part of the letter alerts the recipient to check the enclosed documents. It is usually abbreviated 'Encl' for one document and 'Encls' for more than one. For example:

> *Encls:* (1) *Catalogue*
>   (2) *Rate List*

13. Copy line: Copy line is given at the end of the letter. It gives information to the recipient about the third party to whom the copy of the letter has been sent. In this list, recipients are listed in order or rank if they hold different positions and in alphabetical order if they hold the same rank. Copy notation includes person's title, position, department and complete address along with notation of enclosures. Copy line is indicated by the abbreviation 'CC' which means 'copy circulated' or 'courtesy copy.'

10.5.5   Kinds of Business Letters

1. Letters of Enquiry, Quotations and their Replies: These letters are written to ask for or supply information. They seek general information about the price list, catalogue, quotations, estimate, terms and conditions of the supply of the goods, etc. They begin with a question or a set of questions on which information is based. Information should be given in the form of statements. While writing such letters, inquire about the prices along with proper details of packing, carriage, insurance, time limit by which you need the required goods, provision for accessories and finally the validity period of the quotation.

A well-written response will positively make a good impression while responding to inquiries from potential customers. If an old customer makes an enquiry appreciate it and if a new customer writes to ask for something show gladness and hope for a lasting relationship. Further, draft your letter well and ensure the quality of the product, its proper and timely availability as well as delivery.

2. Letters of Placing Orders and their Execution: In letters of such type, orders for goods are placed or acknowledged. Such a letter is generally a detailed and direct order for the supply of the required goods. Give accurate and full description of the quality, quantity, price, catalogue number, etc., of the goods required. State the price per unit along with the mode and terms of payment. Mention complete address of the place where you want the goods to be delivered, mode of transport, packing details, and the date by which you want the goods to be sent or received. There may be reasons when a supplier may decline the order like he/she may not be satisfied with the buyer's terms and conditions; the buyer's credit may be suspect or the required good may not be available. While rejecting the orders, the supplier should take utmost care so that the goods will and the future business are not affected.

3. Letters of Complaints and Adjustment: A letter of complaint is written to firms to rectify defects and errors regarding poor service, damaged or wrong consignments received, unsatisfactory quality of goods, billing errors, undue delay, discourteous treatment, prices not as agreed, etc. These letters demand a tactful handling of situation as they involve legal matters. Such letters should be polite, careful and firm as well as precise and courteous. Don't doubt the integrity of the people while complaining about an issue. Don't use the words like—dishonest, careless or unfair. While replying them, look into the complaint genuinely and offer the best solution. Write such letters promptly as delays may make your point weak. Be specific regarding information, date, order no, invoice no, description of goods and quantity and don't send the original documents or receipts. Say where and when you bought it, explain the problem you are facing along with the actions you have taken and state what you expect to be done to rectify the situation.

4. Circular Letters: Circular letters are not addressed to a particular individual; rather, they are addressed to all the members of the same group. They are impersonal in style. The main aim of these letters is to advertise a business, offer incentives, push sales, announce changes in the office site, inform the customers about the clearance sale or to send some necessary business information.

5. Letters of Introduction and Business References: Letters of introduction and business references introduce a business friend to another business man or seek assistance and help in some project. Business references are required in opening a bank account or enquiring about financial status of a firm. Personalize such letters by merging individual names into the inside address. Address the recipient by name if you know him/her; otherwise, use singular forms—'*Dear Customer*,' '*Dear Reader*,' not '*Customers*' or '*Readers*.'

6. Letters of Refusal and Acceptance of Business Proposals: In the business world, acceptance or refusal of offers and proposals is conveyed in writing even though it is notified by phone. These letters are based on previous conversation. Confirm officially and show enthusiasm to work for the new business contract. If the proposal does not suit you, refuse it officially even though conveyed through telephone. Be courteous, tactful and appreciate the gestures.

10.5.6 Sample Business Letters

Sample 1: Letter of Inquiry:

56
Sector 24
Chandigarh

29 April 2009
The Centre-In-Charge
Web Training Centre
32 Chandni Chowk
Delhi

Subject: Regarding the computer course

Sir
I saw your advertisement in '*The Indian Express*' of 24 February 2010 about computer programming course. My younger brother is interested in doing a short-term course during the semester break.

I believe this course would suit his requirement. Please send me the following details about the course along with the brochure:

1. Length of the course
2. Date and day of its commencement
3. Nature of the course
4. Affiliation details
5. The eligibility criterion
6. Fee and modes of its payment
7. Timings
8. Hostel facilities for the outsiders

I am sending a self-addressed envelope for the reply.

Yours faithfully

Manish

MANISH KUMAR
Senior executive
SYNTEL India Ltd.

Sample 2:   Letter Inviting Quotations:

NOBLE EDUCATION INSTITUTE
42 MIG Colony, Meerut (UP)
Telephone 01222453457; Mobile 09876543210
Fax: 012254321567

Ref. No. PEL/NEI/342

March 1, 2009

The Executive Manager
Pearson Education Limited
7th Floor, A-8(A) 62
Noida U.P.

Subject: Inviting quotations for purchasing books for library

Dear Sir
We wish to buy some books for our college library on 'Communication Skills' for the students of B.Tech.

We have 'Communication Skills' as a subject for B.Tech. I. In third semester, students face placement interviews; hence, they need guidance on group discussion and job interviews.

Please send us your quotation along with your catalogue at the earliest.

As we have to start our classes from July, we would like to receive the consignment latest by mid-June so that we may have no problem when the session starts.

We look forward to hearing from you soon.

Yours faithfully

Rajeev

RAJEEV KHANDELWAL

Chief Librarian

Sample 3:   Letter Sending Quotation:

Pearson Education Limited
7th Floor, A-8(A) 62 Noida, UP.
www.pearsoned.co.in

Your Ref. PEL/NEI/342
Our Ref. MNB/BE /987

March 8, 2009

The Director
Noble Education Institute
42 MIG Colony
Meerut (U.P.)

Subject: Sending quotation for books

Dear Sir

Thank you very much for your letter inviting quotation for books on 'Communication Skills'. We are pleased to submit the following quotation along with the price list for your consideration.

We assure you that all these books are written by competent authors and are very useful for your requirement. We offer you a discount of 20% on the purchase.

Packing charges and other charges are inclusive in these quotations. We will send the books in good condition and will replace them, if they are damaged during the transaction.

We will dispatch the consignment immediately after receiving your order.

We are waiting to receive your order soon.

Yours faithfully

Harish

Harish Trivedi

Sales Manager

Sample 4: Letter Placing an Order:

ZEN MUSIC INSTITUTE
564 M.I.G. Colony, Yamuna Nagar (Haryana)
Phone: 01732-320789 Mobile: 09898765445
Website: www.zenmusic.com; E-mail: info@zmi.com

Your Ref: MM/ ZMI/543
Our Ref: ZMI/ MM/234

14 February 2010

The Proprietor
Melody Makers
Sadar Bazaar
Ambala Cantt. (Haryana)

Subject: Placing order for musical instruments

Sir

Thank you very much for your quotation. We have approved the price submitted by you along with the institutional discount of 10% you have offered us.

Kindly note our order given with this letter.

Order for the Instruments: Order No. 16/2010

Serial No.	Name of instruments	Quantity	Cost per piece
1.	Sitar	2	Rs 70,000/-
2.	Harmonium	8	Rs 8,000/-
3.	Tabla (set)	4	Rs 5,000/-
4.	Guitar	4	Rs 50,000/-
5.	Tanpura	2	Rs 80,000/-

Please send the instruments within 15 days. I am sure, you will take care of proper packing of the instruments as you have committed in the quotation. I hope you will provide us prompt and satisfactory service in future too.

We will make the payment through a crossed cheque to you within a week of the submission of the bill.

Sincerely

Sunita Desai
Director

Sample 5: Letter of Complaint:

ZEN MUSIC INSTITUTE
564 M.I.G. Colony, Yamuna Nagar (Haryana)
Phone: 01732-320789 Mobile: 09898765445
Website: www.zenmusic.com; E-mail: info@zmi.com

Your Ref: MM/ ZMI/ 544
Our Ref: ZMI/ MM/235

March 1. 2009

The Proprietor
Melody Makers
Sadar Bazaar
Ambala Cantt. (Haryana)

Attention: Mr Narayan Swami, the Sales Manager

Subject: Complaining about the defective instruments

Sir

We express our dissatisfaction with the last order no. 16/2010 you sent us on 27 February 2010. Most of the instruments are defective, broken and are therefore, unusable. I am afraid that we cannot accept these items in this condition.

We remind you that we have been your good old customers for several years and expect better service than this. Please replace the damaged instruments as you have committed.

Could you please confirm when you will be able to replace these goods?

Yours faithfully

MKhurana

Mohit Khurana
Purchase Officer

Sample 6: Reply to the Above Letter:

Melody Makers
Sadar Bazaar, Ambala Cantt. (Haryana)
Phone: 0171-2345678; E-mail: melodymaker@hotmail.com.

Your Ref: ZMI/MM/235
Our Ref: MM/ZMI/545

3 March 2010

The Director
Zen Music Institute
564 M.I.G. Colony
Yamuna Nagar (Haryana)

Subject: Regretting the defective supply of goods

Sir

We have received your letter complaining about the instruments sent on 27 February 2010. We sincerely apologize for the poor quality of the instruments supplied to you.

On inquiring, we found that our dispatch clerk unknowingly mixed the fresh lot of items with the rejected stuff. We have punished the clerk for this negligence.

We are really sorry for the inconvenience that you have faced. We are immediately sending you a fresh consignment and offer you a compensatory discount of 15%.

Hope our business relations will continue to grow as before.

Yours faithfully

Nswami

Mr. Narayan Swami

Sales Manager

Sample 7:   Circular:

Microsoft World, 345, Sector 2, Greater Noida (UP)

Circular

Ref. No. MW/ 42/10

January 5, 2010

Some incidents of thefts have been occurring in the office building frequently. Many employees have lost their laptops, wallets and cell phones. This is a serious issue. All the staff members are requested to attend a meeting in the community hall tomorrow on January 6, 2010 at 2. p.m. to discuss the issue.

Shyam

Shyam Lal

Secretary

Sample 8:   Letters of Introduction and Business References:

R. K. Bedi & Sons

55 Gandhi Nagar, Amritsar – 143001

Phone: 0987654321; E-mail: rkbedi@rediffmail.com

January 30, 2010

Ms. Nivedita Bhatnagar

H. R. Manager

Syntel

Pune

Dear Ms Nivedita

I am sending Mr. Manish Deswal to you. He is very well known to me for the last 10 years. Mr. Deswal is an MBA from Amity University, Noida and has a brilliant academic record. He is confident, hard working and eager to learn.

He is looking for a good opening. Please spare your valuable time and talk to him about the areas of his specialization. In case you have an offer for him and you find him suitable, kindly consider him for job.

Thank you very much.

Yours Sincerely

Rakesh

R. K. Bedi

Task

Answer the following questions:

1. What are the various steps, you will consider while writing a business letter?
2. What is a business letter? How can you write a good business letter?
3. Discuss the structure of a business letter.
4. What are the qualities of a good business letter? Discuss their various types.
5. Write a letter to the director of your college complaining about the bad sanitary conditions of the toilets.
6. As a marketing manager of a company write a letter ordering furniture for your newly set up office.
7. Write a letter to a party reminding them of a due payment which they have to make against the receipt of computers ordered by them.

10.6   Reports

10.6.1   What is a Report?

The word 'Report' has originated from the French words '*reporter*' and '*report*' and Latin '*Re*' (back) plus '*portare*' (to carry). All these words mean 'give an account.' 'Report,' thus, means 'to give people information about something that you have heard, seen, done, etc.' It is a very formal document that is written for a variety of purposes, generally in sciences, social sciences, engineering and business disciplines. However, reports are also written for various types of academic pursuits such as a research report, a book report and project report and include many other kinds of report writing as well.

10.6.2   Purpose of a Report

A report is an extremely official document that is written to serve a range of purposes. Reports play a crucial role in communication in all types of businesses, organizations and professions. They assist people not only in recording the important happenings but also in decision making at all the levels. People are asked to write and present report in every type of profession for different objectives:

→ To keep check and control over a business.
→ To execute new strategies and measures.
→ To keep a record of research work, events and happenings.
→ To meet the requirements of legal and governmental regulations.
→ To study a particular situation to find an effective solution.
→ To discuss, analyze and evaluate data.
→ To make current and future planning and implement it.
→ To evaluate infrastructure, resources and manpower.
→ To compare growth, profit, achievements of an organization with those of its competitors.
→ To give feedback, suggestions or recommendations on a particular problem.
→ To take vital decisions and actions.

10.6.3 Attributes of a Good Report

An effective reporting calls for professionalism, profound knowledge of the subject, attentiveness and outstanding writing proficiency. A good report is essentially:

→ Brief and accurate—facts and figures should be presented in an accurate manner.
→ Clear and logical in structure—indicates clearly where the ideas are leading
→ Relevant and appropriate—concentrates on the particular problem and includes no irrelevant details or misleading ideas.
→ Well-organized, systematic and definite in presentation of facts.
→ Rational, persuasive and specific in analysis and recommendations.
→ Comprehensible—covers all vital details and conveys understandable information.
→ All inclusive—What is the main problem? Who is/are involved in it? When did it arise? Where will the report be presented? How can it be presented the best?
→ Highly objective—no place for prejudices, distortion of facts or personal opinions.
→ Written in good English—uses short sentences, correct grammatical structures and spellings (In report you don't get marks for writing correct language but you lose for writing wrong English.)
→ Using appropriate layout and professional style.
→ Neat and attractive in style and appearance—should make a good first impression.

10.6.4 Types of Reports

Reports vary in style, subject matter and presentation. Reports can be classified on various parameters such as:

→ Presentation—oral and written reports
→ Length—short and long reports
→ Nature—informal and formal reports
→ Purpose—informational and analytical reports
→ Time Duration—routine/periodic and special reports

1. Oral Reports: An oral report is a face-to-face communication about something seen, observed, experienced or investigated. It generally consists of impressions, observations and experiences. It is simple and easy to describe, quick and immediate to present and gives first-hand information but it may not be as objective and as detailed as a report has to be. It saves time for the reporter but may be strenuous for the listener as he/she has to listen and memorise each and every word at the moment. Moreover, it lacks authenticity and is difficult to preserve. An oral report may not be used for taking vital decisions but it is beneficial in judging speculations and impressions and can be used to take an immediate action.

2. Written Reports: A written report provides a permanent record; so, it is always preferred to an oral report. Moreover, a written report is accurate and precise while an oral report may be vague at times. There are no chances of distortion of facts while transferring information from one source to another. A written report is more formal than an oral report and is generally used to communicate complex facts. It is a visual aid to communication as the reporter may organize message into paragraphs highlighting the main points.

3. Short Reports: Short reports can be presented in the form of a letter or a memo. They are concerned primarily with day-to-day business problems as well as their solutions. A short report consists of three parts—an opening, body and ending. Short reports, generally include periodic, situational and progress reports.

4. Long Reports: Long reports describe a problem in detail. They include the process of preparing the outline of the topic, collecting data, making a rough draft, logical and organized presentation of facts, thorough revising, editing and preparing the fair draft, etc. These reports require a deep study of an issue. The important parts of a long report are—preface, introduction, summary, abstract, description, conclusion, appendices, glossary and index.

5. Informal Reports: Certain business reports can be short and informal. In current business dealings, informal reports are more frequent than the formal ones. Basically, informal reports perform the same function as the formal reports—transmitting information, facts or data to someone for taking decision. However, informal reports are quite brief (around one to five pages), that too when you have supplementary material such as bibliography, appendices, etc. The style of writing is positive, personal and conversational. Depending on the requirement, they may have heading, illustrations, footnotes, etc., but may not include all the details like formal reports. Informal reports are written in the form of memo reports or letter reports.

→ Memo Reports: Memo reports play a significant role in an organization. These reports are generally written to: (1) co-workers to give information, express opinion or to state a viewpoint, (2) subordinates to provide information, explain a policy or a procedure, give instructions or to announce changes and (3) your boss to give information, make a request, propose recommendations, give suggestion or to confirm an agreement. The memos are important because they ensure smooth flow of information in all directions in all the organizations.

→ Letter Reports: Reports written in the form of letters are called letter reports. The letter reports combine the features of a business letter as well as a formal written report. They follow the format of a business letter, convey technical information to a company, contain factual information and they are written from the perspective of the readers. However, the purpose of a letter report unlike a business letter is to provide information as it is a technical document in content as well as in tone.

6. Formal Reports: A formal report is the result of thorough investigation of a problem or situation. Formal reports are generally detailed and elaborate. These reports follow a fixed format. The length of the report may vary according to the requirement. (Format is discussed in detail at 10.6.6.). Formal reports include informational, analytical, routine, special, technical, project, research reports, etc.

7. Informational Reports: An informational report presents facts, situations or problems required to take vital decisions. The writer collects relevant information, compiles and organizes it in an orderly manner and presents it as objectively as possible. Informational reports record happenings such as conferences, seminars, tours, and so on and supply details for future planning.

8. Analytical Reports: Analytical reports present data along with an analysis of it. The writer studies facts, situations or problems neutrally, evaluates the information, draws suitable inferences and puts forward his/her recommendations and conclusions. Project reports, feasibility reports and market search reports fall in this category.

→ **Project Reports:** Project reports usually provide pre-investment information required for investments before setting up the project. These reports are based on small investigations. Cost, goods, machinery requirements, etc., given in the report are rough calculations. They also keep the organizations regularly updated about the progress of the long-term projects or bring an important issue in the limelight.

→ **Feasibility Report:** A feasibility report evaluates a proposal designed to determine the difficulty in carrying out a plan. Generally, a feasibility study precedes technical development and project implementation. Market feasibility study involves testing geographic locations for a real estate development project. It takes into account the importance of the business in the selected area. Authorities often require developers to complete feasibility studies before they approve a permit application for retail, commercial, industrial, manufacturing, housing, office or mixed-use project.

→ **Market Search Reports:** These reports contain guidelines for the promoters of the new products, policies, organizations, etc. Market research is an organized effort to gather information about markets or customers. It is done for discovering what people want, need, or believe or how they act. Once that research is completed, it can be used to determine how to market the product. This report collects data on market trends, users and prices of different commodities.

9. Routine/Periodic Reports: Routine reports, also known as form reports, are usually written on a prescribed proforma. The main purpose of these reports is to record the progress of a task, evaluate the performance of its employees and to record the success or failure of a policy. As these reports are written periodically, they are also called periodic reports. They generally include laboratory reports, progress reports, inspection reports, production reports, monthly sales reports, annual confidential reports, etc. All the organizations, institutions, companies and research establishments depend on routine reports for various decisions.

→ **Laboratory Reports:** A laboratory report records the experimental work done in a laboratory to analyze a theory, conclusion or validity of a particular research. One has to record the process, reactions and results accurately to arrive at a convincing conclusion. These reports include title, experiment number, date, purpose, apparatus used, procedure adopted, observations, conclusions and signature.

→ **Progress Reports:** A progress report informs the readers about the progress and status of a long-term project. The project may be about installation of a factory, construction of a bridge or a residential colony or some research work carried out in an organization. These reports are written at the various stages of the project. The essential details included in these reports are title of the project, total work to be done, time allotted, date, work already done, work to be done, time required, future plans, remarks, name, signature and designation of the reporter.

→ **Inspection Reports:** Inspection reports are written to ascertain whether or not the work is going on satisfactorily, infrastructure facilities are sufficient or the quality fulfils the required specifications. These reports are written in factories as well as in educational organizations to check and ensure the quality.

→ **Production Reports:** To control the budget and expenditure, standards are set for a production department based on the capacity of machines, time needed and the manpower employed. To ascertain the efficiency of a factory, production report is prepared. These reports normally give details of the standard production decided in a given time frame, actual production or the comparison of the standard time required and the time utilized.

→ **Monthly Sales Reports:** Monthly sales reports track the sale of a product in the market. They report increase or fall of sale in a particular time period as well as the factors responsible for it and give their recommendations accordingly.

→ **Annual Confidential Reports:** Annual confidential reports are written to evaluate the performance and the general conduct of the employees in an organization. Such reports may be subjective as the human qualities such as alertness, zeal, confidence, etc., may not be measured. However, these reports are used to determine their efficiency, critically appraise their achievements and assess their usefulness before granting them increments or promotions.

10. Special Reports: Special reports are written to convey special information related to a single condition, situation, occasion or problem. These reports do not contain repeated information as they are written about the specific situations. Like other reports, these reports also help in decision making as some of the most important decisions are taken on the basis of special reports. Special reports include inquiry reports, research reports, thesis, dissertations, etc.

→ **Inquiry Reports:** These reports are prepared by the special committees appointed by some government or private organizations to investigate the cases of mishap, carelessness on the part of the officials, charges of corruption, or some antisocial activity. Such reports are prepared in groups because they demand thorough investigation of an issue, objective interpretations and recommendations and systematic presentation of information. These reports are very common in administration as no action can be taken against any one without proper justification.

→ **Research Reports:** Research reports are prepared by the researchers and scholars of various universities, colleges and research organizations to present a concrete proof of the conducted research. While preparing a research report, you must aim at clarity, organization, and content. Research reports are all the more same like technical reports, laboratory reports and scientific papers which follow a consistent format to display information clearly.

10.6.5   Planning and Preparation of a Report

Preparation of a report is also very crucial. It requires careful planning. Keep the following points in mind while preparing your report:

→ The report should be acceptable and intelligible to the readers. To achieve this purpose, build up a clear picture in your mind about your readers—are they technicians, directors or leaders? How many people will read your report? A clear idea about the readers will help you shape your report, decide which points you should include as well as choose a suitable language and vocabulary.

→ Be objective and balanced and give your opinion only if you are asked to do so.

→ Be absolutely clear and consistent about the topic as well as the expected level of commitment. If you have any doubt, ask for clarification.

→ Make a schematic outline—jot down the ideas, study relationship between them and group them under headings and subheadings.

→ The body of your report should include—(1) description of your investigations, experiments, surveys, interviews, documents consulted, etc. (2) an account of your findings and (3) your interpretations of those findings.

→ Be selective as the careful choice of words will enable you to convey the right meaning.

→ Be accurate. Everything you write should be factually accurate and facts should be verified before they are stated in the report. Moreover, arguments should be sound and your reasoning should be logical. You should not write anything that is misleading. Otherwise, you will harm not only yourself but also your organization.

→ Be sure to rely on more than one source of information.

→ When using information from internet, make sure that it comes from a reputable and authentic source.

→ Maintain objectivity and emphasize on the factual material rather on any personal beliefs.

→ Be concise but do not mistake brevity for conciseness. A concise report is short; still, it contains all the essential details.

→ A good report should be simple but you should guard against oversimplifying the facts. Remember your readers are neither ignorant nor they know more than you. You should present information according to the level of their understanding.

→ Always write your report in third person.

→ Use correct spellings, grammar and punctuation marks. Use capital letters for proper nouns and bold, italics and underlines to emphasize main points or headings.

→ Above all don't get distracted. Keep your mind on the goal and you will have a good report.

10.6.6 Structure of a Formal Report

Keeping the above guidelines in mind, draft your report, revise it, check it thoroughly and take some time to refine it; then, compile it under the following heads:

1. Opening Section:
   → Cover
   → Frontispiece
   → Title Page
   → Copyright Notice
   → Forwarding Letter
   → Preface
   → Acknowledgements
   → Table of Contents
   → Table of Charts/Diagrams and Illustrations
   → Abstract or Executive Summary

2. Body of the Report:
   → Introduction
   → Methodology
   → Discussion and Description
   → Conclusions and Recommendations

3. Closing of the Report:
   → Endnotes
   → Appendices
   → References and Bibliography
   → Glossary
   → Index

1. Opening Section: The opening section of a formal report includes the preliminary details that familiarize the readers to the content of the report:

   → Cover: The cover of a formal report is important as it is the first thing the readers notice about the report and it protects the document as well. When a report is placed flat on a desk, the front cover is in view. The cover should be preferably white or some neutral colour and should contain the title, author's name, the name of the department or organization for which it is prepared, date of publication and report number. Space the title, name and date to achieve a nice balance on this page. If possible, type the title in a larger font size than the name and date. Use initial capitals for the title:

ROLE OF COMMUNICATION SKILLS IN JOB SELECTIONS

A Report
By
Seema Chahal
Report No. 15

Guru Nanak Institute of Technology,
Mullana (Ambala)
25 March 2010

→ **Frontispiece:** Frontispiece is generally given in long reports. In includes a map, a logo, an organization chart, a photograph, etc. It arouses curiosity of the reader as well as creates interest in him/her for the report.

→ **Title Page:** The title page of a formal report often contains the same information as is given on the cover page. In some formats, there is a summary also included on this page. It provides the details like heading, subheading, writer's name and designation, name and address of the authority to whom the report is submitted, serial number if any, date, contact number, approval and distribution list:

Report no. 10   Project no. 2

A Report on
ROLE OF COMMUNICATION SKILLS IN JOB SELECTIONS
A Study Based on Job Selections of B.Tech. Students

Prepared for The Department of Training and Placements
MMU Mullana

Approved by: Admission Committee

By V. MENON
Academic Coordinator
MMU, Mullana (Ambala)
27 June 2009

→ **Copyright Notice:** Copyright notice is given on the back side of the title page, if a report is to be published: © 2010 by Pearson Education Ltd. Or sometimes it is given in the form of a note: 'All rights reserved. No part of the report can be reproduced in any form without the written permission of the publisher.'

→ **Forwarding Letter:** 'Forwarding Letter' or the 'Letter of Transmittal,' or 'Covering Letter' is a brief letter by the writer explaining the objectives, scope and other highlights of the report. It contains information like time and areas covered in the research process, difficulties encountered in preparing the report, need for further study or a prompt action, significance of the study, etc.

→ **Preface:** The preface introduces the report describing its salient features and offers it to the readers. It provides an opportunity to the writer to justify his/her approach. A preface is normally written in long reports for the common readers when it is not clear who will read it. If all these features are included in the 'Letter of Transmittal,' there is no point in giving 'Preface' separately.

➜ Acknowledgements: 'Acknowledgements' is the customary necessary part of the report. It gives the writers an opportunity to acknowledge all the major contributors, who have provided financial, moral or emotional support, with their names and designation. '*I am really thankful…. /I take this opportunity to…/I convey my sincere thanks….I express my heartfelt gratitude…/I am indebted…. I acknowledge my thankfulness…./I will be failing in my duty if I don't …../*'—are some phrases which may be used for this purpose.

➜ Table of Contents: The 'Table of Contents' gives complete information regarding the headings, subheadings along with page number on which a particular topic or point is given. In a long report, it not only enables the readers to locate a point or a sub-point but also gives them an overview of the report indicating the relationship between the main points and the sub-elements. You may begin preparing 'The Table of Contents' with page numbers marked by a pencil, and page numbers may be included after completing the whole report. However, be uniform and consistent while numbering the points and sub-points as well as in organizing them. For example:

<h3 style="text-align:center">Table of Contents</h3>

S. No.	CONTENTS	Page No.
1.	Introduction	
	1.1 ------------------	
	1.2 ------------------	
	1.3 ------------------	
	1.4 ------------------	
2.	Discussion	
	2.1 ------------------	
	2.2 ------------------	
	2.3 ------------------	

➜ Table of Charts/Diagrams or Illustrations: The 'Table of Contents' is usually followed by the 'Table of Charts/Diagrams or Illustrations.' It includes all charts, figures, diagrams and illustrations used in the report. If the number of these items is small, they may be combined into one table, otherwise mention them separately giving proper citations.

➜ Abstract or Executive Summary: An abstract or an executive summary is the gist of the report in a single tightly packed paragraph stating aim, results and recommendations of the report. One has to oversimplify facts while condensing a 100-page report to one paragraph but one should not distort facts. Try to convey the salient features as well as the tone and emphasis of the report so that the readers may find the outcome of the research from a glance.

2. Body of the Report: The main body of the formal report contains introduction, discussion and conclusion of the report:

➜ Introduction: The introduction of a report prepares readers for understanding the discussion of the report. Like the title and the summary, the introduction is written for the largest possible readers. It supplies details regarding the general outline of the report—purpose and scope of the study, historical and technical perspectives of the problem undertaken as well as the limitations of the report.

➜ Methodology: Methodology comprises a number of sources through which information has been gathered like internet, libraries, interviews, surveys, discussions, etc., used for collecting information. This section summarizes the method, sources and procedure of data collection as well the criterion of adopting a particular approach.

→ Discussion/Description and Analysis: This part of the report presents facts, analysis and interpretation of data. The details are presented in the same order as they have been collected. Concepts, ideas and facts are made intelligible through comparisons and contrasts; drawing significant relationships among them as well as through objective description, analysis and interpretation of the findings. Discussion part of the report may be divided into sections, subsections, headings and subheadings to provide clarity to the structure.

→ Conclusions and Recommendations: The conclusion section analyzes important results drawn from the discussion and evaluates them in context of the entire work. In your conclusion, you should make recommendations based on those evaluations. It is very much like an informative summary except for one thing—you are writing to an audience who has read your report. In this part, you should mention several techniques employed to solve a problem, propose a course of action to improve a situation and indicate the need of further work in the concerned area.

3. Closing of the Report: The report is concluded with endnotes, appendices, glossary and references.

→ Endnotes: While compiling a report you may use some phrases and terms, which may distract the readers. All these scientific terms, difficult words and technical phrases should be explained along with their sources in detail, immediately after the citation in brackets or as a footnote at the end of the page or after the chapter or at the end of the main body of the report.

→ Appendices: Appendices contain material or data that is relevant to the main text but does not easily fit into the main body, for example, graphs, letters, articles, questionnaires, statistical and technical details, etc. At the end of the report, they do not distract the readers and may be referred to whenever required. If the items included in an appendix are numerous, appendices may also be numbered as 'Appendix A', 'Appendix B' and so on. Some material like slides, models or samples may be recorded in a different way of binding or framing to harmonize with the main report.

→ References and Bibliography: 'References' refer to the works or material—books, research papers, reports, dissertations, thesis, news papers, websites—cited in the report, in the order of their occurrence including author's name, work, publishing details and page number. For instance:

→ Annu Chopra, "New Protection Against Domestic Violence in India" *The Christian Science Monitor*, (March 8, 2007) p. 40

→ *Sunday Times*; "Times Life!" (Sunday: March 4, 2007) p. 1

→ A bibliography is the alphabetically arranged list of the sources used or referred to while preparing it. It mentions the work with the writer's second name first followed by the first name, the name of the source and the publishing details. For example:

→ Hornby, A.S. *An Advanced Learner's Dictionary*. Oxford: University Press, 2005.

→ Bhatnagar, Nitin and Mamta. *Communicative English for Engineers and Professionals*. New Delhi: Pearson Education Limited, 2010.

→ Glossary: A glossary is the list of technical and specialized terms defined in an alphabetical order in a report. It helps the readers understand difficult terms and words and the writer to make key definitions available to the non-technical readers without interrupting the report. Give cross-references of all the words explained in glossary.

→ Index: Index is the final section of the report. It lists all important concepts, topics and subtopics along with page numbers, discussed in the report. In a bulky report, index serves as a quick guide and helps the readers locate all the important aspects of a report.

Task

Answer the following questions:

1. What is a report? Discuss its essential features.
2. Discuss various types of formal reports.
3. What are the various parts of a report? Discuss them in detail with examples.
4. How can you write a good report?

10.7   News Reports

'News' is single new information about a happening presented by print, broadcasting, electronic and cyber media or by word of mouth to a third party or mass audience and 'report' is a short account of the news. A news report is, thus, a version of news sent to press media for circulation. A news report is written about a person, a thing or an event that is considered to be interesting enough to be reported. Reports appear in newspapers or magazines regularly and they are written in an impersonal formal style to attract the readers as well as to convince them.

10.7.1   Characteristics of Good News Reports

→ News reports give facts briefly, precisely and accurately.
→ They deal with real and current happenings and are duly supported with right information.
→ Reporting is done in an extremely clever and highly objective way.
→ Reports are written in a particular style to present the events in a clear and readable way.
→ Good news reports use suitable layout, appropriate vocabulary and correct grammatical structure.

10.7.2   Parts of a News Report

News reports mainly have the following parts:

1. **Headline:**
   A news headline:
   → Is descriptive, interesting and concise.
   → Includes a noun and a verb in present tense.
   → Is short enough to fit in one line within the navigation bar in your system. (An average headline in a newspaper uses around 6 words and 34 characters which convey incredible information into this brief space).
   → Has only the first word in bold letters and the rest of the words are written in small letters, except for proper nouns like Dr. Manmohan Singh, Delhi University, etc.
   → Does not contain full sentences.
   → Uses correct punctuation marks, but does not end a title with a full stop. Question marks may be used, if required.
   → Is simple and direct without extra adjectives or adverbs.
   → Is informative and clearly summarizes the occasion.
   → Incorporates most important keywords for those who often scan only the headlines of the news items.
   → Is understandable out of context as the headlines sometimes appear without articles.
   → Uses abbreviations and short forms for example, 'PM' for 'Prime Minister,' 'SC' for 'Supreme Court,' 'Prez' for 'President' and 'RS' for 'Rajya Sabha' and 'LS' for 'Lok Sabha'.

      Some examples taken from news headlines are: 'India Wins World Cup,' 'Technical Fest at NIT KKR,' 'India to Send Two Astronauts into Space in 2016'.

2. Byline: Byline supplies information regarding the reporter and the location. The reporter's name may be given by his/her name as in 'By Harish Shrivastav'; name of the agency 'PTI' (Press Trust of India); 'TNN,' (Times News Network) 'UNI' (United News of India) or as 'Our City Correspondent.' The location may be given with the reporter's name or on the left hand margin followed by date, for example, 'Ambala, 14 February.'

3. Main Body: The main body of the report has three or four well organized short paragraphs to convey the information effectively. These paragraphs may be divided into the following sections according to their function:

→ Lead/Introduction—First paragraph gives summary of the most important information including 'what happened?' or 'Who did it?'
→ Description: Lead/introduction is followed by detailed description of the happening covering 'when,' 'where,' 'why' and 'how'. This part of the report refers to people and organizations involved; explains situations and circumstances responsible for it and discusses various reasons maintaining cause and effect relationship. The facts are presented either from the most significant to the least important or in a chronological order.
→ Discussion: Discussion follows description. In this part, reporter includes interviews, surveys, eyewitness account or relates to the background of the event.
→ Resolution: News report is concluded with recommendations, appeal, warning or comment as per the demand of the situation.

Headline
Byline (Reporter)

Place, Date:
Main Body
   → Lead/Introduction_____
   → Discussion_____
   → Description_____
   → Resolution_____

10.7.3   General Guidelines

The following guidelines may be followed to write a good news report:

→ You have to be accurate rather sensational, tell the truth not your opinion, no matter how strong your beliefs are.
→ Include every relevant detail that your audience or readers are expected to know. For example, while reporting an accident, the report will be incomplete without mentioning the causes of the accident.
→ Start with an effective lead or introduction. Catch your readers' attention with the most fascinating aspect of the news up front; otherwise, they will not bother reading the rest of it.
→ Avoid the use of passive voice. Use simple declarative sentences with a variety of action verbs and eliminate needless words. Do not try to impress the readers with your learning either.
→ Ensure correct and standard language usage across your text. If your software includes a style checker, use it to assure proper adherence to journalistic guidelines.
→ Avoid long, passionate descriptions. This is a news account, not a travel piece. As such, avoid excessive, flowing accounts of individual places and personalities. Keep your focus on the main event.
→ Use short, concise sentences and paragraphs. News pieces work best when they run through quickly. Keep sentences and paragraphs short and sweet, with plenty of white space throughout the material.
→ You may include fiction elements like suspense and tension into your news piece, if it improves the work. But avoid creativity on the whole, and keep your focus on giving a clear description.
→ Be conversational without being ungrammatical. Make sure that you write in sentences and not in phrases with gerunds that go nowhere. Use adverbs when appropriate.

In a nutshell, your report should be composed of a catchy and powerful headline with a byline or the author's name, dateline, an effective introduction which starts with 'who' and 'what', a body where ample explanations are given answering the questions—'where,' 'when,' 'why' and 'how'—and finally, a brief conclusion.

10.7.4   Sample News Reports

Sample 1

Haryana among 5 states selected for ISRO project

TNN, 26 January 2010, 03:45 am IST

CHANDIGARH: Haryana is one of the five states selected under the major remote sensing and GIS application project entitled 'Space-based Information Support for Decentralized Planning' (SIS-DP) of the Indian Space Research Organization (ISRO).

Haryana chief secretary Urvashi Gulati said the state, only one from the region, has been selected for the implementation of the project in the first phase besides Andhra Pradesh, Assam, Kerala and West Bengal.

National Remote Sensing Centre (NRSC), Hyderabad, director Dr. V Jayaraman apprised of aims and objectives of the project while deputy director Dr. P S Roy gave its detailed presentation during a meeting held on Monday. It was followed by discussions and suggestions from the line department for the effective implementation of the project.

The project would provide ICT-enabled geo-spatial platform involving local bodies to carry out developmental activities under the Panchayati Raj in a decentralized, fast and transparent manner. The project aimed at harnessing the space technology and the information systems at the local bodies to create information base and provide services. The project would include thematic mapping of the state on 1:10 K scale.

The expected output of the project would be a GIS database on various resources and infrastructure, digital resource atlases, reports and development of information system to cater to the needs of various line departments and skate holders.

(Source: *The Times of India*)

Sample 2

IIT topper gives up Rs 22-lakh job to pursue his dream

Bijendra Ahlawat

Tribune News Service

Rohtak, January 25

In an unexpected move, Arun Kumar (23), armed with B.Tech and M.Tech degree from the IIT and CIT California, gave up a lucrative job with an annual income of about 22 lakh for fulfilment of his dream. The dream is to popularize the space science and robotics and to set up an infrastructure for further studies and research in the country itself.

His journey began the day he got selected into the IIT in 2003. Arun hailing from an ordinary family settled at Jamshedpur has recently purchased land in Solan district for setting up an engineering college to teach 'Space science and robotics'. He at present is engaged in a special training course on his pet subjects of space science and robotics in a couple of private schools here.

After completing his engineering from IIT Kharagpur, he went ahead to complete his Masters from California while doing job with one of the MNCs there. But Arun wished to fulfil his dream. "I wanted to do something different and perhaps the best thing was to provide awareness and training in the new fields of space science and robotics in the country and do away the misconceptions surrounding such topics with industry and research as my passion," he said.

"The main motive of my organization is to provide infrastructure and education in the field that include setting up of planetariums and robotics labs," he said. Under this campaign mini-planetariums had been set up in at least half a dozen schools of the region so far. One of such schools has been located at Ambala in Haryana. "The total cost of setting up a mini-planetarium and a robotic laboratory is around Rs 3.5 to 5 lakh," he claimed.

(Source: *The Tribune, Chandigarh*)

Sample 3

Karthikeyan, Rahman, Aamir in Padma list

Tribune News Service

New Delhi, January 25

Nobel laureate of Indian origin Venkatraman Ramakrishnan, Apollo Hospitals chief Pratap Reddy and former RBI Governor YV Reddy were today named for the country's second highest civilian award Padma Vibhushan, as music maestro AR Rahman, Bollywood actor Aamir Khan and controversial Indian origin businessman Sant Singh Chatwal were named for Padma Bhushan.

Awards announced on the occasion of 60th Republic Day included eminent theatre personalities Zohra Segal and Ebrahim Alkazi; and noted mridangam Carnatic artist Umayalpuram K Sivaraman, who were the other three chosen for Padma Vibhushan.

In all, 130 persons, including 13 in the category of foreigners, NRIs and PIOs, were named for the Padma awards—43 for Padma Bhushan and 83 for Padma Shri.

Prime Minister Manmohan Singh's cardiac surgeon RM Panda, eminent neurosurgeon Satya Paul Agarwal, prominent industrialist from Punjab SP Oswal along with Manvinder Singh Banga and real estate czar KP Singh were also named for Padma Bhushan awards.

Cricketer Virendra Sehwag, hockey national Ignace Tirkey, Formula One driver Narain Kartikeyan, badminton star Saina Nehwal, boxer Vijender Singh and Sachin Tendulkar's 'guru' Ramakant Achrekar have been selected for Padma Shri awards in the sports category.

Yesteryear Bollywood diva Rekha and actor Saif Ali Khan have also been named for Padma Shri awards for their contribution in the field of art.

Aamir Khan (44), who made his directorial debut with the critically acclaimed Taare Zameen Par in 2007, recently came out with 3 Idiots that has become the highest-earning movie in Bollywood.

Apart from this, music maestro, Illaiyaraaja has also been selected for the prestigious Padma Bhushan awards. Oscar winner sound recordist of Slumdog Millionaire Resul Pokutty has also been awarded with a Padma Shri.

(Source: *The Tribune, Chandigarh, January 26, 2010*)

Sample 4

SRK spreads awareness on need to protect environment

ANI

Wednesday, Dec 02, 2009 at 1302 hrs

Mumbai:

Bollywood actor Shah Rukh Khan has called for mass awareness on environment protection by saying little drops of water make a mighty ocean.

Addressing a gathering at the screening and a photo exhibition on "Environment Protection" organized by Consulate General of France here on Tuesday, Khan said: "Every individual must be utmost cautious and not to waste natural resources, be it water or any other entity."

"I don't think we are cautious about such small things. But it is necessary to take notice. It might be possible that in our lifetime nothing happens, but as the new years come, I am sure some problems will definitely be there. Although there are talks that the world will end, universe will collapse but I think it might not collapse by some external factor but we ourselves will end up destroying it, like the way we have been doing it. So I think it's an important aspect," he said.

(Source: *Indian Express, December 3, 2009*)

Task

1. Your college participated in 'Youth Festival, 2009.' Prepare a news report for a local daily.
2. Write a news report on the 'Blood Donation Camp' organized in your college.
3. Prepare a news report on 'Technical Fest' organized by the technical society of your college.
4. Draft a report for publication in a reputed newspaper on 'Annual Sports Day,' organized in your college.

10.8 E-mail Writing

An organized system of postal communication started with the establishment of government controlled post offices years ago. People communicated through the postal services for many years for business dealings as well as to reach family and friends without spending much. Then came the internet between the late 1960s and early 1970s and a little later came 'E-mail' or the 'Electronic mail.' In fact, it was invented in 1971 by computer engineer Ray Tomlinson. Initially the use of this technology was considered a luxury. However with time, as the internet became accessible to common man, e-mail started connecting people easier than ever before.

E-mail is a medium of communication that works through computer network. It has replaced the conventional paper mail as a means of official and interpersonal communication to an extent. The incredible high speed, cost effectiveness and efficiency, has made e-mail an integral part of modern communication in all fields, technical as well as commercial and has shrunk the world to the limit that distance does not matter at all. However, this online revolution has come forward with some limitations as it differs in style with the traditional letter communication.

10.8.1 Usefulness of E-mail

1. **Speed:** An e-mail works at an unbelievable speed and this is its greatest advantage. Distance has become immaterial as it reaches anywhere on the globe almost instantaneously.
2. **Cost Effectiveness:** It saves both time and money, which we spend in printing, copying and distributing as the messages can be sent and received within seconds. An e-mail is much more economical than a postal mail, fax or a telephone and its cost viability is not affected by the size of the message, attachments or distance.
3. **Trouble-Free Attachments:** An e-mail may be used in sending personal/official messages attached with documents, files, photographs, presentations, music, sound recordings, video clippings, graphics, software programmes and many more.
4. **Manageability:** The format of the message is easy to manage. The subscribers can delete, revise, store, print, forward or reply the message according to the requirement. We can communicate with individuals as well as groups simultaneously. An e-mail is thus, quite user friendly.

10.8.2 Qualities of a Good E-mail Message

An effective electronic mail message has certain qualities. (a) It is brief and to the point. (b) The message is restricted to one topic and to one screen only. (c) The text is specific, clear and accurate. (d) The language is simple, direct and clear.

10.8.3 What Makes E-mail Different?

In spite of performing the similar basic functions of communication, an e-mail and a paper mail are quite different from each other in their format, approach and purpose. Some of the major differences are as follows:

→ Electronic communication, due to its speed and broadcasting ability, is fundamentally different from paper-based communication, which may take more than 24 hours to reach its destination.
→ In a letter, your recipient may not have an immediate opportunity to clarify the doubts. With an e-mail, your recipient can ask questions immediately; so, it is quite close to face-to-face conversation.
→ The soft copies of e-mail documents may be preserved in the memory of computer and the back-ups may easily be saved in other computers or CDs. The letters may also be stored but the storing may become cumbersome later on.
→ In a postal mail the paper on which you write, the handwriting or the type that you use are the same that your receiver perceives. As the software and hardware that you employ may be different from what your receiver uses, the visual qualities of the message in an e-mail may be quite different by the time it reaches someone else's screen.
→ E-mails are more impersonal and spontaneous than a letter. An ordinary letter may be more suitable for a communication that requires planning and organization before it is dispatched. Conversely, an e-mail will suffice for most business purposes and daily exchanges that are done rather mechanically.
→ Important letters are treasured in personal collections or displayed in the archives of museums as precious documents of the past. Such pride and privilege is not usually given to e-mails.
→ Letters are written more formally than e-mails.

As an e-mail and a letter composition are different from each other, you should tailor your message to the medium used.

10.8.4   How to Send an E-mail?

To send a message through an e-mail follow the steps as under:

→ Log on to a computer network or an e-mail programme by registering your user name and password.
→ Type the e-mail address of the receiver.
→ Compose the message and check it thoroughly.
→ Click on the 'send' button.

10.8.5   How to Receive an E-mail?

→ Log on to a computer network or an e-mail programme by registering your user name and password.
→ Go through the list of your received unread mails.
→ Select the mail you want to read.
→ Choose the suitable step—deleting, saving, printing, forwarding or replying.
→ Then go to the next message.

10.8.6   How Does an E-mail Travel?

A message created by you on your computer and sent, reaches your server and remains there till it processes the outgoing messages. Your server then locates the server for your recipient address and passes on the message to it. The recipient server finally sends the message to its destination. Once it reaches the recipient, it waits there till he/she logs on to read it.

10.8.7   E-mail Writing Tips

Here are some tips for composing and receiving e-mails:

1. Desirables:

→ Check your mail box daily to give an immediate response to the sender. Before responding to a message, read it carefully. Send acknowledgements, if the mail has to be answered later on.
→ Write a short, meaningful and relevant subject line to give the receiver an idea about the e-mail content. Readers with big inboxes will avoid opening the messages like 'Hello,' 'Urgent' 'Hi,' 'Help' or 'Enquiry.'
→ Adopt the normal courtesies of professional letter writing conventions as many people dislike receiving messages without them. Greetings like 'Dear Sir/Madam,' 'Hello Neelam' 'Hi Sandeep,' 'Dear Mr. Khurana,' etc., make the message courteous and confirm that the message is meant particularly for the reader. Similarly, a proper sign off is courteous and it indicates that the message is finished.
→ Although observing formalities in an e-mail depends upon the relationship the writer shares with the reader, replacing the formal 'Dear Ms. Bhardwaj' with 'Hi Ms. Bhardwaj' may offend an Indian receiver. Be careful while being informal in a cross-cultural exchange. However, you may replace 'yours faithfully' with 'regards' or 'best wishes,' if required. Be consistent and do not fluctuate between the formal and the informal approaches.
→ The message should be direct, to the point, clear and short. If it is getting longer, it is better to use a phone or employ a paper communication.
→ Make it convenient for the reader to reply 'yes' or 'no' or give a short answer. Prefer yes/no questions like "Does 4 p.m. suit you on Monday?"
→ Make it easy to read, combine the upper and the lower cases properly. Use a legible font.

→ Even if you want to emphasize a point, do not use all capital letters—this is as if you are shouting at the receiver. Nor do use all small letters, as it shows that you are careless, insensitive and hesitant.

→ Format your message systematically in paragraphs with blank spaces between them. This will impart clarity to it.

→ Show empathy to your readers by appreciating their feelings and using words they understand.

→ Use a conversational, dignified and appropriate tone. Without the right tone, misunderstanding may be created or you may lose the business contacts. For example, you may write for an initial payment reminder: 'Consider it as mild reminder'. Use e-mail to enhance your communication and not to substitute your communication.

→ Use correct English; otherwise, it will indicate your non-serious mood and lack of language abilities.

→ Make yourself look good online because your e-mail can be forwarded to anyone.

→ Follow the rules of good writing. Use crisp sentences, short paragraphs, full words and complete sentences with proper spacing. Make use of simple modern business terminology, instead of long winding old-fashioned sentences.

→ If you are sending an e-mail to multiple people, put their e-mail addresses in the 'bcc' or 'cc' field and your e-mail in 'From: field.' No one likes to share his/her private e-mail ID with strangers.

2. Undesirables:

→ Do not use an e-mail if the message needs to be very private or confidential as it is very easy to forward an e-mail message.

→ Do not leave subject line blank.

→ Do not press the 'send' button in a hurry, in panic or in a fit of anger, otherwise you may have to regret later. Check the mail thoroughly for the content, format and errors. Ask yourself: Do I really have to mail this message?, before actually sending it.

→ Do not give an elaborate reply, if you are pressed with time. This may result in mistakes or make your message sloppy. Remember, an e-mail is an ambassador of your company.

→ Do not forward a message without a brief comment why you are forwarding it.

→ Do not flood your e-mails with smiley faces or other emoticons nor do use excessive punctuation marks like 'Hi!!!!!!!!'

→ Do not use unauthorized short forms like 'r' for 'are'; 'u' for 'you'; '2' for 'to'; 'gr8' for 'great' in official mails.

→ Do not e-mail back the entire message you are responding to.

→ Do not allow e-mail to control your life. Turn off the instant messaging system when you have an important work to do.

→ Do not panic for response as you can always call the person. State the action you expect from the reader then wait for the reply.

→ Never think you are chatting to a computer, write as if you are talking to the recipient.

10.8.8   Structure of an E-mail

An e-mail does not have set standards for its format. We can observe variations in the layouts of different electronic mail service providers. However, the following is the most commonly practiced format for composing and sending electronic mails:

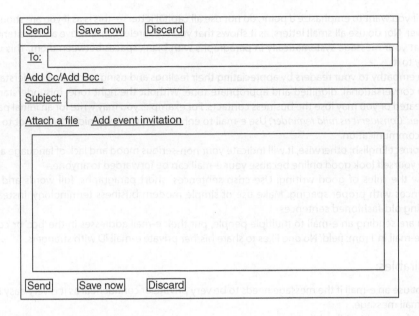

The layout of an e-mail is normally divided into three parts—header; message block and signature block, containing the following information:

→ Header: The header constitutes the details given at the top of the message block. It contains the following entries:
  1. From: The e-mail address of the sender (comes by default).
  2. To: The e-mail address/es of the receiver/s.
  3. Subject: A very brief statement about the contents of the message.
  4. Date: Day, date and time of the message sent (comes by default).
→ Message Block: The message of the mail is typed in this block. It should have a proper salutation, body of the message and complimentary close.
→ Signature Block: The signature block contains name, designation, official address and other details of the sender. Scanned signature of the sender along with his/her other details may be saved in the setting menu of an e-mail programme to save the trouble of typing it again and again.
→ Other Common Features are:

1. Save, send and discard
2. Cc: (courtesy copy) e-mail ID/s of those who receive its copy (optional).
3. Bcc: (blind courtesy copy). E-mail ID/s of those who receive its blind copy, that is, the recipient/s' ID/s will not be visible to the other recipients.

10.8.9   Sample E-mails

Sample 1:   *Your e-mail can be a brief introduction:*

Send	Save now	Discard

To:	<goyal.1708@abccamp.org>	
From:	jatin_ban@rediffmail.com	(Comes by default)
Date:	Monday, February 22, 2010 at 3:52 PM	(Comes by default)

Add Cc/ Add Bcc

Subject:	Application for summer training

Attach a file   Add event invitation

Dear Ms Rudrakshi Goyal

I am writing in response to your ad. posted on jobs.com for summer training at Intelsat. Kindly accept my application along with resume enclosed as an attachment. My skills and experience closely match with the given job description.

I hope to hear from you soon.

Thank you,

Jatin Bansal

Send	Save now	Discard

Sample 2

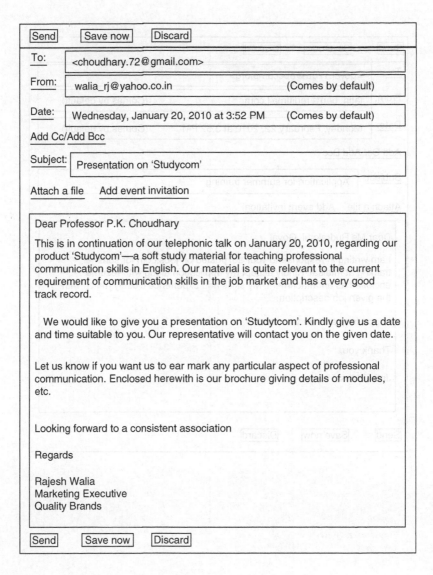

Send Save now Discard

To: <choudhary.72@gmail.com>

From: walia_rj@yahoo.co.in (Comes by default)

Date: Wednesday, January 20, 2010 at 3:52 PM (Comes by default)

Add Cc/Add Bcc

Subject: Presentation on 'Studycom'

Attach a file Add event invitation

Dear Professor P.K. Choudhary

This is in continuation of our telephonic talk on January 20, 2010, regarding our product 'Studycom'—a soft study material for teaching professional communication skills in English. Our material is quite relevant to the current requirement of communication skills in the job market and has a very good track record.

We would like to give you a presentation on 'Studytcom'. Kindly give us a date and time suitable to you. Our representative will contact you on the given date.

Let us know if you want us to ear mark any particular aspect of professional communication. Enclosed herewith is our brochure giving details of modules, etc.

Looking forward to a consistent association

Regards

Rajesh Walia
Marketing Executive
Quality Brands

Send Save now Discard

Sample 3:   Reply to the above mail:

Send	Save now	Discard

To:	walia_rj@yahoo.co.in	
From:	<choudhary.72@gmail.com>	(Comes by default)
Date:	Sunday, January 24, 2010 at 2:52 PM	(Comes by default)

Add Cc/Add Bcc

Subject: Presentation on 'Studycom'

Attach a file   Add event invitation

Dear Mr. Walia

Thanks for your mail. We are surely interested to buy a study software like yours.

You can send your representative for a presentation of your product 'Studycom' on January 5, 2010, at 11.00 a.m. The key areas in which we would be interested are 'phonetics', 'presentation' and 'group discussion.'

Best wishes

P.K. Choudhary

Send	Save now	Discard

Task

1. Suppose you are an engineering student and want to participate in an intercollegiate paper presentation competition on 'Robotics' to be organized at NIT Kurukshetra. Write an e-mail to the organizing secretary enquiring details of the competition.
2. Consider yourself as the purchase manager of an organization. Your company wants to purchase room heaters for its employees. Compose a mail to be sent to the sales person of a company asking for the details regarding the makes, rate list, payment system, freight and handling charges and the supply time. Include other necessary details as well.